SMART TOOLKIT
FOR EVALUATING INFORMATION PROJECTS, PRODUCTS AND SERVICES

This publication has a companion website at www.smarttoolkit.net

partageons les connaissances au profit des communautés rurales
sharing knowledge, improving rural livelihoods

Published by:

ACP-EU Technical Centre for Agricultural and Rural Cooperation (CTA)
Postbus 380, 6700 AJ Wageningen, the Netherlands
cta@cta.int / www.cta.int

Royal Tropical Institute (Koninklijk Instituut voor de Tropen, KIT)
PO Box 95001, 1090 HA Amsterdam, the Netherlands
library@kit.nl / www.kit.nl

International Institute for Communication and Development (IICD)
Raamweg 5, PO Box 11586, 2502 AN The Hague, the Netherlands
information@iicd.org / www.iicd.org

© CTA, KIT, IICD 2009

ISBN: CTA 978 92 9081 427 6; KIT 978 94 6022 027 2

Editing: Patricia Norrish and Kay Sayce, UK
Production: Kay Sayce, Words at Work, London, UK
Review: Karen Batjes-Sinclair, Jenessi Matturi, Gashaw Kebede, Bruce Lauckner and Donna Spencer
Illustrations: Auke Herrema, The Netherlands
Cover design: Anita Mangan, London, UK
Printer: KIT Publishers, Amsterdam, The Netherlands

Sources of tables, figures and diagrams: Unless otherwise stated, these should be credited to the *Smart Toolkit*

Citation: CTA, KIT, IICD (2009) *Smart Toolkit for Evaluating Information Projects, Products and Services*, Second Edition, CTA/KIT/IICD, The Netherlands

All rights reserved. Reproduction and dissemination of material in this information product for educational or other non-commercial purposes are authorised without any prior written permission from the copyright holders provided the source is fully acknowledged. Reproduction of material in this information product for resale or other commercial purposes is prohibited without the written permission of the copyright holders. Applications for such permission should be addressed to CTA, KIT or IICD.

CONTENTS

Foreword — v

Acknowledgements — vi

Introduction to the second edition — vii

About the toolkit — viii

PART 1: The Evaluation Context — 1
- Background — 2
- Stakeholder participation — 3
- Learning — 5
- The project cycle — 8
- The project plan — 10
- Monitoring — 16
- Evaluation — 18
- Impact assessment — 21
- Setting up a monitoring, evaluation and impact assessment system — 24

PART 2: The Evaluation Process — 29
- Introduction — 30
- Preparing the evaluation terms of reference — 32
- Designing the evaluation — 46
- Implementing the evaluation — 58
- Following up the evaluation — 61

PART 3: Evaluation Tools — 65
- Introduction — 66
- Project planning tools — 67
- Evaluation planning tools — 99
- Evaluation implementation tools — 106
- Applying evaluation findings — 163

PART 4: Evaluation Guidelines — 175
- Introduction — 176
- Training course — 177
- Newsletter — 191
- Website — 205
- Question-and-answer service — 219
- Small library / resource centre — 231
- Online community — 243
- Rural radio — 255
- Database — 268
- Selective dissemination of information service — 281

Annexes 293
    1 Toolkit background 294
    2 Toolkit contributors 295
    3 Workshop participants 298
    4 Information sources 300
    5 Glossary 313

Acronyms and abbreviations 316

Index 318

FOREWORD

CTA, KIT and IICD are all involved in improving information products and services for developing countries. In a world so full of information, but with many questions unanswered, this is a challenging task. Monitoring and evaluation are an essential part of this task.

Of the many challenges faced by development agencies, two in particular relate to monitoring and evaluation. The first is to strengthen the learning capacity of the development sector itself. Lessons learned and best practices need to be shared in order to improve performance and avoid costly re-inventions of the wheel. Evaluation provides learning. The second challenge relates to transparency. 'Accountability' is guaranteed a slot on the agenda at most international development fora, not just 'vertical accountability', vis-à-vis policy-makers and donors, but also 'horizontal accountability' to the beneficiaries in the South and the taxpayers in donor countries. Again, there is a pivotal role here for evaluation.

Learning and accountability are two sides of the same coin, and good monitoring and evaluation tools should serve both of them. Development agencies need to learn from previous experience and to demonstrate the impact of their efforts. This is particularly true for information professionals in the development sector, with the ever-changing ICT environment posing a range of new opportunities and new challenges. Conversely, information is key to monitoring and evaluation. Without the relevant information, neither learning nor accountability would be possible. Good information and good evaluation are therefore interdependent.

In recent years, the emphasis in the evaluation debate has shifted. Initially, it was on output; then it moved to outcome and, more recently, to impact. There is a growing demand from both donors and the general public for feedback on the contribution of development activities towards improved livelihoods in developing countries. Measuring the impact of information products and services is particularly difficult. How can one demonstrate using verifiable indicators, for example, the contribution of information towards the achievement of the Millennium Development Goals? This book does not purport to have all the answers, but it will give information professionals insight into applying evaluation tools to information-focused activities and assessing the impact of those activities.

The first edition of the *Smart Toolkit for Evaluating Information Projects, Products and Services* was published in 2005, mainly for use in training and to generate feedback. The response was favourable and the edition remains in much demand, but the feedback indicated that there was room for improvement. CTA, KIT and IICD therefore set about producing a revised, updated and expanded edition of the *Smart Toolkit*, a highly participatory process involving many partners in the South. We hope that this second edition will give information professionals even greater insight into the tools they need to evaluate information projects, products and services for development.

Dr Hansjörg Neun
Director, CTA

Dr Jan Donner
President, KIT

Ms Caroline Figuères
Managing Director, IICD

ACKNOWLEDGEMENTS

This second edition of the *Smart Toolkit* has been an immense collaborative effort involving many people from development organisations throughout the ACP and EU. Although important to the management and effectiveness of information services, evaluation is often not seen as a mainstream activity. As such, we are grateful to the many writers and reviewers who have so willingly contributed their time to transforming the document into a valuable resource for individuals and organisations alike operating in the field of information.

Special thanks are due to our colleagues for their input in various capacities. We would also like to express our appreciation and thanks to the management of CTA, KIT and IICD for their unwavering support in facilitating our partnership and in the production of this revised edition of the *Smart Toolkit*

Dr Ibrahim Khadar, CTA
Harry Heemskerk, KIT
Riet Nigten, IICD

INTRODUCTION TO THE SECOND EDITION

The response to the publication of the first edition of the *Smart Toolkit for Evaluating Information Projects, Products and Services*, in 2005, showed clearly that it met a great need among information practitioners for guidelines on the evaluation process and on appropriate evaluation tools. Suggestions on how to improve the first edition, emanating both from users in the field and from a workshop in Bonn, Germany convened especially to assess the toolkit, encouraged us to produce this revised and updated second edition.

The focus of this edition remains the same as that of the first edition – learning. The importance of evaluation in enhancing organisational learning is widely acknowledged in development literature. Without this learning, through well-planned and implemented evaluations, development organisations are unlikely to build the capacity to respond effectively to the changing needs of their target groups. They will, in other words, have little or no impact. Peter Senge, a leading proponent of organisational learning, wrote in his book *The Fifth Discipline* (1994; see Annex 4):

> Learning organisations are organisations where people continually expand their capacity to create the results they truly desire, where new and expansive patterns of thinking are nurtured, where collective aspiration is set free, and where people are continually learning to learn together.

There is increasing demand for information practitioners to evaluate their products and services themselves, for learning purposes as well as for accountability, and not rely on external evaluations, which are often little more than a rubber-stamping exercise. But in many cases they lack a firm grounding in evaluation – its place in the project cycle, who to involve in its planning and implementation, how to plan it, how and when to implement it, how and when to follow it up and, above all, how to learn from it. In *Evaluating Capacity Development*, Horton *et al.* (2003; see Annex 4), wrote of the benefits of project 'self-evaluation':

> …people who are responsible for the organisation, management and operation and stakeholders with a strong knowledge and interest in the organisation, gain in-depth understanding of what works well and why and where improvements are needed. With this knowledge, they are extremely well prepared to address the necessary changes in practical ways.

The *Smart Toolkit* is therefore timely. It seeks to provide information practitioners with an insight into self-evaluating their products and services, with the view to improving learning and, ultimately, impact. It adds significantly to the limited body of literature on the evaluation of information, and should be seen as a work-in-progress, with its use in the field contributing further insights to be incorporated into subsequent editions.

ABOUT THE TOOLKIT

The *Smart Toolkit* focuses on the evaluation of information projects, products and services from a learning perspective. It looks at evaluation within the context of the overall project cycle, from project planning and implementation to monitoring, evaluation and impact assessment, and then at the evaluation process itself, the tools involved and examples of their application. The theme running throughout the toolkit is:

Participatory evaluation for learning and impact

The emphasis is on internal evaluation – or 'self-evaluation' – rather than external evaluation. Internal evaluation contributes to organisational learning and represents a significant shift from traditional evaluation, which has tended to be donor-driven to meet the demand for accountability and compliance. If evaluation is to achieve its ultimate objectives of enhancing learning and demonstrating impact, it needs to be applied with confidence in a systematic and coherent way.

Why 'smart'?

In 2001, a group of information practitioners from various development agencies, led by CTA, KIT and IICD, began working together to produce a manual that would support self-evaluation by information practitioners. At their first meeting the word 'smart' was chosen to emphasise 'best practice' and as an oblique reference to the SMART indicators (specific, measurable, achievable, realistic, time-bound) common in evaluation literature.

Who is the toolkit for?

The *Smart Toolkit* is aimed primarily at information practitioners in development organisations, particularly those working at grassroots level, who are involved in planning and managing information-related projects and generating new knowledge and key lessons from them. Many of these people would readily acknowledge that not only are they 'non-experts' in evaluation, but also that they lack the basics in how to evaluate information-related projects.

The field of information and communication management (ICM) has become central to much development thinking, boosted by the huge growth in information and communication technologies (ICTs) in recent years and the potential that ICTs have for development. But there is a noticeable gap in the literature when it comes to identifying evaluation methods and tools that can be applied specifically and successfully to information-related projects. The toolkit seeks to fill this gap to some extent and to encourage practitioners to contribute to this effort.

The toolkit should also prove useful for development project managers in general, as well as for funding agencies and other stakeholders in the production and delivery of information products and services.

Who should read this book, and why

- Are you managing an information project, product or service, such as a library, newsletter, rural radio, training workshop or website?

- Do you prepare information products and services for the wider public?

- Are you in the business of disseminating information?

- Are you an evaluator who has been challenged to evaluate information projects, products or services?

- Do you ever wonder what more you could be doing to meet the needs of your target groups, and whether or not you're providing them with the 'right' information?

- Have you ever wondered:
  - why your researchers and scientists don't have access to up-to-date credible information?
  - why many of the reports prepared by government ministries and research institutions never find their way to the libraries?
  - how you could get more people to use your information services?
  - why your website doesn't provide the information it should?
  - why you can't find the information when you need it?

If you have answered 'yes' to some of these questions, then this toolkit is for you.

What is the toolkit for?

If you are new to the evaluation process, the toolkit is a good place to begin. It will help you to organise your thoughts and prompt you to seek the answers to such questions as:

- How is the information product/service performing?
- Are the right things being done?
- Why did that work?
- Why did that not work?
- How can I use these insights to improve the performance and impact of this and future projects?

The toolkit guides you step by step through the evaluation process — why evaluation is necessary, who to involve in it, how to plan it and how to follow it up — and describes the tools available for evaluating a range of information products/services. It warns you of pitfalls you might encounter on the journey, but also demonstrates that evaluation can be invigorating, empowering and, above all, essential to learning and impact.

We hope that the toolkit will:

- add to the body of knowledge on project evaluation, particularly in relation to information products/services
- build the capacity within development organisations for evaluating information products/services
- develop among information practitioners a culture of internal evaluation for information-related projects

What does the toolkit contain?

The book starts with an overview in **Part 1** of the evaluation of information projects, products and services within the context of the project cycle and project management. It stresses two central tenets of evaluation – stakeholder participation and learning – and provides an outline of what evaluation involves and how it links with monitoring and impact assessment.

Part 2 explains the evaluation process as it relates to information projects, products and services. It describes how to prepare the terms of reference for an evaluation, covering such aspects as deciding its scope, methodology, data sources and work plan. It then discusses how to design and implement an evaluation and how to communicate the evaluation findings and translate them into action.

In **Part 3**, we provide a range of tools that can be used in all stages of the evaluation process, from planning and implementing an information-related project to reporting and follow up. The ways in which the tools can be applied will depend on resources, the environment in which an evaluation is being conducted and the type of evaluation.

Part 4 provides evaluation guidelines for nine information products and services – training course, newsletter, website, question-and-answer service, small library/resource centre, online community, rural radio, database and information dissemination service. For each product and service we look at its concept and objectives, data needs and stakeholder participation, evaluation focus and indicators, data collection and analysis, and the plan for communicating the evaluation findings.

The figure here shows the toolkit structure as an integrated whole, with some evaluation guidelines.

The *Smart Toolkit* – the context, process and tools of evaluation, as an integrated whole, with guidelines for evaluating selected information products and services

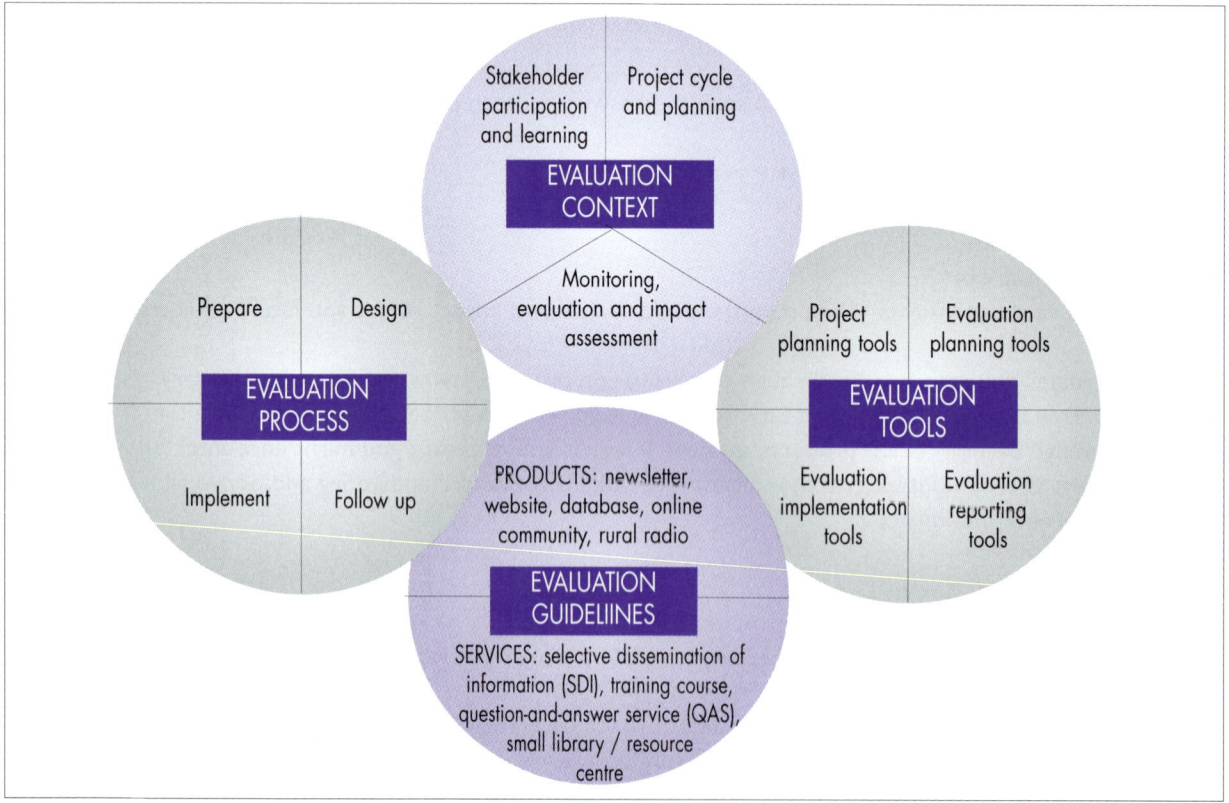

Since the idea of compiling this toolkit was first mooted in 2001, the process has been a highly participatory one. We would like to keep it that way, and to encourage all those using it to provide feedback so that we can continue to revise and update it. To that end, users are invited to contribute to the discussion on **www.smarttoolkit.net**.

You will find in the Annexes some background to how this toolkit was compiled, who was involved in the compilation, an extensive list of information sources (publications and websites) on evaluation, and a glossary of terms.

Part 1
THE EVALUATION CONTEXT

Background

Stakeholder participation

Learning

The project cycle

The project plan

Monitoring

Evaluation

Impact assessment

Setting up a monitoring, evaluation and impact assessment system

The evaluation of information projects, products and services geared to reducing poverty and improving livelihoods in developing countries takes place within the context of a set of standard activities. Experience shows that it is difficult to understand, implement and follow-up evaluation without understanding these contextual activities – from project planning, implementation and management to monitoring, impact assessment and follow up.

In Part 1, we start by providing some background to monitoring, evaluation and impact assessment, what the terms mean, and recent changes in approach. We then look at the two fundamental ingredients of good evaluation – stakeholder participation and learning. Having laid these foundations, we move on to the context in which evaluation takes place – the project cycle, a widely used management tool, and the importance of planning. We then look briefly at monitoring, evaluation and impact assessment before moving on, in Part 2, to an in-depth discussion of the evaluation process

Throughout Part 1 you'll find information on best practice, as well as examples of applying the various activities in a project cycle to information projects, products or services.

Background

Monitoring and evaluation relate to the assessment of project planning and implementation. Monitoring focuses mainly on the *operational issues*, whereas evaluation is often more concerned with the *strategic issues* and it uses information generated by monitoring. Impact assessment is, in effect, the final part of evaluation, concerned mainly with looking for the changes in the lives of people as a result of a project or programme.

> **Box 1.1**
> **Definitions**
>
> MONITORING
> Monitoring is a continuous process of collecting and analysing project information to assist timely decision-making, ensure accountability and provide the basis for evaluation and learning. It usually consists of a standard set of activities. It is used to provide management and key stakeholders with an indication of progress and achievement of objectives, measured against set indicators and expected results.
>
> EVALUATION
> Evaluation is a systematic assessment – as objective as possible – of a planned, ongoing or completed project. It aims to answer specific management questions, to judge the overall value of a project and to provide lessons learned to improve future actions, planning and decision-making. Evaluations commonly seek to determine the accessibility, efficiency, effectiveness, impact, sustainability, relevance, usability and utility of a project to the organisation's objectives.
>
> 'M&E' is a commonly used way of referring to the combination of 'monitoring and evaluation', which together provide the knowledge and information needed for effective project management, organisational and stakeholder learning, reporting and accountability purposes.
>
> IMPACT
> Impact is the change in the lives of people as perceived by them at the time of evaluation, as well as sustainability – enhancing changes in their environment to which the project has contributed. Changes can be positive or negative, intended or unintended. These perceived changes in people's lives could correspond to either the goal or the purpose level of the intervention (see pages 68-83).

Monitoring, evaluation and impact assessment processes have traditionally been seen mainly as a means of accounting to funding agencies for expenses on inputs and activities and have frequently been carried out by an outside evaluator. The role of these processes in managing for impact is often neglected, and the information and insights they generate remain unused.

Increasingly, however, it is being recognised that these processes can be used not only to meet funding requirements, but also for self-assessment and learning and that they should include stakeholders, and especially primary stakeholders – those who use the information products/services. This means doing things in a different way with implications for planning, evaluation skills and budgets. Table 1.1 summarises this change in the approach to monitoring, evaluation and impact assessment.

Table 1.1
Change in the approach to monitoring, evaluation and impact assessment

OLD APPROACH	NEW APPROACH
Monitoring, evaluation and impact assessment mainly for external funding body	Monitoring, evaluation and impact assessment for everybody involved in the project
Focused mainly on the logframe activities and on financial reporting	Provides feedback, generates learning and supports changes in direction
Lots of data and little analysis (lengthy reports)	Strong on analysis of how to make improvements
Little learning	Learning is the key
Little stakeholder participation	Lots of stakeholder participation in decision-making and inclusion in the evaluation team
Seen as boring and not very useful for project staff or stakeholders	Seen as active, interesting and useful

If the ultimate goal of an evaluation is managing for impact – and it should be – then that evaluation needs to reflect a strong commitment to stakeholder participation and to learning. How to involve stakeholders, especially primary stakeholders, and how to achieve learning should be built into project management, from start to finish.

Stakeholder participation

Stakeholder participation is the active involvement of stakeholders in the planning, management, monitoring and evaluation of a project. Stakeholders are individuals, groups or organisations who have a direct or indirect interest in a project, and/or are affected by its implementation and outcome. They are often divided into primary and secondary stakeholders. Examples of stakeholders include project target groups, NGOs, community leaders and donor agencies.

Primary stakeholders are the people who will be using the information product/service, and therefore the only group who can really talk about project impact. If a product/service is not easily accessible and usable at the primary stakeholder level, there is unlikely to be impact. Involving primary stakeholders in the project cycle will enhance usability by helping to ensure that:

- the information product/service is complete, relevant and sustainable

- it is accessible both physically and in terms of its delivery (e.g., the language and language level used to deliver and promote it)

The involvement of different groups of stakeholders should be appropriate and mutually agreed. Primary and secondary stakeholder participation can improve the quality and impact of information products/services by:

- helping to establish agreement on the situation to be addressed and the proposed course of action

- giving stakeholders a clear idea of what should be done and why, thus enhancing their support for and involvement in the project

- improving the quality of information collected

- improving the quality of the analysis, with stakeholders often providing a better insight into the strengths and weaknesses of a project

- helping to create more interest in and understanding of the project and thus enhancing its impact

There are various ways you can include stakeholders in the various stages of a project. Participatory approaches have gained increasing popularity since the 1960s, with those coming under the generic term 'participatory learning and action' (PLA) proving to be most effective (see points 5, 6 and 7 in Box 1.2). Older approaches to evaluation tended to see stakeholders as either passive or as sources of information; their active participation was not encouraged (see points 1, 2, 3 and 4 in Box 1.2).

Stakeholder participation is not just about including stakeholders in the project cycle. It is also about ensuring that the level of their participation is meaningful and involves the sharing of ideas, information and decision-making. Stakeholder participation should not be passive, with the stakeholders simply being informed about a project, asked questions, consulted from time to time and/or asked to provide resources to help the project, such as labour or transport.

For stakeholder participation to be effective, it needs to be:

- **Functional:** This involves stakeholders influencing decisions in projects where the general nature of the project might have already been decided upon, but there is a lot of room for further and more detailed decision-making.

- **Interactive:** This involves stakeholders participating in joint analyses, which lead to action plans, new projects and institutional development, as well as an increased sense of ownership of the project

Only with a combination of functional and interactive participation, and the inclusion of primary stakeholders, can stakeholder participation be truly participatory.

Box 1.2
Stakeholder participation in the context of the old and new approaches

OLD APPROACH

1. PASSIVE PARTICIPATION: People are simply told what is going to happen or what has already happened. *EXAMPLE: Health officers are informed that a training course on HIV/AIDS will be organised for them over the next couple of months*

2. PARTICIPATION BY INFORMATION GIVING: People participate by answering questions, without being able to influence the process. *EXAMPLE: Visitors to a library are asked to fill in a questionnaire in order to assess their interest in a range of books*

3. PARTICIPATION BY CONSULTATION: People participate by being consulted, being able to give their opinion and to comment on the process, but don't share in the decision-making. *EXAMPLE: Readers of a newsletter are asked to give their opinion on its content and format. The publishers decide which suggestions to implement*

4. PARTICIPATION BY MATERIAL INCENTIVES: People provide resources such as labour, knowledge and transport in return for food, cash or other material incentives. They have a say in deciding whether or not to become involved but can't influence the activity as a whole. *Example: Information project managers write an article for a newsletter, sharing their experiences and being paid a nominal fee for their contribution*

NEW APPROACH

5. FUNCTIONAL PARTICIPATION: People participate and influence decisions in projects where the general content has already been decided upon, but there is a lot of room for further decision-making. *EXAMPLE: Extension officers participate in developing an extension approach and trainers participate in developing the methodology for a training course on the new approach*

6. INTERACTIVE PARTICIPATION: People participate in joint analysis, which leads to action plans, new projects and institutional development; this increases their sense of ownership and stimulates them to take control over local decision-making. *EXAMPLE: Guided by radio programme makers, young girls are encouraged to identify specific issues they think a radio programme for young people should deal with and get assistance in developing their own programmes*

7. SELF-MOBILISATION: People are able to identify their own problems and come up with their own solutions, but might need some external help to effect these solutions. *EXAMPLE: Villagers have carried out their own needs assessment and have asked for a meeting with local authorities to help them organise a training course*

Adapted from Pretty (1994)

Getting stakeholder participation right is not easy. It can often take a lot of time and resources that may not be available, and you need to be open to different ideas and opinions once you give people a chance to influence decision-making. It is therefore important to think through the process of stakeholder participation, carefully considering both the benefits and the challenges.

Learning

Here we are talking about learning throughout the project cycle, including the evaluation phase of the cycle (see Figure 1.2, page 8). Learning involves reflecting on project experiences and using the lessons from that reflection to improve future actions.

It is important to integrate learning into planning, monitoring and evaluation and to include primary and secondary stakeholders in this process. Using participatory learning-oriented methods in project planning, implementing, monitoring and evaluation will encourage stakeholders to share their views. The aim is to create an active learning process, or cycle, that helps to improve your information projects, products and services. Kolb's learning cycle (see Figure 1.1) is a commonly used model.

**Figure 1.1
The learning cycle**

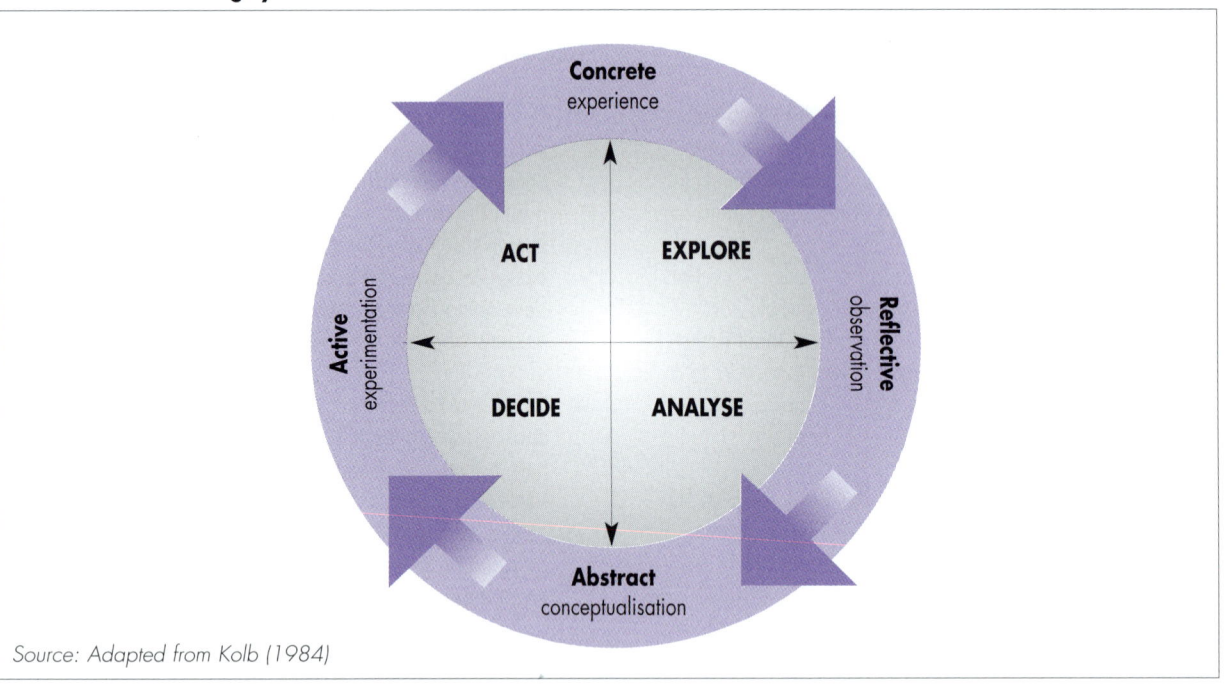

Source: Adapted from Kolb (1984)

In this model, 'concrete experience' is followed by 'reflection' on that experience, carried out on a personal or group basis. 'Reflection' is followed by 'abstract conceptualisation', which involves describing the experience and applying known theories to it, and then moving to 'active experimentation'. This involves constructing ways of modifying experience, leading in turn to the next 'concrete experience'. This whole process might happen in a matter of minutes, or over days, weeks or months, depending on the topic, and there may be a simultaneous 'wheels within wheels' process. It is a good idea to start the cycle by reflecting on experiences you've already had (see the example in Box 1.3) and then proceed through the other stages.

It is worth noting that, often, different stakeholder groups find themselves at different stages of the learning cycle. Whereas one group might have already decided to apply some lessons learned, another group might not yet have completed its review or explored solutions to problems revealed by the review. Keeping all parties in step with each other through the learning cycle is important if there is to be impact on the way in which changes are made to the existing project and to future, similar projects. There are many ways in which learning can be enhanced throughout a project. These include:

- involving stakeholders in all stages of the project and providing them with relevant and timely information throughout its planning and implementation

- developing the capacity of stakeholders to contribute to all stages of the learning cycle

- providing continuous learning opportunities (e.g., workshops, training, exchange visits)

- encouraging dialogue, openness, creativity and experimentation

You also need to be aware of factors that could adversely affect learning in an organisation (see Box 1.4).

Box 1.3
The learning cycle applied to farmer training

REFLECTION: The learning in this case applies to a national fisheries extension department that had been working with farmers for many years using the Training-and-Visit (T&V) approach. It did not seem to be working, so the extension workers set aside time with some farmers to reflect upon what might be going wrong and what to change in the next round of training.

LEARNING: From the reflection they learned that farmers wanted training that enabled them to adapt new practices to their own farming methods, and wanted support after the initial training. The farmers were literate and were happy to have support provided via written and illustrated materials. And they wanted materials written at their level of language and understanding, with illustrations related to their environment, and complete in all technical details.

APPLICATION: Based on this reflection and learning, the extension service realised that they needed to work in a participatory way with farmers to develop the materials and that they needed the expertise of writers and illustrators to produce really useful and usable materials. Together they decided to work with the farmers as teams both before and during the training.

ACTION: Before the training, the teams went to the farmers' areas to get to know their working environment and information sources. During the training, the writers and illustrators worked with the farmers to get the language and illustrations right and with the extension workers to ensure that materials were technically correct and complete. The draft versions were tested with a selection of farmers, and were then produced and distributed to the farmers who had attended the training, as well as to those who had not attended but were aware of the training through word-of-mouth, the extension service, the promotional posters developed during the training course and the radio broadcasts arranged by the extension service.

THE NEXT CYCLE: After this initial phase, the extension service went through two further cycles of reflection and learning. From these they learned that providing the materials alone proved almost as effective as providing training and materials. To implement the project in other regions they needed to go through the full cycle of putting teams together, getting to know farmers and their environments, and writing and illustrating specifically for them.

Box 1.4
Factors affecting the learning cycle

ORGANISATIONAL CULTURE: In some organisations, accountability tends to be associated with blame. This discourages openness and learning. This culture should be changed, encouraging people to see that there is often as much to learn from poorly performing projects as there is from successful ones.

PRESSURE TO SPEND: Learning takes time, and the pressure to meet disbursement targets can lead to shortcuts being taken during the project planning stage, with lessons from previous experiences being ignored or only selectively applied, in haste.

LACK OF INCENTIVES TO LEARN: If accountability is not built into the project cycle, there will be little incentive to learn. This is particularly so when staff rotation or turnover is frequent, with people often having moved on long before the shortcomings of a project in which they were involved become evident.

LOSS OF INSTITUTIONAL MEMORY: This also stems from frequent staff rotation or turnover, as well as from a reliance on short-term consultants and the weakening or disbanding of specialist departments.

TUNNEL VISION: People, departments and organisations can get stuck in a rut, carrying on with using familiar procedures and approaches even when their shortcomings are well known.

INSECURITY AND CHANGE: If people are unclear about an organisation's objectives, or these objectives appear to change frequently, this will not encourage learning.

INEQUALITY IN THE DONOR RELATIONSHIP: If donors take the driving seat, rather than working on an equal footing with the recipient organisation and sharing decision-making, this can inhibit the incentive to learn.

Adapted from OECD (2001)

The project cycle

Monitoring, evaluation and impact assessment operate within the context of a project cycle. Before we look at what a project cycle is and how it works, it is important to be clear first about what a project is, and what exactly we mean by 'information products and services', the main focus of this *Smart Toolkit*. These definitions are given in Box 1.5.

Box 1.5
Some important definitions

What is the difference between a project and a programme?

- A **project** is a one-off activity undertaken to create or deliver a product/service aimed at bringing about beneficial change or added value. It contrasts with processes or operations, which are permanent and seek to create or deliver the same product/service over and over again.

- A **programme** can consist of several projects and is therefore more complex and likely to be spread over a longer period of time. Collectively, these projects are usually intended to contribute to a higher level objective (e.g., improving the livelihoods of the programme beneficiaries).

The terms 'information **products**' and 'information **services**' usually mean project deliverables, such as training courses, newsletters, information databases and libraries. Unlike projects, which tend to have a beginning and an end, services are often continuous, with no declared end.

Figure 1.2
The project cycle

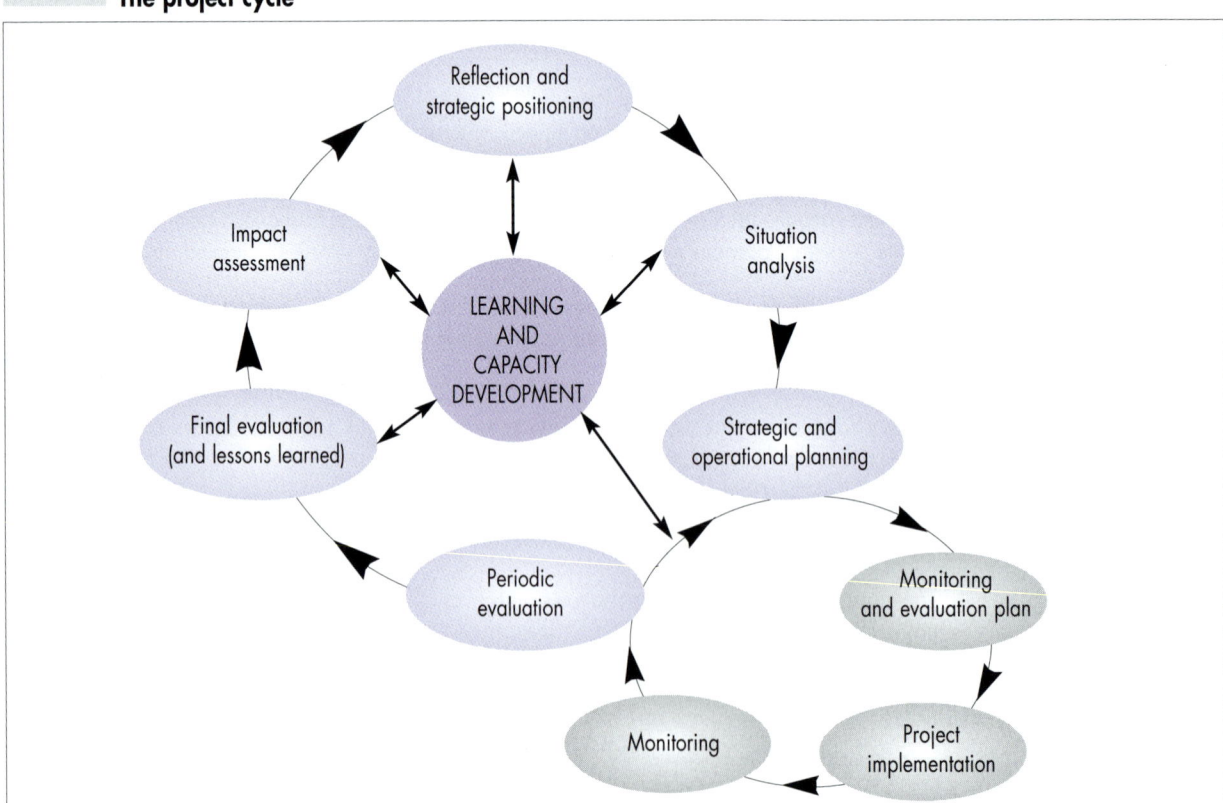

The activities in a project cycle should relate to each other within an overall, coherent management process. If opportunities for stakeholder participation and learning are built into the cycle, the lessons learned can be integrated into subsequent project cycles, not only to increase the impact of each project, but also to improve overall capacity development.

Figure 1.2 illustrates the project cycle. At the hub of the cycle, and relating to each stage of the cycle, is learning.

> **Box 1.6**
> **The project cycle applied to a farmers' training course**
>
> Take as an example, a training course on improved agricultural practices for small-scale farmers. This project is part of a long-term programme to improve agricultural production in the area, with other elements of the programme including such measures as providing seed and supporting irrigation initiatives. Applying the project cycle stages to this project would involve:
>
> REFLECTION AND STRATEGIC POSITIONING: Be clear about your organisation's vision and policies, and how these relate to strengthening the capacity of farmers to increase agricultural production. At this point, lessons learned from previous project evaluations and impact assessments should be brought in to contribute to strategic positioning.
>
> SITUATION ANALYSIS: Take a critical look at issues constraining agricultural production. These might show that offering a course in improved agricultural practices will probably contribute towards increased agricultural production. Or it may not. Assuming that it does, however, you now move on to planning the project strategy and operations.
>
> STRATEGIC PLANNING: Working with stakeholders, decide what you want to change at farmer level. This provides the information you need in order to decide on such strategic factors as course content, form and participants. It should also be fed into the monitoring and evaluation plan, which should be developed at this stage.
>
> OPERATIONAL PLANNING: Sort out practical matters such as the budget, roles and responsibilities, resource persons and participants. You need to make a detailed operational plan. This stage should also include finalising the monitoring and evaluation plan, which should include how and when to conduct the evaluation and who is to conduct it.
>
> MONITORING AND EVALUATION PLAN: Monitoring is concerned mainly with operational issues, whereas evaluation focuses on the more strategic questions A monitoring and evaluation plan involves defining the plan's purpose and scope, reviewing the project concept and objectives, assessing stakeholders' key information needs, formulating indicators, organising data collection and analysis, and deciding on the communication and reporting process.
>
> IMPLEMENTATION: This relates first to project implementation, and then to the implementation of periodic evaluations. The evaluations can be conducted before (*ex ante*), during and/or after (*ex post*) the project is implemented. In the case of the training course, this could translate into running the course (project implementation), then asking trainees for feedback at the end of the course, and following this up some months later with an evaluation of how they applied their learning.
>
> MONITORING: Monitoring should start as soon as the project is implemented. It is a continuous process that should focus on the project inputs (e.g., resource persons), activities (e.g., field trip) and outputs (e.g. number of farmers trained). It can be carried out in a variety of ways, including observations and/or interaction with the participants.
>
> EVALUATION: Evaluation focuses on immediate (short-tem) project outcomes (e.g., participant satisfaction, course relevance). The training course evaluation could be done at the end of the course by asking participants to fill in a questionnaire, score the course against given criteria and/or discuss what worked and what did not. They could also be asked whether they can put into action what they have learnt.
>
> IMPACT ASSESSMENT: The focus here is on what (long-term) changes occurred in the lives of the target group. Impact assessment can be time consuming and complex requiring, in this case, not only good baseline data about the area's agricultural production, but also a clear idea from the outset of the change the course was intended to have.

Used correctly, the project cycle can be a powerful project management tool, helping to improve the delivery of information projects, products and services and to increase their impact. Box 1.7 gives you some ideas about how to work with a project cycle in order to achieve learning and impact.

> **Box 1.7**
> **Working with the project cycle to achieve learning and impact**
>
> In order to facilitate learning during the project cycle, there are several issues you need to be aware of:
>
> SHARED LEARNING: Involving stakeholders in learning opportunities (e.g., exchange visits, progress meetings) is crucial to the effectiveness of a project. Learning can be stimulated by encouraging people to try out new ideas and new ways of working, to review and analyse project activities, and to participate in decision-making
>
> STAKEHOLDER INVOLVEMENT: Stakeholder involvement in the project cycle ensures that different perspectives and views are taken into account, thus enhancing the relevance and effectiveness of the project. It also helps to create a sense of ownership of the project, particularly among the primary stakeholders.
>
> LINKING PLANNING AND EVALUATION: It is important to ensure that evaluation is focused on what is necessary to know in relation to the planned activities and objectives of the project. Evaluation findings can assist in making decisions at both the strategic and operational level.
>
> DOCUMENTATION: It is important to document project activities and to collect project information in a well-structured and systematic way, ensuring that the information is reliable and valid. Poor documentation will detract from effective evaluation. It is also important to record project failures as well as successes, if the project is to have credibility
>
> FEEDBACK AND DISSEMINATION: The findings of the different stages of the project cycle need to be fed back and disseminated in a targeted way, ensuring that the right people receive the right information at the right time.
>
> COST-EFFECTIVENESS: It is important to be aware of the extent to which project activities are carried out effectively in terms of cost.

We now look at the core stages of the project cycle – planning, monitoring, evaluation and impact assessment, bearing in mind that all of them should reflect a commitment to learning and stakeholder participation.

The project plan

A project plan is a formal, approved document used to guide project implementation and management. It covers such elements as objectives (expected results), assumptions, processes, activities, costs and timing.

Project planning is the process of drawing up a project plan, and it is important to get it right. As the term suggests, it involves planning the whole project, not just individual parts of it. It should provide:

- a **strategic** outlook on how the project can make a difference – its outcome and impact

- an **operational** outlook on how to implement and manage the project – its inputs, activities and outputs

- a clear reference **framework** for strategic monitoring and evaluation

Project plan components

The components of a project plan should include:

- **Background and problem statements:** Explain the context in which your project will operate and the problems it intends to address

- **Objectives:** The *goal* (overall development objective) is the ultimate change in the lives of the beneficiaries that you wish to bring about through the project intervention; and the project *purpose* (specific objective) relates to the change in the behaviour of the beneficiaries you wish to happen in order to contribute towards the goal

- **Assumptions:** These are the external factors that influence the success of your project, but that you can't control; being clear about your assumptions will give your project plan the flexibility it should have

- **Inputs:** These include human and material resources, and their cost

- **Activities:** Specify exactly what you will do in order to deliver the outputs

- **Outputs (expected results):** These include the core product/service you wish to provide that will contribute to the project purpose

- **Indicators, and means of verification:** Indicators are variables that help to measure the success of a project; methods and sources of verification describe how and where you intend finding the required information to verify the measurements

Theory of action

Underpinning all these components should be your theory of action. By this, we mean an idea of what changes the project is expected to bring about and what is needed to bring about that change.

Every project plan should have a theory of action. If your theory of action is clearly spelled out, it will also show what you need to evaluate in order to determine whether expectations are becoming reality. A theory of action is more than just a plan; it helps you to see all the links relating to how the information project will be carried out. It will give you and your stakeholders a clear picture of what you want to achieve, the path to take to get there, and what you need to evaluate to measure your performance.

A visual diagram is a helpful means for creating shared understanding about a project's theory of action. Figure 1.3 provides an example of the theory of action, the project example being the development of this toolkit. Although this pathway was not developed at the outset of the project, it is useful to see the path taken and how it is expected to evolve with time.

Logical framework

Every project plan should also have a logical framework, linked to the theory of action. A logical framework is often used to provide a summary of a project plan. It is meant to create shared understanding among key stakeholders about the thrust and logic of the plan. The standard outline

Figure 1.3
Example of a theory of action, applied to the development of this toolkit

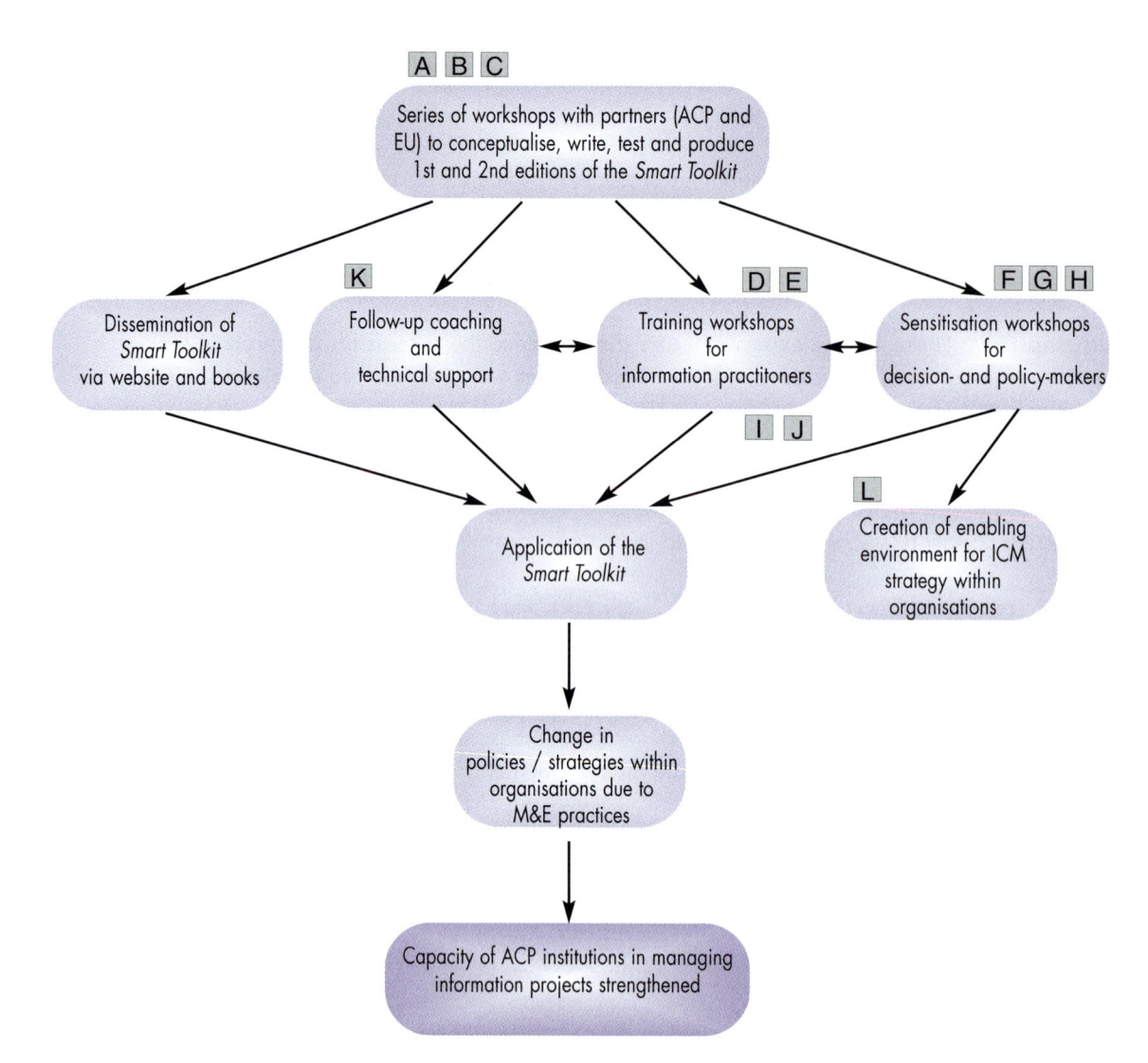

LEGEND

A Lack of awareness about monitoring and evaluation (M&E) and impact assessment
B Lack of general information on M&E
C Writing a book increases the information available on the evaluation of information projects, products and services
D Workshop participants work in the area of information projects, products and services
E Training increases the awareness and importance of evaluating information projects, products and services
F Increasing the awareness of policy-makers increases their support for M&E within their organisations
G Access to policy-makers to convince them to attend the workshop
H Local organisations lobby key organisations, and their policy-makers in particular, to attend the awareness-raising workshops
I Trainees are willing to learn and put in place a system for the M&E of their information projects, products and services
J Trainees take the initiative to develop their own skills further
K Other M&E experts can be called upon for support
L Policy- and decision-makers are convinced of the value of M&E and allow and support it

for a logical framework is shown in Table 1.2. People use different terms, sometimes, to those shown in the table (e.g., instead of 'Intervention Logic', which we use throughout this toolkit, you might see 'Narrative Summary' or 'Objective Hierarchy'). Whichever heading is used, it covers the various levels of objectives from inputs to activities, outputs (expected results), purpose and goal. These objectives should be linked in a well-designed and logical manner, such that if all of them are achieved there is a good chance of the goal being fulfilled.

Table 1.2
The logframe matrix

	INTERVENTION LOGIC	OBJECTIVELY VERIFIABLE INDICATORS	MEANS OF VERIFICATION	ASSUMPTIONS
GOAL				
PROJECT PURPOSE				
OUTPUTS (EXPECTED RESULTS)				
ACTIVITIES				
INPUTS				

A logical framework provides some information that is useful for monitoring, evaluation and impact assessment, but it should not be seen as the plan for these processes. It should be used as a flexible planning tool that can be revised regularly to reflect monitoring, evaluation and impact assessment findings.

Table 1.3 gives an example of a logical framework, as applied to the process of developing this toolkit (compare this with Figure 1.3, which shows a theory of action applied to this toolkit).

Developing a project plan

A good project plan is important because:

- it helps you to think through the changes you want to bring about through your information project
- it provides a basis for your monitoring, evaluation and impact assessment
- it makes it easier to develop strategies and operations, including mechanisms for learning and stakeholder participation, that really contribute towards impact
- it provides the basis for obtaining funding

Table 1.3
A summarised logical framework for the development of this toolkit

	INTERVENTION LOGIC	OBJECTIVELY VERIFIABLE INDICATORS	MEANS OF VERIFICATION	ASSUMPTIONS
GOAL	Contribute to agricultural development by building the capacity in the ACP			
PURPOSE	The capacity of ACP institutions in the management of their information projects strengthened	By the end of 2013 there is evidence of change in the way information projects are run through better targeting, improved content	- Annual reports showing changes in the way they provide services - Budget for M&E - Survey	
EXPECTED RESULT 1	Application of the toolkit	Usefulness of the toolkit in promoting M&E	- Stories - Survey	There is institutional support for the toolkit
ACTIVITIES FOR RESULT 1	Produce the toolkit through the holding of writing workshops, testing and reviewing of the toolkit	Toolkit prepared	Publication	
ACTIVITIES FOR RESULT 1	Organise training workshops on how to use the toolkit in ACP countries	Information specialists in partner organisations trained	Number of beneficiaries trained; plan of action	
EXPECTED RESULT 2	Policy- and decision-makers sensitised on the importance supporting environment for M&E	Policy- and decision-makers aware of importance and role of M&E in the functioning of their organisations	Post-workshop survey (6 months) Policy- and decision-makers are able to cite reasons why M&E is important	'Right' people attend the workshops
ACTIVITIES FOR RESULT 2	Organise workshops in ACP countries to sensitise policy- and decision-makers on the importance of M&E in managing information projects, products and services	Sensitisation workshops held in the ACP	Feedback from the workshop	
EXPECTED RESULT 3	Technical support available to partner organisations	Development of some type of framework which supports the carrying out of M&E	Annual reports Feedback	
ACTIVITIES FOR RESULT 3	Contract consultants to provide technical backstopping	Organisations using this support	Report on feedback of work done and the achievements	
ACTIVITIES FOR RESULT 3	Develop website to support the workshops, training activities, strategy development, etc. and to carry an online version of the toolkit	Website and supporting portal	Feedback via the Q&A	
INPUTS	Funds, technical			

When formulating the steps in developing a project plan, you should invite stakeholders to contribute to this process.

Important steps in the process are:

- Define the basic question, problem field or area of concern. Some possible examples are: What is your vision for an improved future situation? What do you consider your objective to be in relation to the identified problem area? What existing policies might affect your intervention?

- Conduct a thorough situation analysis, including an analysis of external factors (e.g., the policy environment). What is the core problem and how is this affected by other factors?

- Conduct a stakeholder analysis. Who are the stakeholders? In particular, who are the primary stakeholders? How are the stakeholders involved? Can they be included in the analysis? If so, how?

- As part of the stakeholder analysis, information projects need to carry out an 'information analysis' in relation, in particular, to their primary stakeholders (e.g., What information products/services already exist, and which ones are used, and to what extent and why? What means of communication are already available to deliver information, and which ones are used and why? How do people prefer information delivered to them? What language do they prefer?)

- Analyse possible approaches to addressing the problems that have been identified, and develop a strategy.

- Formulate objectives (goal, purpose, outputs), activities, indicators, means of verification, and assumptions.

- Develop a clear and viable plan for monitoring and evaluating the project, and for assessing its impact

- Develop a work plan and budget that include defined tasks and responsibilities, a budget overview and a time frame.

- Consider the need for capacity development for performing project tasks.

Common mistakes that can occur when developing a project plan include:

- not enough strategic thinking on which to base it
- not involving key stakeholders
- not relating the budget to the activities
- not realistically assessing the risks in implementing the plan
- using existing project plans without considering the specifics of a new project
- planning in too much detail too soon
- formulating an unrealistic set of objectives as a 'wish list' for the desired impact
- failing to review the project plan at regular intervals
- not learning from past experiences in planning

> **Box 1.8**
> **Some key points in project planning**
>
> - Define the boundary of the project by being clear about your vision, objectives and policies, as well as existing policies relating to the area of concern; specify expected impact and objectives as SMART objectives (see pages 50 and 96)
>
> - Conduct a thorough situation analysis that looks not only at current problems and issues, but also at possible future directions and opportunities
>
> - Consider issues of usability for all information products/services. Work with primary stakeholders to find out what forms of information products/services they want and can handle
>
> - Be clear about your assumptions, the external factors that might influence your project; the success or failure of a project often turns on these factors
>
> - Work in collaboration with stakeholders as much as possible to ensure shared learning, ownership and commitment and to increase the effectiveness, relevance and impact of the project
>
> - Be explicit about roles and responsibilities
>
> - Use your project plan for monitoring and evaluation, adapting it when necessary at both the operational and strategic levels
>
> - Use the plan for communication with all stakeholders, ensuring that everyone involved knows what they have to do, when, where, how and why

Monitoring

Monitoring helps you to find out if the delivery of your information projects, products and services is going according to your plan. It focuses on assessing project effectiveness and efficiency, especially at the levels of inputs, activities and outputs.

'Effectiveness' means the extent to which activities (e.g., a question-and-answer service, QAS) have contributed to delivering the service (e.g., answers to questions posed by QAS users). 'Efficiency' means the extent to which the project resources (time, people, materials, money) have been used to maximum benefit (e.g., the extent to which the QAS could have functioned with fewer resources).

If the project is not going according to plan, you might need to take additional measures to get it back on track. If that is not realistic, you might need to review your plan. Monitoring also provides you with the necessary background information to help explain evaluation information. Ultimately, monitoring helps you to learn from your experiences during the implementation process and this information is essential for making evaluations.

Monitoring is not an easy task, partly because people often lack the necessary skills and capacity. It involves:

- keeping records and following up all activities and products

- analysing and using what comes out of this work

The monitoring process

Monitoring is a continuous process of assessing what is happening with the project plan. It is mainly about answering the question: 'Are we doing things according to plan?' Monitoring can be conducted at different levels:

- **Individual level:** To what extent is what you're doing in line with the activities that are your responsibility? What is going well and what do we need to improve?

- **Project level:** To what extent are the activities being implemented and the resources being used in line with the project plan? What is going well and what do we need to improve?

- **Organisational level:** Where do we do well as an organisation and what can we improve?

- **Stakeholder level:** To what extent are stakeholders actively engaged in the project (e.g., in design, implementation, monitoring and evaluation)? What is going well and what needs to be improved?

Before conducting monitoring, you need to be clear about what aspects you want to monitor and how often to monitor them. For example, will you be monitoring all activities or only those that relate to stakeholders? Will your monitoring focus mainly on assessing how interim results contribute to the overall objectives and goal? Will you monitor activities weekly, monthly, or at some other interval?

Other key issues you need to consider when developing a monitoring process include:

- **Agreeing on the data** that you and other stakeholders need: Who needs what data and when? How do they intend to use the data? Remember that you should collect the data you need, not just data that make the project look good.

- **Agreeing on methods** for data collection and processing: How will data be collected (e.g., via interviews, questionnaires)? Who will collect the data? How will the data be processed (e.g., will the data be analysed using statistics software and then critically reviewed at a monitoring team meeting?

Box 1.9
Some key points in monitoring

- Ensure that the time and costs of your monitoring system are in balance with total time and costs of the project

- Link monitoring to your operational plan

- Involve stakeholders in the monitoring process. This will help to create understanding, ownership and commitment when making changes in the operational plan.

- Decide on what is essential data to be collected, as well as how to go about collecting, processing and reflecting on it together with the stakeholders involved in the project

- Organise shared learning events with stakeholders during the monitoring process

- Use monitoring data as a management tool, particularly at the level of operations (inputs, activities, outputs/expected results), to inform management and stakeholders about possible action that needs to be taken

- Ensure adequate and timely reporting to management and stakeholders, addressing their specific information needs

Implementing monitoring involves collecting and analysing the data, and reviewing and reporting the findings. Sometimes, findings can be acted upon immediately to improve project implementation. In other cases, they might be more substantial and should be fed into the evaluation process.

Project staff and stakeholders should be involved in designing and implementing the monitoring process. Ideally, the monitoring team should include representatives of the stakeholder groups.

Common mistakes in monitoring include:

- a lack of a clear reference framework in terms of what you will call success and what you will call failure; these are often defined through indicators

- defining too many indicators, making it a huge task to gather data and making interpretation difficult

- not being able to assess change, because you never assessed what the situation was like when you started (people often use baselines for this purpose; see pages 24 and 76)

- not involving stakeholders in defining what data they need and how to go about collecting and processing it

- collecting data, but not analysing them to understand their significance for management decision-making

- lack of clarity about the validity of the data collected and inadequate capacity to verify the data collected

- not organising learning events where the monitoring data are critically reviewed by various stakeholders

Evaluation

Whereas monitoring is concerned mainly with operational issues, evaluation focuses on the more strategic questions about the information projects, products and services. It involves:

- **generating data** on the progress and results of a project

- **reviewing this data** for current and future use and learning

- taking into account the **interests of the stakeholders** (e.g., beneficiaries, target groups, funding agencies, NGOs, partners, policy-makers, networks) who have a direct or indirect interest, positive or negative, in the project

Evaluation gives you the tools to explain what happened, and how and why things happened as they did. Evaluating information projects, products and services is particularly challenging. Whereas evaluating them from a management and accountability perspective is fairly straightforward, trying to determine their benefits, particularly in the medium to long term, is difficult. The picture becomes even more complex when information and communication technologies (ICTs) are involved and with the increasing globalisation of information products/services.

It is important to distinguish between external and internal evaluations:

- **External evaluations:** These are conducted by organisations or independent evaluators outside the organisation which is implementing and managing the project

- **Internal evaluations:** These are conducted by people within the organisation which is implementing and managing the project

A combination of both, with stakeholder participation, is usually best if real learning and impact are to be achieved. The focus in this toolkit, however, is on internal evaluation.

Evaluations can be conducted at various times in the project cycle:

- At the **beginning** of the project planning stage (also known as *ex ante* evaluation). The focus here is on assessing the project proposal in terms of relevance, feasibility, potential impact or expected benefits. The evaluation is like a second opinion on whether or not the project is viable. It includes checking to see if the needs of the stakeholders have been assessed properly and if the strategies and plans have developed adequately.

- At the **mid-way** (or other) point during the project. The focus here is on looking at project progress and performance and identifying changes in the environment that affect its effectiveness. The evaluation involves collecting and analysing data for performance indicators, to compare how well the project is being implemented against expected results. Sometimes a mid-way evaluation is conducted to explain an unusual event (e.g., the monitoring data might be showing a disturbing or remarkable trend).

- At the **end** of the project cycle (also known as *ex post* evaluation). The focus here is on reviewing the whole cycle within the context of its background, objectives, results, activities and inputs. The evaluation looks at how well the project did in terms of the expected outcomes, how sustainable these outcomes appear to be and what factors led to the results.

As far as possible, evaluation events should also be learning events. This can be done, for example, by organising stakeholder workshops to generate information as well as to communicate and discuss key findings of the evaluation.

The evaluation process

The key steps you need to consider when developing an evaluation process are:

- **Preparing the evaluation terms of reference:** This involves defining its scope and purpose, identifying data sources, deciding on methodology, communication, the evaluation team, the work plan and budget, and the terms of reference

- **Designing the evaluation:** This involves reviewing the project and the data needs, deciding on the focus of the evaluation and the key questions to address, selecting appropriate data collection and analysis methods, and drafting the communication strategy

- **Implementing the evaluation:** This involves collecting and analysing the data, and reviewing and reporting the findings

- **Following up the evaluation:** This involves drafting a plan to act on the findings, monitoring the implementation of the plan and managing any follow-up activities or consequent changes

Project staff and stakeholders should be involved in organising and designing the evaluation, and it is important to think through who will conduct the evaluation. Ideally, the evaluation team should include representatives of the project's stakeholder groups.

In Part 2, we go into detail on all these steps of the evaluation process.

As in monitoring, many mistakes can be made in evaluating a project. It is important to understand what mistakes are possible and how to avoid them. Common mistakes in evaluation include:

- not planning the evaluation in advance, and leaving no time and resources for it

- carrying out an evaluation for the sake of a donor, rather than for learning and development

- collecting data without a clear picture of the evaluation design and expected outputs

- not seeing evaluation as a learning process, and forcing conclusions upon stakeholders, rather than facilitating stakeholders to draw conclusions themselves

- producing too many or irrelevant recommendations

- writing an evaluation report without a clear idea on how the recommendations could be implemented

Box 1.10
Some key points in evaluation

- Evaluations should be planned assessments that focus on the extent to which a project has realised its objectives

- Ensure that, as far as possible, evaluations are viewed by the project implementers and stakeholders as a learning mechanism to enhance strategic and operational management

- Plan evaluations carefully at the start of a project, preferably with stakeholders, ensuring that there are enough resources to conduct the evaluations properly, and also to create ownership and commitment

- Develop the evaluation process in collaboration with stakeholders, ensuring that their specific information needs are integrated and their views on data collection and analysis are considered; this will contribute positively to relevance, impact, usability, accessibility, sustainability, utility, effectiveness and efficiency

- Evaluation questions should be broad questions that help you focus on what you need to know, both positive and negative

- Involve stakeholders in implementing the evaluation process (e.g., by setting up a stakeholders' evaluation committee and organising stakeholder workshops)

- Consider an evaluation as an important opportunity to learn and interact with stakeholders

- Relate the recommendations back to the original evaluation questions

Impact assessment

Impact assessment helps you to make strategic choices about your information projects, products or services and assess whether or not they are having an impact on behaviour, lives and livelihoods. Impact assessment is, in essence, an evaluation that focuses primarily on the changes a project or programme brings about. It is related to the highest level of project objective – the goal.

Assessing impact means looking for the changes in people's lives as a result of a programme or project. Often, impact assessments relate to a broader set of interventions (e.g., a programme with interlinked projects), not just one project. They involve looking not only for the expected changes, but also for the unexpected ones, both positive and negative. Impact assessment is usually done when a project or programme has been completed, or at least well on its way towards completion.

In the case of an information project or programme, an impact assessment will look at the broad, long-term effects of the information product/service, at whether the product/service has actually influenced the activities of the target group or led to a change in society. It will ask such questions as: To what extent has the project helped to improve the livelihoods of the farmers? How has it helped – or not helped? What are the unexpected positive and negative side-effects of the project? These questions will generate a better understanding of success or failure.

Although it is difficult to prove that an information product/service has had a demonstrable long-term impact at the level of socio-economic development, it is acceptable in some cases to make assumptions that there is a link between the changes observed and the project or programme, on the condition that the link is plausible. An example is given in Box 1.11.

Box 1.11
Impact assessment of extension booklets on aquaculture

In collaboration with the national fisheries department, an international development agency funded the production of a set of extension booklets to improve aquaculture practices among small-scale farmers. The booklet sets were developed with the farmers following a carefully designed participatory process that ensured they suited the farmers' lifestyle, culture, language, resources and objectives. Some 6,000 booklet sets were printed and distributed.

About 3 years later, the impact of the extension booklet sets was assessed. The impact assessment was conducted among three groups of farmers:

- those who heard about the booklets and came to the project office to get them

- those who received training in using the booklets, and were given the booklets during training

- those who received training but were not given any booklets

The farmers were asked to complete questionnaires designed to find out if they understood the booklets, had followed the recommendations in the booklets, had told other farmers about them, and had seen changes in levels of production. More than 70% said they had followed the recommendations, with higher levels among those who had received the booklets during training. Over the 3-year period, from a region where fish production among small-scale farmers had been static for many years, there was an average annual increase in production of 27%.

The impact assessment drew a direct link between the extension booklets and this increase in production, and attributed much of the success of the project to its inclusion of the farmers in developing the booklets.

The impact assessment process

The reasons for conducting an impact assessment can include:

- it is required for accountability purposes

- it is needed to help convince stakeholders (e.g., donors, partners and target groups) that the project is relevant to the intended changes

- it will improve the understanding of the effects (both positive and negative) on target groups

- it will help reformulate the strategy not only of the project, but also of the organisation implementing the project

Impact assessment can be time consuming and costly as it requires assessing changes at the level of the target groups, which can be quite complicated. The first step to take before conducting an impact assessment is to revisit the strategic framework of the project or programme. This should spell out what the intended impact is, the process leading to it, and the factors contributing to the change.

The key information needs of the different stakeholders then need to be addressed, and these will help determine the appropriate methods to be used for the assessment. The method chosen will also depend on the purpose and scope of the impact assessment. Often a combination of quantitative (e.g., statistics) and qualitative (e.g., perceptions, narrative) information will be gathered. If the purpose is not only accountability but also learning and empowerment, and the scope of the assessment is very participatory and there are adequate financial resources, then more participatory and qualitative methods will probably be appropriate, not least because they can be used to enhance learning.

Common impact assessment methods include:

- **Using available data on the target group:** These data might have been collected by the project organisation or stakeholders, or from external sources such as a bureau of statistics. If the data required are available, this is a cost-effective basis for an impact assessment. Often, however, the available data might not be exactly what are needed and therefore do not clearly show what changes the project has brought about. Taking as an example the farmers' training course referred to in Box 1.11, if there has been increased production this might be attributable to the course, but it could also be attributable to more effective extension services or simply to the weather being more favourable. Will the available data distinguish adequately between these various possible reasons for increased production?

- **Surveying the target group:** This involves conducting the assessment among a sample group of the intended project beneficiaries. If the target group is extensive, the sample should be large, but the cost of this needs to be taken into account compared with the total cost of the project.

- **Self-assessment:** This can be conducted on various aspects of changes (e.g., change in capacity). A range of tools can be used, preferably participatory and learning-orientated ones, in line with PLA (as discussed earlier, under 'Stakeholder participation', see page 4).

- **Impact stories:** Here the emphasis is on collecting in-depth qualitative information ('stories') from a limited number of people in the target group. The stories can provide rich information that helps to interpret the impact of the project on the target group. A useful methodology for this is the Most Significant Change (MSC) technique (Davies and Dart, 2005), based on finding out what people consider the most important change to have occurred as a result of a project, and being prepared for changes that were not envisaged in the original project plan. This technique has the added advantage that the key indicators are chosen not by outsiders but by the people in the target group.

- **Participatory methods:** An example of a participatory method is an impact flow chart. Here, people in the target group (and other stakeholders) are asked to describe the key elements of the project and how these have contributed to observed or perceived changes.

It is often advisable to use a mixture of methods. Increasingly, engaging primary and secondary stakeholders in impact assessment is seen as good practice. Interactive methods such as self-assessment and story-telling can facilitate such involvement.

Making impact assessment participatory is important because the only perspective from which to see impact is that of the target group itself. The impact the target group sees is the impact that matters. The typical characteristics of participatory impact assessment are given in Box 1.12.

Box 1.12
The core issues of impact assessment

The core issues to be aware of when designing an impact assessment include:

- communication (the information needs of all stakeholders)
- context (the effect of the environment on the assessment)
- scale and scope (where the assessment is conducted and how much it seeks to address)
- attribution (who takes credit for change)
- indicators (what indicators are used and how they are selected)
- learning and accountability (why the assessment is being done)
- participation (who is involved in the assessment)
- resources (what is available in terms of human, material and financial resources)
- time and timing (when the assessment is conducted and how much time is need to implement it)

Common mistakes in impact assessment include:

- waiting for the results of an impact assessment when you could have already understood many key lessons about the outcomes from earlier monitoring and evaluation

- not planning enough time and resources for conducting the impact assessment

- confusing attribution and contribution; at the level of impact, usually you will not be able to attribute change to your project alone, as there could be many other influencing factors

- not giving enough attention to communicating the assessment findings to stakeholders and not encouraging them to analyse the findings

- conducting the impact assessment too early for project impact to be shown, or too late, when changes could have been affected by many other intervening factors

> **Box 1.13**
> **Some key points in impact assessment**
>
> - Gather baseline data as early as possible (ideally, at the start of the project) to be able to measure change against these data
>
> - Ensure that the resources needed for the impact assessment are available
>
> - Involve stakeholders in the design and implementation of the impact assessment
>
> - Combine quantitative and qualitative, participatory and conventional, and individual and group-based methods of data collection
>
> - Ensure adequate feedback of the findings to all stakeholders
>
> - See the assessment as an important tool for strategy development
>
> - Link the evaluation of project outcomes to impact assessment

For a more detailed understanding of impact assessment, its core issues and how these issues are played out in actual impact studies conducted around the world, it is worth reading the CTA publication *Perceptions and Practice: An Anthology of Impact Assessment Experiences* (2006). The book describes a number of impact stories.

Setting up a monitoring, evaluation and impact assessment system

This involves the following steps:

1 **Define the purpose and scope** of the system: The purposes could include: accountability to funding agencies (upward accountability is most common), to partners (sidewards accountability) and to beneficiaries (downward accountability); informing strategic directions, to make changes if necessary; informing operational directions, to make changes if necessary; and empowering key stakeholders. Each purpose has different consequences for the process (e.g., where the purpose is to empower the stakeholders, the process will be more participatory and learning-oriented). By 'scope' we mean the level of detail required, the level of stakeholder participation and the level of funding available (e.g., you might want to make the system highly participatory, but funding constraints limit the extent to which you can involve stakeholders).

2 **Review the project concept and objectives:** This involves asking such questions as: What is the project about? What is the theory of action underlying it? What does it intend to achieve? What are the assumptions about critical success factors?

3 **Assess the stakeholders' key information needs:** The most important question here is: What do management, other project staff, beneficiaries and other stakeholders need to know and when? Information needs usually relate to project relevance, impact, sustainability, effectiveness and efficiency. Evaluation questions focus on relevance, impact and sustainability at the level of goal/impact and specific objective/outcome. Monitoring questions focus on effectiveness and efficiency at the expected results and activity levels. Table 1.4 illustrates how information needs relate to different levels of objectives, with some sample questions.

Table 1.4
Linking information needs with different levels of objectives in a farmer training project

OBJECTIVES	LEVEL OF OBJECTIVES	EVALUATION CRITERIA	SAMPLE QUESTIONS
GOAL To improve farmers' livelihoods	IMPACT	Impact Relevance Sustainability Utility	*Evaluation questions:* To what extent have farmers' food security situations improved as a result of the project? Why/why not? What are the unexpected positive and negative side-effects? To what extent is improving food security relevant to farmers' livelihoods? To what extent is the change in the food security a lasting change? Why/why not?
PURPOSE To increase the number of farmers who apply improved farming practices	OUTCOMES	Effectiveness Relevance Usability	*Evaluation questions:* To what extent has the training contributed to good farming practices? Why/why not? To what extent are good farming practices relevant to the needs of the farmers? Why/why not?
EXPECTED RESULTS Farmers trained in improved agricultural farming practices	OUTPUTS	Effectiveness Accessibility Usability	*Monitoring questions:* Are farmers using the new practices? If 'Yes', then ask why and with what result? If 'No', then ask why not?
ACTIVITIES - Assess needs - Develop training course - Organise training course - Run training course - Follow up trainees	ACTIVITIES	Efficiency	*Monitoring questions:* Could the activities be implemented with less money and fewer materials and human resources? Why/why not?

4 **Formulate indicators and other data requirements:** You need to formulate a list of criteria against which to measure effectiveness and efficiency, and determine the type of data (quantitative and qualitative) you will need to carry out this measurement (e.g. 'number of farmers applying good farming practices' and 'reasons for not applying good farming practices').

5 **Organise the data collection, recording and analysis:** What methods will you use to ensure the right data are being collected and properly recorded and analysed? They can be qualitative/quantitative, individual/group based, participatory/conventional; there is more on all these methods in Part 3 (pages 106-114). How will the various stakeholders be involved in these processes? There is more information on different types of stakeholder involvement in Part 2 (pages 35-37).

6 **Organise critical reflection of events and processes:** Critical reflection means asking not only 'what happened' and 'why', but also 'what does this mean?' and 'what are we going to do about it?' This assists in learning and in managing for impact.

7 **Develop the communication and reporting process:** You should decide whom you need to communicate with and report to during the monitoring and evaluation and impact processes, and how to do this. Different stakeholders have different information needs and different reporting requirements.

8 **Assess capacities and conditions for implementing the system:** You need to be clear about what you need in terms of human capacities, incentives, structures, procedures and finance. You also need to assess the potential risks in the process of data collection, recording and reporting. Training farmers in participatory data collection methods will help to build the human capacity and also be an incentive for them to be involved in participatory monitoring and evaluation. A low level of support for a project will have implications for the capacities and conditions necessary to conduct monitoring, evaluation and impact assessment, so it may be necessary to think about how to motivate stakeholders about the importance of these processes.

A well-designed and organised system will ensure that:

- the right data are being collected at the right time during and after project implementation
- the data collected will help guide project implementation and strategic decisions
- project staff and stakeholders will not be overwhelmed by the amount of data gathered
- the time and money spent in collecting and analysing data, and collating and reporting the information derived from this, will be reasonable

Box 1.14
An example of using a monitoring, evaluation and impact assessment system to shape communication activities

Healthlink Worldwide is a specialist health and development agency with a strong focus on:

- communication: supporting partners and clients to share health information effectively
- information and knowledge management (IKM): helping people find solutions to specific IKM problems
- networking and learning: sharing learning through interactive local, national and global networks

Monitoring, evaluation and impact assessment have always been an important component of Healthlink's work, but the nature of these processes has changed over the years:

- they are now more participatory, all being done in consultation with the beneficiaries or their representatives, from the point when the evaluation plan and indicators for a project are developed, to the analysis of results and implementation of learning

- a qualitative approach is now more common; although Healthlink still keeps track of numbers, these are linked to qualitative changes that have taken place in projects, in the belief that marrying up qualitative and quantitative indicators gives more meaning to the numbers

- Healthlink now looks beyond immediate results of a project, at the wider implications of its achievements and actions on a broader group and across sectors

- while reporting to donors is a requirement of projects, Healthlink also works with beneficiaries to analyse the findings and draw out results that can help inform future decisions related to the beneficiaries

- findings are also now used to determine the type of resources or activities that may be of use to beneficiaries

Box 1.15
Some key points in monitoring, evaluation and impact assessment

Stakeholder considerations

1. SHARED LEARNING BETWEEN STAKEHOLDERS: To involve stakeholders in reflective learning sessions and opportunities (e.g., exchange visits, progress meetings) is crucial in making decisions that are owned, effective and sustainable in the long term

2. INVOLVEMENT OF STAKEHOLDERS: To promote trust and acceptance of the findings and agreement relating to what has been learned; to ensure that different perspectives and views are taken into account, thus enhancing relevance and effectiveness of the information projects, products and services

3. OWNERSHIP: To ensure that evaluation is owned as much as possible by the project implementers and by stakeholders as a learning mechanism and to assist in strategic and operational management

4. SHARED PROCESS DEVELOPMENT: To develop the processes in collaboration with stakeholders, ensuring that their specific information needs (key issues) are integrated and their ideas for collecting, processing and reviewing data are included

5. STAKEHOLDER INVOLVEMENT IN IMPLEMENTATION: To encourage shared learning and to ensure strategic decisions are understood and supported in the next phase of the project

6. LEARNING EVENTS: To encourage stakeholders to see monitoring, evaluation and impact assessment as important opportunities to learn together and enhance the impact and sustainability and efficiency of the project

Planning

7. PLANNING THESE PROCESSES CAREFULLY: To ensure there are enough resources to implement them and to create ownership and commitment. This is done with stakeholders at the start of a project

8. DEVELOPING THE MONITORING, EVALUATION AND IMPACT ASSESSMENT SYSTEM: To ensure that all three processes are part of a wider system that is designed during project planning

Data collection and documentation

9. DATA COLLECTION: From project inception, data relating to the information product/service should be collected in a way that is well structured and systematic so that it allows for regular monitoring of results, as well as ensuring preparation for an evaluation and impact assessment

10. COMBINING METHODS: Consider combining quantitative and qualitative, participatory and conventional, individual and group-based methods of data collection

11. FOCUS: Monitoring, evaluation and impact assessment should be focused on what it is necessary to know rather than what you think you might like to know

12. CREDIBILITY: Document both the successes and failures of the information project

Feedback

13. FEEDBACK AND DISSEMINATION: the findings emerging from the different stages of the project cycle need to be fed back and disseminated in a targeted way, so that the 'right audiences' receive the information most appropriate to them

14. RELATE RECOMMENDATIONS BACK TO ORIGINAL QUESTIONS: the findings from monitoring, evaluation and impact assessment can assist in making decisions at both strategic and operational levels

Part 2
THE EVALUATION PROCESS

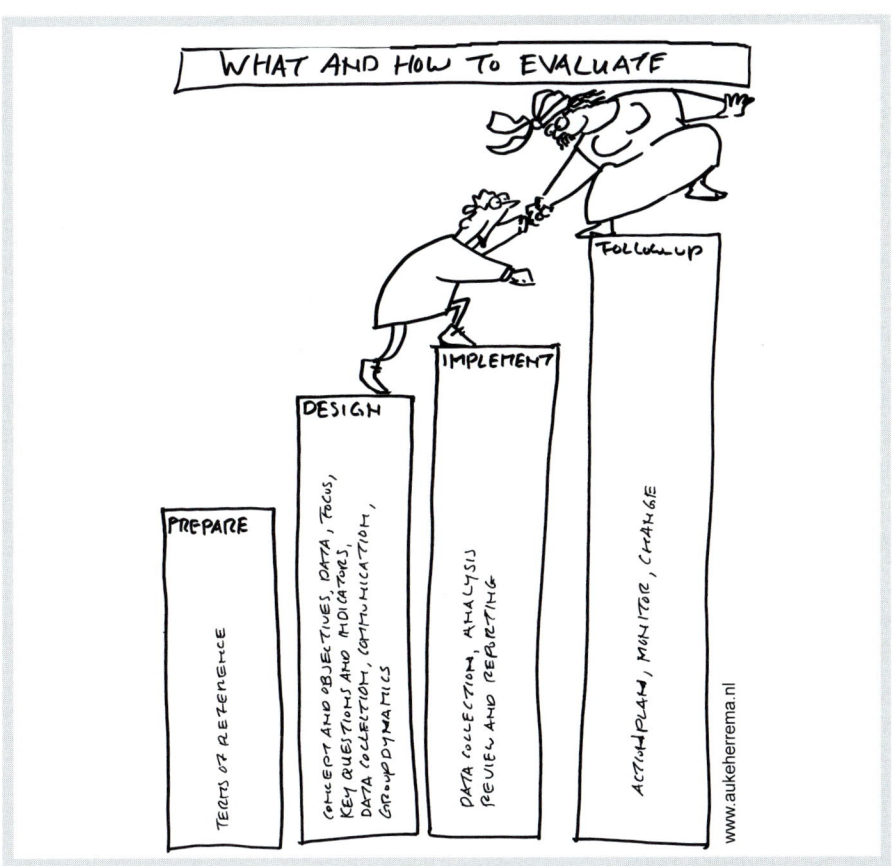

Background

Preparing the evaluation terms of reference

Designing the evaluation

Implementing the evaluation

Following up the evaluation

In Part 1 we looked at the definition of evaluation, its purpose, trends and core ingredients, and at the context in which it occurs – the project cycle. We also looked briefly at the closely related processes of monitoring and impact assessment.

Now, in Part 2, we move on to the evaluation process itself. This process can be grouped into four phases:

- preparing the evaluation terms of reference
- designing the evaluation
- implementing the evaluation
- following up the evaluation

What are the main issues you have to think about when organising the evaluation of an information project, and how do you reflect them in your terms of reference? How do these issues affect the way you design the evaluation? How do you select the evaluation tools? Do the tools you select match the objectives set and the resources available? What does evaluation follow-up involve?

The process described here is intended mainly for self-evaluation, involving you and key stakeholders in the whole process. As we noted in Part 1, self-evaluation enhances the learning experience and makes it easier to apply the lessons learned to a project, with the overall aim of increasing its impact. We look both at the evaluation process in general and at how it applies, specifically, to information projects, products and services.

The four phases in the evaluation process can be subdivided into a clear set of stages:

Phase 1: Preparing the evaluation terms of reference
- Define the reasons for and purpose of the evaluation
- Define the scope of the evaluation
- Organise stakeholder participation
- Identify existing data and sources of data
- Choose a methodology for data collection and analysis
- Formulate a communication strategy
- Select the evaluation team
- Prepare the work plan and budget
- Formulate the terms of reference

Phase 2: Designing the evaluation
- Review the project concept and objectives
- Determine the data needed to evaluate the project
- Determine the evaluation focus, key questions and indicators
- Design the data collection methods
- Design the data analysis methods
- Design the communication plan
- Integrate group dynamics issues

Phase 3: Implementing the evaluation
- Collect the data
- Analyse the data
- Review and report the findings

Figure 2.1
The evaluation process

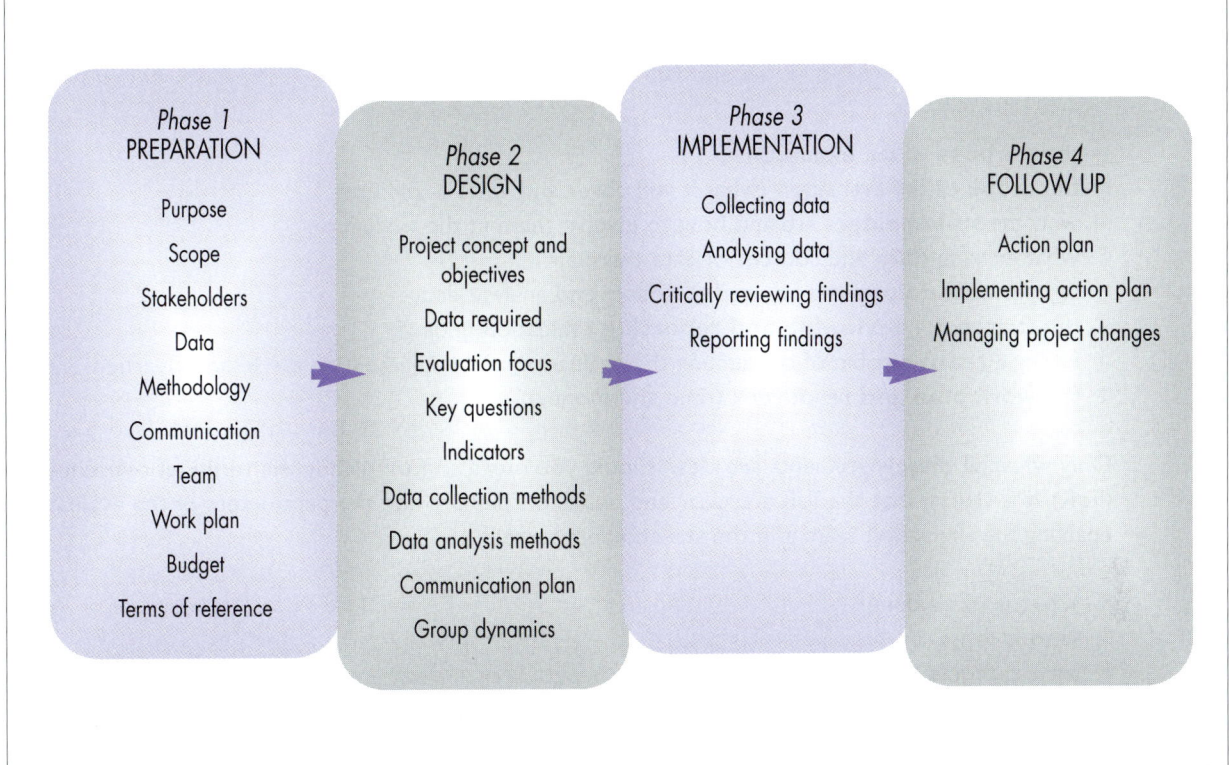

Phase 4: Following up the evaluation
- Formulate the follow-up action plan
- Implement and monitor the action plan
- Make changes where necessary

We have listed these stages in chronological order. In reality, however, you might find that in order to go to the next stage you need to revisit an earlier one, to improve it. For example, in Phase 2, when designing your evaluation and in your discussions with stakeholders, you might find it necessary to go back to Phase 1 to refine the terms of reference so that they match your stakeholders' information needs more closely. Also, there is likely to be some overlap between the phases.

The evaluation process involves selecting data collection tools. Here in Part 2, we discuss the process of selection, but do not go into detail on the tools themselves. That is the subject of Part 3, where we describe the tools you can consider for project evaluation, with Part 4 focusing on examples of how specific tools are applied to specific information projects, products and services.

Every evaluation process is unique. You need to design a process that best fits the project being evaluated and the purpose and scope of the evaluation. Whatever process you design, however, it needs to involve your stakeholders from start to finish. Without this level of stakeholder participation, the value of the evaluation in terms of learning and impact will be considerably reduced.

Preparing the evaluation terms of reference

The first phase in evaluating an information project, product or service is preparation. Getting the preparation right is crucial to the success of any evaluation. Getting it right means being clear about:

- the **purpose** of the evaluation
- the **scope** of the evaluation (what it will cover, and what it will not)
- who the **stakeholders** are and how to involve them in the evaluation
- what existing **data** and sources of data there are
- what **methodology** will be used to collect and analyse data
- the strategy for **reviewing and reporting** evaluation findings
- having a **team** capable of conducting the evaluation and implementing the lessons learned
- the **work plan and resources** (time and money)

Only when all these ingredients are clear should you move to formulating the terms of reference (ToR). It is crucial that the ToR are clear and detailed. They provide the parameters of the evaluation, enabling the evaluation team and the stakeholders to see:

- **what** is to be done
- **who** is to do it
- **how** it should be done
- **when** it should be done

The process of formulating the ToR should involve both the team and the stakeholders, not only because this is more likely to produce a viable set of ToR, but also because it will enhance the commitment of all those involved in the evaluation process.

Defining the purpose

If you do not know why you are conducting an evaluation, and for whom, it is unlikely that you will make the right choices for the evaluation process (e.g., which stakeholders to involve, how to collect data, what communication strategy to use).

To define the purpose of the evaluation, you need to know why the evaluation was required in the first place. There might be one reason or several. It might have been initiated, for example, to:

- **Empower stakeholders:** There are mechanisms that can be used to empower stakeholders in an information project. One of them is to organise an evaluation with strong stakeholder participation. This enhances their understanding of the project and commitment to it, and encourages them to actively contribute to its success.

- **Build stakeholder capacity:** Participatory evaluation enables stakeholders to learn more about a project, and also to acquire new skills related to project implementation, management and evaluation.

- **Improve project implementation:** An evaluation should show where improvements can be made in the way a project is being implemented, particularly if it is an honest appraisal of both failure and success.

- **Assist project re-orientation:** The project might be facing new challenges, which require a change of course and a new strategy. An evaluation should provide the insight needed to formulate a new strategy.

- **Ensure accountability:** An evaluation is a useful way of keeping people informed about the progress and effectiveness of a project. These people might be the donors (this is sometimes called 'upward accountability') or the primary stakeholders ('downward accountability') or both.

> **Box 2.1**
> **Some key points in defining the purpose of an evaluation**
>
> - Ask yourself these questions: Who wants this evaluation? Why do they want it? How is the project likely to benefit from the evaluation?
>
> - Use the answers to these questions to make the right choices in your evaluation methodology.
>
> - Every evaluation is unique. So ensure that the purpose you define suits your evaluation, and avoid the temptation to lift a purpose statement from another evaluation.
>
> - Defining the purpose of your evaluation is, in itself, a good opportunity for learning, improving your project and strengthening your relationship with the stakeholders.

Defining the scope

If you want to evaluate your information project, you need to know what criteria (or main areas of concern) you want to assess. Establishing these evaluation criteria will help you to define the scope of your evaluation.

Various organisations use different sets of evaluation criteria. Important and frequently used criteria include:

- **Accessibility:** The extent to which your project reaches the primary stakeholders (i.e., how easy it was for them to access the information product/service in terms of its availability, distribution and timeliness).

- **Impact:** The positive and negative changes produced by your project, directly or indirectly, intended or unintended (i.e., the extent to which primary stakeholders have successfully used the product/service to improve their lives).

- **Relevance:** The extent to which the product/service is suited to the priorities and needs of the primary stakeholders, and the priorities of other key stakeholders, the project managers and the donor (i.e., the extent to which the project was a good idea).

- **Sustainability:** The extent to which your organisation will be able to continue to provide the product/service after the completion of the project. (i.e., the extent to which the primary stakeholders will continue to benefit from the product/service when the project funding ends).

- **Usability:** The extent to which the primary stakeholders are able to use your product/service. This depends on such factors as completeness of the product/service, accessible language (the language itself, and its level and style), accessible images (diagrams, pictures, etc. relevant to the lives of the primary stakeholders), technically accurate information, and design relevant to the context in which it will be used.

- **Utility:** The extent to which your project could be successfully replicated in another location or among different primary stakeholders. Utility also relates to lessons learned from the project, and how they could be usefully applied to other projects.

- **Effectiveness:** The extent to which your project has achieved its objectives (this is similar to impact, but whereas impact covers both intended and unintended changes, effectiveness is concerned with the intended objectives).

- **Efficiency:** The cost-effectiveness of your project in terms of outputs – qualitative and quantitative – compared with inputs (i.e., has it used the least costly resources possible in order to achieve the desired results?).

Choosing which criteria to use in defining the scope of your evaluation will depend on:

- your organisation's policy and core values
- the policies and interests of other major stakeholders, including your donors
- the current state of your project and the key issues that you need to address
- the level of stakeholder participation you envisage
- the resources (time, money, people) you have

Table 2.1
Applying evaluation criteria to a farmers' training course

EVALUATION CRITERIA	KEY QUESTIONS TO ASK
Accessibility	Did the farmers have access to the training course? If not, why not?
Effectiveness	Were farmers able to use the training on their own farms? If not, why not?
Usability	Was the training course delivered in a language which was understood by all participants? Was the training complete in all details so that farmers could implement it? Was sufficient time given to the training for farmers to be able to absorb the information? Was support provided after the training?
Efficiency	Was the training course implemented in the most efficient way, compared with alternatives? Could the same impact have been achieved with fewer resources?
Impact	Has the training resulted in a change in farmer practices? If so, have these improved practices resulted in better yields for the farmers?
Relevance	Was the training course consistent with the farmers' needs and priorities?
Sustainability	When project funding ends, will the implementing organisation be able to continue providing the training? If not, why not? Are the changes made by farmers sustainable? Have the farmers been able to pass on the knowledge gained?
Utility	Would the training be suitable for other farmers in similar situations?

> **Box 2.2**
> **Some key points in defining the scope of an evaluation**
>
> - It is important to carefully select your evaluation criteria to suit your project and resources. This will help to make the evaluation more focused and manageable.
>
> - An important and often overlooked factor in deciding on the scope is to make sure it matches the resources you have available
>
> - Don't include criteria that go with key questions that can't be answered (e.g., don't select 'impact' if the project has only just started)
>
> - Be aware of the possible conflicting interests among the project stakeholders

Organising stakeholder participation

Who are the stakeholders in your project? And why should they participate in the evaluation?

To answer the first question, in any project there are two sets of stakeholders (see Figure 2.2, overleaf):

- **primary stakeholders** (the end-users of the information product/service)

- **secondary stakeholders**, who can be subdivided into:
    - those who provide the inputs for your information product/service (e.g., donors, partner agencies)
    - those who help to ensure that your product/service reaches the intended end-users (e.g., distributors, media organisations)
    - those who are involved in developing and implementing policies relating to the product/service (e.g., government agencies).

Now to the second question: Why should the stakeholders participate in the evaluation? As we saw in Part 1, stakeholder participation in the project cycle is crucial to project success. We also saw that the level of that participation should be extensive and meaningful, and include exchanging ideas and sharing decision-making.

In the old mode of external evaluation (see Table 1.1 in Part 1, page 3), stakeholder participation tended to be top-down and to be seen as:

- **informing** stakeholders about the evaluation process and results
- using stakeholders as a **source of information** (e.g., through questionnaires and interviews)
- **consulting** stakeholders to obtain their views on the evaluation process and/or results

Today, however, participatory evaluation implies a far more active role for stakeholders, in which they:

- are part of the **evaluation team**
- **actively contribute** to the design and implementation of the evaluation
- help conduct a **joint analysis** of the findings and recommendations

Figure 2.2
Stakeholders in farmers' newsletter project

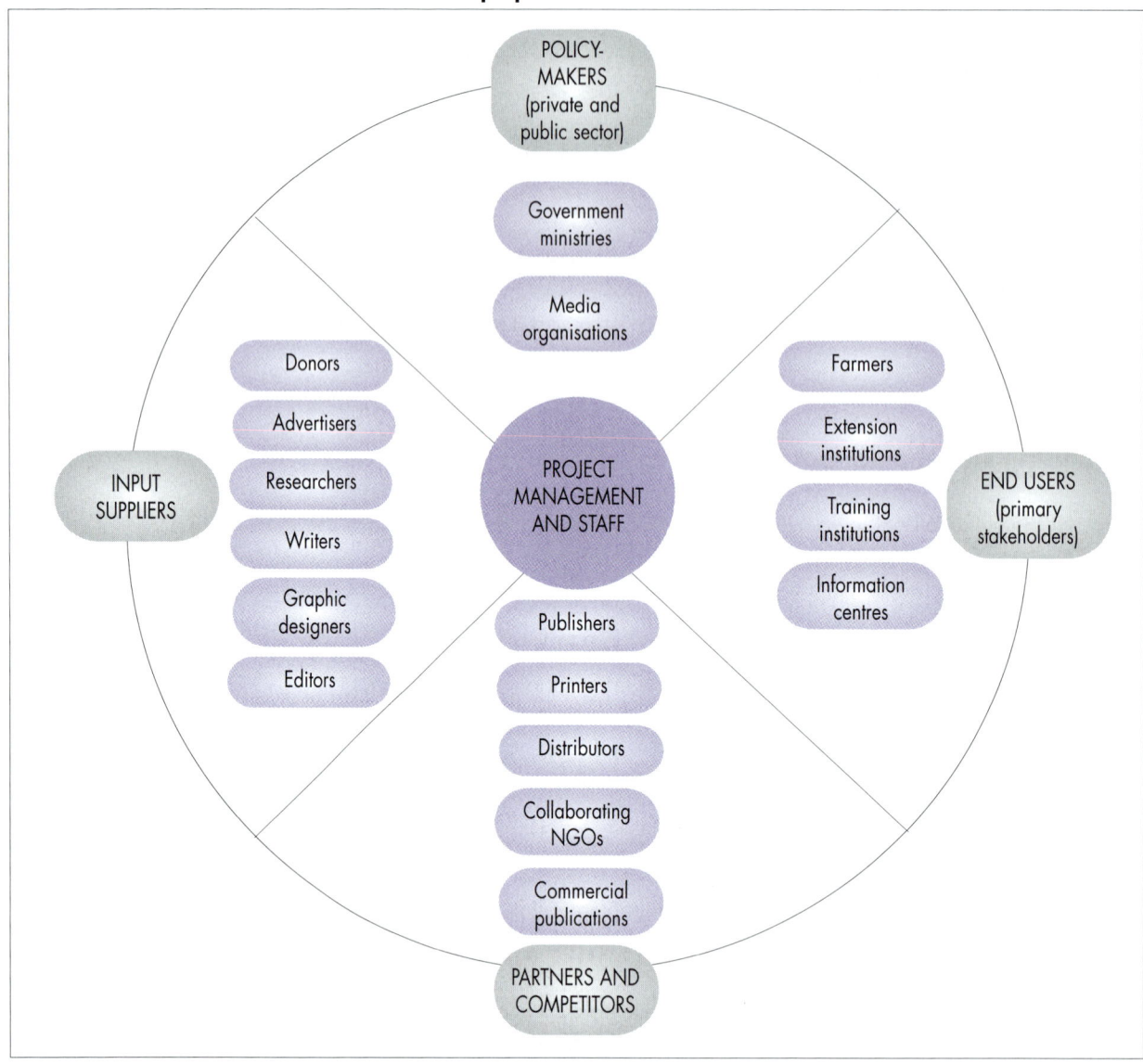

In order to identify the stakeholders who should participate in the evaluation, you need to conduct a stakeholder analysis. This requires analysing such factors as those shown in Table 2.2. Whichever groups of stakeholders you identify, there is one group that should always participate in an evaluation – the primary stakeholders.

Issues to consider that relate specifically to the stakeholders participating in the evaluation include:

- their involvement in, and influence on, the information product/service
- their contribution to the information product/service
- how they benefit from the information product/service
- how they should be involved in the evaluation
- their willingness and ability to be involved and to learn from the evaluation
- the most appropriate ways of communicating with them during the evaluation
- the dynamics and conflicts of interest among the participating stakeholders
- the budget for stakeholder participation in the evaluation

Table 2.2
Example of a stakeholder analysis for the evaluation of a farmers' newsletter

STAKEHOLDERS	INVOLVEMENT IN NEWSLETTER	CONTRIBUTIONS TO NEWSLETTER	BENEFITS FROM NEWSLETTER	INVOLVEMENT IN EVALUATION
Readers (primary stakeholders)	Reading the newsletter; providing feedback through questions and comments on articles; word-of-mouth promotion	Time (reading the newsletter); money (buying the newsletter)	Improved knowledge on agricultural production	Represented on the team Valuable source of information
Editors, writers and publishers	Compiling content; designing layout	Time; professional input	Occupation, status, experience	Represented on the team
Partners (e.g., donors, Ministry of Agriculture units, research institutes, printers, distributors)	Providing information, printing newsletter, distributing newsletter	Time; professional and technical input	Disseminating knowledge; income	Represented on the team Involved in analysis and decisions on action
Management	Establishing newsletter concept/objectives; committing resources; overseeing production and distribution	Time and resources (operating newsletter; dealing with partners and donors)	Organisational goals; status	Work with team on ToR, on data analysis and on recommendations Ensure recommendations can be implemented by the organisation

Box 2.3
Some key points in organising stakeholder participation in an evaluation

- Don't be tempted to copy the way another evaluation organised stakeholder participation. Your stakeholders (types, groups, interests, availability, etc.) will be different from those in any other project

- Be sure to involve the primary stakeholders, the users of your product/service, especially in relation to usability

- Make a clear decision about who to involve and when, and avoid involving everyone in everything. Time is valuable; if you ask too much from stakeholders you may not get their co-operation a second time

Identifying existing data

Knowing what data exist that are relevant to your evaluation will help you decide what data you still need to collect, given your time and resources.

Also, looking at existing data may refresh your memory, and give the evaluation team a better understanding of the project background and any earlier recommendations that might have been made. Often, such recommendations get 'lost' and are not acted upon, or are only partly acted upon.

Where would you look for these data? Possible sources include:

- initial strategic and work plans for the information project
- brochures or descriptions of the information product/service
- baseline data collected before the project was implemented
- desk studies

- earlier evaluation reports
- annual reports
- monitoring and follow-up reports
- stakeholder documents
- official statistical information
- financial reports

Box 2.4
Some key points in identifying existing data

- Make a point of looking for documents that describe why the project exists (rationale), what it is supposed to do (objectives and expectations), its assumptions, its planned activities, problems it has faced and any earlier recommendations made to improve it

- Ask project managers and staff for documents; not everything will necessarily be in an archive or library

- Ask stakeholders what data they hold that could be useful. This is often an overlooked source of existing data

- Take stock of all data available in order to decide what additional data need to be collected through a desk study and other data-collection mechanisms

Choosing the methodology

Choosing your methodology for data collection and analysis will be influenced by many factors. To ensure the methodology fits the evaluation, you need to be clear about:

- the **key questions** you want to answer: this relates to the scope of the evaluation, and what the main concerns are (see Table 2.1)

- the **data needed** to answer these questions: this relates not only to the amount of data but also to the type of data – primary and secondary (see Box 2.5)

- the level of **stakeholder participation**: extensive but carefully managed involvement of both primary and secondary stakeholders is crucial (see Table 2.2)

- the **existing data**: this relates to learning more about the project and not wasting resources on collecting data that is already available

- the available **resources** (time, money, skills) to ensure that the methodology matches your resources

There are a variety of data collection methods to consider. You will usually need to choose a mixture of these. The most common methods include:

- **Quantitative methods** produce quantitative (numerical) data that are relatively easy to summarise and compare. The data can be generalised (scaled up) to a larger population if you choose a representative sample; although this can be very efficient, it is not always easy to do in resource-poor settings. It requires trained people to design the questionnaires, administer and analyse them, and then interpret the findings. It is not enough to present tables of numbers without interpretation and explanation. The main limitation of the quantitative approach is that you may gain only a limited understanding of why things happened.

> **Box 2.5**
> **Types of data to collect**
>
> The types of data to collect fall into two groups – primary data and secondary data:
>
> - PRIMARY DATA are collected directly and for a specific purpose: methods could include questionnaires, interviews and focus groups
>
> - SECONDARY DATA have already been collected for some purpose other than the current evaluation: sources could include routine records, reports, newspaper articles, project monitoring sheets and progress reports.
>
> Examples of routine records are data from log books, registers, personnel lists, receipt books, accounts and contact databases. These data are collected during normal activities, such as data on who is using your information product/service, when they use it, and what they are using it for. If your project is not already keeping these types of records, it should start now; staff should be trained to keep accurate, complete and up-to-date information. Routine records can be used to manage the project and to reduce the amount of data collected during evaluations.

- **Qualitative methods** are used to find out why and how people use your information product/service. They draw data from a variety of non-numerical sources, such as words, pictures and plays, and can be used to elaborate the facts provided by quantitative data. The main limitations of the qualitative approach are that it is relatively labour-intensive and time-consuming, requires good facilitation skills, and the findings can't usually be generalised.

- **Individual methods** involve getting data from individual respondents without interaction with other respondents (e.g., questionnaires and interviews).

- **Group methods** seek to encourage interaction between respondents so that they add to each other's knowledge. This can produce a more in-depth picture of the situation (e.g., focus groups).

- **Participatory methods** are based on using stakeholders as part of the evaluation team and involving them in collecting data. This brings them into direct contact with other stakeholders and thus enhances their understanding of the project, its aims and its impact.

> **Box 2.6**
> **Some key points in choosing the methodology**
>
> - It is often worth selecting a multi-method approach, combining quantitative and qualitative data collection and analysis methods. Known as 'triangulation', this will bring greater understanding and increase the reliability of the findings
>
> - Data collection tools such as questionnaires should be pre-tested to ensure that they produce the data you need. The pre-test might show, for example, that there are ambiguous questions that need to be rephrased, that the language used is not understood, or that some of the questions are embarrassing for the respondents
>
> - Use the sources of secondary data, as far as possible, to provide the quantitative information, and use qualitative methods if the evaluation seeks to learn why, how and where you can improve a project
>
> - Consider whether time is an important element. If you want to measure change, time is obviously important. Often, however, all you want to know is what is happening currently (with the time element becoming important only later when you compare results in the longer term)

Table 2.3
Examples of data collection tools

TOOL	DESCRIPTION	MAIN USE	REQUIREMENTS
Self-administered questionnaire	Questionnaires filled by respondents themselves	Useful for collecting quantitative (numerical) information	Interested, motivated respondents capable of filling in the answers. Questionnaire should be short and easy to complete, to prevent boring, tiring or confusing the respondent
Interviewer-administered questionnaire	Interviewer reads the questions aloud and fills in the answers Could be conducted face-to-face, by telephone or via the internet	Useful for collecting quantitative and qualitative information Different kinds of questions can be asked in the same questionnaire	Interviewers need training to ask questions in a positive, respectful way and avoid misinterpreting answers; for qualitative data, they need good listening and recording skills
Focus group interview	Allows interviewer to find out what a group of users think about a project, product or service	Generating qualitative information quickly	Good preparation and an experienced facilitator skilled in accommodating group dynamics
SWOT analysis	Identification and analysis of the strengths, weaknesses, opportunities and threats (SWOT) of a project, product or service	Useful in group discussion and brainstorming sessions	Important to prepare well for this exercise as it is easy to confuse the various categories (i.e., strengths/ weakness/ opportunities/ threats). Need clear guidelines and everyone involved to agree to them
Case study	An in-depth, longitudinal examination of a single instance or event	Useful to identify and reflect on lessons learned from a case, to apply to others	Ability (skill and knowledge) to compare case with others. Good analytical and writing skills
Creative participatory technique	A participatory technique involving such devices as role play, video and drawings to get views and data	Useful for stimulating participation, especially among less literate people	An experienced facilitator aware of cultural meaning of images
After-action review (AAR)	A quick and simple way to gather data on project performance and output	Useful for identifying whether or not the project strategy and processes were adequate	A tactful facilitator who can create an environment where everyone can share their opinions openly
Rapid appraisal (RA)	Range of tools and techniques including focus groups, case studies, semi-structured interviews with key informants, participant observation and use of secondary sources	Useful in complex situations where quantitative data are limited	Ability to conduct interviews and having good knowledge of the subject area being investigated
Participatory learning and action (PLA)	Involves participation of stakeholders in group sessions, with a facilitator, in preparing, e.g., schedules, impact flow charts, village and resource maps, well-being/wealth ranking, seasonal diagrams, problem ranking and institutional assessments	Useful in complex situations where quantitative data are limited	Creation of an environment where everyone can share and participate equally. Facilitation needs to be done in such a way that the opinions obtained are a true reflection of the group.
Direct observation	Physical observation of actions and activities	Useful for seeing how project activities are being carried out in reality; especially useful for training purposes	Discretion and careful management, to prevent participants finding the presence of an observer restricting

Each method brings with it certain evaluation tools. Examples of some of these tools are given in Table 2.3. Selected tools are dealt with in more depth in Part 3.

Some of the tools listed in the table require good listening and recording/note-taking skills, as well as facilitation skills. You need to take account of the skills you have in your evaluation team when choosing tools, or consider training in those skills which you really need.

Formulating a communication strategy

Reviewing and reporting are essential features of an evaluation. Your communication strategy needs to cover:

- how and when the evaluation strategies, activities and findings will be critically reviewed, and who will be involved in this review

- how and when evaluation findings will be reported, and to whom

This takes us back to stakeholder participation, and the importance of including the stakeholders in the design and implementation of the evaluation and in analysing the findings. This means you need to be clear about what the stakeholders want to know, why they want to know it, and how they want it presented.

Stakeholders differ in many ways, including:

- interest in the project
- commitment to the project
- involvement in the project
- access to means of communication
- expectations about feedback
- time available

So it is important to develop a critical review strategy that involves the right people at the right time. For example, in an evaluation of a farmers' newsletter, the strategy should allow for the readers – farmers – to be involved in formal meetings convened to critically review the newsletter, its content, production and distribution.

Similarly, it is important to develop a reporting strategy that ensures that everyone receives feedback that is relevant to them and in the format they require. For example, farmers might prefer feedback in the form of a video rather than a lengthy written report, and a Minister might prefer a summary of the report.

You should be aware that people often don't read reports. Sending reports will not necessarily elicit much in the way of comment and is not really part of participatory working. It might be better to provide feedback in a workshop setting. Here, the main points or even the report itself can be presented as posters on which the participants can write comments on post-its. These can then be reviewed by a facilitator and form the basis of discussion for the rest of the workshop.

There are various communication methods you can use for reviewing and reporting. Some of them are listed in Table 2.4.

Table 2.4
Communication methods for (a) the review process and (b) the reporting process

COMMUNICATION METHOD	USE IN REVIEW PROCESS	USE IN REPORTING PROCESS
Workshops	Make a joint analysis of data collected Create a shared understanding of the situation Assess joint lessons learnt	
Meetings/discussions	Discuss findings from data collection and analysis	Present findings from data collection and analysis
Individual meetings	Provide ongoing feedback to individuals	Provide findings to individuals
Role-play	To visualise the problems and solutions of specific situations and approaches (e.g., how advisors deal with clients)	
Internet pages	Discuss findings with stakeholders or peers	Present main findings to stakeholders, peers and the public
Videos	To visualise the problems and solutions of specific situations and approaches	Present findings to users
Articles (often more for public relations purposes than for communication)		Present main findings to stakeholders, being aware of what will interest primary stakeholders and what will interest secondary stakeholders
Brochures		Present findings or main changes in project, product or service to users and the public
Summary report		Present findings to managers
Full report		Present findings to key stakeholders

Box 2.7
Some key points in formulating a communication strategy

- Involve the primary stakeholders in every stage of your communication strategy – they provide the most valuable feedback

- Often, it is not appropriate send the same report to all the stakeholders. Some information might be sensitive, other information might not be of interest to everybody. Your stakeholder analysis, if done well, will show you who needs what

- When reporting to a stakeholder, concentrate on the consequences of interest to that stakeholder and be aware of potential problems that stakeholders might have in implementing recommendations

- Make sure that the way you disseminate the evaluation findings suits the recipients. That will give more chance of those findings being read, absorbed and acted upon

Selecting the team

A strong team that includes stakeholders will help generate relevant and accurate data. It will also create a shared understanding of the project, which will help in drawing up recommendations that are relevant to stakeholders.

The size of the team depends on the scope of your evaluation and the resources available. If you are conducting a self-evaluation of a small-scale information product/service, the team will probably be a small one.

The main factors to consider when you're selecting an evaluation team are:

- purpose and scope of the evaluation, and the budget available
- evaluation methodology
- knowledge and skills of the team members
- relationships between the team members
- capacity of team members to influence project implementation

Specific questions to ask when selecting a team include:

- Do you need the team to make an independent judgement?
- Do you need the team to act as group facilitators and work with stakeholders to help them take the learning on board?
- Would including other key stakeholders facilitate the learning process and are they willing to spend their time on the evaluation?
- To what extent are gender/age and other balances required in establishing the team?
- What skills are needed in the team (e.g., facilitation, communication, organisational, technical, statistical)?
- How will you reward and/or motivate the team members?

> **Box 2.8**
> **Some key points in selecting the evaluation team**
>
> - If the funding agency wants an external evaluation to be conducted, as opposed to a self-evaluation, negotiate for project staff to be included in the evaluation team. This is important for learning and for facilitating understanding between the various parties
>
> - If you are the sole evaluator, consider setting up an evaluation committee of people who could provide you with feedback on your evaluation design, implementation, analysis and reporting
>
> - Apart from including stakeholders in the evaluation team, consider asking stakeholders to help carry out specific tasks, such as data collection, data analysis and reporting

Preparing the work plan and budget

An evaluation process can involve a complex set of activities. To ensure that the process runs smoothly, it needs good planning and adequate resources. As resources are usually limited, drawing up a work plan and budget helps in assessing what realistically can and can't be done in the evaluation.

Activities that you need to consider in your work plan include:

- selecting the team (including stakeholders)
- arranging team meetings and training
- pre-testing data collection tools
- collecting data
- analysing data
- arranging critical review meetings
- preparing and communicating findings
- formulating the follow-up action plan

The work plan should be clear about who is responsible for the various activities, and about the timeframe, both overall and for each activity (the schedule).

Budget items that should be considered include:

- costs of the various activities
- allowances for team members
- training for team members
- consultancy fees
- transport costs
- workshop venue costs
- workshop materials
- communication costs (telephone, internet, postage)
- printing costs

Box 2.9
Costs to consider when preparing an evaluation budget

Evaluation budgets vary depending on the scope and objectives of the exercise. As such, there is no 'typical' budget for evaluating an information project. As a first step, however, you need to think about how to get your evaluation funded if a budget has not already been allocated.

If you are conducting your own evaluation, you will be doing most of the work, possibly with help from your colleagues, using existing office facilities, transport and supplies. It will therefore be difficult to itemise the costs; on the other hand, the more they are internalised, the easier it will be for you to go ahead with the evaluation. However, you might want some outside expertise in, for example, analysing the data, or additional resources such as statistical software packages. These items will form part of your direct costs and you should have some provision in your budget to cover such expenses. The likely in-house and external costs, if you're conducting your own evaluation, include:

IN-HOUSE COSTS
- your time
- time provided by other staff involved in the evaluation
- time provided by support staff for such tasks as data entry
- meetings (e.g., briefing meetings, stakeholder meetings, validation workshops)
- transport
- office supplies (e.g., stationery)
- communication (e.g., fax, telephone, postage, photocopying, printing)

EXTERNAL COSTS
- consultants (e.g., for evaluation, data analysis, publishing)
- other experts (e.g., IT experts)
- transport and accommodation for these external advisers

> **Box 2.10**
> **Some key points in preparing the work plan and budget**
>
> - Don't be too ambitious in your planning; this could raise expectations that you might not be able to meet
>
> - Be sure to check the skills available to you in your team and budget for training if it is needed
>
> - If possible, plan and budget for additional activities that could be carried out once the initial results from data collection, analysis and review are known
>
> - Ensure that your budget matches the activities you need to carry out

Formulating the terms of reference

The terms of reference (ToR) for an evaluation provide the guidelines for your evaluation team. Even if you are the sole evaluator, it is useful to formulate the ToR, as this will provide an opportunity for an overall view of the organisation of the evaluation before you begin.

The ToR will serve as a blueprint to show why the evaluation is being conducted, how it will be conducted and what it is expected to produce. They are not a wish list. Resources are nearly always less than wanted, and the ToR should reflect the reality of what is available and what can be achieved. Realistic, detailed and well-formulated ToR are useful when seeking approval for the budget and approaching prospective team members.

You should include the following elements in the ToR:

Background
- reasons for conducting the evaluation
- parties involved in commissioning the evaluation

Evaluation
- purpose
- scope
- expected outputs

Stakeholder participation
- who to involve, for what purpose, at what stage, and how

Existing data
- project documents (primary sources)
- records (secondary sources)

Methodology
- data collection
- data analysis

Communication
- critical review process
- reporting
- who to involve, and how

Team
- composition
- expertise represented
- stakeholder groups represented
- roles and responsibilities

Work plan and budget
- activities and schedule
- detailed costing

Box 2.11
Some key points in formulating the terms of reference

- Avoid copying the ToR from another evaluation. Each evaluation is unique and you should take the time to formulate your own ToR

- Don't make the ToR a wish list. Ensure that the terms match your resources

- To get approval for the budget and to sustain commitment from evaluation team members, make sure that your ToR are realistic, detailed and well formulated

- If possible, involve team members and key stakeholders in formulating the ToR. This will enhance their commitment and improve the quality and comprehensiveness of the ToR

Designing the evaluation

Once the terms of reference have been agreed upon and the budget approved, you can move on to designing the evaluation. This is where you have to get down to planning each aspect of the evaluation in detail – exactly who is going to do what, and when, and how, and what resources will be used at each stage.

It is important to remember that all decisions made in relation to the detailed planning will depend on resources, especially the skills and time available. There is no point in choosing certain methods or tools if you have no skills in the team for them and no way of getting access to training.

Designing the evaluation involves going through the following stages:

- reviewing the project concept and objectives
- determining the data needed to evaluate the project
- determining the evaluation focus, key questions and indicators
- designing the data collection methods
- designing the data analysis methods
- designing the communication strategy

Reviewing the project concept and objectives

You can't evaluate an information project, product or service if you don't know what it is about. Even if you're conducting a self-evaluation, you will probably need to refresh your memory about the idea behind the project, how the project was intended to be implemented and what it was intended to achieve. Unless you know this, you can't make the comparisons between what was intended and what has actually happened, and so you can't really evaluate the project. Studying available documents will help you find out about:

- key issues the project is expected to address
- purpose of the project in relation to these issues
- specific objectives to be achieved within the project time frame
- indicators used to measure performance
- work plan (activities)
- staff and stakeholders
- management structure and budget

As we saw in Part 1, every project should have a theory of action and a logical framework. These documents will, if well conceived and compiled, tell much of what you need to know about the project purpose, objectives and performance indicators, as well as the assumptions made when the project was initiated.

If the project documents you need are not there, or are incomplete, or if the project objectives have changed, you will need to discuss with the project staff and stakeholders how the objectives and indicators should be interpreted for the purpose of the evaluation. Only if this interpretation is clear will it be possible to compare expectations with actual performance.

If your information product/service is more of an ongoing activity, rather than a project, you might find it useful to reflect on the background and purpose of the product/service. This could involve asking such questions as:

- Why was the product/service initiated and what problems does it seek to address?
- What is the long-term goal of the product/service?
- What is the core assignment or purpose of the product/service?
- What are the short-term objectives to be achieved by the product/service?
- What is the main approach in delivering the product/service?
- What are the core values of the product/service?

Box 2.12
Some key points in reviewing the project concept and objectives

- Be clear about what the key issues of the project are, and how they relate to the project concept and purpose

- If some of the information you need is not available from documents, ask project staff and stakeholders

- If you are new to the project, it might be worth conducting analyses (e.g., situation analysis, SWOT analysis) to help you understand the project, its political and cultural environment and the needs and resources of the stakeholders

- Benchmarking will help you to compare the performance of the product/service with other comparable products/services, and to identify best practices. This will help in ensuring that any value judgments in your evaluation will not be arbitrary, and in formulating recommendations to improve the quality of the product/service

Determining the data needed

Identifying what data are needed and who is likely to provide them is critical to the success of an evaluation. You will need data that relate to the evaluation criteria you have identified. As discussed earlier in relation to the scope of the evaluation, these criteria could include: accessibility, impact, relevance, sustainability, usability, utility, effectiveness and efficiency.

It is important to ensure that the data collected are of good quality. Avoid the common mistake of collecting too much data, some of it of limited quality. Less good-quality data will produce a better evaluation than too much data of dubious quality.

And be flexible about what data you need. As the data collection process gets under way, you might have to revise the type of data you need.

To obtain the data required from the various stakeholders, you need to determine what questions to ask them. It is a good idea to make an inventory of these questions and then to design your selected data collection methods (e.g., interviews, questionnaires, focus groups) around them. An example is given in Table 2.5.

Table 2.5
Sample questions to obtain data from the key stakeholders in a newsletter

STAKEHOLDERS	QUESTIONS	POTENTIAL USE IN THE EVALUATION
Readers (primary stakeholders)	Does the newsletter meet your information needs? Is the newsletter timely?	To improve content and thematic focus. To decide whether or not to recommend the newsletter to others. To decide whether or not the newsletter should be continued
Editors, writers and publishers	How effective and efficient is the newsletter? Is it meeting the needs of the readers? Are the articles well written? Is it cost-effective? Can it be produced on a sustainable basis? Do staff have the capacity needed to produce the newsletter?	To identify ways in which the newsletter can be improved. To identify ways in which costs could be reduced. To decide whether or not the newsletter should be continued
Partners (e.g., donors, Ministry of Agriculture units, research institutes, printers, distributors)	Are the topics of the newsletter in line with your priorities? Does the newsletter reach the target groups?	To decide upon collaboration on the newsletter
Management	Is there an incentive for you to promote the newsletter? How sustainable is the newsletter given the available resources? Do staff have the capacity needed to produce the newsletter?	To determine what resources are needed to continue to produce the newsletter and/or to build capacity

> **Box 2.13**
> **Some key points in determining the data needed**
>
> - In formulating the questions, consult stakeholders extensively to find out what questions are most likely to elicit quality data
>
> - Consider all potential stakeholders, not only those with whom your project has good relationships or are easier to reach than others
>
> - As the evaluation progresses, be prepared to adjust your assessment of data needed, to add/delete needs as appropriate
>
> - Avoid the common mistake of collecting too much data

Determining the evaluation focus, key questions and indicators

The focus of an evaluation is a further specification of the scope. Every evaluation exercise has to be limited in focus because time, skills, and budget are limited. And it is not possible to cover all elements of the project every time you carry out an evaluation. It is therefore strategic to make a deliberate choice of the areas of focus of the evaluation.

It is useful to formulate specific questions for each of these areas of focus. Focus and questions need to be linked to indicators. A common mistake in evaluations is to compile the indicators solely on the basis of the logframe objectives, without having a clear idea about the evaluation focus and the specific questions that relate to different areas of the focus. This could lead to producing indicators that are irrelevant, unfeasible and unreliable, and therefore do not produce the data you need to conduct a useful evaluation of a project.

The steps involved in this process are:

- **Focus:** The first step is to determine the areas of focus of the evaluation. This means looking at the criteria that you are using to define the scope of the evaluation (e.g., accessibility, impact, relevance, usability, effectiveness, utility and sustainability) and getting down to more detail about these criteria. Which criteria would you prioritise? What time and budget limitations might determine how many criteria you can focus on? How do the various criteria relate to the different stakeholder groups, to the product/service, to its promotion and distribution? For example, if a service does not appear to be achieving the objectives that have been set for it, the focus will need to be on *why* this is so.

- **Questions:** The next step in the process is to identify the specific questions that relate to the different areas of focus of the evaluation. You will need to phrase key questions that are simple, that can be answered easily and that will provide the required information. This means that you need to be clear about the product/service performance and the changes that it might have brought about. For example, if the product/service is not achieving its set objective, the questions would relate mainly to the content of the service and whether or not the end-users had the skills and resources to make the best use of it.

■ **Indicators:** Indicators are quantitative and/or qualitative measures that enable you to answer your key questions and help to assess the extent to which project activities and impact have been achieved. Quantitative indicators relate to changes in numbers (e.g., the number of people listening to a particular radio programme), whereas qualitative indicators relate to changes in perception (e.g., the opinion of users on the content of that programme). Indicators need to be based on a clear idea of which stakeholder group(s) they will be applied to, and to be feasible both technically and financially.

In general, you can divide indicators into:

■ SMART indicators, where the quantitative component is important
■ SPICED indicators, where the subjective interpretation of various different stakeholders is important

And whether your indicators are SMART or SPICED, or a mixture of the two, they should all be clear, realistic, economical, adequate and easily monitored (CREAM).

Table 2.6
Qualities of SMART and SPICED indicators

SMART			SPICED		
S	=	Specific, yet simple	S	=	Subjective
M	=	Measurable	P	=	Participatory
A	=	Achievable (sometimes, Area-specific)	I	=	Interpreted and communicable
R	=	Realistic	C	=	Cross-checked and compared
T	=	Time-bound	E	=	Empowering
			D	=	Diverse and disaggregated

Again using the example of a newsletter, Table 2.7 illustrates how focus, key questions and indicators can be determined.

Box 2.14
Some key points in determining the evaluation focus, key questions and indicators

■ Ensure that the focus of your evaluation reflects the resources you have to carry out the evaluation in terms of time, skills and budget, all of which are often limited

■ Check that the indicators link closely to the focus

■ Check that all the relevant questions of your project plan and of your stakeholders are included in the overview and that the questions will give you the answers you need in terms of the evaluation focus and indicators

■ Don't try to include everything. It would be a waste of time and money to collect, analyse and report on issues that no one is really interested in

Table 2.7
Determining the focus, key questions and indicators for evaluating a newsletter, using some standard evaluation criteria

EVALUATION CRITERIA (SCOPE)	FOCUS	KEY QUESTIONS	INDICATORS	INFORMATION SOURCES
IMPACT	Readers (primary stakeholders)	To what extent have readers successfully used the newsletter to improve their practices?	% of readers indicating benefits from reading the newsletter	Readers
RELEVANCE	Livestock farmers	To what extent are the contents of the newsletter relevant to livestock farmers?	No. of articles per issue targeting livestock farmers	Newsletter archive
ACCESSIBILITY	Reach of material	Are some livestock farmers not receiving the newsletter? If not, why?	No. of newsletters distributed to livestock farmers % of livestock farmers who don't know about newsletter or find it difficult to access Reasons for their not knowing or finding access difficult	Reader registration and statistics Readers who are livestock farmers
USABILITY	Use of material	Do the farmers understand and use the material in the newsletter? If not, why (wrong language, language too difficult, content not detailed enough, etc.)?	% of livestock farmers satisfied with the information in the newsletter % not satisfied and reasons why The reasons for their satisfaction, or lack of it	Readers who are livestock farmers
EFFECTIVENESS	Readership	To what extent do the farmers read the newsletter?	No. of farmers who say they read the newsletter No. of articles read per issue No. of farmers who share the newsletter with others	Readers
	Accuracy	Does the newsletter provide accurate information?	No. of comments/questions per issue related to inaccuracies	Comment registration
EFFICIENCY	Article writing	How much time is spent on writing an article?	No. of hours spent per 300-word article	Time register Time estimates by staff and partners
	Contributions from partners	What contribution do partner organisations make?	No. of articles written by staff No. of articles contributed by partners	Newsletter archive
	Costs	What are the newsletter production/distribution costs?	Unit cost per newsletter	Accounts department
SUSTAINABILITY	Newsletter as a service	Will the newsletter financier be able to support the continuation of the newsletter?	Budget commitment in the coming years	Strategic plans

Designing the data collection methods

Evaluations can fail because too little or too much data were collected without the right questions being asked. It is therefore important to prepare properly for your data collection so that:

- the necessary data you need are available during the evaluation
- the data you collect do answer your key questions
- no more data than necessary are collected

As noted earlier, there are many types of data collection methods, including quantitative, qualitative, individual, group and participatory methods. Each method brings with it a selection of tools which elicit particular types of data. You need to be clear about when you want qualitative data (e.g., when you want to know how some aspect of a project is affecting primary stakeholders) and when you need quantitative data (e.g., the project donors or potential donors will want to see statistics).

In selecting the tools, you need to be clear about how they are going to be applied. For example, you need to specify:

- source of information
- major questions to be addressed
- indicators related to these questions

Having worked on the evaluation focus, key questions and indicators, providing this detail should not now be difficult. Table 2.8 provides an example of the data collection design for a newsletter. There is more detail on data collection tools in Part 3.

You should always bear in mind that apart from using the data for the evaluation, at a later date stakeholders and others (e.g., potential donors) might want to see the data.

> **Box 2.15**
> **Some key points in designing the data collection**
>
> - Prepare your combination of methods well so that you don't collect more data than you need and that you don't overlook data needed for answering key questions
>
> - Remember that analysing qualitative data can be very time-consuming. On the other hand, analysing quantitative data can often be done using statistical software packages
>
> - At the local level, in-depth, qualitative information may be more suitable than quantitative information if the aim of the evaluation is to assess where to concentrate efforts to improve the information project, product or service
>
> - The money, time and human resources available limit the sort of data collection tools you can use and how to use them

Designing the data analysis methods

Once all the data have been collected and collated, they need to be analysed. This means that the relationships between the data have to be clarified and conclusions drawn.

You should always be clear about how the data are going to be analysed before starting to collect them. This will help to ensure that you collect the right data and do not overlook any data you need.

Table 2.8
Data collection design for a newsletter for farmers

TOOL	INFORMATION SOURCE	KEY QUESTIONS	INDICATORS	COMMENTS AND CONCERNS
DESK STUDY	Letters to the editor Subscriptions Recent issues of the newsletter	How satisfied are readers with the newsletter? Does the newsletter provide accurate information?	% of readers satisfied with the newsletter No. of comments/ questions per issue related to inaccuracies	Only active and/or dissatisfied readers will write a letter Will not help you to find out why people are not satisfied
	Newsletter archive	To what extent is the content of the newsletter relevant to farmers? What contribution do partner organisations make?	No. of articles per issue targeting farmers No. of articles written by staff No. of articles contributed by partners	Useful as a starting point; once you know this you can do some qualitative data gathering to find out which articles have been useful
	Subscription register	To what extent does the newsletter reach the different user groups?	No. and % of target users who are subscribers	
	Accounts department	What is the cost of producing the newsletter?	Cost per reader	Staff time on the newsletter is not adequately registered
SELF-ADMINISTERED QUESTIONNAIRE	Readers and ex-readers	Are you satisfied with the contents? How many articles per issue do you read on average? Is the newsletter easy to read? Which other topics would you like to read? How has the newsletter helped you?	% of users satisfied with the newsletter	Many readers might not return the questionnaire
INTERVIEWS	Staff and partners	How much time is spent on writing an article? How do we improve the quality, but reduce time spent?	No. of hours spent on a 300-word article	
MEETINGS	Staff and partners/ stakeholders	What are the strengths, weaknesses, opportunities and threats (SWOT)? How can collaboration be strengthened?		Some partners may not want to participate in the meeting
WORKSHOPS	Primary stakeholders – representative sample of individuals Groups of primary stakeholders, if possible	Are you satisfied with the newsletter contents? How many articles per issue do you read on average? Is the newsletter easy to read? Which other topics would you like to read about? How has the newsletter helped you?	No. of readers satisfied and using information	Will give you reasons why things are working or not May be difficult to get groups together, but small groups will do (3-4 people) even if all are from the same organisation

When you are designing your data analysis methods, you need to answer these questions:

- Which tools can be used to analyse the data?
- Which data collection methods will provide the data for these tools?
- What types of observations and recommendations can be made from each tool?
- How will the analysis be verified?

Quantitative data are often analysed with the aid of a computer using a spreadsheet and/or a statistical software package. These analyses can be presented in tables, graphs, bar charts or pie charts. Qualitative data are often best analysed using tools such as a problem tree or a SWOT analysis. All these tools are described in more detail in Part 3.

An example of the data analysis design for a newsletter is provided in Table 2.9.

Table 2.9
Data analysis design for a newsletter

ANALYTICAL TOOLS	COLLECTION METHOD	TYPE OF OBSERVATIONS	TYPE OF CONCLUSIONS
Statistical analysis	Desk study Questionnaire	Increase/decrease in number of readers in different categories	Target groups that need more attention
Statistical analysis for formal qualitative part of questionnaire	Questionnaire, face-to-face with readers	General satisfaction	General conclusions on content, presentation, language, etc. and on distribution
Costs and income	Desk study Accounts	Increase/decrease in costs/revenue	Where to reduce costs? How to increase revenue?
SWOT analysis	Meeting(s) with partner(s) and users (primary stakeholders) Readers' letters	Strengths, weaknesses, opportunities and threats (SWOT) regarding the use and sustainability of the newsletter (e.g.: - usefulness - timeliness - easy to read - subjects of interest - subjects that don't interest readers)	Strategies for improvement Opportunities for collaboration (e.g., topics to include or avoid, topics to highlight)

Designing the communication strategy

The communication strategy for critically reviewing and reporting findings was formulated in Phase 1. Now it is time to develop a more detailed communication plan. Preparing an effective mix of communication methods is an important factor in ensuring a common understanding and commitment among stakeholders. These methods include workshops, meetings, articles and reports. The communication plan is also likely to influence your data collection and analysis activities.

Initially, you need to answer the question: What do you want to achieve through the critical review and reporting processes?

> **Box 2.16**
> **Some key points in designing the data analysis**
>
> - Ensure that enough resources are allocated to data analysis. Sometimes, a lot of time and effort is spent collecting data that are never properly analysed because of a lack of resources
>
> - Allow plenty of time to analyse qualitative data. Although software is available to help in the analysis of qualitative data, considerable human effort is needed to understand what has been collected
>
> - Keep looking for data that contradict your assumptions, so that they are fully tested. Test out alternative explanations. Bear in mind that the purpose of analysing data is to understand
>
> - Stay focused on the objectives of the evaluation
>
> - Don't attempt complex statistical analyses unless you have a good knowledge of the statistical analysis process
>
> - Don't overdo the analyses
>
> - Include in the data analysis process the people who took part in data collection

Having answered the question, you then need to focus on the two areas of the communication plan:

- **Critical review:** Questions to ask when selecting the critical review methods include: Who will be included in reviews? What will be the main focus of the reviews? Which communication methods best suit the different groups involved?

  When designing the critical review plan, it is important to note the basic questions that lead to critical review, such as: What is happening? Why is it happening? What are the implications for the project? What do we do next?

- **Reporting:** Questions to ask when selecting the reporting methods include: Who are the target groups for reports? What will be the main focus of the findings? Should some parts of the findings be omitted from the report, depending on the target group? Which communication methods best suit these target groups (e.g., oral presentations, articles, videos, brochures, reports)?

  When designing the reporting plan, you should ensure that the message being delivered is clear (in terms of content, language, graphic illustrations, etc.) and timely (at agreed times and while the momentum is there).

An example of a communication plan drawn up for the evaluation of a newsletter evaluation is given in Table 2.10.

Evaluation findings can lead to an increase in knowledge and skills, as well as a change in attitudes that can influence the way people behave within the organisation. The tendency is to assume that evaluation results will be used to guide decision-making and improve the project. But this is not always the case. To stand a far greater chance of being acted upon positively, the findings should be analysed with the primary and secondary stakeholders.

Smart Toolkit for Evaluating Information Projects, Products and Services

Table 2.10
A communication plan for a newsletter evaluation

COMMUNICATION METHOD	STAKEHOLDERS TO REPORT TO	MAIN ISSUES TO DISCUSS / REPORT ON
Workshop on SWOT analysis of key findings and ways forward	Representatives of primary stakeholders (farmers/readers) and newsletter staff	Critical reflection on the results from the data collection
Workshop to brainstorm key findings and ways forward	Staff and management of the newsletter and selected stakeholders	Creative solutions to problems identified
Full report, including executive summary	Funding agency Partners Staff and management	Readers' development Readers' satisfaction Topics Costs and income Conclusions and recommendations
Face-to-face meeting	Management	Conclusions and recommendations Feedback on individual staff members
Article in newsletter asking for readers' comments	General readership	Major findings and ways forward

Box 2.17
Some key points in designing the communication plan

- An effective plan should contain a mix of communication methods, to ensure all stakeholders are reached in ways that best suit them

- Special emphasis needs to be placed on the critical review and feedback as part of the communication plan. This is key to ensuring quality of the results and their acceptance by stakeholders

- Involve management, colleagues and other key stakeholders in the critical review process, to maximise the learning from the evaluation

- Although not all the results can be shared or will be acceptable to all stakeholders, try to take on board the key recommendations and find ways to put them into action

Integrating group dynamics issues

When organising and interacting with groups during an evaluation, you need to be aware of group dynamics issues and how to integrate them into the evaluation design. How well the groups involved work together will have an influence on the value of the findings.

The way in which groups work together and develop is known as 'group development'. All groups working together face a number of problems, defined within the context of phases of development.

The phases are:

- **Inclusion:** This relates to the need to belong and be accepted. This phase is characterised by a lot of 'small talk'. Group members observe whether they are important to the group leaders, and the degree of involvement of the leaders strongly influences members' behaviour. Once the members have assessed the leaders' involvement, they turn to each other to assess their commitment to and participation in the group.

- **Control:** In this phase, group members seek the level of influence they are used to having. They become concerned with power and test other members of the group. If a group has control problems, there will be endless conflict and shifting loyalties, with some members avoiding responsibility and others wanting it all. In this phase it is best not to rush to accept the views or opinions of any member, as this might exacerbate the problem.

- **Affection:** As group cohesion develops, members are more willing to co-operate with each other, using the words, 'we' and 'our group' and becoming interested in each other at the personal level. The danger here is that negative feelings get hidden, which may hinder the work. Also, subgroups often form, threatening group co-operation. There is a need for clarity regarding where loyalty to the group ends and personal autonomy begins. Cultural differences in terms of such factors as openness and sharing personal information can also cause problems.

You must recognise that although there could be conflict in a group, not all conflict should be considered as 'bad'. A positive effect of conflict is that it can lead to the group performing better if they are able to explore the issues fully and openly. Table 2.11 lists sources of conflict that could be regarded as positive and others that might have negative effects.

If you are the group facilitator, you need to ask yourself these questions:

- What keeps the group from functioning well?
- Is the group behaviour at this moment a problem, or is it part of healthy group development?
- What can you do to help the group to go through this phase? Would an assignment in which certain behaviour is allowed help them to get past the identified problem and develop further?

Table 2.11
Sources of conflict in groups

POSITIVE	Focused on task issues
	Legitimate differences of opinion about the task
	Difference in values and perspectives
	Different expectations about the impact of decisions
NEGATIVE	Competition over power, resources, rewards (in the control phase this may be healthy, but in other phases it can be unhealthy)
	Conflict between individual and group goals
	Poorly run meetings
	Personal grudges from the past
	Faulty communication

You also need to be aware of how to promote the healthy development of the group, by:

- providing favourable conditions (e.g., voluntary membership, setting clear goals)
- recognising the group development phases and stimulating the group to look at their behaviour
- having a good mix of skills to support the group
- having a working environment conducive to members working together as a group
- creating a sense of unity within the group
- modelling and supporting relevant processes (e.g., if involvement is required, show involvement yourself)

In the event of conflict in groups involved in your evaluation, there are five possible routes (Levi, 2001): avoidance; accommodation; confrontation; compromise; or collaboration. Although avoidance, accommodation and confrontation can resolve the conflict, they can also create winners and losers. In brokering compromise, everyone wins a little and loses a little; this is not an ideal situation. Collaboration is time-consuming but allows everyone to win, and encourages creativity and performance.

In essence, you should try to create an environment that promotes affection, inclusiveness and room for each member of the group to participate equally and openly.

Implementing the evaluation

Having prepared the evaluation terms of reference and designed the evaluation process, the evaluation should now be implemented. If you have given enough attention to the design, implementation will be much easier.

The main steps in the implementation process are:

- collecting the data
- analysing the data
- critically reviewing and reporting the findings

Collecting the data

It is useful to start by collecting all the relevant data available, and this is best done via a desk study. This exercise might also highlight areas where more primary data are needed, and it could involve checking available data with stakeholders.

Once the secondary data have been collected, you need to start collecting the primary data, using the tools you selected in Phase 2. This involves:

- designing the tools (e.g., a questionnaire, an interview checklist)
- training interviewers, if necessary, to ensure a common approach
- identifying and motivating your respondents
- testing the tools with selected respondents
- developing a time schedule and organising logistics (e.g., transport)
- applying the tools
- reviewing experiences with interviewers

You need to be aware of the sort of problems that can occur with the data from questionnaires and interviews. Pre-testing your questionnaire and training your interviewers can help to overcome these problems. This will show you where, for example, it is necessary to rephrase questions, or to choose to use a questionnaire rather than an interview.

Common problems with data collection tools are:

- **Lack of clarity:** This is probably the area that causes the greatest source of error in questionnaires and interviews. Questions need to be clear, short, simple and unambiguous. The aim is to eliminate the chance that the question will mean different things to different people. If the questionnaire designer does not do this, then essentially participants will be answering different questions. The problem can be exacerbated if there are different interviewers.

- **Use of jargon:** Jargon (including technical terms) and colloquial expressions might not be used and understood by all participants.

- **Leading questions:** A leading question is one that encourages a certain type of answer. Leading questions should always be avoided, as they produce unreliable data.

- **Words or phrases with positive or negative connotations:** Two words that sound similar might have quite different connotations (e.g., 'childlike' is a positive, affectionate term that can be applied to men and women, and young and old; 'childish', however, has negative connotations – no one wants to be thought of as childish).

- **Embarrassing questions:** These can make respondents uncomfortable, and close a potentially useful source of information.

- **Hypothetical questions:** These tend to be based on conjecture (e.g., 'If you were governor, what would you do to stop crime?'). They should be avoided as they do not produce consistent data representing real opinions.

- **Prestige bias:** There can be a tendency for respondents to answer in a way that makes them feel better and puts them in a better light.

Box 2.18
Some key points in collecting the data

- Do not assume your questions are clear and unambiguous. Pay attention to pre-testing and to training your interviewers

- Review the initial results of the data collection with other interviewers, in order to identify any problems quickly

- Change a data collection tool if it does not appear to be generating adequate, useful and good-quality data

- Be prepared to organise additional data collection if the initial results indicate that there is a need for more data

- Always keep your ToR in mind

Analysing the data

Once you have collected all your primary and secondary data, you can start analysing it. There are two approaches you can adopt:

- **Quantitative analysis**
    - Make relevant calculations (totals, averages, spread)
    - Analyse the statistical significance
    - Present the data in suitable formats (e.g., tables, graphs)

- **Qualitative analysis** (and critical review)
    - Organise the relevant results
    - Identify the stakeholders to involve
    - Organise a meeting or workshop to analyse the findings
    - Prepare a report on the meeting or workshop outcome

After you have analysed your quantitative and qualitative data, you need to check if the findings are credible. This has implications for the quality of the evaluation report and whether or not it is accepted. To verify the findings, you could:

- talk to people who know about the product/service (expert views)
- compare your data with those of other surveys
- include a verification method in your data collection design (e.g., a control group)
- compare findings from different methods used to collect data (triangulation)

Box 2.19
Some key points in analysing the data

- Consider verifying your data analysis design
- Use a statistician to see if any differences are significant. Interpreting the relevance of significant difference is not a task for people with no statistical background
- Involve stakeholders in analysing and interpreting the data
- Combine data analysis and verification with a first critical review involving stakeholders

Critically reviewing and reporting the findings

The communication process can be seen as a sequence of events, each of them with its own objectives, target groups and characteristics aimed at ensuring that the evaluation findings are critically reviewed and effectively reported to stakeholders.

You will have established in your communication strategy what events and tools you're going to use to review and report findings. Implementing this strategy involves:

- preparing a **presentation** of the final findings from the data analysis
- preparing an **event** at which the findings will be presented

- formulating **questions and assumptions** related to these findings
- formulating the expected **outcome** of the event
- identifying **participants** in this event
- developing the **programme** to address the questions and assumptions
- organising the **event**
- addressing the questions and assumptions, and agreeing upon the **recommendations**
- **reporting** on the findings and recommendations for improving the project, product or service

> **Box 2.20**
> **Some key points in critically reviewing and reporting evaluation findings**
>
> - Participants in communication events might have different interests; be aware of where bias prevents open, objective discussion; create an atmosphere of openness by being open yourself
>
> - Be aware of which stakeholders are likely to be most affected by the evaluation findings
>
> - Make the event action oriented, so that the next stage becomes implementing the findings
>
> - Be flexible in your communication plan. You should always leave space in the plan for any changes based on the early results of the data collection
>
> - Write up the report in a timely fashion and as soon after the event as possible, while the enthusiasm and momentum is still there
>
> - Avoid writing too lengthy a report because you think it carries more weight. It is the content that matters. Most people would rather read less than more

Following up the evaluation

Too often, an evaluation report is produced but, for various reasons, little or no action is taken to implement its recommendations. It is important to build the follow-up action plan into the overall work plan and to ensure that it includes consideration of how the action plan is to be monitored and how the changes it brings to the project are to be managed.

The main post-evaluation activities, therefore, are:

- formulating the action plan
- monitoring the implementation of the action plan
- managing the resulting project changes

Formulating the action plan

Formulating the action plan should start from the time you discuss the evaluation findings. Specific manageable actions (matching existing skills and budget) need to be agreed, responsibilities defined and a time frame developed for these actions.

Important elements of an action plan should include:

- a clear goal (what do we want to achieve)
- a clear description of activities (what are we going to do)
- clear deadlines (when should the activities be done)
- clear responsibilities (who is responsible for implementing the plan)

When formulating an action plan you should ensure that:

- the stakeholders involved are committed to carrying out the plan
- the plan is realistic and manageable, and not just a wish list
- it includes short-term wins as well as long-term gains, so that stakeholders see improvements quickly
- it is implemented without delay, so as to keep up the momentum of the evaluation

Box 2.21
Some key points in formulating the action plan

- Ensure that major elements of the action plan are included in the organisational strategy
- Use a pilot approach to test planned actions that might meet with resistance
- Make sure your key stakeholders are committed to the action plan, so that any major changes to the project do not later meet with resistance to these changes
- Communicate the action plan and its goals through various channels

Monitoring the implementation of the action plan

The implementation of the action plan should be monitored in order to see if the recommended changes are being made and are improving project performance and impact. Monitoring the implementation, following the standard monitoring process (as described in Part 1, pages 16-18) will also contribute to learning for future evaluations.

Monitoring the implementation of the plan will involve setting out the planned actions and the changes they should lead to (the indicators for success). It is only in this way that an assessment can be made as to whether or not the change contributed to improvements in the project. If the changes are substantial, it might be useful to set up a steering committee consisting of different stakeholders who can monitor progress.

Box 2.22
Some key points in monitoring the implementation of the action plan

- Do not monitor everything. Concentrate on the most important actions
- To avoid losing momentum, react quickly if actions are not being implemented according to the action plan
- Be ready to change the action plan if it becomes clear that some actions will not generate the desired results

Managing change

Evaluation is all about improving the performance and impact of your information project, product or service. This improvement means changes. And changes mean that the stakeholders might need to adapt their behaviour. Different stakeholders have different positions and might not agree on some of the evaluation findings. They might also have had different levels of involvement in the evaluation.

The implementation of the action plan therefore needs to take into account the different reactions that stakeholders might have to the findings of the evaluation. Possible reactions include:

- **Accepting the findings and recommendations, and ready to act upon them.** This is the easiest situation. Nevertheless, there may still be various barriers to implementation (e.g., other people might resist changes in the way they need to work).

- **Accepting the findings and recommendations, and willing to see them implemented, but unable to act upon them.** In this case, you will need to find out what the obstacles are. They might include a lack of necessary skills, staff or financial resources. If these problems can't be dealt with, implementation of the action plan is unlikely to succeed.

- **Accepting the findings, but not the recommendations, and not willing to act upon them.** This can happen when the recommendations appear to create more negative effects (extra time and costs) for this stakeholder than positive improvements. Negotiation might be needed to minimise the negative effects and enhance the positive ones. This can also happen when a stakeholder is unable to see the benefits of implementing the recommendations and therefore hesitates to support them. In this case, more information and exposure to successful examples might be required.

- **Rejecting the findings and the recommendations.** It is likely that this reaction is based on the relationship the stakeholder has with the evaluators and/or the information project, rather than on the report itself (assuming the evaluation and the report were adequate). Other reasons for this reaction could be that the stakeholder was not involved in the evaluation, that there are personality clashes or that there is disagreement between the stakeholder and the unit implementing the project. In these cases, relationships need to be improved before any co-operation from the stakeholder can be expected in the implementation process.

To anticipate how a stakeholder might react to the evaluation findings and recommendations, you could do a new stakeholder analysis. The focus would be on assessing the benefits and contributions of the recommended changes.

A useful tool for assessing the willingness and ability of stakeholders to change is the ADKAR model (Hiatt, 2006). This model lists five factors for successful change at an individual level:

- **Awareness** of why the change is needed
- **Desire** to support and participate in the change
- **Knowledge** of how to change
- **Ability** to implement the change
- **Reinforcement** to keep the change in place

The model can be used to find out why a stakeholder is resisting change and to help the stakeholder move through the change process. It can also be used to create an action plan for personal and professional advancement during change, and to develop a change management plan for your stakeholders.

Managing change successfully requires keeping these factors in mind:

- different people react differently to change
- everyone has fundamental needs that have to be met
- change often involves loss, and people facing changes might feel a sense of loss
- expectations need to be managed realistically
- fears need to be dealt with

If the evaluation recommendations call for a fairly complex set of changes involving various stakeholders, it might be worthwhile considering using the services of a change agent who can guide and lead the change process. It should be someone who is committed to the change process, has the capacity to lead it and has good relationships with the stakeholders.

Box 2.23
Some key points in managing change

- Use a communication strategy that ensures that stakeholders are kept informed efficiently and comprehensively; don't let the grapevine take over. In this strategy, include individual interviews with stakeholders to guide them through changes that will affect them personally

- Be open and honest about the facts. Avoid creating unrealistic expectations

- Give stakeholders choices to make, and be clear about the possible consequences of those choices

- Give stakeholders time to express their views and concerns. Support their decision-making process, and provide any reassurance, guidance or information they might need

- Where the changes involve loss, identify what could replace that loss. This will help assuage potential fears

- Where the change process is complex, consider using a change agent. If the evaluation was conducted by an external evaluator, experience has shown that it is not a good idea to use the same evaluator to manage the project changes

Part 3
EVALUATION TOOLS

Introduction

Project planning tools

Evaluation planning tools

Evaluation implementation tools

Applying evaluation findings

In Part 1 we looked at what evaluation is – its purpose and the context in which it occurs. We moved on in Part 2 to the evaluation process itself, especially as it applies to information projects, products and services. The discussion looked at the four major steps in the evaluation process: preparing the evaluation terms of reference; designing the evaluation; implementing it; and following it up.

In Part 3 we look at the evaluation tools. The tools featured here are those that we consider to be well suited to evaluating information projects, products and services. With the increasing demand for information practitioners to evaluate their projects themselves, and not rely on external evaluations, the tools chosen are also seen as suitable for self-evaluation and for fostering learning and stakeholder participation.

The term 'tools' applies to the range of tried-and-tested approaches you can use to evaluate your product/service. Most of them can be used at all stages of the evaluation process. We have divided them here into:

- **project planning tools** (planning frameworks, benchmarking and indicators): as their name implies, these are used to plan a project and, if done properly, can be invaluable reference points and sources of information when the project is subsequently evaluated

- **evaluation planning tools** (terms of reference and logic model): using these tools, and drawing on the project planning frameworks, will establish a strong base from which to select the most appropriate evaluation implementation tools and to conduct the evaluation

- **evaluation implementation tools** (data collection, SWOT analysis, questionnaires, focus groups, flowcharts, case studies, interviews, creative tools, reviews and data analysis): usually a mix of tools will be used to evaluate a product/service, but the particular mix depends on a range of factors, including evaluation purpose, time, finance and available skills

- **applying evaluation findings** (report writing, dissemination channels, promotional approaches, using force-field analysis and brainstorming to create action plans): we put particular emphasis on these tools because, all too often, a great deal of work is done on planning and implementing an evaluation and producing findings and recommendations, but poor reporting and promotion results in little, if any, effort to translate the findings into action

All the tools described here feature in Part 4, where we provide evaluation guidelines for selected information products/services.

PROJECT PLANNING TOOLS

The planning tools described in this section include planning frameworks, benchmarking and indicators.

The two most commonly used project planning frameworks are:

- **logical framework** (logframe)
- **results-based management**

Both are covered here because some development agencies use one, some the other, so it is a good idea to be familiar with both of them. For example, in 1992 the European Commission (EC) adopted project cycle management (PCM), based on the logical framework approach, using PCM design and management tools. Other organisations such as CIDA, World Bank and USAID use results-based management.

Another framework, but which is used primarily for 'evaluation' planning, is the **logic model** (see pages 103-105).

Table 3.1 shows the main elements of these three frameworks, the different terminology used and general evaluation criteria (see Part 2, pages 33-34).

The **benchmarking** tool helps you to set targets against which you can evaluate the performance of your project. By comparing your organisation's activities with those of comparable organisations, you can learn from their experiences and use these to improve your performance.

Project planning also involves selecting the **indicators** that will enable you to measure the degree to which your project has been successful.

Table 3.1
The main elements of the project and evaluation planning frameworks

LOGICAL FRAMEWORK	RESULTS-BASED MANAGEMENT	LOGIC MODEL	EVALUATION CRITERIA
Goal	Results (long term)	Long-term impact	Impact Relevance Sustainability Utility
Project purpose (outcomes)	Outcomes (short and medium term)	Outcomes (short and medium term)	Effectiveness Relevance Usability
Expected results / outputs	Outputs	Outputs	Effectiveness Accessibility Usability
Activities	Process	Activities	Efficiency
Inputs	Resources/inputs	Inputs	Efficiency

Logical framework

The logical framework – which we will refer to as the 'logframe' from now on – was developed in the late 1960s. It is the project planning and management tool now most commonly used by development agencies.

Funding agencies tend to use the logframe for assessing, following up and evaluating projects. Implementing organisations use it for planning, implementing and following up projects.

WHY?
The logframe can be used at all stages of project planning and implementation, right through to the evaluation stage. This integrated approach ensures that the same criteria are used throughout the project cycle and that the framework for all phases of the cycle has the same format.

HOW?
Until the 1990s, project planning tended to be done by external consultants, but since then there has been a clear change in approach, with more and more organisations adopting an internal participatory approach.

There are two phases in preparing a logframe:

- **analysis** phase
- **planning** phase

We look at these two phases in detail, and then at the use of the logframe in the evaluation process.

Analysis phase

The analysis phase of a project is a pivotal part of the planning process. The key potential stakeholders need to be involved in this phase in order to ensure that the needs, concerns, views and perspectives of the various stakeholder groups are represented and understood.

Among the techniques you can use in this phase are SWOT analysis (see pages 115-119), Venn diagrams (see pages 152-154) and rich pictures (see pages 150-152).

Here, we go through the various types of analyses that are part of this phase:

- stakeholder analysis
- problem analysis
- objectives analysis
- strategy analysis

All these types of analyses will be used to compile the logframe.

Stakeholder analysis

Stakeholders are groups of people with an interest in a project and the problem it seeks to address. They can be directly or indirectly linked to it, and might be positively or negatively affected by it. They include policy-makers, input suppliers, partners and, of course, the end-users themselves – the primary stakeholders. Examples of the individuals or groups who could be stakeholders in an information project are given in Part 2 (Figure 2.2, see page 35).

Conducting a stakeholder analysis helps to identify:

- who exactly the stakeholders are
- their perceptions of the problem the project is addressing
- the resources (e.g., political, human, financial, legitimisation) they bring to the project
- their expected roles in resolving the problem that the project seeks to address
- the potential power they have to influence the process of the project
- their expected roles in resolving the problem
- areas of possible conflict
- their needs in relation to the accessibility and usability of your product/service

Table 3.2 shows how to structure a stakeholder analysis. Table 3.2 (a) summarises how different stakeholder groups are affected by the problem the project is addressing. Table 3.2 (b) summarises how the project intervention might affect these groups. Both examples can be adapted to include additional information about the stakeholders, depending on the scope and focus of the issues being addressed.

Table 3.2
Stakeholder analysis to assess (a) stakeholders' relationship to the problem being addressed and (b) how they are likely to be affected by the project

(a)

Stakeholders	How are they affected by the problem?	Capacity / motivation to help address the problem	Relationship with other stakeholders

(b)

Stakeholders	How are they involved in the project?	Expected positive impact and benefits	Expected negative impact and costs	Net impact

Table 3.3
Gender analysis among the primary stakeholders

Production of products / services	Who does the work? Women	Men	Frequency of activity		
1					
2					
3					
Household tasks					
1					
2					
3					
Community tasks					
1					
2					
3					
Resources	Who has access? Women	Men	Who has control? Women	Men	Other*
1					
2					
3					
Benefits	Who has access? Women	Men	Who has control? Women	Men	Other*
1					
2					
3					

* Government, private organisation, etc.

Gender analysis among the primary stakeholders is a key part of stakeholder analysis. An example of how to include gender analysis is given in Table 3.3.

Once completed, the stakeholder analysis should be reviewed and, where necessary, updated throughout the project planning stage, as the scope of the project becomes clearer and new information becomes available.

The stakeholder analysis is an important source of information for the evaluation of a project, both in its own right and within the context of the logframe.

Problem analysis

Problem analysis strongly influences the design of a project. Without an in-depth analysis of the problem that a project seeks to address, the project planning stage will probably not provide the firm basis upon which the success of a project depends. Too often, projects are implemented with a pre-defined solution to a problem about which not enough is known.

Brainstorming using SWOT analysis (see pages 115-119) is a useful technique for problem analysis. If it is difficult for some stakeholders to attend a brainstorming session in person, you could consider setting up an electronic discussion forum.

A useful way of illustrating the analysis of the problem is to draw a 'problem tree'. This requires identifying the causes of the problem and its intermediate and ultimate effects. The problem tree defines the links between the causes and the effects, it helps to improve the project design and also to improve its monitoring and evaluation. Box 3.1 (overleaf) presents a case study of what can go wrong if there has been inadequate problem analysis.

**Figure 3.1
An example of a problem tree**

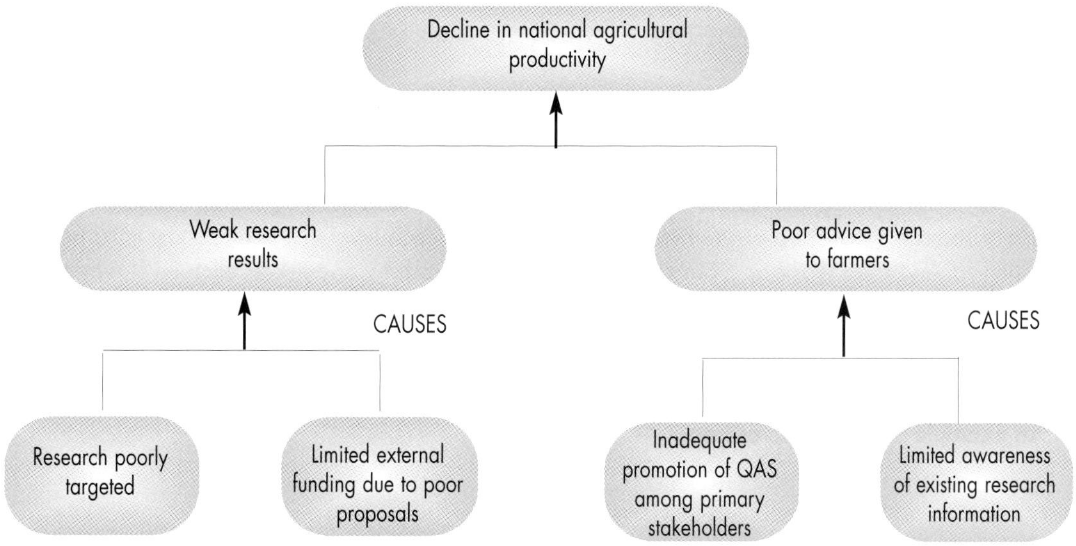

Note: This problem tree assumes that there are linear causal relationships between causes and effects. It's important to note, however, that the cause–effect relationships in your project might not be as evident or clear-cut.

Objectives analysis

Carrying out an analysis of the objectives of a project is like mapping the vision of the future. A useful way of illustrating this analysis is to draw an 'objectives tree'. This involves:

- translating each negative statement (problem) in the problem tree into a positive statement (objective)
- testing the logic of the hierarchy of objectives

Box 3.1
Case study of the consequences of poor problem analysis

In 1995, a pan-African information service based in Southern Africa began to decentralise its activities. Part of this involved establishing an Eastern African regional QAS (Question-and-Answer Service) node, in addition to the QAS node covering Southern Africa.

The Kolomari area was served by the Southern Africa node, but in 1998 it became part of Eastern Africa. It continued, however, to be served by the Southern Africa node. It had been overlooked in the changes. As a result, Kolomari farmers were still being provided with a service that no longer addressed their specific needs. It also meant a lack of timely information, and this led to a decrease in the use of the service. This affected the activities of the research institutes in the area, which began to find it difficult to attract enough external funding, and it had a negative impact on national agricultural output.

A good problem analysis conducted at the time of the decentralisation exercise, and again when Kolomari became part of Eastern Africa, might have prevented this situation.

The top of the tree is the overall objective, and the lower levels are the means to achieving that objective. All the objectives will be used to assess the performance of the project. Figure 3.2 provides an example of an objectives tree.

So, whereas the problem tree shows the cause–effect relationship between problems, the objectives tree shows the means–end relationship between objectives.

Having drawn the objectives tree, you now need to test the underlying logic. A simple way to do this is to start at the top of the hierarchy and ask how each level in the hierarchy is to be achieved. And then work up from the bottom of the hierarchy and ask at each level why this objective is being undertaken.

Figure 3.2
An example of an objectives tree

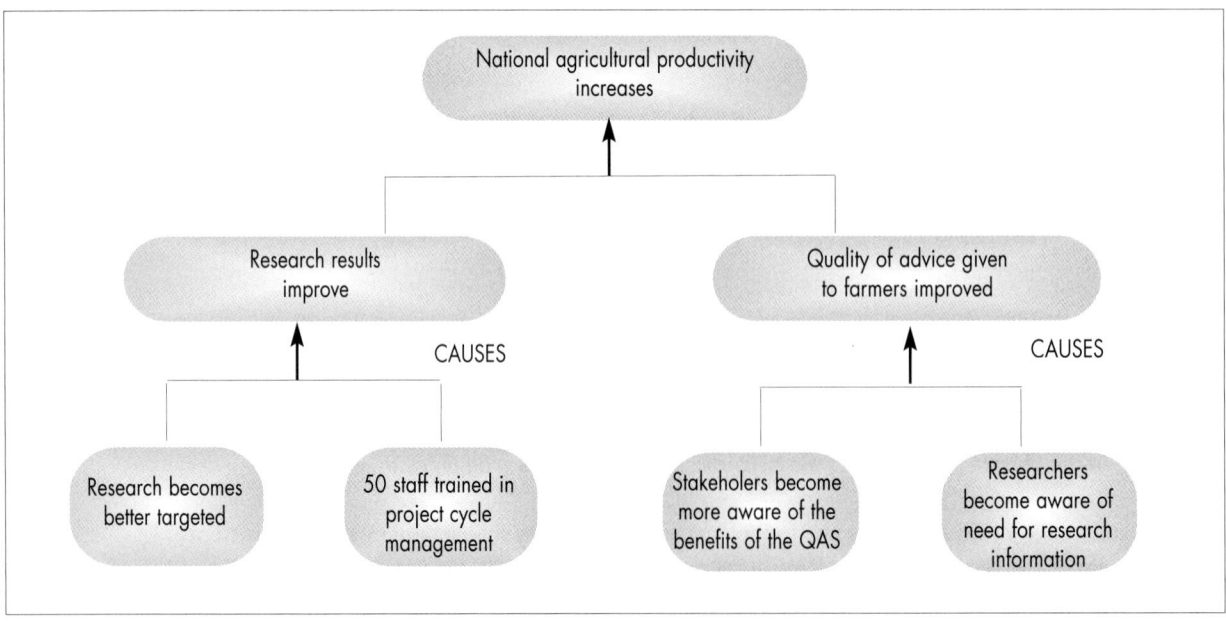

Strategy analysis

The purpose of a strategy analysis is to reach decisions on how to solve the identified problem. It involves clustering the objectives and examining the feasibility of various options, taking into account the resources available.

This is also useful for designing the strategies for various actions that will contribute to achieving the overall objective of the project. In short, it is a prioritisation exercise.

Choosing a strategy requires thinking about:

- how the strategy will contribute to your overall **goal**
- how it will benefit the **primary stakeholders**
- how it complements your organisation's current or intended **projects/programmes**
- its capital and cost implications, and available local **resources** (human and financial)
- its potential contribution to **capacity building**
- its **technical feasibility**

Figure 3.3
An example of a strategy analysis tree

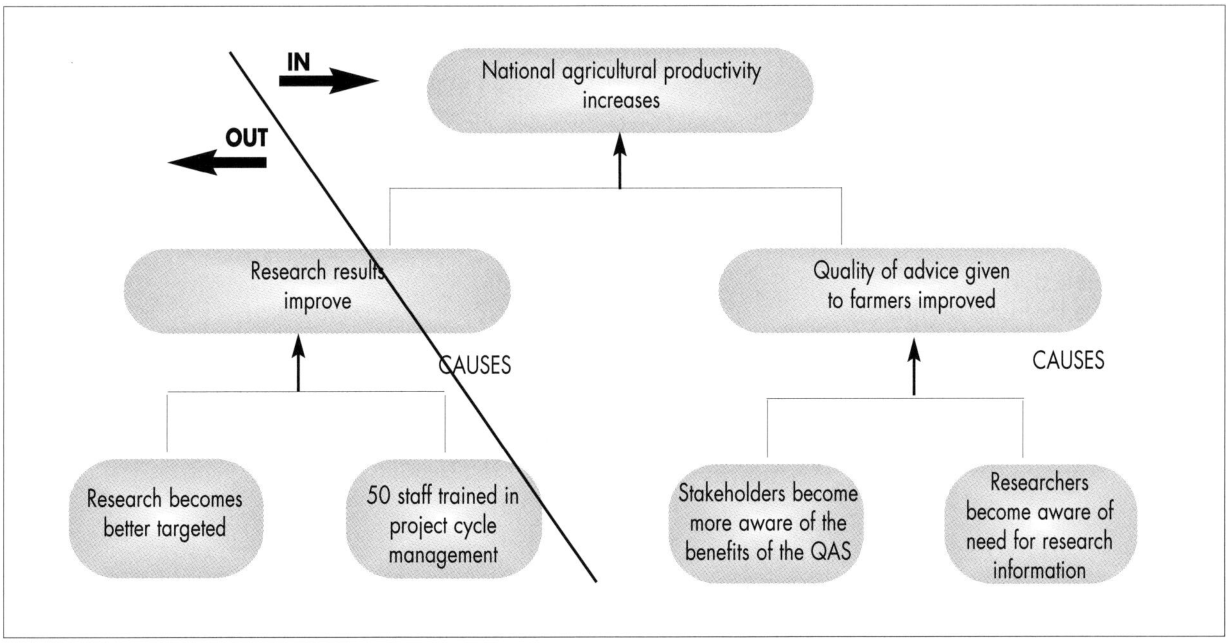

Planning phase

The planning phase involves constructing the logframe matrix and preparing the implementation plan and the budget.

We also need to mention the system called 'cascading projects', which relates to a situation when projects have a complex set of goals.

Constructing the logframe

A logframe is a matrix of four vertical columns and five horizontal rows, as shown in Table 3.4. Although the matrix implies a linear process, constructing it is an iterative process.

Let's now look at each of the elements in the logframe matrix:

Intervention logic: This term is used to cover the different levels of objectives, from inputs to activities, outputs, purpose and goal. These objectives should all be linked in a well-designed and logical manner, such that if all are achieved there is a good chance of the goal being fulfilled. The term 'intervention logic' is sometimes replaced by 'narrative summary' or 'objective hierarchy'.

Goal: The project goal is usually stated in broad terms, encompassing a set of initiatives and looking at the long term. For example, referring to Box 3.1, the goal is: 'To improve agricultural productivity in Eastern Africa'. But this does not mean that the QAS node contribution alone is enough to achieve this; other initiatives – international, national, regional and local – will be needed to help improve the situation.

Purpose: The project purpose describes the intended benefit of the project. It should always be stated in one complete sentence, which includes the target group and a realistic time frame. The project will achieve its purpose if the outputs are achieved and the assumptions associated with these outputs are met.

Outputs (expected results): The project outputs are the products of the activities undertaken. Together, these products are the benefits accruing to the primary stakeholders and represent the achievement of the project purpose. A logframe may specify outputs over time; that is, the envisaged outputs in the first year, the outputs in the second year, and so on. Thus, new outputs can be added as time progresses. Similarly, unanticipated outputs can be added over time.

Table 3.4
The logframe matrix

	INTERVENTION LOGIC	OBJECTIVELY VERIFIABLE INDICATORS	MEANS OF VERIFICATION	ASSUMPTIONS
GOAL				
PROJECT PURPOSE				
OUTPUTS (EXPECTED RESULTS)				
ACTIVITIES				
INPUTS				

Activities: The project activities should specify the means (actions) and costs of producing the outputs. Each objective at the output level should have an activity or group of activities associated with it.

Inputs: This relates to the funding, skills, time and materials available for the project. It is an aspect which, although crucial to project success, is often not taken into account enough when setting the project goal and activities.

Indicators: The project indicators provide a measurement for evaluating the progress of the activities towards attaining the objectives. 'Objectively verifiable' means you must be able to verify whether or not the objectives have been reached, and to what extent. As we saw in Part 2, indicators should be SMART (specific, measurable, achievable, relevant and time-bound) and based on good baseline data (see Box 3.2). The process of identifying indicators, especially when they have a strong qualitative component, should include stakeholders, especially primary stakeholders. A community's perspective of an improvement in their quality of life might differ from that of an outsider. It could also be relevant to distinguish between women's and men's perspectives.

Means of verification: The source of data should be established for each indicator for each level: goal, purpose, output and activity. The purpose of this is to test whether or not an indicator can be measured realistically.

Assumptions: Projects are never isolated from external events. They are always subject to influence by factors outside the control of project management, such as unstable environments. Being clear about the assumptions about the environment in which a project will operate is crucial to good project design. Failure to identify assumptions realistically is a common source of project failure.

The importance of the assumptions becomes clear when considering the link between them and the intervention logic, as shown in Table 3.5. The link between these elements is referred

Table 3.5
Linking intervention and assumption

INTERVENTION LOGIC	OBJECTIVELY VERIFIABLE INDICATORS	MEANS OF VERIFICATION	ASSUMPTIONS
Goal			Assumptrions for achievement of sustainability
Project purpose			and
			Assumptions for contribution to overall goal
Outputs			and
			Assumptions for achievement of project purpose
Activities			and
			Assumptions for achievement of results

to as the 'if [ ] then [ ] logic path'. Key questions to be raised when completing the column are:

- If the activities are undertaken, what other factors need to be in place in order for the outputs to be achieved?

- If the outputs are achieved, what other factors need to be in place in order for them to lead to achieving the purpose?

- If the purpose is achieved, what other factors need to be in place in order for it to contribute to the goal?

It is also important to be aware about who has control over the assumptions and whether the assumptions are critical to success. If an assumption is critical to project success, but you can't influence it in any way, then you might need to have another look at what you can achieve.

Box 3.2
Building baseline data

You can't record the changes a project brings about unless you have a starting point against which to measure them – that is, what the situation was like before the project started. This information is called baseline data.

Baseline data are usually gathered at the start of a project. If you don't already have these data in place you must collect them. Make sure the data you collect relate directly to the indicators that you have identified; don't waste time getting other information, as you probably won't use it.

When identifying data sources, ask yourself the following questions:

- Can the data source be accessed on a practical, timely and regular basis?
- Will the source provide quality data?
- Is collecting data from the source feasible and cost-effective?
- How should the data be collected? (e.g., sample surveys, administrative records, focus groups)
- Who should collect the data? (e.g., field officers, project officers, stakeholders)
- When and how often should the data be collected, analysed and reported? (e.g., monthly, annually)
- What formats are needed to record the data being collected?
- Who will analyse the data?

Cascading projects

A project should have a single purpose. If the problem analysis reveals a situation that is too complex to be addressed by a single project, what can you do? The answer is: Adopt the system called 'cascading projects' by designing a series of parallel projects with the same goal but different purposes. This requires amending the logframe, as in the example in Table 3.6.

The advantages of cascading projects are:

- they avoid the need to design very complex projects
- each project and sub-project has a clearly defined purpose
- each project purpose has clear responsibilities

Table 3.6
A logframe matrix for cascading projects

	IL	OVI	MOV	A
GOAL	G			
PROJECT PURPOSE	P1			
OUTPUTS (EXPECTED RESULTS)	O1.1 O1.2 O1.3			
ACTIVITIES		Means	Cost	

Project 1

	IL	OVI	MOV	A
GOAL				
PROJECT PURPOSE				
OUTPUTS (EXPECTED RESULTS)				
ACTIVITIES		Means	Cost	

Project 2

	IL	OVI	MOV	A
GOAL	P1			
PROJECT PURPOSE	O1.1			
OUTPUTS (EXPECTED RESULTS)	Z1 Z2			
ACTIVITIES		Means	Cost	

	IL	OVI	MOV	A
GOAL	P1			
PROJECT PURPOSE	O1.2			
OUTPUTS (EXPECTED RESULTS)	X1 X2 X3			
ACTIVITIES		Means	Cost	

	IL	OVI	MOV	A
GOAL	P1			
PROJECT PURPOSE	O1.3			
OUTPUTS (EXPECTED RESULTS)	Y1 Y2			
ACTIVITIES		Means	Cost	

IL: intervention logic
OVI: objectively verifiable indicators
MOV: means of verification
A: assumptions
G: goal
P: purpose
O: outputs

Source: Schiefer et al. (2001)

- each project has a clearly defined intervention logic
- each project has its own indicators for monitoring and evaluation
- each project and sub-project takes account of its own external environment

Project implementation

For planning the implementation of a project, a Gantt chart can be used. The chart is linked to the project outputs specified in the logframe.

Table 3.7
A sample Gantt chart for planning project (a) implementation and (b) resources

(a)

Ref. no	Results and indicative activities	Person responsible	Comments	2009-2010										
				N	D	J	F	M	A	M	J	J	A	S	O
1.1	Stakeholders become more sensitised to the benefits of using QAS	Contractor: Tango & Co.													
	Activities														
1.1.1	Preparation of sensitisation activities				■	■	■								
1.1.2	Prepare pamphlets on services offered by QAS nodes and distribute via local newspapers							■	■						
1.1.3	Announcement of open-day in local newspapers and on prime-time local radio									■	■				
1.1.4	Organise two open-day sessions to sensitise the stakeholders (preferably on a Saturday when most people are free)											■	■		
1.1.5	Prepare and distribute feedback leaflets to obtain feedback about the open-day sessions													■	■	■

(b)

1.1	Activities	Days	Unit price	Quantity	Total euros
1.1.1	Preparation of sensitisation activities				
1.1.2	Prepare pamphlets on services offered by QAS nodes and distribute via local newspapers				
1.1.3	Announcement of open-day in local newspapers and on prime-time local radio				
1.1.4	Organise two open-day sessions to sensitise the stakeholders (preferably on a Saturday when most people are free)				
1.1.5	Prepare and distribute feedback leaflets to obtain feedback about the open-day sessions				

A Gantt chart is a list of activities plotted against a specific timeline, showing start and due dates for each activity (milestones), and who will be responsible for which activities. It makes it easier to be clear about the relationship between activities (e.g., whether the start of Activity B requires the completion first of Activity A). A typical Gantt chart is shown in Table 3.7.

Project budget

The project resources are the means – physical and non-physical resources – you need in order to carry out the planned activities and manage the project. They include human and material inputs, time and funds. They should form the basis of your project budget, which provides the financial framework for project implementation. The checklist in Box 3.3 will help you to determine what and what not to include in your budget.

Box 3.3
Checklist for a project budget

- Identify the most important project budget lines in terms of their share in the overall budget. Is it acceptable within the project (and according to general standards) that these project budget lines make up the main share?

- Is the budget within the agreed budget line of the funding agency?

- Is there a policy regarding the types of costs to be financed by each funding agency (e.g., running costs, salaries for local staff)? Are the types of costs for this project within that policy?

- Did you incorporate the overhead costs within the budget? If yes, has this been agreed in advance with the funding agency?

- Are some intermediate activities expensive? What makes them expensive? Are there other less expensive ways to achieve the same results?

- Is it possible to ask for a contribution from the primary stakeholders in order to reduce the funds requested from the funding agency?

- Does the project generate any income that returns to the project?

- What is the cost-efficiency of the project? What is the cost per beneficiary? Is this cost acceptable when compared with similar projects in the region or the sector?

- Is the budget cost-effective (i.e., is it likely to achieve given objectives at the lowest possible cost)?

Logframes and evaluation

An evaluation challenges the original assumptions of the project design and considers how far the project purpose has been achieved. The main difference between using a logframe to design a new project and using one to evaluate an ongoing or completed project is that in the analysis phase, instead of using primary data sources, for the evaluation you use existing project documentation.

Figure 3.4
Relationship between logframe elements and evaluation criteria

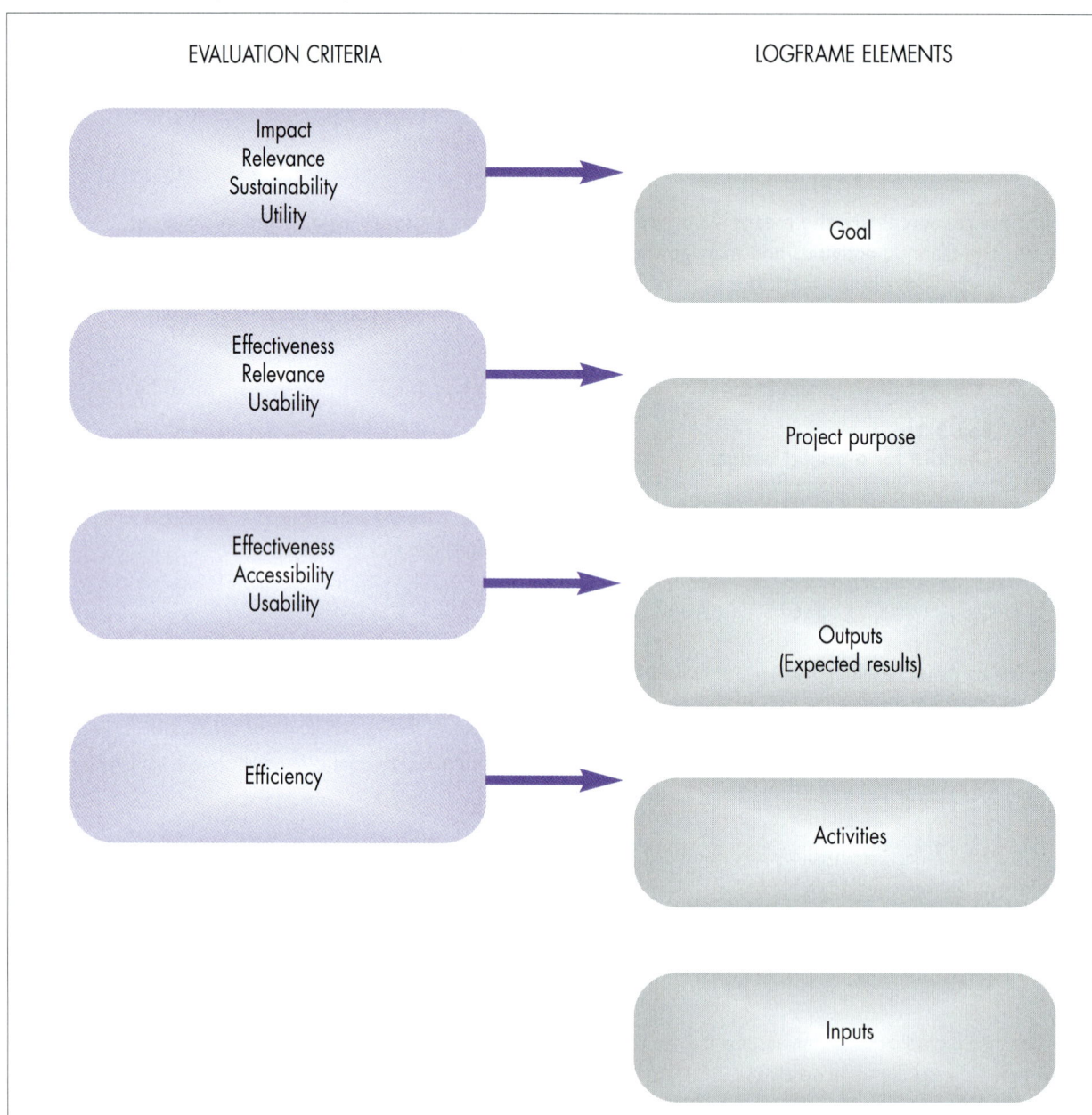

Figure 3.4 shows the main links between key evaluation criteria and the key logframe elements.

A key evaluation question to ask when matching the evaluation criteria with the logframe elements is: Was everything done as planned? To answer this question, you need to focus on:

- quality of the day-to-day management
- cost-effectiveness
- level of contribution from stakeholders
- quality of monitoring
- suitability of indicators

Let's look at some of the most important evaluation criteria as an example of how they link to the logframe elements:

Relevance: This relates to how far the project's stated objectives correctly address the identified problems. The main issues to be addressed are the:

- extent to which products/services suit the priorities of the primary stakeholders
- complementarity and coherence with other activities/projects being undertaken in the region
- overall design of the project (strengths and weaknesses)

Accessibility: This relates to the extent to which your project reaches the primary stakeholders. The main issues to be addressed are:

- the distribution of the product/service
- the availability of the product/service
- the timeliness of the product/service

Usability: This relates to the extent to which the primary stakeholders are able to use your product/service. The main issues to be addressed are:

- the completeness of the product/service in relation to its intended use
- the ease of comprehension of the language used (the language itself, and its level and style, if delivered in written form)
- the relevance to the lives of the stakeholders, ease of comprehension of diagrams and pictures, and technical accuracy of information

Effectiveness: This relates to whether the project's outputs achieved the project purpose. The main issues to be addressed are:

- the extent to which the development objectives have been achieved
- the extent to which the planned benefits have been delivered
- the appropriateness of the indicators relating to benefits
- whether the assumptions at outputs level were inadequate or invalid
- how unplanned outputs might have affected the benefits delivered

Impact: This concerns the relationship between the project purpose and the project goal, and involves both quantitative and qualitative analyses. The main issues to be addressed are the:

- extent to which the planned overall objectives have been achieved
- appropriateness of the logframe indicators at this level
- appropriateness of any specific impacts (e.g. those which are gender related)

Sustainability: This relates to whether the positive outcomes at purpose level are likely to continue after funding ends. The main issues to be addressed are:

- ownership of objectives and achievements
- policy support, and responsibilities of the beneficiary institutions
- institutional capacity
- adequacy of the budget
- socio-cultural factors
- financial sustainability

Utility: This relates to the extent to which the information project, product or service could be successfully replicated in another location or among different primary stakeholders. The main issues to be addressed are:

- the suitability of the information product for use with other, similar groups of people
- the conditions which made for success and whether they hold good in other locations or with other groups
- what would need to be done to ensure that the product is suitable for use with other people in other areas (e.g., translation of language and contextualising of illustration)
- lessons learned and how they could be usefully applied to other projects

Efficiency: This relates to the cost-effectiveness of the information project, product or service in terms of outputs (quantity, quality, timeliness) compared with inputs. The main issues to be addressed are:

- the extent to which the objectives have been (or are expected to be) achieved without using more resources than required
- quality of day-to-day management
- level of contribution (financial/human) from partners
- quality of monitoring
- suitability of indicators

In your evaluation, some criteria would be more important than others. This depends on the focus of your evaluation.

Box 3.4
Some key points in constructing a logframe

- Set clear, plausible specifications about the envisaged impact of the project

- Formulate project objectives that can realistically be achieved through a defined set of activities

- Link the resources (inputs), activities and impact to the goal and purpose

- Consider carefully the external factors that could affect the project

- Constantly monitor and periodically evaluate the indicators and sources of verification, and adapt the logframe if necessary

- Don't assume that because the logframe is well constructed the project is likely to be successful

- Don't simply fill in the boxes in the logframe matrix and then file it away; it should be referred to constantly if the goal and purpose are to be achieved

Box 3.5
The strengths and weaknesses of the logframe approach

WEAKNESSES	STRENGTHS
■ Can be very time-consuming to construct and apply	■ Clearly shows means–ends progression of project inputs leading to outputs for set purposes in support of the project goal
■ Can oversimplify objectives	
■ If not formulated in a participatory way, it might not reflect agreed solutions	■ Clearly shows objectives, responsibilities, measurability and sources of verification
■ Can downgrade less quantified objectives and unintended effects	■ Is specific about the inputs and costs for project activities
■ Is based on determining the project outcome in advance, although development contexts tend to be complex and full of uncertainties	■ Specifies the key assumptions and risks surrounding the project
	■ Supports the systematic and effective collection of information
	■ Supports better decision-making
	■ Plays an important role in all phases of the project cycle, including planning, implementation and evaluation
	■ If formulated in a participatory way, it can take into account the multiple perspectives of stakeholders

Results-based management

Results-based management – also sometimes referred to as 'performance management' or 'outcome measurement' – is a project planning framework that seeks to address the growing demand for evidence that funded activities are producing long-term benefits. This demand comes especially from publicly funded organisations.

In the evaluation context, it reflects the move away from focusing on evaluating the input side of a project (e.g., financial efficiency, use of human resources) to evaluating the output side, giving more weight to how a project affects the lives of its primary stakeholders.

Among the organisations that are leading proponents of results-based management are the World Bank, USAID and CIDA. For project managers it is a very useful tool for managing and monitoring projects. For beneficiaries, it is an indicator of what exactly they should expect from a project. And for evaluators, it is the most straightforward way of assessing the outcome of a project.

WHY?

Results-based management is the best way to link performance measures to the intended result of a project. The establishment of specific intended results at the planning stage facilitates the later stages of management and monitoring and, most importantly, makes an evaluation study relatively easy to carry out.

HOW?

Organisations vary in the way they carry out results-based management, but in all cases the focus is on achieved results. This is ensured by:

- analysing the existing situation
- clearly identifying specific objectives
- choosing the strategy for meeting objectives
- determining the success criteria
- analysing the assumptions and the potential hindrances to success

Results-based management is seen as an essential link between evaluation and planning. When an evaluation is carried out during project implementation, the results can be fed into the ongoing planning process. When an evaluation is carried out at the end of a project, the results can be fed into subsequent strategic planning and reporting.

We will look first at the framework itself, and an example of how to apply it. We then discuss results-based management within the context of monitoring and evaluation.

The framework

Results-based management relates to the way an organisation is motivated and how it applies processes and resources to achieve targeted results.

It generally refers to outcomes that convey benefits to the community. The key issue is that results differ from activities. Many people, when asked what they produce, describe their activities rather than the results of their activities (the products).

The main features of results-based management are:

- specified results that are measurable, relevant and can be monitored
- resources that are adequate for achieving the targeted results
- organisational arrangements that ensure that responsibilities are aligned with results and resources
- processes for planning, monitoring, communicating and resource release that enable an organisation to convert resources into the desired results

The assumptions in a results-based management framework are exactly the same as those for the logframe. No project is independent of what is happening in its environment, and much of what does happen is beyond the control of the project officer. Understanding and assessing the important assumptions in a project environment is an essential part of good project design. Failure to realistically identify, address and continuously monitor assumptions is a common reason for project failure.

Part 3: EVALUATION TOOLS: Project planning

**Figure 3.5
The results-based management framework**

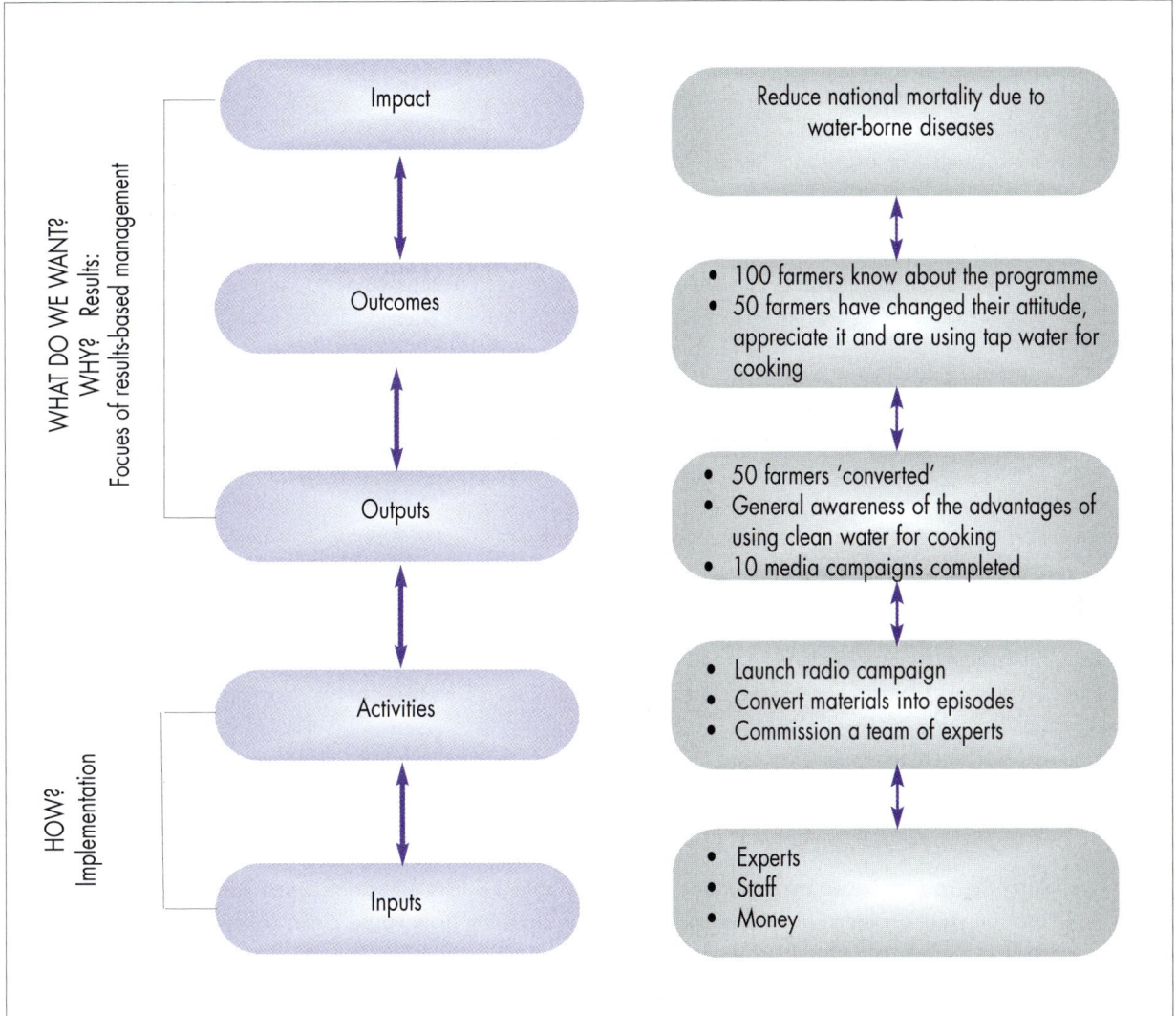

An example of applying results-based management is given in Box 3.6. The example highlights two important characteristics of results-based management:

- This approach **differentiates between achievements (results) on the one hand, and activities and implementation on the other.** In the example, conducting the primary survey to assess people's views and levels of knowledge, preparing the project materials and raising awareness of the project are all part of the activities - they should not be considered as achieved results.

- This approach **emphasises the need to determine what the project intends to achieve**. In the example, if it aims only to increase people's knowledge of the importance of using clean water, then the project can't be held accountable if none of the farmers has stopped using irrigation water for cooking purposes. If the aim is to change farmers' behaviour, then the result that counts here is the number of farmers who started using clean water.

Box 3.6
An example of the application of the results-based management approach

In this example, the project is about setting up a radio programme to raise the awareness of farmers in a particular area of the need to use clean tap water (not irrigation water) for household activities.

The **project objective** would be:
- to raise the awareness of x number of farmers, through a new local-language radio programme, to use clean tap water instead of irrigation water for cooking, drinking and washing

The **project strategy** would be:
- to launch a radio programme to be aired when farmers are listening to radio; seen as an effective way of telling them about the advantages of using clean water for household needs, and the risks of using irrigation water for these purposes

Examples of **project activities** would be:
- conducting a survey of the number of farmers who have access to clean water but don't use it
- investigating why they are not using the clean water, and listing the reasons for this
- commissioning a team of experts to prepare scientific material for the programme, and convert this material into a set of episodes that would appeal to the farmers
- determining the best times to promote and air the radio programme

Examples of the **results** at various levels could be:
- Stage 1: x number of farmers know about the programme and have started following it
- Stage 2: x number of farmers understand it and have a better idea why to use clean tap water
- Stage 3: x number of farmers have changed their attitude and now think it's better to use clean tap water for cooking, drinking and cleaning
- Stage 4: x number of farmers have changed their behaviour and have stopped using irrigation water for cooking, drinking and washing; they now use clean tap water instead

Using the results-based management approach, Table 3.8 lists eight questions you could use to describe your project. This is a useful exercise in learning how to be clear, concise and specific about the envisaged results of your project.

Table 3.8
An exercise in describing a project using results-based management

QUESTION	KEY WORD	YOUR ANSWER
What is the problem your project seeks to address?	Problem	
Who stands to benefit?	Who?	
What are the major activities in the project?	Activities	
What are the outputs of these activities?	Outputs	
What outcomes will these outputs produce?	Outcomes	
Toward what single impact is the project contributing?	Impact	
What key constraints will influence the project as you move from activities to outcomes?	Constraints	
What indicators will you use to measure progress toward achieving the project outputs and outcomes?	Indicators	

Monitoring and evaluation

Results-based management advocates that, to become truly results-oriented, monitoring and evaluation needs to be aligned with annual plans and other work plans of the implementing organisation. It helps the organisation to focus on achieving outcomes, with the emphasis on the effective use of resources, not just their efficient use.

Monitoring

Monitoring is generally described as the collection of data over time, as described in Part 2. It helps to identify day-to-day problems during the implementation of activities. It looks at whether the activities are likely to achieve the planned target and, if not, what corrective measures need to be taken before the evaluation.

Results-based management places strong emphasis on monitoring. In this approach, the acronym used to describe a good indicator is **c**lear, **r**elevant, **e**conomic, **a**dequate and easily **m**onitored (CREAM).

The key issues here are:

- results information needs at the project, programme and policy levels
- the demand for results information at each level should be identified
- results information should move both horizontally and vertically in the organisation
- the responsibility at each level for data collection needs to be clear

Evaluation

The key evaluation questions that are addressed by the results-based management approach are:

- **Strategy:** Are the right things being done, strategically? This relates to *rationale* and a clear *theory of action*

- **Operations:** Are things being done properly? This relates to *effectiveness* in achieving expected outcomes, *efficiency* in optimising resources, and *client satisfaction*

- **Learning:** Are there better ways to do things? This relates to *alternatives*, *best practice* and *lessons learned*

Results-based management prescribes four instances that warrant gathering evaluation information to support management decision-making:

- divergence between planned and actual performance
- need to differentiate between the contributions of design and implementation to the outcomes
- need to determine what is or is not working efficiently and effectively
- conflicting evidence of the outcomes

Smart Toolkit for Evaluating Information Projects, Products and Services

Box 3.7
Some key points in constructing a results-based management framework

- Be clear about the parameters of the project

- Remember that the environment in which your project operates is probably full of uncertainties which might affect the project, so you will need to continuously update the framework

- Don't design your project and then try to identify the 'problem owners'

- Show clearly how the people involved in project activities are linked to the improvement expected in the long term

- Don't describe the project 'goal' in terms of what is to be done, but rather how it will make a difference

Box 3.8
The strengths and weaknesses of the results-based management approach

WEAKNESSES	STRENGTHS
- It is sometimes confusing because of the different names that people use to refer to it	- Requires the participation of all key stakeholders as well as those involved in implementing the plan
- The terms differ from those used for logframe, which can be confusing	- Is objective and results-oriented, focusing on what is to be achieved, as well as on what is to be done
	- Has a logical sequencing of inputs, activities, short-term outputs, medium-term outcomes and long-term outcomes
	- Is flexible

Benchmarking

Benchmarking is a project planning tool that provides information on how well a particular product/service is doing, compared with similar products/services. It's important to know that what you compare it with has the same or similar function and similar primary stakeholders. You also need to know how it has been evaluated, and whether the primary stakeholders were consulted. In other words, you need to compare like with like, using the same parameters.

The process of benchmarking involves identifying 'best practices' in relation to an organisation's procedures, products and services. You need to understand these procedures, products and services in detail before you undertake the benchmarking process.

Benchmarking was developed in the USA in the 1970s and was used mainly by companies operating in an industrial environment. It is now increasingly used by public sector organisations, universities and development agencies.

WHY?

Benchmarking helps you to improve the efficiency and effectiveness of your project, which contributes to improved performance. It does this by helping to identify and adopt higher standards and best practices.

HOW?

The benchmarking process has several steps, as shown in Figure 3.6. Although the figure implies that the process should be done in a sequential manner, benchmarking should not be seen as a linear process. For example, there might be occasions when you will need to revisit activities from previous steps (e.g., re-examining your own process), and there might also be circumstances where you will be implementing activities in multiple steps simultaneously.

Whatever the sequence you decide to use, however, you should ensure that all the steps are followed.

Types of benchmarking

There are various types of benchmarking, as outlined in Table 3.9.

The benchmarking process

The benchmarking process is illustrated in Figure 3.6. The figure outlines the eight steps in the process. Step 8 of this process is particularly important. CTA's flagship magazine *Spore* – available to

Table 3.9
Types of benchmarking

TYPE	WHAT IT DOES	EXAMPLE
Internal	Compares activities among similar operations in one's own organisation	Between departments within the same organisation. The main advantage is that sensitive data and information are easily accessible, but innovation might be lacking
Competitive	Compares activities with the best of similar activities implemented by direct competitors	A UK training institute benchmarks its activities against those of the Open University, which has a reputation for providing excellent training through distance learning
Functional	Compares methods with organisations in various areas of activity to find ways of improving functions and work processes	Often used where there is no counterpart (e.g., a development agency that has a unique approach to implementing information projects in ACP countries will need to look beyond the development information sector if it wants to benchmark its activities)
Generic process	Compares processes used in unrelated activities (e.g., innovative, exemplary work processes)	A development agency could benchmark against a lobbying agency, to compare how it uses its network to influence decisions made at the policy level

people involved in ACP agricultural and rural development – is used as an example. Some of the areas in which *Spore* excels are: its usefulness, cost-effectiveness, content quality, timeliness and dissemination (both the printed and online versions).

Figure 3.6
The steps involved in the benchmarking process

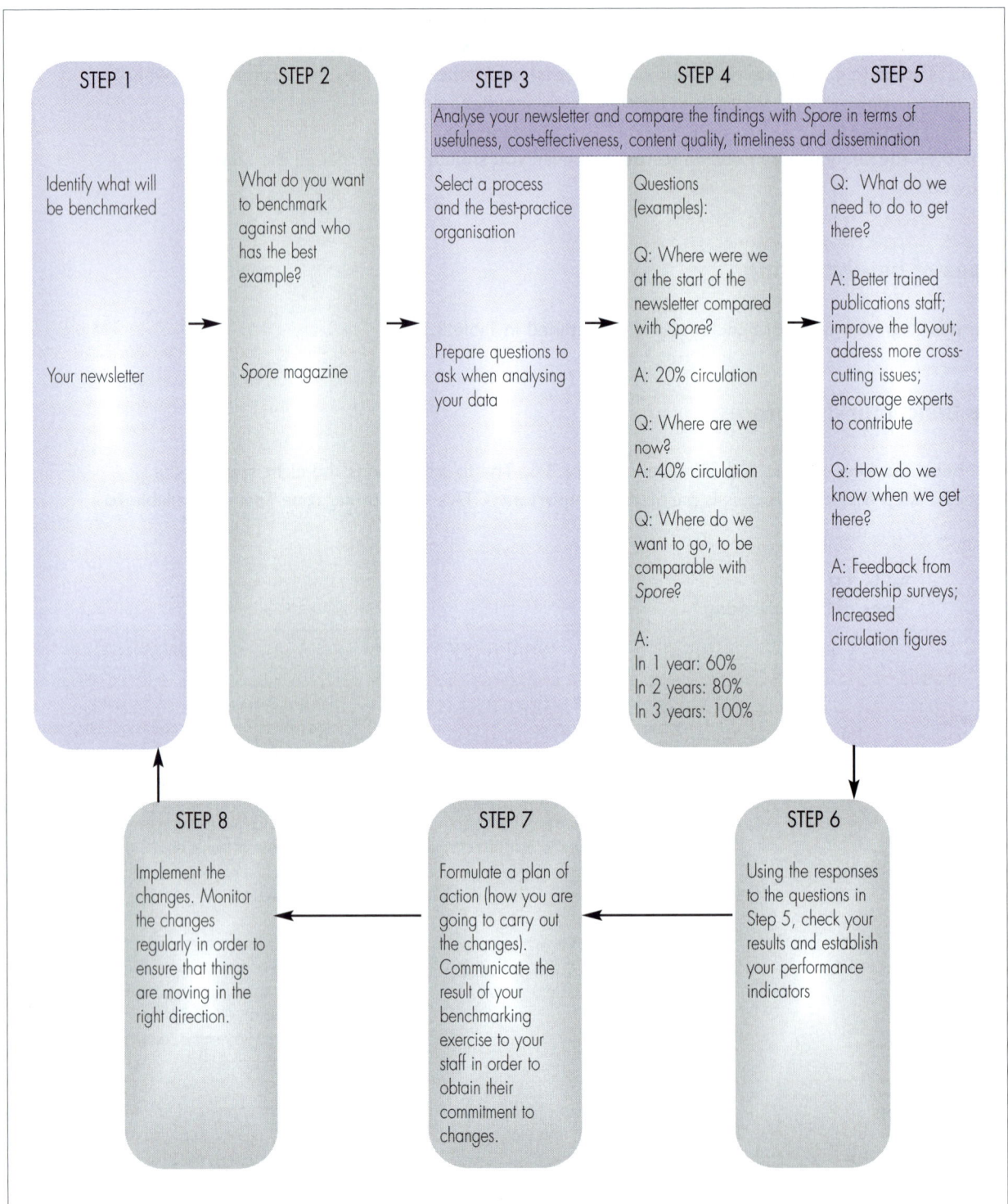

Part 3: EVALUATION TOOLS: Project planning

Box 3.9
Some key points in carrying out a benchmarking exercise

- Make sure you get management's commitment before you embark on the benchmarking exercise
- It is a good idea to involve people of mixed skills in your internal benchmarking team
- Avoid relying on pre-existing benchmarks
- Don't try to benchmark a total system; break it down into smaller, manageable components
- Don't carry out a benchmarking exercise just for the sake of it
- Choose topics that are tangible and are not too difficult to measure

Box 3.10
The strengths and weaknesses of benchmarking

WEAKNESSES	STRENGTHS
■ Can be time-consuming and requires good skills and knowledge	■ Provides an opportunity to build on the work of others, reducing the need to reinvent the wheel and facilitating more efficient use of resources
■ Might be difficult to persuade partners to share information because of confidentiality issues	■ Helps to identify what needs to be improved and how (e.g., higher standards, quality)
■ Communication failure between partners can occur	■ Helps to identify weak areas and what needs to be done to improve them
■ Management sometimes do not support benchmarking because it might expose the organisation's weaknesses	■ Identifies best institutional practices
■ There might be difficulties in transferring best practices to other organisations because of cultural, environmental and other factors	■ If the process is carried out in a participatory way, it enables employees to visualise the improvements, which can be a catalyst for change
■ Quantifiable results may take much longer, depending on the scope and nature of the changes introduced	■ Encourages organisations to find ways of measuring their products/services in terms of inputs and outcomes, thereby promoting a focus on the most beneficial aspects of a project

Identifying indicators

This project planning tool will help you to identify appropriate indicators to measure how near you are to what you planned to achieve.

Indicators are quantitative or qualitative measures that enable you to assess the degree to which project outputs and impact have been achieved. They also help you to focus on what exactly you're trying to achieve, and why. They reflect those areas of your product/service that you consider to be most important. They may be quantitative (e.g., how many people listened to a particular radio programme?) or qualitative (e.g., what was their opinion about the content of that programme?) Some things are fairly easy to measure (e.g., number of people using your product/service). Others are less so (e.g., how did these users benefit from the product/service?). Because of the imperfect 'fit' between indicators and what they are meant to capture, it's often better to use several indicators to capture different dimensions.

To evaluate the performance of your information product/service, you first identify the product/service, and then describe to whom and how it is provided. This will give you indicators of the efficiency or effectiveness of this provision. Over time, repeated measurements will show if changes are in the direction you intended – and if not, you can take action to make further changes.

To evaluate the impact of your product/service, the procedure is similar. Here, indicators will relate to the output, the outcome for the primary stakeholders and the impact in the wider social and economic environment. For example, the impact of weekly radio broadcasts might be seen in the farmers' increased knowledge about market prices; an indicator here could be the change in farmgate prices at the local market compared with those in a bigger city market. This improved knowledge might lead to the farmers growing higher-priced crops; an indicator here could be the percentage change in the production of certain crops over a specific period.

WHY?

Indicators are a way of making the issues that are important to you measurable. They allow you to answer questions such as:

- Are we providing a useful product/service that the primary stakeholders want/need?
- Are we getting value for money?
- Are we getting the best possible use out of our resources?
- Should we do this differently?

So you need to be clear about why you want to evaluate specific issues, and what dimensions are important to you. The choice of indicators will determine how you collect data, and then how you analyse, interpret and report these data.

HOW?

First, you need to be clear about what you want to know. Then you need to think about how best to find out this information and which dimensions of this information can be measured. For example, if you're interested in 'listener satisfaction', you could conduct an audience survey that includes the question 'Did you like programme X?' You then measure the proportion of listeners who replied 'yes'. But you might also want to know about what parts of the programme they enjoyed most; if this is the case, then you may be able to more easily get this information by interviewing people separately, rather than using a questionnaire.

Creating indicators

There are five steps involved in creating indicators:

- *Step 1:* Make the project issues (objectives) measurable
- *Step 2:* Select the indicators
- *Step 3:* Specify the type of indicators
- *Step 4:* Determine the reference points
- *Step 5:* Assess the quality of the indicators

Step 1: Make the project objectives measurable

Some issues are obvious indicators (e.g., number of users of an information service). Others are more abstract (e.g., terms such as the 'quality' of the information service, and the 'learning' created by providing it). So you need to define the issue and the activities related to it in concrete terms. Box 3.11 provides an example of making an abstract issue measurable.

> **Box 3.11**
> **Making an abstract issue measurable**
>
> To measure the 'quality of the information service', you might need to look at:
>
> - **Accessibility** (distance from the point of service, time taken to respond to demands, technical requirements to access the service)
>
> - **Usability** (whether all the information needed to complete a task was present, whether material was in a language that people could understand, whether pictures and diagrams were comprehensible to them etc.)
>
> - **Relevance** (focuses on real problems faced by the primary stakeholders, offers choices, offers new perspectives, points to other sources of assistance and complements them)
>
> - **Efficiency** (logical presentation, use of didactic and illustrative material).
>
> To measure 'learning', the direct benefit of an information service, you might need to look at:
>
> - Improved knowledge (improved ability to identify and solve problems)
>
> - More confident behaviour (more able to provide the service)
>
> - Regular use of skills (number of occasions when new knowledge is applied).

In order to assess the abstract concept, you look for specific items to measure. Each of them could become an indicator. How many you choose will depend on the time and resources you have available.

The items to measure should reflect the views of stakeholders. Whether an information product is really useful depends on the values of the community served. In order to arrive at an appropriate representation of the issues, seeking the views of the stakeholders can be very helpful. Using a participatory approach may also save time in the long run.

Step 2: Select the indicators

Step 1 will produce many possibilities for defining the issues at stake. The second step is to select the set of indicators to be used. You are trying to provide as many reference points as necessary to capture the essential issues to be evaluated. The evaluation of the performance of a product/service should include indicators on the services provided, their intended benefits and the target group. The evaluation of the impact of a product/service should include indicators on the project outputs, the immediate beneficiaries and the changes in the wider community.

The number of indicators to choose depends on the resources available for the evaluation. About 10–15 indicators should be the maximum, except for very large studies. Generally, it's better to have a small number of significant indicators.

The indicators should also be selected on the basis of a set of methodological rules (see Box 3.12). To determine which of the issues identified in Step 1 should be reflected as indicators, you should check this list. Ensure that there is no overlap or duplication in the final set of indicators chosen.

Box 3.12
Methodological rules for indicators

The commonly used criteria defining good indicators are:

VALIDITY	Does the indicator measure the condition/result?
RELIABILITY	Will it be a consistent measure over time?
SENSITIVITY	Will it be sensitive to changes in conditions?
SIMPLICITY	Will collecting and analysing the information be easy?
UTILITY	Will the information be useful for decision-making and learning?
AFFORDABILITY	Can the project afford to collect the information?

Step 3: Specify the type of indicators

Step 3 involves deciding whether an indicator should be qualitative or quantitative:

- **Qualitative** indicators present descriptive information. Their purpose is to capture processes and qualitative differences, rather than count items. The information for these indicators is often derived from individual or group observations and judgements. Qualitative indicators can be transformed into quantitative information (e.g., having asked survey respondents if they would describe a newsletter as relevant, easy to read, attractive to look at, etc., you could use this information to quantify the number of generally positive or negative statements made).

- **Quantitative** indicators are used mainly for things that can be counted. The data are relatively easy to obtain. Often they are generated during the process of implementing a project, and simply need to be analysed (e.g., the number of downloads from a website). Other data require explicit measurement based on available statistics or formal questionnaires.

Both qualitative and quantitative indicators are refined by adding the unit of analysis in terms of the level of the social system (who – individuals, communities, organisations, networks etc.), the period of measurement (when) and, if relevant, geographical coverage (where). This could be done as shown in Box 3.13.

Whereas quantitative indicators are more precise, qualitative indicators provide a richer picture of reality and a better understanding of the reasons for change. Both types are 'objective' in their own way. Quantitative data are less easily challenged, but qualitative data help to show the relevance of

> **Box 3.13**
> **Examples of qualitative and quantitative indicators**
>
> Quantitative indicators for the 'accessibility' of an information service':
>
> - Distance of rural communities from a low-cost telecentre with a helpdesk
>
> - Percentage change in the number of visitors to the telecentre over a defined period
>
> Qualitative indicators for the 'improved knowledge' resulting from an information service:
>
> - The telecentre is close enough to a range of communities for them to use it when they need to
>
> - Positive and negative experiences of the users of the information in solving the problem for which information was sought
>
> - Ability of the users to discuss the problem in question

the 'hard facts'. In the context of an open and dynamic learning process, qualitative data are often more useful for convincing people about the value of a project. A mix of qualitative and quantitative indicators can be used; often, this is the most appropriate approach.

It's worth noting that it's often not possible to get the detailed data that, ideally, you might like. In the case of the example in Box 3.11 for instance, instead of looking at the different items determining the 'quality of the information service' (accessibility, usability, relevance, efficiency), it might be more realistic to use a qualitative indicator that simply seeks users' overall perception and level of satisfaction with the information service.

Step 4: Determine the reference points

Whether an indicator is qualitative or quantitative, in order to interpret its value it is necessary to set a point of reference against which the measurement can be compared. The ideal reference point would be baseline information that refers to the exact items specified in the indicator.

For quantitative baseline data, apart from some simple measurements (e.g., the circulation figures for a newsletter) such information is usually not available. Qualitative baseline data are much easier to find. Usually, development projects have documents concerning the problems they are supposed to address and supporting baseline data.

Apart from baseline data, there are alternative reference points against which measurements can be compared, as shown in Box 3.14.

Step 5: Assess the quality of the indicators

The next step is to assess the quality of the indicators selected. A commonly used formula for doing this is to apply the SMART and SPICED criteria to the indicators (see Part 2, page 50). These

Box 3.14
Reference points for comparison

- **Trends** (e.g., a consistent increase or decrease in requests for support; increasing feedback from readers of a publication)

- **Thresholds** (e.g., at least three districts covered by a database; the minimum number of students on a course)

- **Targets** (e.g., the number of documents distributed by a stipulated deadline; the proceedings of a conference available in printed form by a given date)

criteria are used for a final check on the indicator. It is not easy to satisfy all criteria at once. For a cost-effective evaluation, it's better to drop indicators that are too ambitious or costly to measure.

Creating indicators is an iterative process. From Step 5, you might find it necessary to return to some of the earlier steps. Often, establishing indicators is, in itself, already part of the evaluation, especially if you do it in collaboration with stakeholders.

Box 3.15
The SMART and SPICED criteria for measuring the quality of indicators

Check that your selected indicators are:

Specific and simple	S
Measurable	M
Achievable	A
Realistic	R
Time-bound	T

An example of a SMART indicator:
If the project objective is to promote the use of better seeds and farming techniques in a particular area, a good indicator would be the percentage of farmers who, over the long term, used the improved seeds and the cropping techniques recommended. The information is specific, measurable, should be available, is realistic and has a time-bound element.

Check that your selected indicators are

Subjective	S
Participatory	P
Interpreted and communicable	I
Cross-checked and compared	C
Empowering	E
Diverse and disaggregated	D

An example of a SPICED indicator:
If the project objective is to promote the use of better seeds and farming techniques in a particular area, good indicators would be why farmers had used or not used the new seeds and practices, and which farmers they were (age, gender, health, poverty, etc.).

Applying the indicators

Once you have created the indicators, you use the data obtained to judge the performance of your product/service. The data provided by the indicators will gain meaning only through your understanding of their significance.

Other data obtained during the evaluation process, apart from those derived from the indicators, could turn out to be extremely important in understanding the results. Qualitative indicators offer more possibilities in this regard.

Box 3.16
Sources of more information on indicators

Professional agencies and associations have compiled lists of key performance indicators and codes of conduct.

Examples include the Library Performance Measurement and Quality Management System for electronic libraries (http://equinox.dcu.ie), and the work on performance measures by the International Federation of Library Associations and Institutions (IFLA) (http://www.ifla.org/VII/s22/annual/sp22.htm). Another example is the ethic standard of the International Federation of Journalists (http://ifj.org/).

It is also useful to look through specific evaluation guidelines, such as those provided by the International Development Research Centre (IDRC) on evaluating telecentres (Whyte 1999a, b).

Box 3.17
Some key points in creating and applying indicators

- Ensure that indicators are defined when planning an activity

- Remember that you need qualitative indicators to explain what is happening and why

- Remember that indicators should be used critically

- Ensure that the stakeholders agree on the selected indicators. The value of an evaluation is easily discredited if indicators are not seen to be measuring the right thing. Every indicator can be challenged (e.g., an indicator shows that 80% of the readers of a publication find it useful, but are these readers able to apply the knowledge gained from the publication?)

- Explain quantitative indicators. The significance of the numbers generated should be made clear by describing in qualitative terms what a particular amount means in a given context.

- Using standardised indicators or copying indicators from previous studies saves time, but use them with care and make sure that they are well understood and suit your purpose.

- Don't jump too quickly from issue analysis to measurement. Sometimes it is better to formulate questions rather than indicators. This is particularly so in the case of social learning, which is characterised by gradual change, people's differing views and the cultural dimension of social change.

Box 3.18
The strengths and weaknesses of using indicators

WEAKNESS	STRENGTHS
■ Measuring change without understanding the context in which the data were collected can lead to inappropriate conclusions	■ Well-formulated indicators are a key element of all evaluations and impact assessments ■ Creating indicators can lead the participants in an evaluation (including the primary stakeholders and the project staff) to reflect on project objectives and disclose their expectations about the project

EVALUATION PLANNING TOOLS

Now you're ready to start planning your evaluation. The first thing you need to think about is why you want to do the evaluation. This is important because it will affect decisions you take later, so it really is worthwhile taking some time to be clear about what it is that you want to achieve.

The next thing you need to think about is how you're going to do the evaluation. Part of this involves a decision about participation in the evaluation: Who will be involved? How much will their views influence decisions about the evaluation's objectives? What indicators should be measured? And how? Whether you share some or all of this decision-making with your colleagues, or even with your primary stakeholders is a value judgement. It is less time-consuming to take the decisions yourself, or with a small management group, but it may be at the cost of obtaining useful knowledge or building organisational capacity.

If you decide to involve the primary stakeholders, there are a variety of tools that you can use (e.g., role-play, drawing, video) to encourage participation and elicit useful information. While more time-consuming, it's generally worthwhile to be as participatory as possible. This is because the quality of the learning achieved is much richer.

The tools to use to plan your evaluation include:

- **terms of reference**
- **logic model**

In this section we describe what these tools are and how to use them, before moving on to describe the tools you will need to implement your evaluation.

Terms of reference

The terms of reference (ToR) is a document setting out the work and the schedule that needs to be carried out by the evaluation team. The document describes:

- **background** of the project to be evaluated
- main **reasons** for the evaluation
- **objectives** and expected outputs of the evaluation
- key **issues** and the **scope** of the evaluation
- evaluation **method**
- **roles and responsibilities** of those participating in the evaluation
- **work plan and budget** for the evaluation
- process for **reporting and feedback**
- key **documents** to be consulted during the evaluation

Although written for the evaluation, the ToR can be used for other purposes, such as developing a business plan or proposing research studies.

WHY?
A ToR is a key document that needs to be prepared with care. It is the document against which the performance of the evaluation team will be judged. The team needs to ensure that all issues raised in

the ToR are covered in the final report. If it is not possible to do this, because of constraints beyond your control, you need to inform management and other key stakeholders as soon as possible.

HOW?
The content of a ToR varies, depending on the scope of the project and the key evaluation issues to be addressed. Nevertheless, there is a generally accepted format for ToR, and a standard process involved in preparing a ToR.

Preparing the terms of reference

The main steps involved in preparing the ToR are described here.

Step 1: Background to the evaluation

Prepare a profile of the information product/service to be evaluated – its historical background, its evolution, and how it relates to the goal of the programme or to your institution. Clearly identify the primary stakeholders, their problems and the needs that led to the provision of the product/service, and their role in the evaluation.

Step 2: Reasons for the evaluation

You need to indicate why the evaluation is being carried out. This should refer to the initial motivation for the evaluation (e.g., learning purposes; improvement in product/service; accountability to the funding agency). If there are other reasons for the study, add them here.

Step 3: Evaluation objectives and expected outputs

Describe the objectives clearly. They could be:

- to determine if the project is on track
- to obtain baseline data that will serve as an input in similar activities
- to provide the funding agency with enough information to make an informed judgement about project performance

Describe the expected outputs clearly. They could include:

- an analysis of the evaluation findings in terms of the evaluation criteria (see Part 2, see 33-34)

- identification of the strengths and weaknesses of the project recommendations for future strategies for similar projects

Step 4: Key issues and evaluation scope

This step builds on Step 3, as the evaluation objectives will determine the key issues of the evaluation. For example, you may be concerned about issues relating to:

- whether accurate information is getting to the people who need it; this involves looking at **relevance** and **accessibility**

- how the primary stakeholders use the product/service and how satisfied they are with it; this involves looking at **usability**

- what the long-term consequences (positive and negative, intended and unintended) of the product/service are; this involves looking at **impact**

- whether the positive outcomes of the project at purpose level are likely to continue after external funding ends; this involves looking at **sustainability**

- how well the information product/service is performing within the context of its objectives; this involves looking at **effectiveness** and **efficiency**

- whether the product/service could be provided successfully to other similar communities in the region; this involves looking at **utility**

The scope of the evaluation relates to the breadth and depth of the study — what the evaluation will cover and to what extent. The scope can be defined in terms of themes (e.g., focusing on cross-cutting themes such as gender or youth); geography (the area to be covered); and/or the timeframe (the period over which the evaluation will be carried out).

Step 5: Evaluation method

You need to take care to ensure that there is agreement on the evaluation techniques to be used, as this will affect the quality of the exercise. In the ToR you need to specify:

- the type of data to be collected
- how the data will be collected
- where the data will be collected
- who will collect the data

Step 6: Roles and responsibilities

Defining the roles and responsibilities is where team-building comes into its own. No one person will have all the necessary skills, so you will need to look for the skills in each person that set them apart from others, and build a team of people with complementary skills (e.g., you might look for someone who is good at problem solving, someone who works very logically, someone who is good at mathematics, someone who can speak the local languages, and so on).

The ToR should show that:

- the skills needed for the evaluation are represented in the team
- you have taken important factors (e.g., gender) into consideration in the composition of the team
- the team includes people from outside your department, to foster wider ownership of the evaluation process
- the roles and responsibilities of each team member are clear
- the team leader has the necessary skills (e.g., management experience, communication skills)

Step 7: Work plan and budget

The ToR should contain a detailed work plan - a list of the planned evaluation activities, their start and end dates and who will be responsible for each activity. The Gantt chart described in project planning can be used for evaluation planning as well. Points to remember when preparing the work plan include:

- ensuring that the work plan is realistic
- avoiding being over-ambitious with targets
- checking the availability of everyone (e.g., their planned holidays or missions), and getting agreement on important milestones
- taking into account the time needed for briefing, debriefing meetings, report writing, etc.

The ToR should include a detailed budget. Costs should be kept as low as possible; some experts suggest that evaluations should cost about 5% of the budget of the project being evaluated.

Step 8: Reporting and feedback

The format, style, language, presentation, target audience and deadline for the submission of the evaluation report should be defined in the ToR. The number of copies required should also be specified. In general, there are three sections to the evaluation report: an executive summary; the main report (methodology, findings, conclusions and recommendations); and the annexes (work plan, lists of people involved, list of documents consulted).

An example of the sort of details a ToR should contain on reporting and feedback is given in Box 3.19. Note that a decision will have to be made about the ways in which to present the report according to the needs of the various stakeholders.

Box 3.19
A sample 'Reporting' section in a ToR document

The ToR document related to a performance evaluation of CTA's location-based seminars. The aim of the evaluation was to improve the performance of the programme.

The document was divided into: Background and reason for evaluation; Objectives and scope (including indicators); Expected outputs; Issues to be addressed; Evaluation method; Expertise required; Reporting; Implementation schedule; Co-ordination; and Key documents.

The section on 'Reporting' read:

- Desk study (mainly at CTA): *one report*
- Regional reports (based on surveys in ACP regions): *six reports*
- Summary of desk study and regional studies: *one report* (main findings, conclusions and recommendations will be summarised in one report (maximum 20 pages); this task to be undertaken by CTA staff in collaboration with one or two external consultants)
- In order to facilitate follow-up to recommendations, all the reports will make a clear distinction between the various programme components

The 'Implementation schedule' set a date for the submission of the report.

Part 3: EVALUATION TOOLS: Evaluation planning

Step 9: Documents

The ToR should list the key documents to be consulted during the evaluation, as well as their sources of verification. These documents could include:

- the project logical framework
- annual work programmes
- financial and project management documents
- monitoring reports
- field visit reports
- previous evaluation reports
- annual reports
- training materials and reports

Box 3.20
Some key points in preparing the terms of reference

- Start the process of writing the ToR in good time; it often takes more time than planned to obtain consensus on various aspects of the ToR from the stakeholders

- Keep your project logframe up-to-date, as this will form the basis of the evaluation ToR

- Don't try to address all the evaluation criteria in a single ToR; in a post-project evaluation, keep to criteria relating to this type of evaluation, and likewise for a mid-term evaluation

- Seek input from your colleagues when preparing the ToR – they might have valuable ideas

Box 3.21
The strengths and weaknesses of a terms of reference

WEAKNESS	STRENGTHS
■ A weak ToR will probably produce a weak evaluation report, which is a waste of resources	■ A ToR sets out clearly what is expected from the evaluators and from the evaluation
	■ Writing a ToR provides you with an opportunity to step back and reflect on your project

Logic model

A logic model is a logical chain of connections showing what a product or service is expected to accomplish. It highlights how the evaluation is expected to work, what activities need to come before others, and how desired outcomes are achieved. It is an essential part of the planning for an evaluation because it offers the flexibility of starting at any point during the project (e.g. if no planning documents are available for the project you're evaluating, the logic model can help you to restructure the project prior to the evaluation).

A logic model can be illustrated in several ways, including:

- descriptive form, using words
- line diagram
- table
- hierarchy of objectives
- flow diagram

WHY?
A logic model will show you how to get from the start of an evaluation to the intended end. Think of it as a series of 'if…then…' events. You can use it not only to describe the chronology of an evaluation, but also to assess the progress of the evaluation against the original plan.

HOW?
Creating a logic model to guide your evaluation involves adopting a cause-and-effect approach, like this: If we do A, then we can achieve B; if we do B, then we can achieve C; if we do C, then we can achieve D; if we do D, then we can achieve E; and so on.

Creating a logic model

A cause-and-effect approach could go like this:

- **Inputs:** What resources have been used? Where have they come from? What activities have they contributed to?

- **Activities:** What have been the main activities? What outputs have they contributed to? Who have been the main beneficiaries?

- **Outputs:** What outputs have resulted from each activity? How does each output connect to a specific outcome?

- **Outcomes:** What outcomes stem from these outputs? What longer-term goal or impact is the programme trying to achieve?

Figure 3.7 is an example of a logic model for a training course on project management.

Box 3.22
Some key points in creating a logic model

- Think of it as a cause-and-effect model
- It is particularly useful for ongoing, rather than one-off, projects
- It offers the flexibility of starting at any point during a project
- Keep to the standard headings, as shown in Figure 3.7

Part 3: EVALUATION TOOLS: Evaluation planning

Figure 3.7
A logic model for evaluating a training course on project management

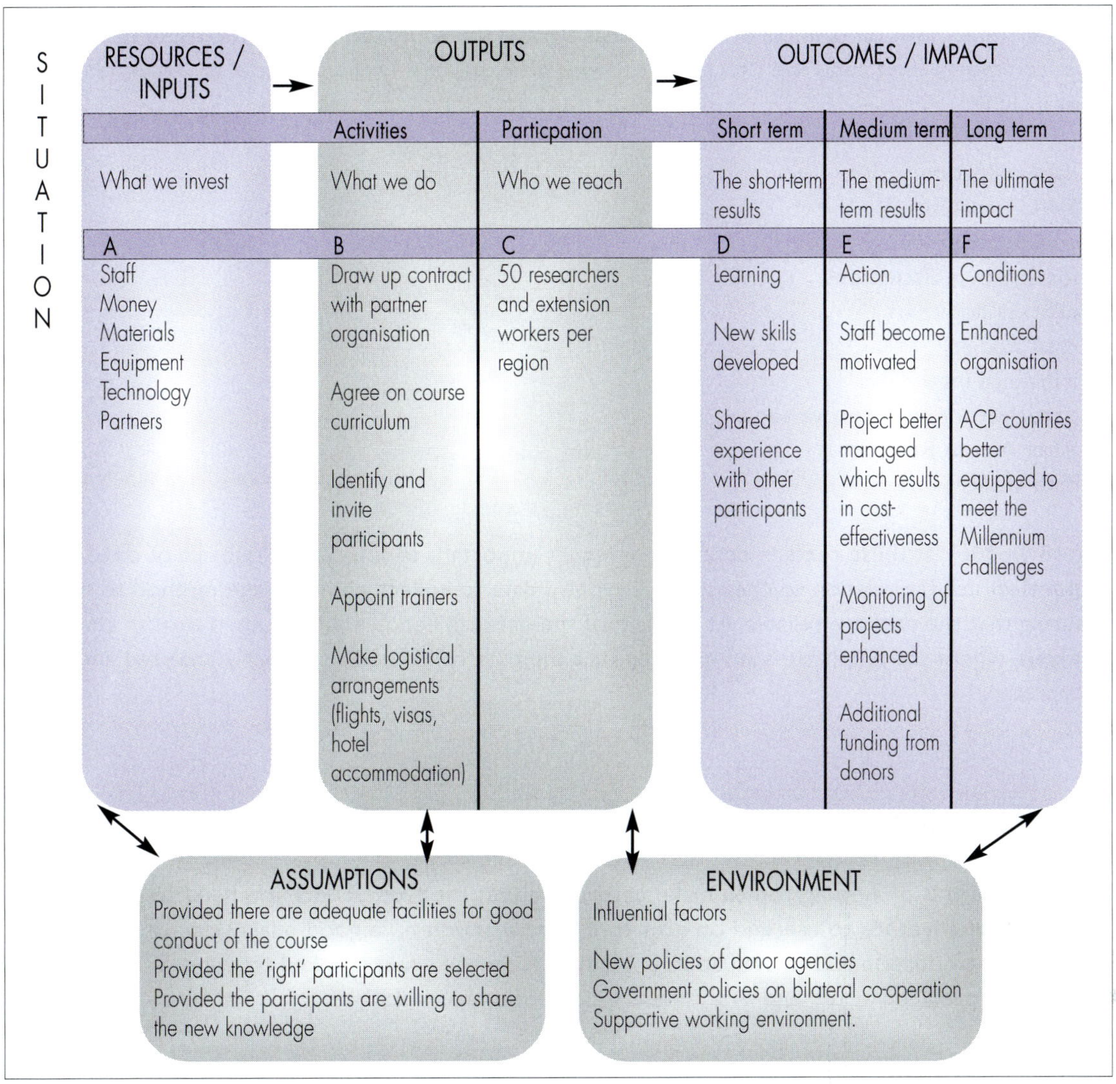

SITUATION	RESOURCES / INPUTS	OUTPUTS		OUTCOMES / IMPACT		
		Activities	Particpation	Short term	Medium term	Long term
	What we invest	What we do	Who we reach	The short-term results	The medium-term results	The ultimate impact
	A	B	C	D	E	F
	Staff Money Materials Equipment Technology Partners	Draw up contract with partner organisation Agree on course curriculum Identify and invite participants Appoint trainers Make logistical arrangements (flights, visas, hotel accommodation)	50 researchers and extension workers per region	Learning New skills developed Shared experience with other participants	Action Staff become motivated Project better managed which results in cost-effectiveness Monitoring of projects enhanced Additional funding from donors	Conditions Enhanced organisation ACP countries better equipped to meet the Millennium challenges

ASSUMPTIONS
Provided there are adequate facilities for good conduct of the course
Provided the 'right' participants are selected
Provided the participants are willing to share the new knowledge

ENVIRONMENT
Influential factors

New policies of donor agencies
Government policies on bilateral co-operation
Supportive working environment.

Box 3.23
The strengths and weaknesses of a logic model

WEAKNESSES	STRENGTHS
■ Can be difficult to understand the logic if people don't share the belief in causality ■ Does not identify resource use ■ Does not specify the scope for an evaluation, apart from showing what should happen ■ Does not identify any support that may be needed.	■ Reveals inter-relationships among project elements ■ Describes project elements in a way that encourages understanding between a variety of projects ■ Can be an effective tool to communicate the effect of a project ■ Conveys the fundamental purpose of a project ■ Shows the intended/anticipated results of a project ■ Depicts the actions/causes expected to lead to the desired results ■ Helps determine whether planned actions are likely to lead to the desired results

EVALUATION IMPLEMENTATION TOOLS

This section focuses on data collection and analysis, and the tools you can use for these tasks. The most commonly used tools are described, showing why they are useful and how to implement them. They include:

- data collection
- SWOT analysis
- questionnaire design
- focus group discussions
- process flowchart
- case studies
- individual interviews
- participatory and creative tools
- After Action Review
- data analysis

Before we look at these tools in detail, however, it's important to look at the subject of **data collection** itself in relation to choosing the type of data to collect, choosing the method to use and ensuring that the data are reliable. At the end of the data collection tools we then turn to **data analysis**, where the emphasis is on ensuring that the data collected are properly analysed and interpreted.

Data collection

The focus here is on helping you to make decisions about the type of data you need to collect, on the collection methods to use, and on how to ensure that you have good quality data. It serves in part as an introduction to the evaluation implementation tools and is linked to the data analysis information provided at the end of the descriptions of these tools.

Choosing the type of data to collect

All evaluations require the collection of data that will inform the decision-making process and promote learning. As we noted when outlining data collection in Part 2, the data to be collected for an evaluation can be divided into primary and secondary data. Primary data are collected directly and specifically for the evaluation at hand, whereas secondary data are the data that have already been collected for some purpose other than the current evaluation.

There are no hard and fast rules for data collection. As the evaluator, you need first to decide *why* you are doing the evaluation and *what sort of questions* you want answered. This will help you decide *what type of data* you need to collect and *which methodology* to use to collect them – qualitative or quantitative, or a mix of the two.

Quantitative data

Quantitative methods, such as surveys seeking 'yes' and 'no' answers, yield quantitative data. Quantitative data are numerical, and are relatively easy to summarise, compare and generalise. The main strength of the quantitative approach is that its methods produce data that can be generalised to a much larger population. Provided you choose a representative sample (see pages 109-112) for more on sampling), you can generalise your findings from a small number of people (say, 50) to a much larger group (say, 1000). This is a very efficient approach in resource-poor settings.

The main weakness of the quantitative approach is that you get a limited understanding of the meanings and context of action and behaviour. It's important to recognise the limits of what you're doing, and interpret your findings cautiously.

Qualitative data

Qualitative methods, such as SWOT analysis and focus groups, use non-numerical sources, such as words, pictures and plays, as data. The advantage of using qualitative data is that they provide rich and detailed information about the stakeholders' perspectives, including a context and explanation for these perspectives. Qualitative methods can also be used to elaborate the facts provided by quantitative data.

The main weaknesses of the qualitative approach are that collecting and analysing qualitative data are fairly labour-intensive and time-consuming, and the findings cannot usually be generalised.

Combining quantitative and qualitative approaches

Combining quantitative and qualitative data collection methods will help you to gain greater understanding and improve the reliability of the findings. Choosing the data to use for your evaluation depends mainly on the answer to the 'why' question of your evaluation. Some elements to take into account are:

- at the local level, in-depth qualitative information will probably be more suitable than general statistics if you want to learn how to improve project performance and impact

- current and potential funding agencies might require valid statistical data at the national or regional level

- the money, time and human resources available will determine what is possible at any one time

- the importance of the time element (if you want to measure change, time is obviously important, but if you simply want to know what is happening currently, it is less so, although it might become more relevant when you compare your results with those analysed a year previously)

Table 3.10 gives examples of the main types of data, and their characteristics.

Choosing the data collection methods

When you have decided what type of data to collect, you need to decide what methods are most suitable for collecting them.

Whatever methods you choose, try to collect information in a participatory way that is responsive to the stakeholders' interests and allows all voices to be heard.

The participatory approach is based on:

- using visual rather than verbal techniques where necessary
- group-based activities
- seeking 'reversals of learning' (where the primary stakeholders become the experts, and the experts become the facilitators)

Table 3.10
Data type and characteristics

TYPE OF DATA	CHARACTERISTICS	ADVANTAGES	DISADVANTAGES
PRIMARY DATA			
Qualitative			
AAR, focus group discussions, SWOT analysis	Multiple perspectives, new insights, facilitator can build on preceding questions	Wide range of different viewpoints	The weak may be reluntant to speak
Creative techniques	Fairly unstructured tool which can provide understanding of the current situation	Assist with clarifying objectives and the roles of different participants	May not provide the most relevant information
Direct observation	Direct observation during some of the activities	Useful exercise	Some participants might find the presence of an observer restricting
Quantitative			
Self-administered questionnaires (mini-survey)	Predefined questions; use structured questionnaires; limited number of mostly close-ended questions	Data can be collected and analysed within a few days	No control for misunderstood questions, missing data or untruthful responses
Individual interviews	Sample users	Data can be collected and analysed quickly; opportunity to gain a first-hand impression; Yield richest data, details, new insights	Expensive in terms of logistics (time, place, privacy, access, etc.); often requires lengthy data-collection period
Questionnaires administered by telephone	Predefined questions: use structured questionnaires; limited number of mostly close-ended questions	Inexpensive. Suited for short and non-sensitive topics	Eliminates those without a telephone. There can be mis-understanding in communication. Intrude on people's privacy
SECONDARY DATA			
Newspaper articles; records in diaries, scrapbooks, findings and recommendations of past evaluations and of similar organisations; records of lunch discussions; plan-and-review days; documentary evidence from community, public events; attendance registers; relevant project documents, etc.	Wide-ranging; provides overview of the topic under investigation	Written from different perspectives	Sources may be unreliable

This participatory approach has the following advantages:

- flexibility in how you can collect data
- receptiveness to new and unexpected ideas
- free flow of communication
- empowerment of the people involved
- facilitation of the validation of information collected

For the evaluation to be successful, the stakeholders should be included at every stage, from conducting research and designing the evaluation approach to collecting and analysing data. They are also valuable as a point of reference for validating the data used in the evaluation.

Primary data collection methods

Here is a brief outline of each of the methods listed on page 106, followed by some notes on obtaining secondary data (consulting routine records, etc.) and on sampling.

- **SWOT analysis:** Used to gather and analyse data on the environment in which the project is operating. It can also be used to analyse the decision-making process behind the product/service and is therefore useful in helping you to develop the evaluation recommendations. A good SWOT analysis is dependent on how the information is gathered for the matrix, and it should include a wide spectrum of stakeholders representing various viewpoints. (See pages 115-119)

- **Questionnaires:** Used to gather quantitative data, mainly, but also to elicit answers that can add to qualitative data Questionnaires are quite commonly used in evaluations, especially for obtaining information about opinions and attitudes of the primary stakeholders. The findings can usually be analysed quantitatively. The cheapest surveys are those that are short, simple and self-administered. The main problem is non-response – people not being there when the questionnaire is distributed, or not wanting to participate in the survey. Creating a good questionnaire requires knowledge and skill; the wording and sequence of the questions are very important in obtaining valid results. (See pages 120-126)

- **Focus groups:** A group interview tool to help you find out what the users think and feel about the project. It's a quick way to generate useful qualitative data. Focus groups comprise a small group of people to be surveyed and/or interviewed to provide information relevant to the evaluation. The usefulness of focus groups depends on the skills of those moderating the group, and the method used to select the group. Focus groups are popular because they are not very expensive and are simple to organise. (See pages 127-132)

- **Case studies:** Used to identify and reflect on lessons learned from past successes and failures of the project, and aimed at ensuring that learning takes place. A case study (which can include stories and anecdotes) is a qualitative analysis of a product/service in terms of how it developed and how it is being used and perceived. Deciding how many case studies to do, and to what depth, is influenced by the purpose of an evaluation. Case studies are usually based on multiple methods (interviews, focus groups, questionnaires, documentary, web research, etc.) and involve multiple sources (the people directly involved, primary stakeholders' representatives, other stakeholders, etc.). The stories and anecdotes the data yield can be understood in context to help your analysis, but they can also liven up a report and give statistics a human touch. (See pages 136-140)

- **Interviews:** Used to identify who to interview and how to ensure you obtain useful information from them. You can ask people questions via different routes and different media. You can conduct interviews (individual or group), either face-to-face or over the telephone, or asynchronously via e-mail, the internet or post. These interviews can be unstructured, semi-structured with a checklist, or based on a questionnaire. Asking your own colleagues to be interviewees can be an excellent starting point for collecting data. Often they will have ideas about what questions should be asked, and of whom. (See pages 141-144)

- **Participatory and creative tools:** Used to encourage stakeholders' active participation in the evaluation process. These participatory techniques include using drawings, role-play, video, rich pictures and Venn diagrams to obtain a range of views from different users about the project. You will need the necessary skills to help people feel comfortable with each other and to open up. These techniques are fairly easy to use and inexpensive, but you need time and energy to get people's co-operation. (See pages 144-154)

- **After Action Review:** Used to obtain data on the performance and output of the project, either during or at the end of the information project. It provides insight into what happened, why it happened, what went well, what needs improvement, and what lessons can be learned from the experience. This is a simple tool to use and is useful in giving various stakeholders an opportunity to share their views and ideas. (See pages 155-157)

Secondary data collection

The routine records of your project can be a cost-effective and valuable source of secondary data for evaluation. They could be data from log books, registers, personnel lists, receipt books, accounts, contact databases, etc., providing information on the number and background of people using your product/service, types of information consulted, when people use the service, ideas and comments, and so on.

If you are not already keeping such records, it is advisable to start now and train your staff to keep them up-to-date with accurate and complete information. In all cases, you should maintain regular (weekly, monthly) tabulations and summary reports. To do this, you can construct tables in which you count and summarise relevant data and perhaps display them as charts or graphs.

These records can be used to spot trends, see which groups of people are using (or not using) your product/service and look at the relative cost-effectiveness of different activities.

Sampling

It is not necessary to examine everybody in the target group to get answers to what you want to know. It's usually more practical to examine a sample of the group.

A sample should be representative of the target group. **Random sampling** is usually the best way to achieve this. It can be done by using lists (e.g., a database of product users) to select the sample; this is useful so long as the lists are complete and up-to-date. You could also use maps to select random places, and then the people living in those places, for your sample. A carefully chosen random sample can make confident generalisation possible.

Many studies - and probably most of those in resource-poor situations - do not use random samples, because it can be an expensive way to conduct sampling. A common, less costly approach is **quota sampling**. This involves dividing the target group into sub-groups, and then, drawing on your knowledge of the group and the project, selecting samples from each sub-group, based on specified numbers (e.g., asking the interviewer to interview 40 women and 60 men between the ages of 50 and 60). The selection of the samples is non-random.

If you choose to do quota sampling, you need to be aware of the mistakes that people sometimes make with this approach. These include:

- using the wrong basis upon which to select the sample
- selecting people who are similar, thus underestimating the variability in the population
- some groups being over-represented and others being under-represented

You cannot be too confident when scaling up the results of a quota sample to the complete target group. But it is almost always better to have a quota sample than no sample, or a sample obtained at an unreasonably high cost. An example of quota sampling is given in Box 3.24.

Box 3.24
A village readership survey using quota sampling

To evaluate the use of a newsletter aimed at children under 18 years old, the team took three equally sized quota samples of 20 children in the village. These samples were:

- 20 children with no formal education
- 20 children who had completed primary school
- 20 children who had completed secondary school

Of the total number of children in the village:

1. 60% did not receive any formal education
2. 30% had completed primary school
3. 10% had completed secondary school

The results of the quota sampled in the survey showed that:

- the highest proportion of readers (10 out of 20) was in category 3 (to be expected)
- the next highest proportion (3 out of 20) was in category 2 (also to be expected)
- the lowest proportion (1 out of 20) was in category 1 (also to be expected)

If you add these numbers together you get a total readership of 14, which is 23% of the quota of 60 children. This gives a distorted view of the overall readership. To get a true picture, the sample data need to be linked back to the percentages of children in each category, as shown below, and re-calculated:

1. 1 out of 20 is for 60% of the total number of children
2. 3 out of 20 is for 30% of the total number of children
3. 10 out of 20 is for 10% of the total number of children

When recalculated the total readership is actually only 13%.

Adding the number of readers in the three groups together, and averaging them, gave an unrealistically high proportion of readers. When the actual distribution of the children in the village who attended school was taken into account, the survey showed a difference of 10% between the original result (23%) and the re-calculated result (13%). Table 3.11 shows how this information was presented to show the difference.

Table 3.11
The results of a village readership survey using quota sampling

	COLLECTED DATA: NUMBER OF READERS PER QUOTA SAMPLE	ACTUAL POPULATION AVERAGE
No formal education	1 out of 20	1 out of 20 – for 60% of the population
Finished primary school	3 out of 20	3 out of 20 – for 30% of the population
Finished secondary school	10 out of 20	10 out of 20 – for 10% of the population
Average number (percentage) of group under 18 years old	14 out of total 60 = 23%	Total readership = 13%

Another type of sampling, to gather qualitative data, is **theoretical sampling**. This involves asking:

- What group (or event) should be investigated next so as to explore the issues in more depth?
- Are there examples to contradict what we believe to be happening?

You should search for infrequent occurrences as well as typical ones and to compare them to detect possible reasons for difference.

No matter what sampling approach you choose, you need to be aware of its limitations when you interpret findings and draw conclusions. Common errors, and their remedies, are given in Table 3.12.

Table 3.12
The most common types of sampling errors and their remedies

TYPE	CAUSE	REMEDY
Sampling error	Using the sample and not the population	Use larger samples; this reduces but doesn't eliminate the problem
Sample bias	Those selected to participate did not do so, or did not provide adequate information	Try to reach the non-respondents
Response bias	Responses do not reflect the true picture, possibly because the questions were misunderstood	Carry out careful pre-testing to revise questions if necessary

Adapted from Westat (2002)

Ensuring good-quality data

Every effort needs to be made to ensure that the data from which conclusions will be drawn are good quality. This means checking their reliability and testing their validity, and then subjecting them to proper analysis.

Reliability

By 'reliable' we mean that the data-collection method used should give comparable results when used repeatedly. For example, does the way you pose questions in the questionnaire help you to gather reliable data? To determine the resource materials borrowed from a library, you might ask: 'How many books did you borrow the last time you visited the library?' But the person might have borrowed pamphlets and magazines, as well as books.

A better question to ask is shown in Table 3.13.

Table 3.13
Example of a question to find out how people are using a resource centre

'How many of the following did you borrow? Tick every box that applies and enter the number of items if it was more than 1.'	
RESOURCE MATERIALS BORROWED	QUANTITY
Books	
Pamphlets	
Reports	
Magazines	
Other – please specify	

Another reason why your data might not be reliable could be the way in which your questionnaire is designed. For example, there might be printing mistakes.

Can you see how the example given in Table 3.14 might cause confusion?

Table 3.14
Example of a confusing question

The 'faces' are in the wrong order, so a respondent might hesitate about which face to put the 'x' under				
	☹	☺	😐	
How satisfied are you with the newsletter?				X

One way of ensuring reliability is to test your data-collection tool on a small number of people (preferably, similar people to those who will be involved in your evaluation) so that you can identify any difficulties before you use the tool, and make the necessary changes.

Validity

Your evaluation results will be useful only if they are based on accurate data. Using valid methods for collecting data ensures that the variables selected are appropriate measures of the concepts, and that accurate results are produced. Box 3.25 contains two examples of ways to obtain valid data.

> **Box 3.25**
> **Examples of ways to ensure valid data**
>
> EXAMPLE 1. In an effort to find out if a particular radio programme is proving popular, you might ask: 'Do you like this radio programme?' The respondent might reply 'Yes', to be polite. It would be better to ask first: 'Do you listen to the radio?' If the answer is 'Yes', then your next question would be: 'What do you like listening to most?' This will show, perhaps, that the target programme is mentioned more often than others. If this is further confirmed by an independent study, the results would be further validated.
>
> EXAMPLE 2. Your data show that most people using your product are educated men. Is this because your product is indeed used mostly by them, or is it because your data collection did not reach the women who may be using it? To check the validity of your data, you will need to look closely at the design of your study, how you selected the sample and how the data were collected, to ensure they did not unwittingly cause women to be under-represented for any reason.

Expertise

Having reliable and validated data will not be much use unless the analytical and interpretative tools applied to them are used with care and expertise.

- **Statistical analysis:** You need to ensure that your data do not contain errors. If possible, consult a statistician in the early phases of study design (unless you are knowledgeable in this field). In general, you will get a good sense of what is going on by counting totals per group. Computer spreadsheet programs such as Excel are capable of calculating frequencies, percentages, measures of central tendency (mean, median and mode) and doing cross-tabulations.

  For in-depth analyses of data, you will need more complex statistical tests such as t-test, ANOVA, correlations and multivariate methods. These can be calculated using a good statistical software package. However, a more profound knowledge of statistical analysis is needed as it is easy (using software) to do an inappropriate analysis. Fortunately, most evaluations don't need this level of analysis.

- **Qualitative data analysis:** There are several ways to analyse the qualitative reports, notes and transcripts that have been collected. The data should be structured and prepared in such a way as to facilitate analysis to the level of detail needed for your purpose. Then you need to carry out the labour-intensive task of coding and categorising your data in order to identify themes and patterns. You need good analytical skills to analyse qualitative data properly.

- **Data interpretation:** Several problems can arise in the interpretation of data. One might relate to confusion over the results of significance testing which should be seen as a continuous (rather than discrete) scale of probability that a statement is likely to be true. Another problem is that there is a difference between 'significance' in the statistical sense and 'significance' in the practical sense. Something that is 'statistically significant' might have no practical relevance. Another problem relates to 'precision and accuracy'. These two terms tend to get confused. Estimates can be precise without being accurate, a fact often glossed over when computer output contains results specified to the fourth or sixth decimal place. A third problem relates to 'causality'. This can be tricky because causality is the actual reason why most statistical correlations are done. Yet correlations, however strong, are only indicative; there may be associated variables that are the real cause, yet nothing is known about them.

Conducting data analyses is dealt with in more detail at the end of this section on evaluation implementation tools.

> **Box 3.26**
> **Some key points in collecting data**
>
> - Be clear about the sort of primary data and secondary data you need
>
> - Before deciding on what data you need, be clear about why you're doing the evaluation and what sort of questions you want answered
>
> - It is often worthwhile combining quantitative and qualitative data collection methods
>
> - Whatever data collection methods you choose, try to collect data in a participatory way
>
> - Make every effort to ensure that the data from which conclusions will be drawn are good quality

SWOT analysis

The acronym 'SWOT' stands for 'strengths, weaknesses, opportunities, threats'. SWOT analysis is a valuable and versatile tool for organisational analysis and for strategic decision-making.

A SWOT analysis identifies how to maximise the potential strengths and opportunities of a product, service or process, while minimising the impact of its weaknesses and threats. The analysis usually takes account of internal factors such as human resources, management, staff commitment and obstacles (strengths and weaknesses), and external factors such as a change in government policy, stakeholder resistance, complex funding agency requirements, and a reduced budget (opportunities and threats).

WHY?
The SWOT technique is useful for assessing the external environment in which the information product/service is provided, as well as for reviewing, in a simple and straightforward way, how well you have planned your evaluation and what factors could influence the success of your evaluation. In particular, using a SWOT analysis to evaluate an information product/service helps you to:

- understand the environment in which you are operating
- look critically at how you will turn your findings into action
- identify where resources need to be allocated, both within the organisation and externally
- identify those stakeholders who may or may not be useful to the evaluation exercise
- provide a basis for assessing core capabilities and competencies
- provide a platform for sharing different perceptions among different groups
- draw on a wide set of experiences, ensuring that most of the key points are taken into account
- produce an output that forms an agreed basis for subsequent analysis and decision-making
- make a coherent contingency plan for the evaluation

A particularly useful time to do a SWOT analysis is when you're carrying out an evaluation for the purpose of organisational learning. Participants can then reflect both on the organisation and its activities. But you should be aware that a SWOT analysis may in itself be perceived as a threat.

Box 3.27
A case study showing why SWOT analysis is useful

This case study shows the point at which a decision was made by Gabrima Development Centre (GDC) to conduct a SWOT analysis of the institution to clarify issues and improve its work. It also demonstrates how the GDC went about setting up the SWOT.

GDC is a management training institution. The level of enrolment was dropping considerably, resulting in a loss of revenue and staff redundancies. Two other management training centres nearby, however, were operating at a profit, their enrolment figures quadrupling in 3 years. They were equipped with the latest technologies and state-of-the-art libraries.

In 2004, a new Director, described as 'dynamic', was appointed at GDC. His immediate objective was for GDC to become viable within 2 years. He consulted a strategy planner who advised him to conduct a SWOT analysis of the institution.

One of his first actions was to encourage the staff to conduct a self-evaluation exercise to identify the strengths and weaknesses of the institute, and the opportunities and threats facing it. A brainstorming workshop was convened and an external facilitator engaged for it.

From the discussions, a list of strengths, weaknesses, opportunities and threats was compiled and entered into a SWOT analysis matrix, as shown in Table 3.16. The findings of the SWOT analysis were used by GDC in future planning and as a basis for a subsequent mid-term evaluation, to provide some background for the evaluation team and to help GDC draft the ToR for the evaluation.

HOW?
A SWOT analysis is a strategic balance sheet where strengths can be thought of as assets (resources), and weaknesses as liabilities, and where opportunities and threats could become future assets or liabilities, respectively. Careful preparation is needed so that people participate constructively. A SWOT analysis is usually drawn in the form of a matrix, as shown in Table 3.15.

Table 3.15
A SWOT analysis matrix

	POSITIVE	NEGATIVE
Internal	Potential strengths	Potential weaknesses
	Positive characteristics and advantages of the information product/service	Negative characteristics and disadvantages of the information product/service
External	Potential opportunities	Potential threats
	Factors which can benefit, enhance or improve the information product/service	Factors which can hinder the information product/service

Conducting a SWOT analysis

There are four main steps involved in conducting a SWOT analysis, based on inviting participants to attend a brainstorming workshop to carry out the analysis.

Step 1: Doing the groundwork

Establish the **objective** of the analysis. Are you thinking of offering the product/service to a new group of people? Are you looking at one product/service or many?

Select **participants** in the SWOT analysis who reflect an appropriate mix of skills. They should know about the topic addressed by your objective. The more stakeholders that are involved, the more comprehensive the analysis is likely to become. However, you need to bear in mind the costs of involving more people.

Gather enough **data** on the topic and distribute background information to participants well in advance of the first meeting so that they have time to think about it.

Step 2: Preparing the workshop

If you don't have a good **facilitator** in-house, try to find someone who can fulfil this role effectively. Good facilitators create an atmosphere conducive to the free flow of information, they listen carefully and respectfully, and they know how and when to stop participants from drifting away from the subject.

The size of the **groups** can be decided on the basis of the overall number of participants (large groups can be broken into smaller groups of around 10 people to maximise output).

Among the **resources** you will need are a flip chart and markers, or some other means of keeping a record of the discussion so the groups can refer back to points made earlier.

Step 3: Briefing the participants

Provide the participants with information about the **workshop objective** and **issues to be discussed**, the **evaluation purpose** and type, the **stakeholders** who will be involved in the workshop, the **evaluation scope**, time frame and geographical coverage, the **resources** available, and how the **evaluation results** will be disseminated and lessons learned acted upon.

Step 4: Analysing the workshop results

A lot of information can be generated during a brainstorming workshop. For this information to be useful, set the priorities by:

- reducing the list of strengths and weaknesses to no more than five distinctive strengths and debilitating weaknesses

- reducing the list of threats and opportunities to the five most important issues.

Table 3.16 shows an example of a SWOT analysis before it has been finally reduced.

The greatest challenge in SWOT analysis is to make a correct judgement that will benefit both the project implementing organisation and the community. To achieve this, you need to be clear and focused about the threats and opportunities. They are not absolute. What might at first look like an opportunity might not emerge as such when considered against the organisation's resources or the community's expectations.

Table 3.16
An example of a SWOT analysis matrix

	POSITIVE	NEGATIVE
	Strengths	Weaknesses
	Internal positive aspects under your control and on which you may wish to capitalise	*Internal negative aspects under your control (to a large extent) which you could plan to improve*
Internal	Years of proven experience in training Established training facilities and infrastructure Availability of extra-curricular activities Good proximity to train station and shops Good management structure Established systems and procedures Effective cost-control programme Experience in collaborating with other organisations New, dynamic and visionary leader	Outdated technical knowledge High rate of staff absenteeism Heavy dependence on part-time lecturers No procedure for monitoring success or failure Poor competitiveness Exorbitant school fees Non-motivated staff Weak planning Insufficient funds to invest in technologies Lengthy courses of 3 months No reliable access to computers Poor PR and marketing strategy Limited sports facilities and other campus activities Limited accommodation on campus
	Opportunities	Threats
	Positive external conditions you don't control which you could take advantage of	*Negative external conditions you don't control but you could minimise their effects on the project*
External	New government policies favour training organisations Government encouragement of the use of distance education New possibilities for co-operation New target groups High demand for new courses and for the specialised courses such as those GDC offers Reduced import duties on learning materials Higher expatriate quota for training institutions Availability of latest technology Diversification of revenue sources through better exploitation of consultancy assignments Strategic alliances and partnerships with institutions of international repute Exploitation of multilingual assets to become a regional centre	Negative trends in the training sector Unstable political situation Unfavourable tariffs on importation of computers Poor economic environment High crime rate in the region Competition from other management centres Free management courses provided by Ministry of Education for its staff Proliferation of management training centres Absence of an effective national regulatory framework for management training centres Inadequate public transport facilities

Box 3.28
Some key points in conducting a SWOT analysis workshop

- Choose participants who represent the appropriate mix of skills
- Choose a suitable facilitator
- Ensure that there is no hidden agenda
- Ensure all participants support their points with concrete examples
- Avoid simply listing errors and mistakes
- Don't lose sight of external influences and trends
- Don't try to disguise internal weaknesses
- Don't allow the SWOT analysis exercise to become a blame-laying exercise
- Record the workshop minutes and distribute them among the participants
- Prioritise the points raised when identifying the strategic options
- Use the outcomes of the SWOT analysis throughout the evaluation

Box 3.29
The strengths and weaknesses of SWOT analysis

WEAKNESSES	STRENGTHS
■ Can be misused to justify a previously decided course of action, rather than used as a means to open up new possibilities	■ Provides a structured and concise format that helps you plan an evaluation
■ Can provoke disagreements and a tendency to lay blame	■ A lot of information can be included in a small amount of space
■ Discussions about threats and opportunities are only as good as an organisation's awareness of the external environment	■ Is a good basis for assessing core capabilities and competencies
	■ Is a stimulus for stakeholder participation
	■ Takes account of multiple perspectives
	■ Is not complicated to use as an outline

Questionnaire design

Questionnaires are used to gather data from a large number of respondents. They are often the only feasible way to ensure the number of respondents is large enough to allow statistical analysis of the results. They ensure that different respondents answer the same questions on the same topics. A well-designed questionnaire can gather information both on the overall performance of the product/service and on specific components. If it includes demographic questions about the participants, you can correlate performance and satisfaction among different groups of users.

WHY?
Questionnaires are used to put information obtained from many sources into a uniform data structure, which can then be entered into a template for analysis. The template now is almost always a computer spreadsheet (e.g., a spreadsheet programme such as Excel, or attached to specialist statistical analysis software such as the Statistical Package for the Social Sciences, SPSS). When computer access is limited and not too much data have been collected, questionnaire responses can be collated by hand on sheets of paper.

HOW?
Designing a questionnaire is part of a multi-stage process that starts with clearly defining what you want to know, why you want to know it and how you will use your results. This will determine what information you need and at what level of detail. Once you have done this, you will be in a position to ask the right questions and to interpret the results correctly. Ensure that all members of the team are involved in the design of the questionnaire, but do focus on common core issues so that the questionnaire does not become unmanageably long. Thus, although questionnaires might be cheap to administer compared with some other data-collection methods, they can be relatively expensive in terms of design time.

Designing a questionnaire

There are five steps involved in designing a questionnaire: defining its objectives and identifying the respondents, drafting the questionnaire, testing and finalising it, administering it, and reviewing the completed questionnaires.

Step 1: Define the objectives and identify the respondents

Start by reviewing why you're doing the evaluation and what you hope to accomplish by it, and then articulate clearly how you intend using the questionnaire answers. This provides a focus on what information you need, what questions to ask and who to get answers from. There is an example of a questionnaire on pages 124-126.

You might want to group the respondents (e.g., by their role or age) because you believe different groups use the product/service in different ways. Some groups might not be able to answer the same questions as other groups, so you might need to structure the questionnaire in such a way that respective groups can answer the parts relevant to them. In some cases, it might be necessary to design more than one questionnaire to accommodate the different groups.

In designing a questionnaire, be aware of respondents' cultural practices and beliefs, what vocabulary is appropriate, who may need to be approached for permission to ask questions (or be informed about the survey), whether gender or other factors affect respondents' accessibility and whether interview training is needed.

Step 2: Drafting the questionnaire

Responding to a questionnaire should be an interesting, stress-free experience. If respondents become bored, confused or irritated, their answers might be of little use. They are more likely to co-operate if they are told why you're asking the questions, and that their answers will be treated in strict confidence.

The main things to think about when designing a questionnaire are:

- **Order and layout:** Arrange the questionnaire as if you had to answer it. If it is to be self-administered, is it attractive and professional looking? Is it easy to read? At the beginning of the questionnaire have a short introductory section that explains the purpose of your evaluation, and assures respondents that their answers will not have any negative implications and will be kept confidential.

- **Tone and content:** Are the questions interesting? Are many of them on the same subject, or are the subjects varied? Are some questions asked more than once? Are some irrelevant? Are there questions that need to be asked which are not? Focus each question on one issue. Leave sensitive questions about personal information (e.g., income) to the end.

- **Vocabulary:** Is it appropriate for the age and level of education of the respondents? Could a different choice of words make the question clearer?

- **Closed and open questions:** Do you know enough about the range of possible answers to use closed questions (i.e., where the possible responses are specified in advance). An example of a closed question in Box 3.30 is 'How do you receive information?' Closed questions can all be converted to quantitative data and produce results that are easy to summarise, compare and generalise. However, open-ended questions can be very useful for drawing out respondents and really finding out their views. But the answers need time and effort to analyse. It is often useful to end a questionnaire with a final open-ended question, like this: 'Do you have any further comments?'

- **Number of questions:** How many questions you ask is not only affected by what you need to know. People are more willing to complete a short questionnaire than a long one, and you should bear in mind the costs of analysing large numbers of questions, particularly if they are open-ended. In the pre-testing stage, you will find out how long it takes to complete the questionnaire and whether the respondents can spare that amount of time.

- **Self-administered / interviewer-based questionnaires:** Self-administered questionnaires require respondents to be interested in, and capable of, filling in the answers. A covering letter explaining how the questionnaire results will be used and why the respondent has been approached should be worded persuasively. If respondents feel their views are valued, they are more likely to participate. Interviewer-based questionnaires should be easy for the interviewer to read aloud, and must have instructions that reduce the chance of an interviewer making a mistake. Interviewers should be trained how to approach a respondent and how to ask questions in a positive and respectful way. Try to avoid including questions that could embarrass either the interviewee or the interviewer or both.

- **Answer categories:** Take great care when designing answer categories. Examples are given in Box 3.30.

> **Box 3.30**
> **Designing the questionnaire answer categories**
>
> Ensure the categories in the questionnaire don't cause confusion, e.g.:
>
> How many years of education have you received?
>
> *Design 1*
> a. Less than 5 years
> b. 5–10 years
> c. 10–15 years
>
> *Design 2*
> a. 0–4 years
> b. 5–10 years
> c. More than 10 years
>
> In Design 1, somebody with exactly 10 years or with more than 15 years of education would not know which answer to choose. Design 2 is better. However, both designs fail to differentiate those with no education at all from those with a few years of education.
>
> Ensure the categories in the questionnaire cover all possible answers, including a final category e.g.:
>
> How do you receive information? a. Radio/TV; b. Newspaper; c. Library; d. Word of mouth; e. Internet; f. Other (please specify)
>
> Ensure that you have indicated what people have to do, for example, if respondents need to tick more than one answer you need to specify that this is so.
>
> When you design your answer categories, there is no fixed rule about whether you should give respondents an even number of choices (forcing them to choose whether they are more positive or more negative) or an odd number of choices (providing them with neutral ground), e.g.:
>
> a. Very good
> b. Good
> c. Poor
> d. Very poor
>
> a. Good
> b. Moderate
> c. Poor

A note of caution. Be very careful with 'skip logic'. This assumes that not all questions are relevant to all respondents. Those who answer a question one way may be required to answer the next question(s); those who answer another way may be told to skip over inappropriate questions. For example, if the answer to the question 'Have you read this newsletter?' is 'No', then the respondent skips the next few questions. The questionnaire needs to be very clear and unambiguous, particularly if it is self-administered.

Step 3: Test and finalise the questionnaire

Test the draft questionnaire with a small number of people who are similar to your future respondents. This will reveal any difficulties that respondents have in completing the answers, and which questions are not yielding the data needed.

This will help you to amend the draft before the final version of the questionnaire is completed, and will alert you to any practical difficulties, including the needs of your survey staff.

Step 4: Administering the questionnaire

If the questionnaire is interviewer-based, the interviewers should be trained how to complete it. This could be done during the testing stage. It's also important for interviews to be conducted at times and places that are convenient for the respondents.

Interviewees need to be given:

- an idea of how long the interview is likely to last
- a brief explanation of the purpose of the questionnaire
- an assurance that their answers will be treated as confidential
- instructions (for self-administered questionnaires) on how to fill out the questionnaire and what to do with the completed questionnaires
- thanks at the end of the interview

If interviewees ask to be informed of the outcome, take their contact details and send them the information.

Step 5: Reviewing the completed questionnaires

Questionnaires should be checked as soon as possible after an interview to ensure they have been completed properly. Ideally, they should be checked before the evaluator leaves the area where they were filled in, so that if there are any issues to be clarified, this can be done on the spot.

Box 3.31
Some key points in designing a questionnaire

- Begin with easy general questions, to put the respondent at ease, establish interest and build rapport

- Keep it simple. Complex questions can confuse respondents and produce inaccurate results. Generally, the more words to a question, the more likely it is that the wording itself will influence the response. Try breaking up a long question into two shorter ones. Use words that everyone can understand easily

- 'Yes' and 'no' answers do not always adequately measure the range of opinion on something, so avoid them if this is likely. For example, instead of asking 'Are you satisfied with the newsletter?', ask 'How satisfied are you with the newsletter: very satisfied, fairly satisfied, not very satisfied, or not satisfied at all?'

- Leave sensitive questions till the end (e.g., some people are uncomfortable being asked about their income or educational qualifications)

- Don't assume knowledge (e.g., if you ask a technical question, some people might answer without really understanding what it means)

- Avoid using slang, cultural-specific or technical words unless they will help respondents understand the question

- Avoid asking leading or loaded questions (e.g., ask 'What do you think of the services?' not 'Are the services good?')

- Avoid using judgemental words that might influence the response (e.g., 'highly effective government')

- Don't ask more than one question at a time. If the word 'and' is in your question, it might indicate that you are trying to ask several questions at once

Box 3.32
The strengths and weaknesses of questionnaires

WEAKNESSES
- Creating a questionnaire takes time and resources

- Good questionnaire design is more difficult than most people realise. Badly constructed questions will yield poor, unreliable data

- Questionnaires can't be used when researchers are unsure about the range of questions they wish to explore

- You need skilled people to administer questionnaires

STRENGTHS
- Questionnaires are relatively cheap

- They are the best option when there are a large number of people to collect opinions from

- They ensure that responses of different people can be collated and compared

- When they are well designed they are easy to use

- They can be re-used at different times to build a picture of trends

- They can be distributed widely using e-mail and analysed quickly using readily available software

---

SAMPLE EVALUATION QUESTIONNAIRE
(for participants in a training course)

Kindly fill in the entire questionnaire

1. Family name: ....
2. Other names: ....
3. Profession: ....
4. Name of organisation: ....
5. Position: ....
6. No. of years in present position: ....
7. Official address: ....
   Country: ....
   Telephone: ....
   Fax: ....
   Email: ....

8. Gender: Male............. Female................

9. Age bracket: (a) 16–25 (b) 26–35 (c) 36–45 (d) 46–55 (e) Over 55

10. Educational level (please tick the highest level from the options below):

    Technical Certificate/Diploma   Undergraduate Degree   MSc   PhD
    ☐   ☐   ☐   ☐

11. Working language: .... Other languages: ....

12. To what extent were the objectives of the training course made clear to you before you participated in the event? Please tick one of the options below:

Not clear at all	Partly clear	Clear	Very clear
1	2	3	4

13. To what extent were you satisfied with the way the course was organised? Please tick one of the options below:

Not satisfied	Partly satisfied	Satisfied	Very satisfied
1	2	3	4

14. Please state one strong aspect of the organisation of the course:
....
....

15. Please state one weak aspect of the organisation of the course:
....
....

16. To what extent were the objectives of the course consistent with your own expectations? Please tick one of the options below:

Not consistent	Partly consistent	Consistent	Very consistent
1	2	3	4

17. To what extent did the course provide opportunity for networking with participants?

Did not provide an opportunity	Partly provided an opportunity	Significantly provided an opportunity	Very significantly provided an opportunity
1	2	3	4

18. To what extent did you benefit from one another's experience during the course?

Did not benefit at all	Partly benefited	Significantly benefited	Very significantly benefited
1	2	3	4

19. Which of the following benefits did you gain from the training course? Please tick all the appropriate options:

I obtained new and significant information on the topic	
I acquired new techniques/skills	
We reached consensus on appropriate strategies/policies relating to course content	
I made useful new contacts	

20. Give two examples of the most significant information/skills that you acquired on the course
....
....
....

21. Indicate two ways in which you have been able to apply the information/skills acquired
....
....

22. Did you share the lessons learned from the course with other people?
    Yes/No

23. If yes, which of these methods did you use? (Please tick all that apply).

Back-to-office report	Face-to face discussions	Teaching	Writing	E-mail	Websites	Other (please specify)

24. Do you think your efforts in applying and/or sharing the lessons learned from the course have led to improvements in the performance of your organisation?
    Yes/No

25. If yes, please give an example of the improvements
....
....

26. Have you benefited from any of our institution's other services since attending the training course?
    Yes/No

27. If yes, please indicate the type of service(s)
....
....
....

28. Has access to our service(s) helped you to make better use of the information/skills acquired during the training course?
    Yes/No

29. Since the training course, have you attended any other courses dealing with a similar topic?
    Yes/No

30. If yes, please indicate the title, date and location of the course(s) referred to in Question 29.
....
....

31. Who funded your participation at the course mentioned in Question 30?
....
....

32. To what extent did you feel that the information/skills acquired from the course(s) referred to in Question 30 reinforced those you acquired through this training? Please tick one of the options below.

Not at all	Partly	Significantly	Very significantly
1	2	3	4

Please state any other observations you might consider pertinent to this evaluation exercise
....
....
....

Thank you for taking the time to fill in this questionnaire

Focus group discussions

Focus group discussions are group interviews carried out in a systematic way with selected members of the target group to provide information on a particular topic. They can be used at all stages, from project planning to evaluation.

Information from focus group sessions is qualitative. The sessions explore knowledge, beliefs, concerns and attitudes, rather than collect statistical facts. The aim is to gather as many diverse points of view as possible. When you want to understand what the target group believes, and their perceptions and questions, focus group discussions are a good way to do this.

A focus group usually has between four and eight participants. Groups larger than this are difficult to manage because a record needs to be kept of what is said by each person. Even if the session is tape-recorded, it can be difficult to make out what individual people are saying if two people speak at the same time.

The discussion is led by a facilitator, based on carefully designed questions. The interaction between the facilitator and the group, and among the participants, is what makes focus groups work. Several focus groups (two to four) on one topic will provide a more complete view about the product/service.

WHY?
You can use focus groups if you're looking for:

- the range of opinions held by the users of your product/service
- perceptions and ideas, rather than numbers or percentages of users holding those opinions
- ways to improve your product/service
- background information on quantitative data already collected
- opinions about the accuracy or relevance of data generated by other means (e.g., a questionnaire survey found that 70% of villagers had access to a radio which they listened to daily; one focus group might confirm this finding, but another might qualify it by pointing out that generally women are working in the house while the radio is being played outside)
- an idea of important issues for a future questionnaire-based survey to evaluate the product/service; this includes finding out about the vocabulary used by the users of the product/service, to enable phrasing of the questions so that they are easily understood.

HOW?
There are three distinct stages in running focus groups: preparation, implementation and analysis. With each stage are a series of steps that should be followed, from drafting the plan and developing the questions to identifying group participants, holding the discussion and analysing the results.

Organising focus group discussions

Step 1: Draft a plan and make logistical arrangements

Draft a plan for the focus group discussions that includes criteria and specifications about the participants. It should set dates and times that you expect to be suitable for the participants. Identify a comfortable and convenient meeting place, preferably where people can sit in a circle. Choose a neutral meeting place that will allow participants to express their opinions freely and openly.

Step 2: Develop the script

Develop a script that you feel will get people talking in a way that serves your purpose. A script for a focus group discussion usually has 10-12 open and clearly worded questions, ordered from the most general to very specific questions.

There are several different types of questions:

- **Opening questions** to get people talking: (e.g., 'Tell us something about yourself. For instance, what do you enjoy doing in your spare time?')

- **Introductory questions** to introduce the topic and the participants' connection with it: (e.g., 'What is the first thing that comes to your mind when you hear ... [name of product/service being evaluated] ?')

- **Transition questions** to link to the key questions (e.g., 'What were your first impressions when you first got involved in ... [name of product/service being evaluated] ?')

- **Key questions**, the most important questions (usually 2-5) to obtain the data you need (e.g., 'Did your organisation have any benefits from using ... [name of product/service being evaluated]? If so, in what ways?')

- **Ending questions** to ask participants for advice and comment on possible omissions in the discussion (e.g., 'If you could give some advice to the project leader what would it be?')

Remember that a focus group discussion is not an interrogation or a quiz — it is a discussion. The questions should stimulate participants to respond and talk among themselves. Prepare some prompts/probes for each question to assist when additional discussion is needed.

Also, make sure questions do not assume anything. For example: 'What is the most helpful service the resource centre provides?' assumes that it provides helpful services. This series of questions would allow you to get the information you want without making assumptions: 'Have you used the resource centre? What for? Did you find it helpful?'

As well as asking questions, having a flip-chart with a diagram on it or drawing a picture gives people something to discuss.

Step 3: Recruit the participants

A group of four to eight participants is manageable and productive. Some people prefer to have fewer than six people as this fosters greater in-depth discussion. When recruiting the participants, allow for some non-arrivals and invite one or two more.

Important points to remember when recruiting the participants include:

- **Number of groups:** This depends on your time and budget, but you should hold at least two groups. If you have only one, there is the risk of such problems as people not showing up, not all questions being addressed, all participants sharing the same opinion, and so on. If you have more groups, it's worth inviting different types of participants for each one (e.g., different age groups). It's more useful to have two groups of females (e.g., girls and elderly women) than to have one group and find that the girls are silent in the presence of their seniors.

- **Homogeneity:** This is advisable. Try to identify people with a similar background, as they are more likely to talk freely and share experiences if they feel they have a lot in common with the others. They should be typical of the product/service target groups. Select according to such criteria as occupation, use of product/service, age and gender. Ideally, they should be strangers to one another.

- **Using existing lists:** The easiest way to recruit is from an existing list (e.g., subscribers to a newsletter, a registered members' website). Send a personal invitation and follow up with a phone call to confirm their attendance. Explain what is involved (and how they feel about a tape-recorder being used if you plan to use one). Ask if there are any special requirements, and tell them how long the meeting is expected to last. As they are volunteering their time, it's worth thinking how you could show your appreciation in a culturally sensitive way.

- **Provisions:** Offer refreshments and, where necessary, try to arrange such things as transport or childcare. It should not be necessary to offer money to get people to attend a focus group discussion - people like to be consulted for their opinions - but you do need to arrange to serve them drinks and snacks and, if necessary, cover travel costs.

Step 4: Select a facilitator, note-taker and observer

Facilitators are responsible for guiding the participants through the meeting. They look after the group dynamics and make sure all participants join in the discussion. They should:

- be unbiased, empathetic, positive, respectful and good listeners

- have experience with focus group discussions in general and with the specific subject

- not be connected with delivering the product/service.

Using an external facilitator has advantages and disadvantages:

- **Advantages:** Facilitating the discussion is a major challenge of focus groups, so it's important to have a good facilitator, and external ones are usually skilled and experienced. Also, they are not part of your organisation; participants might feel more comfortable about making critical comments to an external person than to a representative of your organisation. It is also possible that they will lead the discussion to interesting topics that you might not have considered. And finally, having an external facilitator allows you to be an observer and thus get more out of the discussion.

- **Disadvantages:** It means additional costs. Also, many external facilitators work for the private sector and might not necessarily be good at facilitating in other sectors, so check their experience in your sector. It can be difficult to explain to an external person exactly what you have in mind for the discussion, so it could mean more time spent on discussing the script. And finally, external facilitators don't necessarily write the report of the focus group; if you write it, make sure their comments are included in it.

Ensure that you recruit someone to take notes, operate the tape-recorder and handle logistics. Note-taking demands capturing what was said and expressed (verbally and non-verbally), by whom, what the tone of the discussion was (particularly for sensitive or controversial issues), who was actively participating, who was not, and factors that might explain any reactions or attitudes. The note-taker should document group composition and dynamics.

If the group is large, and resources permit, another observer could be used just to record observations. It's good to have one or two observers (not more than two) from your organisation present to discuss the findings with afterwards. Tell them not to contribute to the discussion unless asked to by the facilitator. Depending on the venue, the observers should be seated outside the circle of participants.

Even if you're the only person available to conduct the focus group discussion, go ahead as long as you are a good listener with an ability to facilitate group discussion.

Step 5: Facilitate the discussion

A focus group discussion usually takes between 1? and 2 hours. The basic requirements are chairs, a table, a flip-chart, a tape-recorder, and drinks and snacks. Check that the tape-recorder is working before people arrive, Other good practices include:

- Greet people on arrival and offer them refreshments to make them feel comfortable

- Start the session with a welcome, presenting yourself, giving a brief overview of the topic and the objective of the discussion. Also explain how the session is being recorded (in writing and/or on tape); check that everyone agrees to this before starting. Explain who will have access to the information and how anonymity and confidentiality will be ensured

- Agree to some ground rules before the discussion starts (e.g., only one person speaks at once; people treat each others' opinions with respect even if they disagree; if the facilitator interrupts the speaker will finish the sentence and then stop talking; smoking is not allowed; cellphones must be turned off or switched to silent mode)

- Assure participants that all their contributions are valuable and important, and that you're keen to hear about differences in the group. Emphasise that there are no 'correct' answers

- Don't be afraid of silence. You can often use it to your advantage. A pause can encourage people to speak (particularly people who usually talk less in groups) or to expand upon an idea

- Summarise before moving from one subject to another. The best way to do that is to say: 'If I understand your point of view, you mean that…' And don't pass judgement or give an opinion

- Remember that the facilitator is the listener and recorder, and should not be too actively involved in the discussion except to guide it and keep it focused

- Discourage questions from the participants in the beginning, but encourage them at the end, and explain any misunderstandings only after the discussion has finished

- Thank people for their contributions and take care of any logistical problems they might have. They should leave feeling positive about their experience

Step 6: Analyse the results

Immediately after the discussion, when the participants have left, the facilitator, note-taker, observers and any others involved should review the discussion and findings. This will reveal any different interpretations there might be. Check that the tape-recorder worked properly and that the written notes covered everything. Write down anything you notice is missing.

Depending on time and resources, the analysis can be based on a complete transcript of the focus group, a tape-based summary transcript or the notes of the note-taker. Review of notes taken at the time and listening to the tape-recordings are practical ways of doing the analysis.

Cut and paste the transcript or notes onto either paper or the computer, ordered by question. Be careful not to lose the source. Set aside comments that don't answer any questions, and group similar comments together. Write a summary for each question, separating different sources if you used different categories of participants.

Step 7: Report your findings

The report normally consists of a summary, the purpose and procedures of the focus group discussion, the findings, conclusions and recommendations. The 'findings' sections should contain summaries per question, and some verbatim reports (quotations) of what participants said, as data.

It is a good idea to use visuals in the written report and consider an oral presentation for your colleagues and/or other interested people.

Box 3.33
Some key points in organising a focus group discussion

- Prepare the script and questions carefully (only very experienced facilitators can improvise the script during the session), but this shouldn't mean you can't be flexible during the session

- Address all participants equally, and try not to let any of them dominate the discussion; however, some might be more 'information-rich' than others, so it might be good to let them talk a bit more than others

- Stick to the time set for the discussion and estimate the time needed for each question

- Make very clear to the participants what will happen with the results of the discussion, including whether or not you will share the final report with them. It will be encouraging for them to know they are collaborating with important research. If the objectives of the discussion are not clear, people might not be willing to share their opinions

- Avoid passing judgement or expressing opinions. Participants tend to see facilitators as experts and might be tempted to adopt their opinions

- Don't be tempted to answer questions about the product/service. This disturbs the process. Try to assess the knowledge level of the participants beforehand, and use the introduction for necessary explanations; and, if necessary, at the end of the session, discuss queries with the individuals who raised them

- Don't let too much time elapse before analysing and reporting on the focus group discussion. Start cutting and pasting the notes or transcript soon after the session and summarise the main findings. Use the tape recording to check the findings and to get quotations

- Before finishing the conclusions and recommendations, ask other people involved to read it, and include their insights in the report. Consider organising a meeting to present the results and discuss the evaluation follow-up

Box 3.34
The strengths and weaknesses of focus group discussions

WEAKNESSES	STRENGTHS
■ Focus groups give an indication of a range of views in a community, but should not be used to make generalisations because they are not a representative sample	■ Focus group discussions can help to identify beliefs about a product/service, which can be used in designing questionnaires
■ Some participants might be intimidated either by others or by the experience, which means that either they don't participate, or they give socially approved answers	■ They encourage participants to generate and explore their own questions and analyse their own experiences
■ Unlike personal interviews, the opinions expressed are influenced by the others	■ They are usually more cost-effective than holding individual interviews
■ With only about eight (or fewer) people in a group, their responses will not be as reliable and valid as a structured survey, unless you hold many different focus group discussions on the same topic	■ They allow information to be obtained from non-literate communities
	■ They can reveal opinions and attitudes that would not emerge in a formal questionnaire
	■ They are usually well accepted by the community, as group discussion is a natural form of communication

Process flowchart

The process flowchart tool focuses on the sequence of activities involved in implementing an information project. Almost any information activity can be treated as a process. For example:

- writing a brochure
- developing a website
- making a rural radio programme
- running a training course
- publishing a newsletter
- providing a documentation service

WHY?

Using the flowchart can help you to depict fairly complex information activities in a way that makes clear the components and steps involved and how they relate to each other. It also helps you to:

- identify problems in the sequence of activities (e.g., delays, bottlenecks and responsibility loopholes
- identify ways of improving the process
- identify where misunderstandings between people and units can occur
- explain the information activity process to others (e.g., evaluation team and other stakeholders), giving them a clear picture of the way the project is organised
- see how the work of the different units and people relate to and affect each other

HOW?

To describe the information activity process, the flowchart uses symbols to represent the various activities during the process. There are five steps involved. Here, we describe each step and then feature, as an example, a process flowchart involved for a question-and-answer service.

Using a process flowchart

Step 1: Define your process

Identify the process you want to analyse. Think about what your starting point is and what you intend the outcome/end result to be.

Step 2: Describe the process

Describe the process using the symbols in Table 3.17.

Table 3.17
The symbols used for the steps in a process flow chart

SYMBOL	EXPLANATION
(rounded rectangle)	Starting point and outcome
(square)	Divide the process into 5-10 important activities that are roughly the same level of importance. Don't mix activities and their sub-activities.
(diamond)	Identify critical decision moments. Describe these decision moments in the form of yes/no questions. Ensure that both the 'yes'-side and the 'no'-side have a follow-up activity, e.g., E.g.: 'Request accepted?' Yes = Invite client. No = Inform client
(circle)	For each activity, identify the responsible person and/or unit. All activities/decision moments that follow the symbol are the responsibility of the person and/or unit indicated
(flag/document shape)	Identify the information flowing into the process and the information flowing out of the process. The arrows (see below) connecting lines indicate the flow of information.
(arrow)	Connect the symbols with arrows indicating the sequence of steps and include loops to show that an earlier activity should be repeated.

Step 3: Identify (possible) bottlenecks

For each activity and at each decision point, ask yourself:

- Why is this activity taking place?
- Why is it taking place at this point in the sequence?
- What is the volume of work at this point?
- How much time does it take? Why is it taking that length of time?
- Is the activity difficult to carry out? If so, why?
- Why is this specific person responsible for this activity?
- What are the risks involved in this activity? What could go wrong?

Step 4: Identify improvements

Based on your answers in Step 3, ask yourself:

- Could some activities, decision points or information be left out?
- Could some activities, decision points or information be combined or changed?
- Could some activities, decision points or information be simplified?
- Could any of the responsibilities involved be changed?

Step 5: Evaluate the potential improvements

Evaluate your ideas for improvement by asking yourself whether or not they result in:

- some activities requiring less effort and less time
- an improvement in the quality of the information project
- fewer resources being required
- an improvement in working conditions

From Figure 3.8 you can see that there could be delays between:

- receipt and registration
- registration and assessment
- assessment and compiling the answer
- compiling the answer and sending it

Box 3.35
Some key points in compiling a process flowchart

- Use a flowchart wherever a process seems to be complex, or when many people are involved in the activity

- Involve key stakeholders in developing and verifying the flowchart

- Don't try to include everything in one chart; if necessary, make different charts for the different main activities in the process

- Don't make a flowchart for everything; if a process is clear for all stakeholders, it does not need further explanation

- Avoid using a flowchart as the only means of communication; some groups of stakeholders might not be able to read them adequately

**Figure 3.8
Example of a process flowchart for a question-and-answer service**

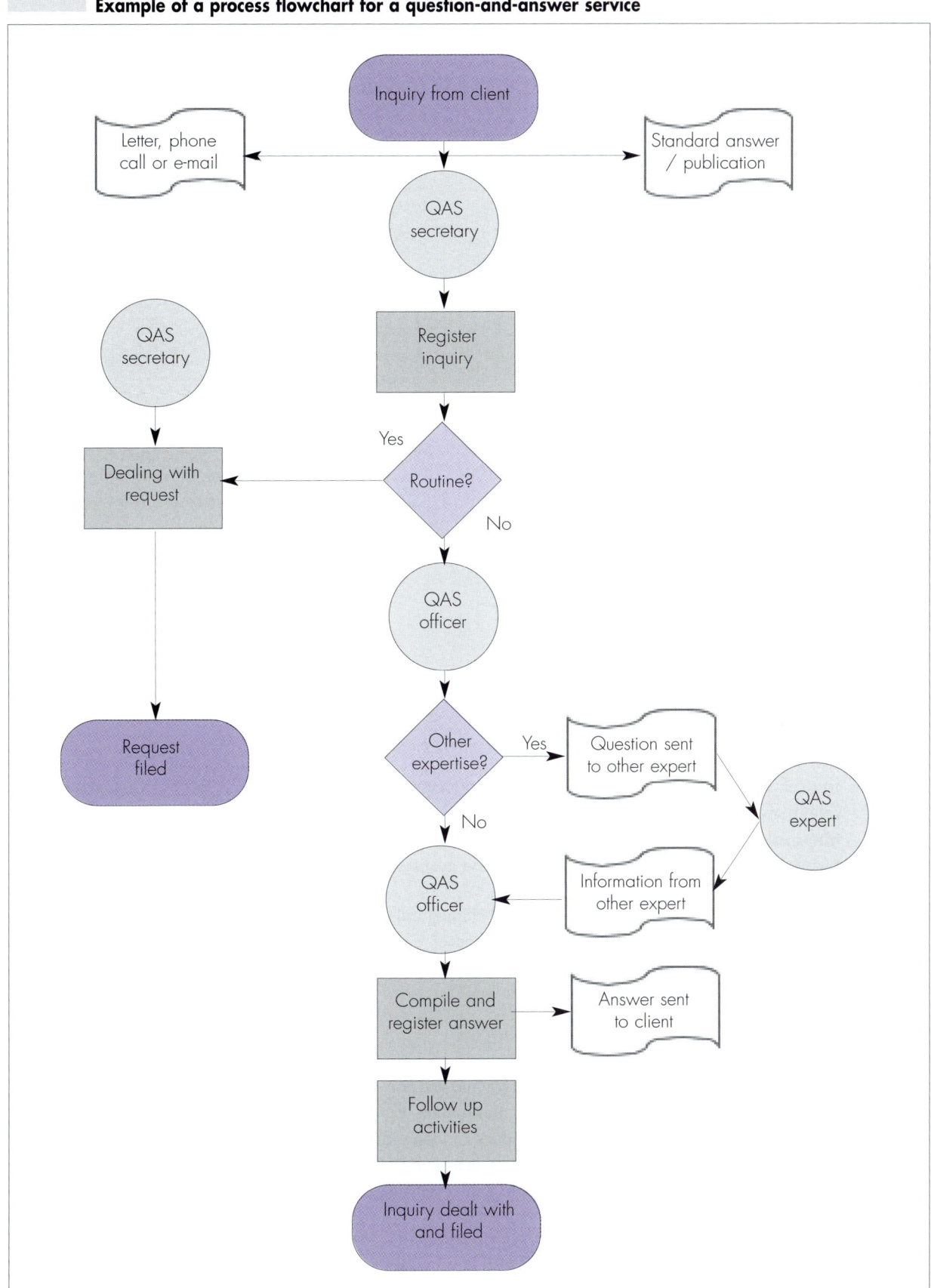

Box 3.36
The strengths and weaknesses of process flowcharts

WEAKNESSES	STRENGTHS
■ It is often difficult to distinguish between the levels of activities (activities and sub-activities)	■ A process flowchart is a relatively simple tool that can be applied to a variety of information products/services
■ Some activities are cyclic, without a clear beginning and end	■ It gives a spatial overview of the process and helps you to identify bottlenecks and see where improvements are needed
■ If not used properly, simple activities can be depicted as a process	■ You can develop a flowchart alone or in a group (not more than 20 people) on a participatory basis; if it is developed with the limited involvement of a few key people, try to include all the other stakeholders in the process by inviting their comments
■ If the process of developing the flowchart is participatory, there is the danger that participants confuse the present situation with the desired outcome	■ It is a useful tool for presentation purposes, showing what procedures should look like
■ If not explained properly, a process flowchart can easily be misinterpreted	■ Depending on the complexity of the activity, it usually takes a relatively short time to develop a process flowchart

Case studies

You can use case studies to evaluate your product/service. A case study is a qualitative analysis of something (e.g., a product, event or organisation) within its wider context. It is particularly useful when you want to assess processes and impact. How many case studies are undertaken in an evaluation, and to what depth, depends on the evaluation purpose.

Case studies are based on multiple tools, including individual interviews, focus groups, questionnaires and website research; they also make use of other data sources, such as records. They provide valuable insight into the past, especially when there is a high staff turnover resulting in institutional memory loss.

WHY?
Case studies collect and present qualitative information about a chosen subject. They are often the only way to demonstrate use, outcomes and impact. Evaluations based on an experimental design (specifying the test units, sampling procedures, independent variables, dependent variables and how external variables are to be controlled) are usually not feasible or affordable for non-research purposes. The accessibility of both people and reports is an important precondition for generating insights from case studies.

Case studies can expose contradictions and complexity. Sometimes they follow on from a broader survey, to focus on issues of special interest highlighted by the survey. It is often more convincing to show case study evidence than to give a theoretical summary of advantages and disadvantages without concrete examples.

HOW?
There are several steps involved in a case study. Depending on what you want to know, the time a case study takes can vary from hours to months. As a guide, a case study that produces a report of 5-10 pages will take about 5 days for the preparatory activities (steps 1 and 2 below); 2-3 days for conducting the study (step 3); 2-3 days for analysing the data and writing the report, and 1-2 days for distribution (steps 4 and 5).

For multiple case study research (conducting more than one case study), steps 1, 2 and 5 will take proportionally less time per case, but you will need extra time to write a synthesis report. An understanding of the subject and context of the case study is important, as well as writing skills and the analytical capacity to draw conclusions from the material gathered.

Organising a case study

Step 1: Prepare an outline and identify contacts

The outline is a brief plan describing the rationale of the study. You need to be clear about the objectives of the study, as the case study themes will be derived from your objectives. The outline should also describe the methods to be used to gather data (e.g., interviews and reviewing reports) and the sources of data (e.g., community representatives, a newsletter). Decide whether you will study one case (for the time being) or more. The advantage of conducting more than one is that you will have comparative data and they will make generalisation possible.

Once these decisions have been taken, you need to identify who needs to be approached and when. Involving key stakeholders in the design of your study outline will help suggest themes and overcome possible obstacles.

Step 2: Design the questions and select the case(s)

For each theme in the outline, draw up a set of questions. A case study tends to start with a descriptive section, where the 'how' questions are asked. These questions help you to establish an image and context and to describe the aspect of the product/service being studied. This is often followed by an explanatory section, where the 'why' questions are asked.

Having formulated the themes and questions, you then define the criteria for selecting a case, such as type of data available, and accessibility of data sources. If you plan to conduct several case studies, possible criteria for selection could include geographical spread, diversity among the cases, different stages of implementation, and amount of funding, and so on. If you're not familiar with the region or the study topic, ask for local/expert help to select the cases.

When approaching the contact person for a case you have selected, you need to be clear about the study objective, the type of people you would like to talk to, the type of material you would like to review, the time you need, and the way the study will be reported and disseminated. You also need to be clear about how the study might benefit them. A (financial) incentive might not be available, but promotion of the case through publication and dissemination is usually appreciated.

At this stage it also is worth thinking about how you would respond if the study uncovered something they might not want others to know about.

Box 3.37
Case study of a city-based resource library

The library had been set up to provide agricultural and environmental information to extension workers and journalists. The aim of the case study was to see if the library was reaching its target groups with information they found relevant. The study took 3 days to complete (over a 2-week period). Routine records of users and withdrawals were examined, resulting in a graph showing a steady rise in use, with a marked peak at certain times of each month. It also revealed who used the centre regularly, and who used it occasionally, and used this data to select the participants in a focus group discussion (two regular users, four occasional users).

The discussion revealed that, out of all the information materials available in the library, the two regular users found newsletters on health-related topics very useful for developing training materials and copy, and would have liked more information about wider issues related to health. Of the occasional users, one found the centre's opening hours inconvenient (she had a young family), another said the materials were not scientific enough for her needs, and the other two said they had not been aware of all the centre had to offer and would now use it more, and encourage others to do so. None of them could suggest why there might be peaks of use. It was decided to design a small questionnaire for the centre's users to complete, including the question: 'Is there any particular reason why you came here today?'

As a result of this case study, the staff changed the opening times on some days of the week, made contact with a local university to access scientific materials on demand, and made more effort to advertise services through the local media. They also subscribed to a newsletter dealing with health, and included teachers, journalists and health staff in their target groups for future publicity.

Step 3: Conduct the case study

A combination of interviews (individual and group) and studying documentary material (leaflets, earlier evaluation reports, website material) is usual for a case study. To get a fuller picture you should interview the people providing what is being studied as well as the intended beneficiaries.

You will find it helpful to draw up a list of stakeholders, as each will have their own experience and perspective (e.g., organisational staff such as the manager or co-ordinator); field staff who have direct contact with the target groups; relevant people from local/national government bodies and partner organisations); and the actual users. The number and variety of people to include in the study will depend on its purpose and the time and resources available.

The questions should be seen as a guide rather than a checklist. Interesting findings are often discovered when unexpected topics are discussed. When conducting a study in a context (geographical or thematic) you're not familiar with, working with a local person (not involved in the case) will add value.

Recording interviews is good for back-up and can help to produce nice quotations. Pictures and video are good tools to visualise the study and can provide a user-friendly means of disseminating the final report. However, before you start recording ensure that it is acceptable to the interviewee and ensure that there is agreement about what can be used, who can be named, etc.

Step 4: Analyse the data gathered

Start by going back to the objectives and themes you defined in the outline of the case study. Use the data collected for the case study as a base, and structure them according to theme. Depending on the complexity and quantity of the data, there are several ways to do this. If your notes are handwritten, the data can be coded using colours or letters matching the different objectives or themes. If notes are typed, you can use the computer to help organise the data. If you recorded interviews and didn't make a transcript, listen to your tapes for any extra findings and for quotations.

When the data is structured according to theme, write up the findings for each theme. This will form the basis for the case study report. If you discuss early drafts with informants and other stakeholders, this will add to the richness of your data, as well as identify factual errors.

If you have conducted more than one case study and you need to do a cross-case analysis, the data you use will probably be the finished reports of each case. Collate all data according to the study theme(s) and analyse the patterns (look for similarities and differences). This could form the basis of a synthesis report, summarising the findings from the various case studies.

Step 5: Write and distribute the report

There are many ways to write up a case study. How you do it depends on who will read it and why you did the case study in the first place. For evaluation purposes, it should be factual. The data gathered for each theme will form both the descriptive and the analytical parts, so a large chunk of the work will already have been done by this stage. A summary and conclusion will make the report attractive for a wider audience.

You should send a final draft of the report to (at least some of) the people interviewed, to give them an opportunity to comment. Generally, comments on facts should be adopted, and comments on your analysis of the facts should also be taken seriously. With multiple case studies, a synthesis report should reflect the patterns in the different cases on the key themes identified, whilst highlighting the similarities and differences.

It is best to have different channels of distribution (e.g., e-mail, websites and printed reports). If you have accompanying multi-media material (e.g., video clips, photos), consider distributing the report on CD-ROM. Presenting the case study findings at special events will help to share the lessons learned.

Box 3.38
Some key points in conducting a case study

- Take time to elaborate the case study objectives and themes, and be prepared to adapt themes when unpredicted issues arise

- Arrange the practicalities carefully. Making appointments for visits and interviews is done most quickly and efficiently by telephone

- Be prepared to be critical; ask for, and report on, challenges and failures as well as positive results. A case study that shows only positive results lacks credibility. Also, an analysis of project weaknesses is just as valuable as identifying project successes

- Get the basics right (e.g., correct spelling of people's names, accurate brief summaries of the project). Getting the basics wrong can undermine confidence in the study

- Plan for multiple case studies, if possible. This reduces the risk that the case study selected turns out not to be as information-rich as expected, and it makes the findings more representative and provides data to compare

- Involve other people in order to challenge your analysis. One of the most difficult aspects of case studies is analysing the data and drawing conclusions, because these are influenced by the observer's perceptions

- Acknowledge your sources, including people interviewed, and websites, newsletters and other documents consulted, so that others can follow up your work at a later date

- Be flexible about changing the key issues and themes of the case study, should new material emerge which suggests this

- Don't give too much space in the report to the descriptive section. In evaluation reports, readers tend to be more interested in the explanatory section, the analysis and the conclusions. Spend some time defining your audience, and consider producing the report in different formats to suit different audiences

- Be clear about how and when you will disseminate the findings, and stick to this if possible

Box 3.39
The strengths and weaknesses of case studies

WEAKNESSES	STRENGTHS
■ Case studies are not representative; when doing multiple case studies, analytical generalisation is possible, but not statistical generalisation	■ Case studies are good tools to get in-depth qualitative information
■ The findings are subjective – they depend on interpretation	■ They are an attractive and illustrative way to highlight an aspect of a product/service
■ Case studies can take up a lot of time, for all involved in them	■ The research is relatively flexible, with plenty of opportunity to discover new issues along the way
	■ They tap into different people's subjective experiences of the aspect under study

Individual interviews

If you want to know what people think about a product/service, or how they use it, you must ask them. Individual interviews can be conducted face-to-face, by telephone or online. You can use a structured questionnaire to record information systematically, or adopt a more informal, semi-structured approach, using a checklist of questions to guide the interview. Semi-structured interviews can seem like a casual conversation in that, where relevant issues arise by chance, they are followed up by further questioning.

When selecting individuals to interview, to avoid bias ensure that they are representative of different class, age, gender and occupational groups within the target community. Individuals can be selected at random, or a group could choose a sample of its members based on criteria provided by the evaluators. If individuals are self-selected, there is a danger that only the more articulate and influential members of the group will come forward.

Lay the foundation for honest assessment by clearly explaining that you want to learn what the respondent really thinks, and that what is wanted is specific, critical feedback. The interviewer must know and understand the reasons for the evaluation. This is especially important with semi-structured interviews, which are flexible interviews, allowing new questions to be brought up during the interview as a result of what the interviewee says.

WHY?
One-on-one interviews enable you to collect data about people's understanding and use of the product/service. They can provide feedback that will give the following type of information:

- whether the product/service is relevant to them
- the extent to which they understand the product/service
- the extent to which their understanding is consistent with what the product/service was intended to do
- their opinion about the way the product/service is provided
- what else they would like to see included
- how they use the product/service

HOW?
The exact number of interviewees depends on what you want to find out, the kinds of respondents being targeted, and the time and other resources you have at your disposal. The typical number ranges from five to 15 people. Even a fairly small number of people can provide a lot of useful information. Generally, once a definite pattern in the responses can be detected, you probably know enough, particularly if you compare it with data from the routine monitoring of activities.

There are a series of steps involved in arranging and conducting individual interviews, from preparing and conducting them to analysing them.

Organising the interviews

Step 1: Identify the objectives and resources

Decide on the interview objectives and review the resources available. The expenses associated with interviewing relate mainly to:

- the interviewer's time to develop questions, prepare materials, recruit participants, conduct interviews, and analyse and write up results of each interview
- reimbursing interviewees' travel costs
- paying fees to use the venue (usually, an avoidable expense)

Step 2: Decide how to conduct the interview

Interviews are typically conducted in person, especially if specific reactions are to be observed (because you can see people's expressions as they answer). But, especially if the respondents are known to the interviewer, they can also be done on the telephone or via an online chat room. For face-to-face interviews, try to find a quiet, comfortable environment.

Step 3: Prepare the interview

Depending on what is wanted from the interview, decide whether to use a formal, structured approach or a more informal, semi-structured approach. In constructing a formal interview, there are likely to be a mix of closed and open-ended questions (as for questionnaire design). You also need to decide how much information you need to collect about the interviewee; sometimes, anonymous interviewees are freer with their responses.

With semi-structured interviews, write down the questions before the interview, but be prepared to take a different path of questioning if necessary. This means you must understand clearly what information is needed and why. The relative informality of this approach can encourage interviewees to 'open up', as well as enabling you to explore unanticipated topics.

Sometimes the first part of the interview follows a structured format with a more informal approach being reserved for the remainder of the interview. This could allow nervous interviewees to gain confidence early in the interview.

Closed questions offer a set of appropriate answers from which the interviewee can choose (e.g., 'Which of these do you prefer, site design x or site design y?'). If possible avoid questions with only 'yes or no' answers: people often say 'yes' just to please. Questions can usually be rephrased to avoid a 'yes' or 'no' response. Open-ended questions enable you to observe the level of understanding (e.g., you can ask interviewees to describe in their own words their use of a service, or how they would describe it to a friend).

Open-ended questions should be worded in a way that promotes an in-depth response in the interviewee's own words (e.g., 'What do you think of the layout of this newsletter?').

Step 4: Identify the interviewees

The people you interview are volunteers. Your choice will reflect your purpose and their availability and willingness. In most cases, you will be selecting the interviewees in advance, but sometimes the selection will be more random (e.g., stopping people when they leave the resource centre you are evaluating). Whenever possible, appointments should be made with the people who are to be interviewed.

Step 5: Conduct the interview

Start by telling the interviewees about the purpose of the interview and how long you expect it to take. Make sure they understand that you would like them to answer honestly and comprehensively, and that you will not be offended if they are critical. Explain why notes are being taken and/or why the conversation is being taped, and reassure them that their responses will be confidential and anonymous. If they object to taping, ask if you may take notes. If they object to that but are still willing to be interviewed, make sure you record notes of what you recall as soon as you can after the interview.

Each interview with pre-selected interviewees should take 20-60 minutes (try not to exceed an hour). Random interviews (e.g., stopping people to ask them questions) should take no more than 5 minutes. Telephone interviews should always be kept short. At the end of an interview, it is worth asking interviewees if they would mind you contacting them again if necessary.

In an interview make sure you:

- are prepared with pen and paper
- ask the questions clearly
- listen carefully
- follow up on anything interesting that comes up
- take good notes and/or record the interview, wherever possible
- explain any differences in procedure if the interview is taped
- obtain all the data needed before ending the interview; if necessary, review your notes with the interviewee
- thank the interviewee for his/her time

Step 6: Analyse and record the interview

Depending on time and resources, your analysis can be based on a complete transcript of the interviews. You can cut and paste copies of the original transcript or notes according to the questions answered by the various interviewees, but be careful to code each fragment (e.g., use the initials of who was answering) so as not to lose track of the source.

Review any comments that don't answer specific questions, and group any similar comments. Write a summary for each question, separating responses if different categories of participants were used (e.g., interviewees divided into users and staff, or into male and female respondents).

Step 7: Report the results

Start the report with background information on the evaluation – the product/service being evaluated, the purpose of the evaluation, the tools used to conduct the evaluation and to reach conclusions. The bulk of the report should consist of the findings, which should be in the form of summaries of the responses to the questions. Use quotes anonymously as evidence; this makes the report persuasive and attractive to read.

Box 3.40
Some key points in conducting individual interviews

- Tell the interviewees about the purpose and process of the interview
- Make sure they understand that you want them to react honestly, comprehensively and critically
- Explain why notes are being taken and/or the conversation is being taped
- Reassure them that their responses are confidential
- Don't interrupt unless it is to bring them back to the point of your question
- Don't volunteer information unless it is to get the interview going, to get it back on track or to give background information relevant to your objectives

Box 3.41
The strengths and weaknesses of individual interviews

WEAKNESSES	STRENGTHS
Individual interviews can be time-consuming and labour-intensive	Individual interviews (especially semi-structured interviews) are a good way to get detailed feedback from a relatively small number of people representing your target group
Some people take the opportunity to speak at length about matters that are not relevant	Most people like to talk about themselves, their work and their interests
People can be reluctant to be overtly critical in a one-on-one situation	Individual interviews are flexible, and can offer valuable insights
Transcripts from interviews can be daunting to analyse	Some people find individual interviews less intimidating than group interviews

Participatory and creative tools

The focus here is on selected participatory and creative methods that can be used to collect data. They are particularly helpful in environments where the participants have difficulty expressing themselves or are reluctant to share their opinions in public. These tools stimulate learning not only for the evaluator, but also for the participants themselves; this is important for commitment to the evaluation process and its outcomes.

We are going to describe five participatory and creative methods:

- drawing
- role-play
- participatory video
- rich pictures
- Venn diagrams

Drawing and role-play are presented together because they are closely related to each other in terms of the way they are implemented. Participatory video, rich pictures and Venn diagrams are presented separately.

Drawing and role-play

WHY?
For the drawing tool, participants are encouraged to draw their impression of something. This is a way of helping them to express opinions and capture thoughts that can't easily be put into words. Drawings help you understand how people perceive their situation. They often contain meanings not consciously realised, and might highlight key issues or identify gaps that need to be addressed.

For the role-play tool, participants are encouraged to act out a scene about a topic of interest. You can obtain information from their acting that might not emerge using any other data-collection tool. Role-play is an interesting way to evaluate people's perception of an information product/service.

HOW?
The steps involved in using drawing and role-play range from ensuring that the target community understands what the evaluation is about, why you need information and how you want to gather it, to encouraging expression of opinions through drawing and/or role-play. The results are then analysed by discussions between the evaluators and participants.

Organising drawing and role-play assignments

Step 1: Awareness of the evaluation

Meet with the community leaders, officials and other key stakeholders, and tell them about the evaluation and what it is you're trying to do. Find a location to hold your meetings with the target group whose opinions and views you want to discover.

Step 2: Prepare the assignment

Prepare the central questions you would like to have answered. For drawing, make sure that you have paper, markers and other material that the participants can use to draw; remember that you can also use soil, sand, sticks and stones creatively. You might also want them to make collages, in which case you will also need such things as old magazines, glue and sticky tape. For role-play, you could provide the group with costumes and props they can use to act out their role.

Think about how you want to divide up the group. This division is important, because it will influence the interaction and expression within the group (e.g., in an environment where women don't speak out when men are around, you might want to separate the men from the women; or if there is a strong hierarchical culture, where a participant is not 'allowed' to enter into discussion with his/her boss, divide the group into the different sub-groups, such as local officials and resource centre managers in one group, and resource centre staff and users in another).

Step 3: Give the assignment

Provide the participants with two or three central questions that they can use and develop in a creative way. Examples of questions about an information service are: Which aspects of the service do you use? How do you use them? Would you change anything about the way they have been provided? If so, what? Then ask the participants to think about how they would draw or act out their answers to the questions.

Step 4: Implement the assignment

Let the participants know how long they have to prepare their drawing or role-play, and while they are doing this, walk around and listen to the discussions. Don't ask questions, just listen; this could provide you with valuable information. But do answer queries they might have about how to prepare for and carry out their assignment. When you think that they have had enough time to prepare, ask them to draw or act out their answers.

Step 5: Analyse the results

After each group's presentation, encourage them to explain their drawing or role-play. Then, with both the 'performing' group and the other groups who have in this case been observers, work together to identify the key issues portrayed. You can do this by asking the participants to comment on or write down the most important issues they drew/enacted; this gives them an opportunity to become more involved in the evaluation and have a say in the analysis.
You should then write down the project objectives and compare them with the issues raised by the groups; this will help to identify any gaps.

Box 3.42
Some key points in using drawing and role-play

- Meet community leaders and local officials to ensure that they support the initiative

- Use simple props; this will help make the participants feel more at ease

- Provide labels for the participants to wear, that identify them in some way (e.g., their occupation); this is a great way to encourage interaction

- Meet in small groups; this makes it more likely that all the participants will participate

- Remember that some cultures might not be entirely at ease with drama as a form of communication

- Don't try to be too specific about what should appear in drawings or role-play; these activities are about creativity, so let the participants be as creative as possible

- Don't give the impression of being an expert. Engage in discussions at the level of the participants and show understanding of their needs and environment

Box 3.43
The strengths and weaknesses of drawing and role-play

WEAKNESSES	STRENGTHS
▪ Being able to use these tools can depend on the co-operation of community leaders and members ▪ People who are too self-conscious to participate might have opinions that differ from those who do participate ▪ People might not take acting or drawing pictures seriously	▪ Drawing and role-play are tools that are simple and easy to use ▪ They don't require a lot of equipment or resources ▪ They are good for multilingual groups ▪ They tap into a range of different communication styles ▪ They can lead to creative insights and solutions

Participatory video

WHY?
Participatory video (PV) is a method which involves groups, communities and organisations shaping and creating their own films. This process is empowering, enabling groups to take action to solve their own problems and communicate their needs and ideas to decision-makers and/or other stakeholders.

Video is a good medium for collecting information from groups and disseminating it to them, mainly because of its visual impact and ability to reach a large audience. Advances in technology have made video production more accessible technically and financially (as shown by the developments in Internet broadcasting, such as YouTube and BlipTV).

Although we focus here on PV mainly as a tool to gather and document data for evaluation purposes, it can also be used for a wide range of other purposes, such as promoting awareness, advocacy, conflict resolution, decision-making, education and training.

HOW?
Creating PVs involves:

- using games and exercises to understand quickly how to produce PVs
- having facilitators guide the process, drawing on PLA (participatory learning and action) methodologies and tools
- having short videos and messages directed and filmed by the participants
- showing footage to the wider 'community'/stakeholder groups
- using a dynamic process of participant-led learning, involving 'sharing and exchange'

There are some examples of PVs on the internet.

Producing video films

Before making a video film, you should go through some general tips for each stage of the production process - pre-production, production, post-production - with the key people involved (e.g., script writer, film-maker, editor, technicians).

Pre-production

- Develop a concept (idea) for your story, preferably one provided by the primary stakeholders
- To develop the concept, ask yourself what it is you want to show, and then ask: why? where? how? who? when?
- Develop a storyboard to determine the shots you need to take. A storyboard is a plan showing the plot and main events through a sequence of drawings
- If you are preparing a video for the web, it should not be more than three minutes long

Figure 3.9
Types of shots to consider

The type of shots you could consider using include: close-ups (powerful, and appropriate for web-viewing); medium shots; wide shots (used to convey a lot of information, and seldom appropriate for web-viewing); cut-away shots (fillers - focusing on something other than the current action).

Close-up shot    Medium shot    Wide shot    Cut-away shot

Photographs reproduced unxder permission © K Batjes-Sinclair

Production

- Avoid camera movement (use a tripod where possible)
- Avoid panning (i.e., moving with an object)
- Avoid zooming as much as possible (it's better to move in than to zoom in)
- Avoid filming where there is a backlight
- Allow 10-15 seconds per shot for editing of the video
- Run the video with the tape for 20 seconds at the beginning and end of the film
- Make sure surrounding sounds are kept to a minimum; the camera microphone will pick up any noises

Post-production

The following aspects are important in the post-production process:

- **Editing:** Ensure that the primary stakeholders are involved to some extent in editing the film and that they have the final say in terms of content and messages (if you have the resources, you can use Windows Movie Maker, available on Microsoft Windows XP, for editing)

Part 3: EVALUATION TOOLS: Evaluation implementation

Figure 3.10
Using the 180 degree rule

The 180 degree rule is a basic film editing guideline stating that two characters (or other elements in the same scene) should have the same left/right relationship to each other, as illustrated here. The figure shows the axis between two characters and the 180° arc on which cameras can be positioned (right-hand side). When cutting from the arc on the right to the arc on the left, the characters switch places on the screen.

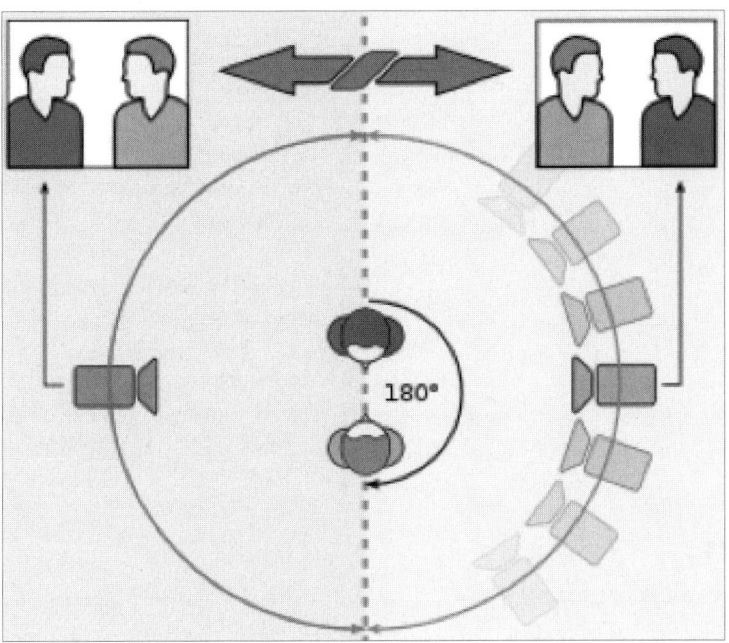

Source: http://en.wikipedia.org/wiki/180_degree_rule

- **Sound:** Make sure that there are no background noises
- **Voices:** Make sure the dialogue is clear
- **Titles:** Use titles to link the story together

Apart from showing the video in venues to which your primary stakeholders have access, you can also show it on the web (e.g., at blip.tv - http://blip.tv, YouTube - http://uk.youtube.com/ or OneWorldTV - http://tv.oneworld.net/).

Box 3.44
Some key points in producing participatory videos

- Meet community leaders, local officials and other stakeholders to ensure that they support the initiative

- Ensure that the primary stakeholders have the opportunity to express their opinions during the process and can see that these opinions are incorporated into the video content and message

- Make the process fun and energetic; this will encourage participation and make the video more appealing

- Let the process have a measure of spontaneity; don't try to pre-plan everything or give specific roles to the participants; PV has to do with creativity

Box 3.45
The strengths and weaknesses of participatory videos

WEAKNESSES	STRENGTHS
■ If not used properly, the wrong messages can be conveyed	■ PV can be used and understood by everyone, including the illiterate
	■ The equipment required is increasingly available and affordable
	■ PV encourages broad participation in the evaluation process and can be used to build consensus in communities
	■ It gives a voice and a face to those who are often not heard or seen
	■ Videos are transportable, easily replicated and easily shared, and therefore have a wide 'spread effect'

Rich pictures

WHY?
Rich pictures were developed to gather information about complex situations. They are particularly useful in illustrating the richness and complexity of a situation in which an information project operates. They allow you to get an idea of all the influences, interactions and connections among various stakeholders, offering a way of making sure nothing important gets left out of your thinking.

Rich pictures involve using cartoon-like drawings to depict ideas, connections, relationships, influences, and cause-and-effect situations. They should also reflect subjective elements such as characteristics, points of view and prejudices. While working with your primary stakeholders you should try to draw these elements from them, rather than rely on your own interpretation of the situation.

Rich pictures provide an excellent tool for group work, and are also a good way for a group to come to a broad, shared understanding of a situation.

HOW?
A rich picture is best developed in a group of between four and seven people. Pictures, text, symbols and icons should all be used to graphically depict the situation.

Developing rich pictures

To develop your rich picture, you need to:

- Get a flip chart or a large piece of brown paper (about A1 size, 594 x 841 mm). The more complex a situation, the larger the piece of paper required. If necessary, join flip chart sheets together

Figure 3.11
An example of a rich picture

Start with the physical features of the situation and the primary stakeholders. In other words, identify the people, organisations and aspects of the project that are important. Then indicate the links between these entities. Once the picture has been drawn, ask the group to write (or tell, if they are illiterate) a story about it, using numbers to link aspects of the picture to the explanations.

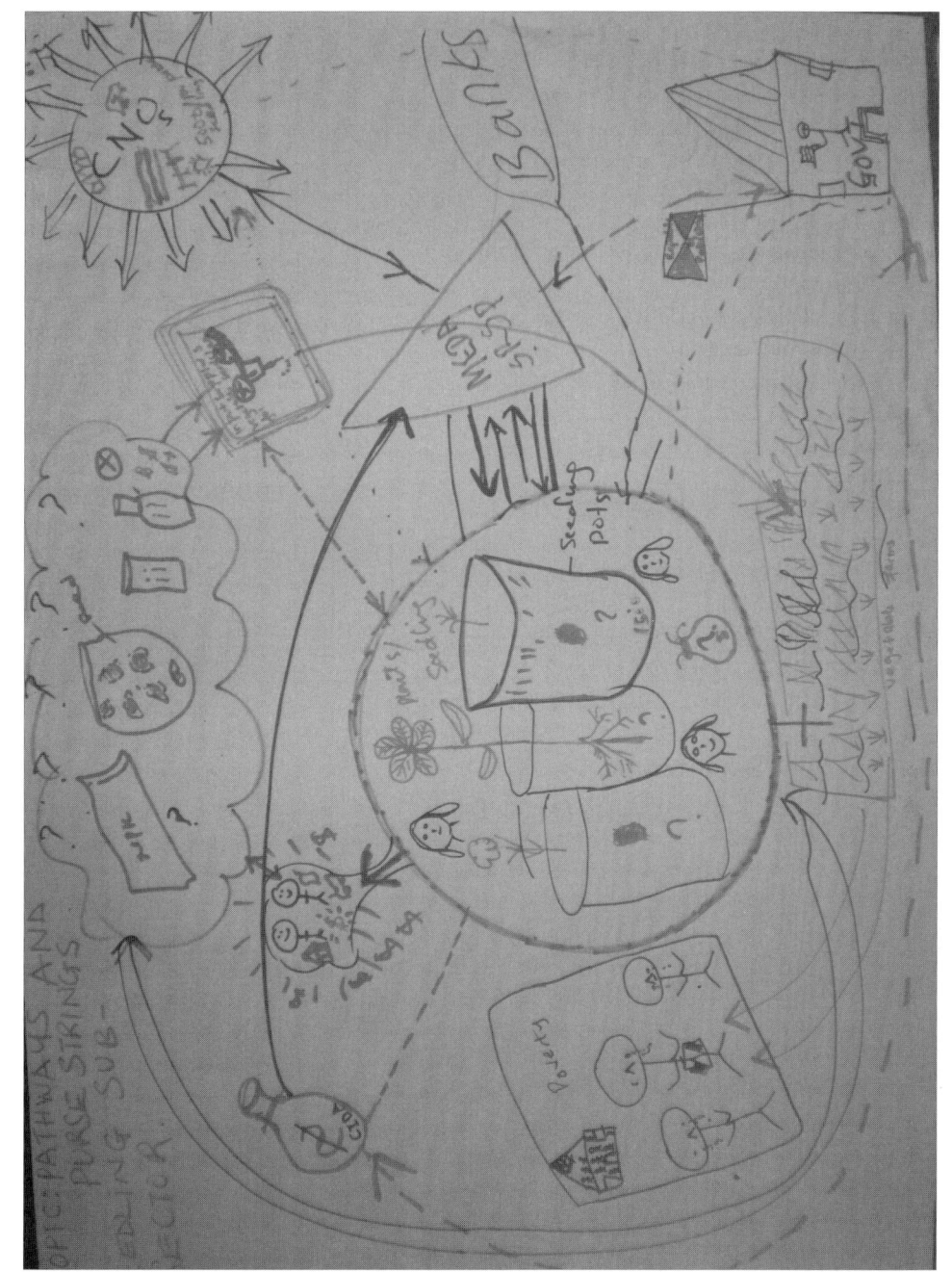

Source: Used with permission from Wageningen UR, Wageningen International

- Put the paper on a table or on a surface where everyone can easily draw on the paper. Make sure that each person has a marker (use different coloured markers)

- Decide on a topic / focus area related to the information project you are evaluating

- Encourage everyone to contribute, making it clear that not being able to draw well is not at all important

Use the following checklist as a guide for developing the rich picture:

- stakeholders
- problems and issues
- vision and opportunities
- biophysical setting
- organisations, institutions, paradigms
- infrastructure
- legal, policy and political institutions
- economic issues
- social and cultural issues

Box 3.46
Some key points in developing rich pictures

- Meet community leaders, local officials and other stakeholders to ensure that they support the initiative

- Don't conduct this exercise as an expert. Engage the stakeholders in such a way as to encourage their active participation and willingness to share their views

Box 3.47
The strengths and weaknesses of rich pictures

WEAKNESSES	STRENGTHS
Being able to conduct the rich picture exercise in a community depends on the co-operation of the community leaders and members	Very few resources are needed to develop a rich picture
People who don't readily participate might hold different and valuable opinions that the exercise will not capture	Using this technique can lead to creative insights and solutions

Venn diagrams

WHY?
Also known as a Chapati diagram, a Venn diagram is a series of circles of varying sizes that provide a map of the key institutions and individuals in a community and their importance and relationships with each other. Venn diagrams are useful for trying to understand the relationships between an

information project and other organisations that you rely on or interact with. They can be used to identify primary stakeholders and to monitor and evaluate changing relationships over time between project, stakeholders and organisations involved.

HOW?

A Venn diagram can be drawn on a large sheet of paper, a chalkboard or other types of marker boards. It is helpful to have pieces of paper (of different colours, if possible) cut into different shapes to represent the various organisations and individuals in a community. These are then taped to the diagram on the paper or chalkboard. If coloured paper is not available, the groups and individuals can be drawn on the paper with a marker. The activity can also be done on the ground using stones of different sizes to represent various groups, but in this case you will need to record it on paper for easy reference.

Constructing a Venn diagram

Ask those taking part in the exercise to identify key institutions and individuals that are important to the information project, and to describe the situation before or during the information project. Other information that you could ask for, depending on the situation, include:

- information on leadership
- relationship between institutions
- decision-making relationships
- issues of conflict

In a Venn diagram, the size of the circle indicates the relative power/influence of the project, stakeholders or organisations - the larger the circle, the more important the entity is. The distance between the circles indicates the relative strength or weakness of the working relationships between the project, stakeholders and organisations - the closer the circles are to each other, the more interaction there is. Overlapping circles represent entities interacting with each other, and a small circle within a larger circle represents a component of the entity.

Figure 3.12
Example of a Venn diagram showing the relationships between stakeholders in an information project

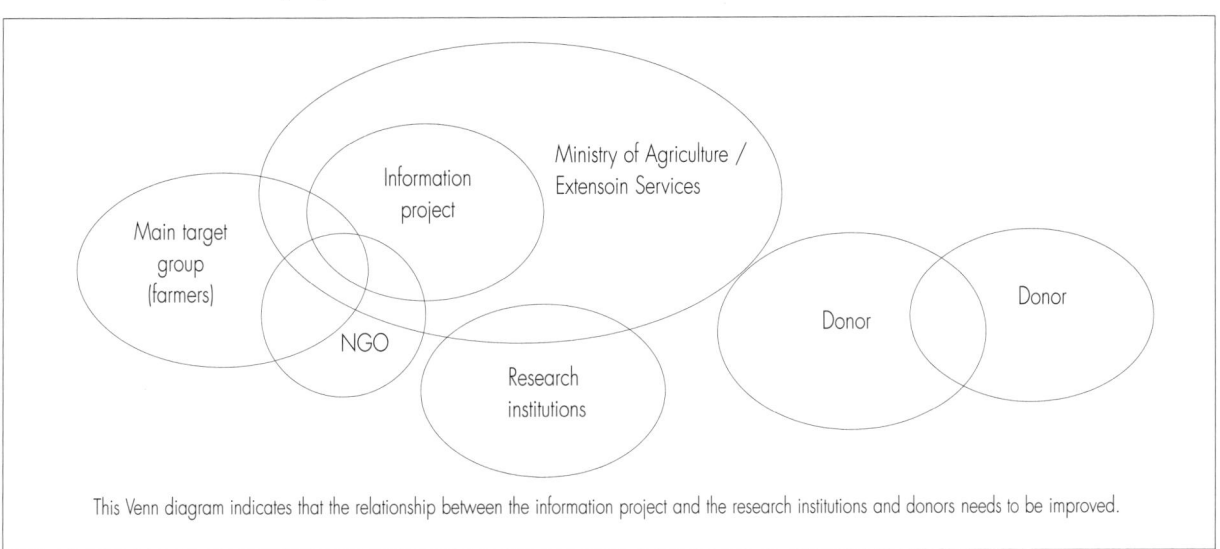

This Venn diagram indicates that the relationship between the information project and the research institutions and donors needs to be improved.

Figure 3.13
Example of a Venn diagram showing the use of pieces of paper cut into different shapes to represent the various organisations and individuals in the community

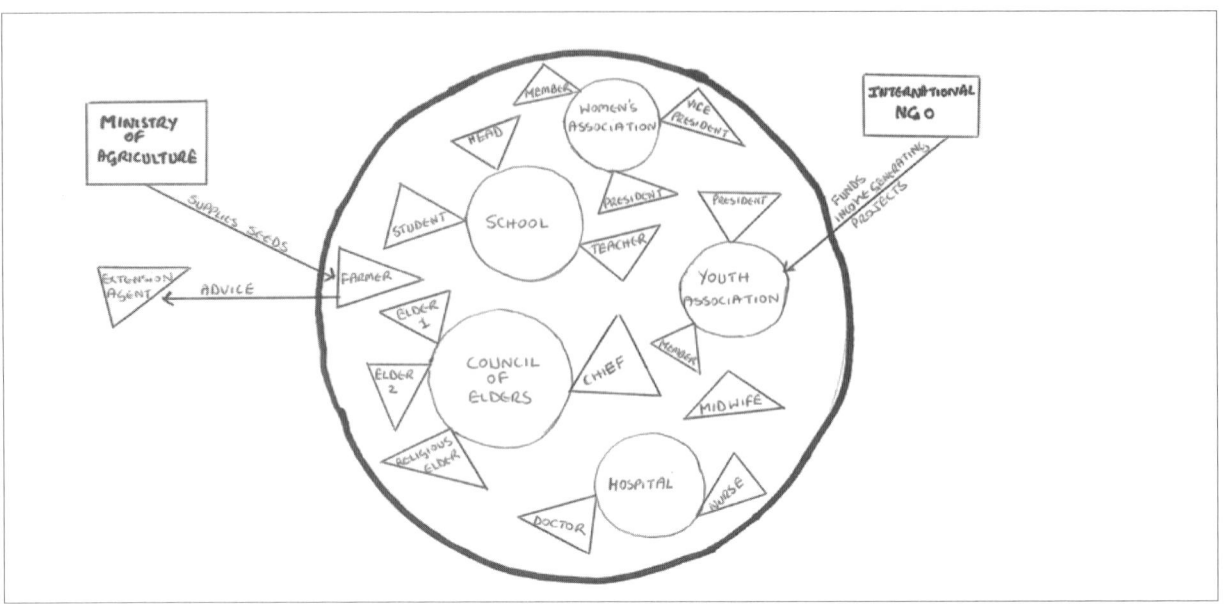

Box 3.48
Some key points in constructing Venn diagrams

- Try to make the process as participatory as possible; this will facilitate a 'buy-in' by the various stakeholders, which will help you to effect changes in the process where necessary

- Ensure that the discussions are well facilitated so that the information obtained is not biased

- Don't let individuals dominate the decision-making process in the group

Box 3.49
The strengths and weaknesses of Venn diagrams

WEAKNESSES	STRENGTHS
■ Circle size can be confused with circle proximity	■ Venn diagrams help you to see at a glance who the primary and secondary stakeholders are
■ Strategic alliances might influence the considerations of group members	■ They often provide more information about the relationships between organisations than that which can be gained from just reading documents about the organisations
■ If not well facilitated, the diagram might reflect the opinions of the dominant members of the group	
	■ They are useful in helping you to analyse and highlight conflicts among stakeholder groups
	■ They provide insight into past and current relationships, and show you where you should be moving in the future

After Action Review

After Action Review (AAR) is a simple tool that you can use to capture the lessons learned from the successes and failures of a project activity, with the main aim of improving future performance and contributing to the success of the information product/service of which the activity is a part. It is also a way of improving the evaluation process, providing an opportunity for you, management, staff and other key stakeholders to reflect on the performance of the product/service.

The review should be carried out when the stakeholders are available and memories are fresh, preferably using a facilitator to help promote discussion and draw out the lessons learned. It can be conducted almost anywhere, and will vary in length (e.g., a 15-minute review can be conducted immediately after a 1-day workshop to reflect on the event and its impact).

WHY?
AAR is a good tool to enhance learning and build trust amongst the key stakeholders. It allows you to ask questions that focus directly on activities that have taken place.

HOW?
AAR involves calling a meeting of key stakeholders to discuss a project activity and posing core questions aimed at learning how to improve the activity. Focus groups could also be used to carry out AARs.

Conducting an After Action Review

You should call an AAR meeting as soon as possible after the activity in question, inviting as many of the key stakeholders as possible. Try to create the right social climate for the meeting, one that is conducive to trust, openness and commitment to learning.

When you invite people to the meeting, you need to make clear to them that:

- the review is not a critique on the performance of the particular people, but rather a **learning event**
- everyone attending the review is an **equal participant** and should feel free to comment on the actions of all involved
- the sole purpose of the meeting is to identify ways in which the **activity could be improved**

Unless the review is intended to be very informal, you should appoint a facilitator. The main reasons for having a facilitator are to help you to create the right social climate and to enable everyone to contribute and draw out opinions.

There are three sets of core questions to be addressed:

- What was supposed to happen? What actually happened? If there were differences, why? These questions are intended to create a shared understanding within the group of the initial objectives of the evaluation and whether they were achieved.

- What worked? What didn't? Why? This set of questions focuses on generating conversations about the details of the activity.

■ What would you do differently next time? This question is intended to help identify specific, actionable recommendations (see Box 3.50). The facilitator asks the group members for clear and achievable recommendations. Arrange in advance for someone to take note of the recommendations, as well as comments that could form the basis of recommendations.

Box 3.50
Examples of specific, actionable recommendations

A comment made by the Project Leader and recorded during the AAR: 'If only we could get proper training, we could provide a better product/service.'

A poor recommendation based on this comment would be: 'More time is needed to better prepare those involved in providing the information product/service'

A good recommendation based on this comment would be: 'Train staff to provide a better quality product/service as soon as possible'

When the review is complete, write it up and circulate it to all the participants in the review, for their comments and feedback. A typical template for this is given in Table 3.18.

Table 3.18
Example of an AAR template

Name of information product/service	
Name of particular activity being reviewed	
Date of review	
Background to the activity	
Name of person(s) who called the review	
Names and roles of review participants	
Name of review facilitator	
Key words (maximum of 10) that would give an idea of the learning derived from the review	
Specific actionable recommendations	Quotations on which the recommendations were based

Box 3.51
Some key points in conducting an AAR

■ Conduct the review as soon as possible after the activity, while memories are fresh and the participants are available
■ Try to include all the key stakeholders in the meeting
■ Create a supportive and open learning environment
■ Post the sets of questions on a flip-chart or board prior to discussing them
■ Don't seek out individuals to blame for any failures in the implementation of the activity
■ Keep the meeting simple, with clear aims and a defined time frame

Box 3.52
The strengths and weaknesses of an AAR

WEAKNESSES	STRENGTHS
■ Don't under-estimate the political nature of AARs	■ AARs can be applied across a wide range of information activities, from two people conducting a 15-minute review at the end of a short workshop to a larger group of key stakeholders spending a morning reviewing a training course
■ Some people consider AARs time-wasting and ritualistic	
	■ They can provide valuable insights into the strengths and weaknesses of an activity
	■ They provide directly actionable feedback in a way that is not linked to the assessment of anyone's performance

Data analysis

Whenever you systematically observe and record variables (e.g., activities, events, people's behaviour, people's opinions), you're collecting data. Do not collect more data than you need, but make sure you have enough to meet the purpose of your evaluation. Data need to be analysed, and how you do this will depend on whether they are quantitative or qualitative, and on what questions you need to answer.

If you want to be able to see clear relationships between variables, and to generalise from this information, you need quantitative data. Think about the tables that will help to inform your decision-making. Establishing relationships between variables might require using certain statistical techniques, but more often you will not require complex statistical analysis.

If you want to understand people's perceptions and why they do what they do, you need qualitative data. Many evaluations use both kinds of data.

WHY?
You will have collected data using various tools (e.g., focus groups, interviews and questionnaires). For these data to be useful, you need to analyse them and draw conclusions that form the basis of an evaluation that can inform future decisions.

If you are clear about the boundaries of your evaluation, this will help you to maintain focus in your data collection and analysis. The steps involved in analysing quantitative and qualitative data are explained below.

HOW?
There are a series of steps involved in analysing quantitative and qualitative data; they range from reviewing and entering the data to running statistical analyses and verifying the data.

Analysing quantitative data

Step 1: Review the raw data

Reviewing the data will give you an overview of what you have. There are specific things to look for. For example, questionnaires should be checked immediately to see if they have been completed properly. If there are problems, try to recover any missing data and also think about re-training the data collector to improve future data collection. Do frequency counts of variables and look for inappropriate combinations or repetitions that might introduce bias, as well as for outliers (observations that are numerically distant from the rest of the data).

Step 2: Enter the data

Quantitative data are often analysed with the aid of a computer and a statistical software package. This entails coding up questionnaire/interview responses on the basis of a previously developed code sheet and then entering the data into the computer. Box 3.53 gives an example of this.

Box 3.53
An example of coding responses

Your questionnaire contains this open question: 'Why did you visit the resource centre today?'

You need to read through the completed questionnaires to see the responses to this question, allocating a code for each type of response and recording the codes on a sheet of paper (code sheet).

An answer 'I wanted to find out about how to raise goats' might be coded as: '1 = Seeking information about goat rearing' (because you had noticed that several people had been looking for information about goats). Another answer, 'Someone told me about it', might be coded as: '2 = Recommended by another person'. Another answer 'I was waiting for a friend' might be coded as: '3 = Other reason' if this cannot be put into another category.

Another way might be to put blue dots against all instances of seeking information about goats, and red dots against answers where there was no particular reason.

When there are only a few variables for a relatively small number of cases, it's as easy to tally by hand. For large quantities of data, particularly if you wanted to do some statistical analysis, it is quicker to enter them directly into a spreadsheet. Most statistical software has a spreadsheet available, but if you use a generic spreadsheet such as Excel it can usually be imported into the statistical software fairly easily.

When entering into a spreadsheet it is best to start at the top of the spreadsheet and you should enter the data case-by-case, using one row for each case. Each column corresponds to a response variable (e.g., reason for coming, male or female, found or did not find what they wanted). The top row should contain labels to describe the response variables. Figure 3.14 shows part of a spreadsheet of data from a telephone-administered questionnaire that was part of a newsletter evaluation. If you use Excel (or similar program) to enter the data, it is a good idea to freeze the panes so that the column labels are always visible.

Figure 3.14
An example of coded responses on a spreadsheet

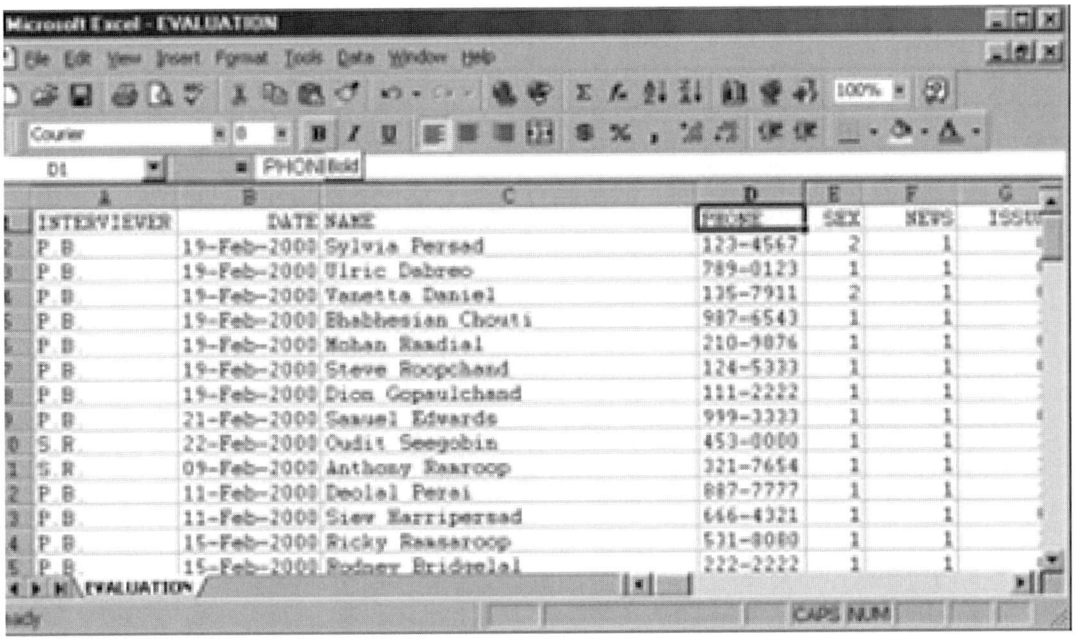
Microsoft Excel - EVALUATION

INTERVIEWER	DATE	NAME	PHONE	SEX	NEWS	ISSU
P.B.	19-Feb-2000	Sylvia Persad	123-4567	2	1	
P.B.	19-Feb-2000	Ulric Dabreo	789-0123	1	1	
P.B.	19-Feb-2000	Vanetta Daniel	135-7911	2	1	
P.B.	19-Feb-2000	Ebabbesian Chouti	987-6543	1	1	
P.B.	19-Feb-2000	Mohan Ramdial	210-9876	1	1	
P.B.	19-Feb-2000	Steve Roopchand	124-5333	1	1	
P.B.	19-Feb-2000	Dion Gopaulchand	111-2222	1	1	
P.B.	21-Feb-2000	Samuel Edwards	999-3333	1	1	
S.R.	22-Feb-2000	Oudit Seegobin	453-0000	1	1	
S.R.	09-Feb-2000	Anthony Ramroop	321-7654	1	1	
P.B.	11-Feb-2000	Deolal Persi	887-7777	1	1	
P.B.	11-Feb-2000	Siew Harripersad	646-4321	1	1	
P.B.	15-Feb-2000	Ricky Ramsaroop	531-8080	1	1	
P.B.	15-Feb-2000	Rodney Bridgelal	222-2222	1	1	

Quantitative data don't always require complex statistical analyses. All the responses should be read carefully and a summary of the responses can be entered directly into the report as a table, pie chart or bar graph showing the relative frequency of the variables in which you're interested. Figures 3.15 and 3.16 give examples of a pie chart and a bar graph.

Step 3: Import data into statistical software

If you need to analyse the data statistically, you can use statistical software packages; there are new ones coming onto the market regularly, but at time of publishing this toolkit, a popular one for analysing evaluation data was the Statistical Package for the Social Sciences, also known as SPSS).

If you use a software package, it will be necessary to define the variables so that the software can understand and label the data.

Step 4: Check the data

However much care has been taken in collecting and entering data, errors might have crept in. Check your data to eliminate the more important errors. This could involve:

- checking that all coded values are within the codes specified
- looking for outliers
- generating maximum and minimum values that are within a sensible range (e.g., no school children under 1 year old, or people 50 years old)

**Figure 3.15
An example of a pie chart**

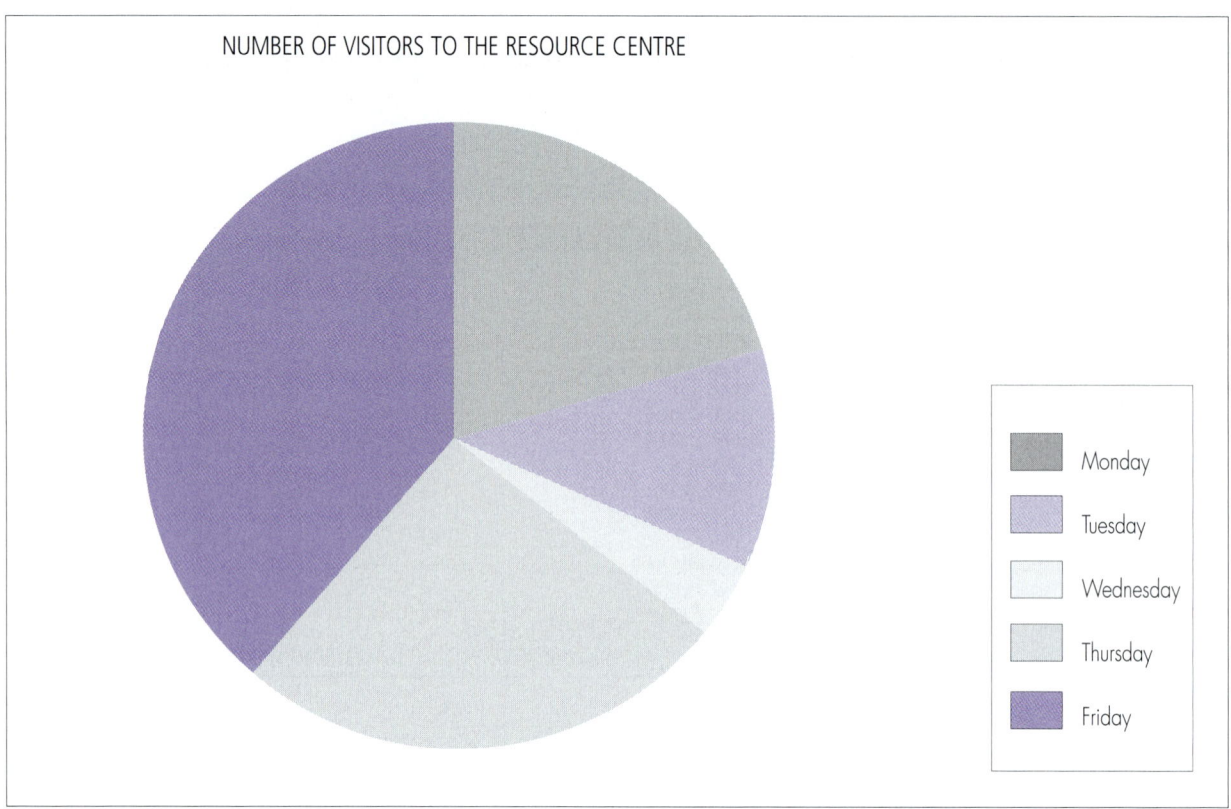

**Figure 3.16
An example of a bar graph**

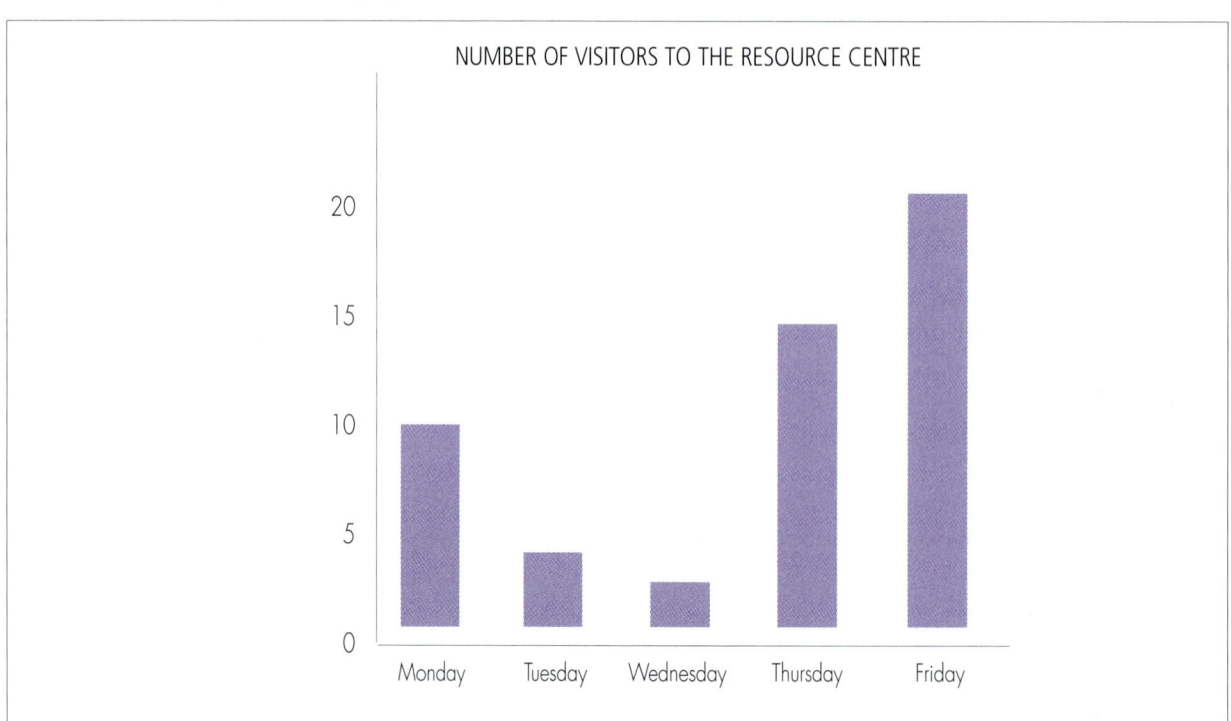

Step 5: Run statistical analyses

The main tasks in most analyses involve obtaining frequencies (finding out how often each response occurs), finding averages and compiling graphs (e.g., bar graphs and pie charts). Cross-tabulations are also useful, but make sure they relate to why you want the information. These basic statistics and graphs will provide enough information for most evaluations.

For more complex analyses you need a good grasp of statistical theory. People who undertake complex analyses, but are not aware of the many pitfalls, can draw misleading conclusions. If you need to do complex analyses, do consult a statistician when you are planning your evaluation.

Analysing qualitative data

Step 1: Review the raw data

Reviewing the data will give you an overview of what you have, and it could suggest initial themes for analysis. The analysis of qualitative data is an iterative process – as you collect data you are also starting to analyse it, and the emerging results influence subsequent data collection. In this way, data review overlaps with data entry (e.g., as interview notes are transcribed, gaps and ambiguities emerge and reveal things that need to be followed up).

Step 2: Enter the data

How the answers to questions are entered will depend on the level of detail regarded as essential for the analysis. Do you want to keep a record of people's exact words, or will a summary be enough? Always remember that the data – not the notes or transcription – are the original source. So any interpretation has to take account of what could be lost through transcription.

You also need to think how you're going to make use of your data. If it's just to get the gist of what people believe and do, then inputting notes each day under headings that reflect what you want to know will be helpful.

Step 3: Check the data

If possible, review the transcripts with the people you interviewed before finalising. Because there is a risk that the person may decide to withhold permission to use the data, you need to consider what is ethical to do, as well as how feasible it might be.

Step 4: Explore relevant themes

There are many software packages that facilitate the analysis of qualitative data, making the process more transparent and more open to team assessment. They also make qualitative data easier to retrieve.

Transcripts of audio- or video-taped interviews or meetings, and notes from observations or documents can be entered, stored and coded in the software (in much the same way as would be done for quantitative analysis). These codes form the basis for categories that can be examined to detect relationships and patterns which generate hypotheses that can be checked against the rest of the data. To check for consistency, check the original contexts of the coded fragments. Recombining fragments is facilitated by the software, and you can search for key phrases or concepts as the analysis develops. Notes about coding decisions and hypotheses generated should be date-tagged.

For relatively small amounts of qualitative data it might be more appropriate to simply sort them into, for example, themes and sub-themes. Having done that, you might notice, for example, that most complaints were linked to how services were delivered, rather than to the services themselves. You could then look at where the services were provided, and when and by whom, and might find that most cluster around a certain place, time or personnel. This might suggest a need for closer supervision and/or training.

Verifying the data

After you have collected and analysed both your quantitative and qualitative data, you need to check if the results are credible, as this has implications for the quality of the evaluation report and whether or not it is accepted. Verifying the findings involves talking to people who know about the information product/service being evaluated.

Box 3.54
Some key points in analysing data

- Make sure you have enough resources for data analysis; sometimes a lot of time and effort is spent collecting data that is never properly analysed because resources are not available

- Allow plenty of time to analyse qualitative data. Although software is available, human effort is needed to become familiar with, and understand, the data that have been collected

- Keep looking for data that contradict your assumptions, so they are fully tested. Think of and test out alternative explanations for apparent patterns emerging from the data

- Stay focused on the objectives of the evaluation

- Find a statistician who can help you, if necessary

- Don't attempt complex statistical analysis unless you know how to do it

- Don't overdo the analyses

Part 3: EVALUATION TOOLS: Applying evaluation findings

APPLYING EVALUATION FINDINGS

The main objective of an evaluation is to learn. In most cases this learning should be shared with a wider audience – colleagues, partners, donors and other relevant stakeholders. This is especially so if you want to see changes in the management and support for your information product/service and/or changes in the implementing organisation as a whole.

Your evaluation design should have included your communication strategy. Writing the evaluation report is a very important part of the strategy. You should already have decided on how you want to address the different audiences so that the results can be used in a meaningful way. You might have decided, for example, to produce a comprehensive evaluation report for your organisation, partners and donors, but a shorter one for other audiences. Whatever strategy you take, if the report is received seriously and appropriate action taken, it can lead to an improvement in resources you need to manage the information product/service better.

This section will help you to address these matters. It shows you how to present the evaluation results, disseminate the findings to the stakeholders, and use the findings for decision-making and management of current and future information products/services. It covers:

- writing and disseminating the evaluation report (how to structure and write the report)
- using the evaluation results (how to promote utilisation of the results)
- translating findings into action (how to apply what you have learned from the evaluation to your project and organisation)

Writing and disseminating an evaluation report

The focus here is on helping you to write and disseminate your evaluation report. The report should convey the main messages of the evaluation, taking into account:

- the different audiences
- the (possibly) sensitive nature of some of the information
- the languages and different levels of comprehension of the audiences
- the need to translate the recommendations into action

WHY?
Writing an evaluation report is done mainly to encourage the results to be used (and so it should be timely) and to provide resource material for other evaluations. The report is also important for learning, capacity building, sustainability and accountability purposes.

HOW?
Writing the report requires being clear about who you are writing it for, what and what not to include in it, how to structure it and what format the final product should take. Once written, you should then obtain feedback from colleagues and other stakeholders before sending it to your target audiences.

Writing the report

There are several points to keep in mind when you're preparing to write an evaluation report:

- the report should be coherent, cohesive, concise and objective, and you should be clear about your target audience (see Box 3.55)

- it should be well structured, building logically from the opening summary through to the conclusions and recommendations; pay attention to the style and layout of the report so that the reader will find it easy to follow (see Box 3.56)

- keep to the scope and terms of reference of the evaluation; not all the data gathered should be used in the report (see Box 3.57)

- the issues covered in the evaluation terms of reference should be covered in the report, and the quantity, quality and variety of the evidence given should support the recommendations (integrate your data into the report to support the points you make)

- although some information can be omitted from a report because of its sensitive nature (e.g., for ethical, commercial or political reasons), ensure that you include enough to explain the recommendations

Box 3.55
Possible target audiences for an evaluation report

- Management of the implementing organisation (decision-makers)
- Project management and team
- Users of the information product/service
- Partners and other linked organisations
- Funding agencies
- Research and development organisations
- Government bodies
- NGOs

The report content

The content of the report is dictated by your decisions on whom the report is for. You need to pay special attention to the sections that people are most likely to read: the executive summary; the lessons learned; and the conclusions and recommendations.

The executive summary should contain the main reasons for writing the report, and the main findings, conclusions and recommendations (see Box 3.58). The findings, conclusions and recommendations can be written in bullet-point form, to make them easier to read and absorb. In many cases this will be the only part of the report read by key decision-makers so take some care with this.

The main points to keep in mind when you're writing the report are:

- think about the main message you want to get across

- write the report objectively, not with the aim of persuading the readers to think in a particular way

Part 3: EVALUATION TOOLS: Applying evaluation findings

Box 3.56
Structure of an evaluation report

Title page (with names of the authors, the date, and the publisher)

Acknowledgements

Table of contents

Executive summary

Main report
- Introduction (purpose and context of the evaluation)
- Evaluation methodology
- Evaluation findings
- Main conclusions and recommendations (cross-referenced to the annexes, where appropriate)
- Lessons learned

Annexes (should contain relevant background material, such as an outline of the information product/service in question; the evaluation terms of reference, team and timetable; names of people interviewed, list of documents/organisations consulted; and detailed results cross-referenced to the conclusions and recommendations in the main report)

Acronyms and abbreviations

Box 3.57
Using information not in the evaluation report

Sometimes, as part of an evaluation exercise, the people involved in the evaluation might be asked to highlight their main findings or impressions; although some of the information gathered could be important, it might not fall within the scope of the evaluation. One way of ensuring that this information is not lost is to prepare an aide memoire.

You might also come across information that can't be included in the report because it's too sensitive but it does call for some action (e.g., information about misconduct, such as the misuse of resources). Try to find ways to deal with it, such as briefing your manager or highlighting your concerns in a confidential report.

Box 3.58
Structure of the executive summary

- One or two opening paragraphs on the rationale for the evaluation
- A paragraph on the main objectives of the evaluation
- Two or three paragraphs on the methods used to conduct the evaluation
- One or two paragraphs on the problems encountered during the evaluation
- List of the main findings of the evaluation
- List of the main conclusions and recommendations
- List of lessons learned
- A concluding paragraph

- ensure that its tone suits the audience and the purpose of the evaluation (e.g., was the evaluation for learning purposes, or for accountability purposes?)

- be aware of the expectations of your audience; readers will expect to find sound analyses backed by data and/or qualitative observations

- use diagrams, figures or tables in a report to illustrate points more clearly, and use quotes or testimonials from stakeholders to support points being made

- state the findings clearly and link them to the stated objectives of the evaluation

- if some of the terms of reference for the evaluation changed during the course of the evaluation, explain why this has happened

- present the main conclusions and recommendations in a way that is easy to read (e.g., using bullet points, using subheadings)

- keep the main report as short as possible, using the annexes for the relevant back-up data

- complete the report in a timely way so that the recommendations can inform plans

Disseminating the report

When you have written the report, send the draft to some of the key stakeholders (e.g., project management and team, and partner organisations) to check the accuracy of the information reported. Specify a time limit for them to send their comments back to you. Be aware that some people you're sending the draft to might think the report reflects unfavourably on them, and take this into account when they provide feedback.

Table 3.19
Presenting the evaluation findings to various audiences

FORMAT	DECISION-MAKERS	MANAGERS	OTHER STAKEHOLDERS*
Published report		■	
Meeting		■	
Confidential note	■	■	
Aide memoire	■	■	
Back-to-office report	■	■	
Presentation	■	■	
Annual report	■	■	
Newsletter			■
Brochure			■
Press release			■
Drama/storytelling			■

* For example, representatives of primary stakeholders, and organisations implementing similar projects

The results need to be presented and disseminated to the various target audiences (Box 3.55). You need to communicate effectively and appropriately with each audience, choosing between providing written, oral and visual presentations (see Table 3.19).

Different elements of the report can be sent to different audiences, taking into consideration the possible sensitive nature of some of the data as well as the interests of the stakeholders. A management summary can be used for wide dissemination.

> **Box 3.59**
> **Some key points in writing and disseminating an evaluation report**
>
> - At the outset, remember to allocate the resources needed for writing and disseminating the report
> - Ensure your report covers only those aspects that relate to the evaluation scope and terms of reference
> - Write in as concise, coherent, clear and objective a way as you can
> - Be aware that compiling and writing the report can take some time (often longer than data collection and analysis)
> - Send the draft report for restricted circulation, to give key stakeholders the opportunity to comment on it and correct any inaccuracies
> - Ensure the draft report is labelled as 'draft' on every page, and indicate that it is not to be copied and circulated
> - Avoid introducing any bias into your findings
> - Don't include sensitive information in the report; include this in a confidential report or brief to your manager

Promoting the use of evaluation findings

Your evaluation findings might indicate changes that need to be made to improve the information product/service. To make these changes requires the co-operation of management, colleagues and other key stakeholders, and this might require some negotiating skills.

The development of a strategy for using the findings of an evaluation is essential. The evaluation itself will not meet its objectives if the findings are not used, the stakeholders will see the whole exercise as a waste of money and time (with negative implications for their future involvement), and the project itself is likely to suffer. Yet it is fairly common for evaluation findings and recommendations to be presented – and then put away and forgotten.

Here we look at promoting the use of evaluation findings among the various stakeholders, seeking their endorsement for translating the findings into action. Underpinning this effort will be a strategy for using the findings.

WHY?
The benefits of using evaluation findings include new knowledge, new skills, new directions and a positive change in attitudes. Timely action can help an organisation improve the efficiency of operations and use of resources. Your strategy for promoting the use of the findings will help to:

- ensure that findings are used in a timely and organised way, without duplication
- show stakeholders that the process is credible, transparent and accessible
- ensure accountability to stakeholders
- enhance the learning to be derived from using evaluation findings
- provide a basis for agreeing on priorities and follow-up actions.

HOW?

The first task is to highlight the importance of using the findings of your evaluation. You also need to ensure that the resources are there for implementing the recommendations that arise from the findings and for encouraging the organisation to integrate the knowledge gained into its general follow-up procedures.

Developing the strategy

The main elements of the strategy should be: promoting acceptance of the evaluation findings, reacting to findings as they arise, disseminating the findings, proposing follow-up actions and getting agreement on them.

Promoting acceptance of the evaluation

If key stakeholders are kept informed from the outset about the evaluation and its progress, they are more likely to be receptive to its conclusions. Try to encourage their commitment to the process all along the way. They need to understand how you conducted the evaluation so they are not sceptical about the results.

The relevance of the report is very important. The report should address the current needs of the information product/service and its target audience. You must know what the target audiences want to know from evaluations, how they will use the information, and how feedback systems can respond better to those demands.

Reacting to evaluation findings

During the evaluation period, react to some of the findings as they arise. For example, if most people on a newsletter subscription list are no longer associated with the institutions that receive it, there is no reason to wait until the end of the evaluation review process before addressing this. At the same time ensure that you do not over-react to some of the interim findings of the report.

Disseminating evaluation findings

You need to make sure that the findings, main conclusions and recommendations emanating from the evaluation are sent to the 'right' audiences.

Timeliness is also essential. Findings that arrive long after an evaluation has ended are less likely to be noticed, let alone acted upon. To ensure timeliness, make the main findings available to the key stakeholders as soon as possible. You could do this by producing a summary of the key points, not more than 2-3 pages long.

Producing a discussion note

Produce a discussion note that puts forward ideas for follow-up action. It should address issues raised in the report, and an attempt should be made to identify and classify the main follow-up actions.

If, when you're writing the evaluation report, some of the findings appear to be incorrect or questionable, you should also raise these in the discussion note so that they can be clarified.

Agreeing on follow-up actions

Assess the stakeholders in terms of those who might be opposed to, or critical of, the evaluation and its findings. If there is strong resistance to the findings, there is very little chance that the recommendations as set out will be adopted. However, depending on your discussions (and negotiating skills), it might be possible to come up with modified recommendations.

The discussion note should be discussed with the key stakeholders in a meeting where the issues can be debated and discussed, with the aim of drawing up an action plan. The plan should be realistic and should include a schedule of priorities, actions, names of people responsible for each action, deadlines, and subsequent action points (such as further analysis/review of specific aspects of the project).

> **Box 3.60**
> **Some key points in promoting the use of evaluation findings**
>
> - Make sure that everyone involved understands the purpose of the evaluation
>
> - Be aware that the way the evaluation report is written and how the messages are conveyed can be misinterpreted
>
> - Involve all the key stakeholders in the process so as to promote acceptance of the findings and stimulate commitment to follow them up
>
> - Prioritise the areas that need to be addressed immediately
>
> - Try to develop an open culture where it is easier to address issues raised in the findings
>
> - Don't spend time trying to patch up the report where some findings are contentious but can't be checked; just agree on what needs to be done about those particular issues

Translating evaluation findings into action

The focus here is on helping you to implement the recommendations arising from evaluation findings. This involves drawing on the ideas of your colleagues and other key stakeholders and offers a systematic framework for addressing areas of concern and building on areas of strength. We look particularly at how to incorporate the evaluation findings into future activities.

The main aim of following up the evaluation findings is to address problems that the evaluation has identified. This task will involve looking at how your strategy and action plan can be modified to improve the impact of the information product/service that was evaluated.

WHY?
The reasons for transforming learning into action include:

- putting in place a system focusing on considering the findings of the evaluation and ensuring they are acted upon
- ensuring that learning takes place within the organisation
- providing a mechanism that involves staff and other key stakeholders in the learning process

HOW?
There are two tools you could use to translate findings into action. One is known as 'force-field analysis' and the other as 'brainstorming'. Force-field analysis was developed by Kurt Lewin, (1943) who believed that situations are maintained by dynamically balanced patterns of forces; when problems arise, it is necessary to modify this balance so that the situation changes itself in the right direction.

Brainstorming was described by Alex Osborn (1953), as '…a conference technique by which a group attempts to find a solution for a specific problem by amassing all the ideas spontaneously by its members, based on a set of rules'. Some basic rules that apply to productive brainstorming are: don't criticise ideas put forward; build on each other's ideas; and do encourage wild and exaggerated ideas.

Force-field analysis

Force-field analysis helps you to define the problems clearly so you can create action plans for strategies and become more productive. You look for what the evaluation found that:

- encourages you to change the direction you would like to go (helping forces)
- constrains you from change (hindering forces)

You need to have a meeting with your colleagues and other key stakeholders (as appropriate) to identify and list helpful and hindering forces. This involves:

- preparing a complete but short problem statement
- developing a solution objective (what you hope to achieve)
- identifying all possible forces that affect the problem (e.g., apathy, poor facilities)
- selecting the ones you think are most relevant to your product/service

A good idea is to draw the forces, as shown in Figure 3.17. Use arrows to indicate the strength of the different forces and group them into the helping and hindering forces.

You then need to consider how you could change the hindering forces. An example of changing a hindering force could be to foster staff morale by offering them more training opportunities. You then develop an action plan and assign responsibility for the different activities to be implemented to change these hindering forces.

**Figure 3.17
Illustrating force-field analysis**

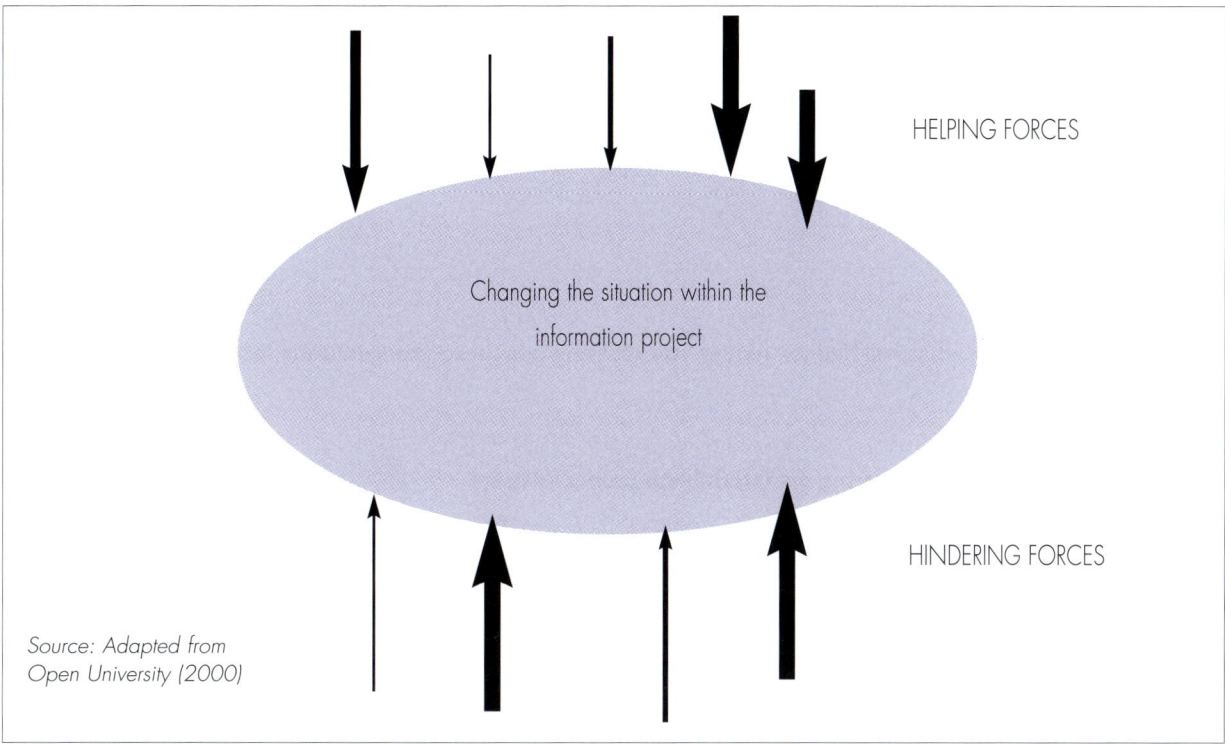

Source: Adapted from Open University (2000)

Brainstorming

Whereas force-field analysis helps you to define the problems clearly so you can create action plans for strategies and become more productive, brainstorming is used to generate ideas. It involves presenting a problem or situation to a group and asking them to come up with as many solutions as possible, without judging them. A good brainstorming session encourages ideas, no matter how silly some of these may seem.

During the brainstorming session you will need to:

- focus on the problems to be addressed, as well as the strengths of the information product/service and the implementing organisation
- be non-judgemental
- be as imaginative as possible
- write down all the ideas that are put forward

Once all the ideas have been written down, the group can start sorting them out. Depending on the situation, they can be clustered into similar areas, given priorities, or tested by asking questions about issues raised and exploring them further (e.g., 'Why didn't the newsletter develop according to plan?').

Applying the force-field analysis and brainstorming tools

You have just completed your evaluation of an information product/service and there is a list of areas that need addressing. Write down three to five areas you need to look at and want to change using a table such as Table 3.20.

Table 3.20
Areas of the information product/service that need to be changed

1	
2	
3	
4	
5	

Now identify what will help or hinder you carrying out these changes, using Table 3.21.

Table 3.21
Forces helping or hindering the information product/service

HELPING (+)	HINDERING (-)

You will now have to consider what can be addressed and who will do it (e.g., Your organisation? Or will you need to get funding in place, or skills training?)

Table 3.22
Identifying the forces that can be addressed

HELPING (+)	HINDERING (-)	WHAT CAN YOU DO ABOUT IT?

Now think about how you will address what needs to be done, and draw up an action plan. Allocate the responsibilities for carrying out the various activities in the action plan, as shown in Table 3.23.

Table 3.23
An action plan template

THINGS TO DO	PERSON RESPONSIBLE

Box 3.61
Some key points in translating evaluation findings into action

- Appoint a group leader or bring in a good facilitator

- Ensure that the climate for discussions is open and relaxed

- Ensure that discussions focus on problem-solving and not on fault-finding

- Don't use the exercise to apportion blame

- Write down all ideas that emerge during the brainstorming session

Box 3.62
The strengths and weaknesses of force-field analysis and brainstorming

WEAKNESSES	STRENGTHS
▪ There might be serious constraints to these tools, such as low morale	▪ Force-field analysis provides a framework for addressing complex problems
▪ There might be too much reliance on the subjective impressions of the people identifying the helping and hindering forces, and not enough on objective factors	▪ Brainstorming is a familiar and well-established technique
	▪ Brainstorming encourages radical or different ideas to emerge
▪ Excluding factors outside the control of those involved in brainstorming might lead to acceptance of something that might be at the root of one or more problems	▪ Brainstorming is easy to use and requires few resources
▪ There can be a tendency to devote too little time to these tools and not to follow them up	

Part 4
EVALUATION GUIDELINES

Introduction

Training course

Newsletter

Website

Question-and-answer service

Small library / resource centre

Online community

Rural radio

Database

Selective dissemination of information service

This Part features case studies of evaluations of selected information projects, products and services. The information activities covered are:

- Training course
- Newsletter
- Website
- Question-and-answer service
- Small library / resource centre
- Online community
- Rural radio
- Database
- Selective dissemination of information service

In each case we describe the activity and its concept and objectives, and look at how to prepare, implement and report an evaluation of the activity.

We include guidelines on compiling logical frameworks and logic models, determining stakeholder participation in the evaluation, defining the evaluation focus and indicators, collecting and analysing data, and communicating the evaluation results.

TRAINING COURSE

> These guidelines relate to evaluating a training course, using the terms of reference (see Part 3, pages 99-103) as the basis of the evaluation and drawing on examples where appropriate.
>
> It is important to make the evaluation process as participatory as possible, involving colleagues and key stakeholders from the outset, including your primary stakeholders (see Part 1, pages 3-5). By doing this, you will find the experience more rewarding and more likely to result in a general acceptance of the evaluation findings, making it much easier to implement change.
>
> The notion of 'critical reflection' is discussed towards the end of the guidelines, but we advise you and your evaluation team to 'reflect' on the main findings and problems at each stage of the evaluation process, for learning purposes and to improve the way you conduct the evaluation. (See Part 1, pages 5-6).
>
> The background to the evaluation process in general – concepts, context, terms, trends and core ingredients – is described in Part 2. Do read that section if you are not familiar with certain concepts or terms that occur in these guidelines. And in Part 3 you will find more on the evaluation tools described here.

Before evaluating a training course, you need to be clear about:

- what the training course is about
- its concept(s) and objectives
- who the primary and secondary stakeholders are
- how to go about identifying the needs of the primary and secondary stakeholders
- what the focus of the evaluation is, the questions to ask and the indicators to use
- how to collect the data and analyse them
- how to communicate with your key stakeholders, to critically reflect upon the evaluation results and to report the results in such a way that they will be accepted and acted upon

What is a training course?

A training course is a single event or process that is designed to improve the participants' skills, knowledge and/or attitudes. It can be a workshop, a course lasting a few hours, or one ranging from several days to several weeks. It can also consist of a series of training events spread out over time. It could be a face-to-face or online activity.

Whether the course is a one-off event or a series of events on the same subject, the main focus of any evaluation will be on learning lessons for the organisation of future courses and how they can be improved.

Determining the course concept and objectives

You can't evaluate the training course unless you are clear what it is about. The concept (idea) behind the course and the objectives it seeks to achieve need to be clearly stated, otherwise you can't compare its actual performance with its intended performance. Also, without a clear concept it is difficult to make the right choices during the evaluation process.

In determining the concept of the training course, you should ask these questions:

- Why was the training course developed?
- What were the main objectives (expected results) and problems to be addressed at the time?
- What is the goal of the training course?
- What is the purpose of the training course?
- What are the core values of the training course?
- Who are the targeted trainees?

In evaluating the course, you need to ask yourself key questions related to the concept, such as:

- Do the expected results achieved reflect its core values and approach?
- Do they reflect the project purpose and contribute to the goal?
- Does the course address the main objectives and problems it was supposed to?
- Are the correct messages being conveyed?

Box 4.1
Sample of the concept behind a training course for agricultural extension workers

Main problem: Agricultural extension officers are not effective enough because they use a top-down approach in transferring knowledge to farmers. Experiences in other countries show that a more participatory approach leads to better results in which farmers are better able to apply the lessons learnt.

Target group: The targeted participants are agricultural extension officers from both government and non-governmental organisations.

Goal: To contribute to improved agricultural extension services.

Purpose: Effectiveness and efficiency of extension officers increased.

Expected results: Extension officers trained in participatory techniques for assisting farmers. (A specific challenge is to overcome the attitude of extension officers seeing themselves as 'the experts' telling farmers what to do, rather than seeing farmers as partners solving the problem together).

Main approach: A participatory training approach is used to develop the training skills of the extension officers. The course uses the practical situations in which the participants find themselves.

Core values: Relevance, effectiveness, usabilty, impact

The logical framework is a useful tool that can help you clarify the training course objectives (see Part 3, pages 68-83). Commonly known as the 'logframe', it helps to summarise a project in a logical sequence. If a project plan does not have a logframe, it is useful to construct one so that you have a good idea of your objectives and the consequent hierarchy of activities. An example of a logframe for a training course is given in Table 4.1

If the training course is not seen as a project, but as an ongoing activity, the logic model (see Part 3, pages 103-105) might be the more appropriate tool to use. It gives an overview of activities associated with the course, the resources used, the outputs/results, the outcomes/effects and the impact.

An example of a logic model applied to a training course is given in Table 4.2.

Table 4.1
Logical framework for a training course for extension officers

	INTERVENTION LOGIC	OBJECTIVELY VERIFIABLE INDICATORS	MEANS OF VERIFICATION	ASSUMPTIONS
GOAL	To contribute to improved agricultural extension services			
COURSE PURPOSE	The effectiveness and efficiency of extension officers increased	After 2 years, 70 extension officers apply participatory techniques	Follow-up reports Survey	Applying participatory techniques contributes to improved farm practices
EXPECTED RESULTS	1. Awareness created among participants 2. Training programme and materials developed 3. Extension officers trained	Feedback from participants saying they are aware of the need to change their approach Programme and materials used for the training In 2 years time 100 extension officers trained	Participants are able to give examples of improved techniques Archives: documentation on training materials No. of extension officers trained	Extension officers willing to apply new techniques
ACTIVITIES	1.1 Identify examples of similar courses 1.2 Organise meeting with extension officers to identify needs and interest 1.3 Organise an exchange visit to extension staff elsewhere 2.1 Identify priority subjects 2.2 Identify resource persons 2.3 Develop training material and exercises material for each subject 3.1 Organise a pilot training course 3.2 Improve the training course 3.3 Run the course on a regular basis 3.4 Organise follow up	(sometimes a summary of resources/means is provided in this box)	(sometimes a summary of costs/budget is provided in this box)	(if the activities are completed, what assumptions must hold true to deliver the expected results)
INPUTS	Project funding from donor agency; core funding from Ministry	List resources available		

Table 4.2
Logic model for a training course for extension officers

FOCUS	RESOURCES	ACTIVITIES	OUTPUTS (indicators of results)	OUTCOMES (indicators of effects)	IMPACT INDICATORS
Planning and development					
1. Training needs identification	Open-minded staff, transport, postage, photocopies. Willingness of respondents to participate	Designing and administering questionnaires and interviews. Conducting meetings. Analysing data and drawing conclusions	No. of questionnaires administered. No. of interviews conducted. No. of meetings conducted	No. of training sessions	
2. Involving stakeholders and partners	External-oriented staff, transport, Willingness of partners	Calls, visits, meetings with external partners. Developing agreements	No. of calls/visits made and meetings organised. No. of new external experts involved	No. of sessions dealt with by external trainers. No. of participants referred by partners	
3. Training programme development	Dedicated staff	Programme formulation. Session design	Training programme. Text for training brochure. Session outlines	No. of relevant sessions increased. Participant satisfaction with content increased	
4. Developing training materials	Own resources (books, reports, databases), Internet databases. Expertise / documentation of partners	Identifying and selecting information resources. Developing background material. Developing exercises	Background materials and exercises	Participants satisfied with training materials	
5. Logistical arrangements	Dedicated staff. Financial resources. Communication and copying equipment. Course venue and transport	Arrangements with venue. Support to transport arrangements /participants. Arranging for training equipment	Reservation of venue. Transport arrangements. Training material ready	Level of satisfaction with venue, transport and equipment increased	
6. Budgeting and financing	Capable staff. Support of management and donor agencies. Organisational guidelines. donor financial guidelines	Making a financial plan. Specifying activities. Calculating the budget	Clear financial proposal. Clear financial report	Funds available. Expenditure within budget limits. Staff and management agree on financial priorities	
Implementation/operations					
7. Promotion and invitation of participants	Motivated, skilled staff. Promotional materials (website, brochures, invitation letters). Relationship with media	Posters/brochures/invitation letters produced and distributed. Meetings organised. Websites maintained. Media informed	No. of brochures/letters distributed. No. of meetings + participants. No. of website visitors. No. of press releases	% of potential participants being aware of the service. No. of partners (experts involved) increases	Increase in number of inquiries/registrations on programme. Reduced % of questions asked outside scope of the course

Table 4.2 (continued)

FOCUS	RESOURCES	ACTIVITIES	OUTPUTS (indicators of results)	OUTCOMES (indicators of effects)	IMPACT INDICATORS
Implementation/operations					
8. Delivery of the training programme Monitoring and evaluation	Motivated, skilled staff Training venue and equipment Training materials Contracts with experts	Conducting training programme	No. of participants No. of training courses conducted No. of training sessions	% of participants following the training Percentage of participants satisfied	% of users able to name participatory techniques to help apply lessons learned % of farmers able to improve agricultural production as result of course
Monitoring and evaluation					
9. Monitoring and evaluation	Capable staff Clear procedures Adequate registration Indicators of quality, effectiveness, efficiency	Defining indicators Designing report formats Organising data collection Generating statistics and reports	Clear evaluation reports produced, per training course, 3-months, year	Improved effectiveness and efficiency of the training course	

Clarifying data needs and stakeholder participation

When preparing for an evaluation, you will need to know who your primary and secondary stakeholders are so that you can determine your data needs and involve stakeholder representatives in the evaluation. The stakeholders should be taken into account at every stage of the evaluation, from its planning and design, to being part of the team as well as sources of information, and providing feedback on the evaluation results. It will be difficult to implement the evaluation recommendations if they are not acceptable to your stakeholders.

The range of stakeholders in a training course could include:

- trainees/course participants – the primary stakeholders e.g., researchers, extension officers, community workers, staff from NGOs, local government and companies
- resource persons, including trainers
- the institution organising the course and the individuals managing it
- collaborating institutions (e.g., those providing the trainees, resource persons, research findings, case studies)
- funding agencies (financiers, donor organisations, banks, student award schemes, research institutions)
- government (providing support and, where appropriate, counterpart funding)

One way of identifying your primary and secondary stakeholders is to conduct a stakeholder analysis. It helps you to identify the key stakeholders, how they benefit from and contribute to the training course and how to include them in the evaluation. Table 4.3 provides an example of a stakeholder analysis.

Table 4.3
Stakeholder analysis for a training course for agricultural extension officers

STAKEHOLDER CATEGORY	BENEFITS FROM THE PROJECT	CONTRIBUTIONS / SACRIFICES	INFLUENCE ON THE PROJECT	POTENTIAL INVOLVEMENT IN THE EVALUATION
Trainees (extension officers)	Improved skills	Time, change of approach	Through needs assessment / evaluation	Represented on the evaluation team. Involved in analysis and decisions on actions for change An information source Informed about main findings
Managers of extension agencies	New approach to show	Time to convince staff of training needs	Sending staff for training	Being informed about and reacting to findings Represented on the team
Resource persons (including trainers)	Extra business	Time, expertise	On developing and implementing the programme	Represented on the team Involved in analysis and decisions on actions for change Valuable source of information
Collaborating agencies	Contact with and feedback from trainees	Time and resources	Through resource contribution	Being informed and reaction to findings
Managers of the training institution	New product to show to others	Time to develop concept / convince funding agency	On project concept and planning	Represented on the team Drawing up terms of reference Decisions on findings
Funding agency	Results to show to their clientele	Finance and time	On project concept and planning	Terms of reference Decision on continuing project financing

When considering the stakeholders' interests in the course, be aware of the kind of questions they would like to have answered. Table 4.4 gives an overview of the kind of key questions that might be asked. If you know your stakeholders really well, you can start the process by working with your colleagues to formulate the questions based on your knowledge of them. However, the stakeholders must become involved at some stage to ensure that you have their views. You can do this using interviews, workshops, and questionnaires with individuals or groups of stakeholders.

Defining the evaluation focus, questions and indicators

Most evaluation exercises need to be limited in focus to reflect time and budget limitations. It is not possible to cover all elements of a training course extensively every time you carry out an evaluation, so you need to choose the focus of your evaluation based on stakeholders' key questions and the time and cost of accessing data.

Choosing the focus will determine the key questions (areas) of the evaluation, taking into account its objectives (stated in the terms of reference) and the concerns of the key stakeholders. To define

Table 4.4
Key questions stakeholders could be interested in

STAKEHOLDER CATEGORY	QUESTIONS THEY ARE INTERESTED IN	POTENTIAL USE OF THE ANSWERS
Trainees (extension officers)	How effective is the new approach? How good is the training institution?	Apply to attend the course Recommend the course to others
Managers of extension agencies	How effective is the new approach? How effective is the training? How good is the training agency?	Send more extension officers Change training strategy Change training institution
Resource persons (including trainers)	How can we improve the training course?	Adjust training course
Collaborating agencies	Do we benefit enough, considering our contribution?	Reduce/increase contribution
Managers of the training institution	How effective is the training course? How effective are the trainers?	Change training strategy Change trainers
Funding agency	How effective is the training course? How effective is the training institution? How sustainable is the training course?	Improve training course Improve training institution Decide on continuing to provide funds

the focus you can use the model developed by Donald Kirkpatrick (1994), which has four levels of measurement of effectiveness and impact.

Table 4.5
Applying Kirkpatrick's model to the evaluation of a training course

LEVEL	MEASURES	WHEN / HOW TO MEASURE
4. Impact	Whether the course improved trainees' performance	Six months after the course, using impact stories and focus group discussions
3. Transfer/adoption	Whether the training resulted in a change in trainees' behaviour	A few months after the course, using questionnaires and observation
2. Learning	How much 'learning' took place	Pre- and post-course, using tests, interviews, questionnaires and focus groups
1. Satisfaction	How satisfied the trainees were about the course	At the end of the course, using a short questionnaire

To use Kirkpatrick's model, start from the bottom

4. Impact
3. Transfer/adoption
2. Learning
1. Satisfaction

The levels of 'satisfaction', 'learning' and 'transfer/adoption' can also be considered as being part of the evaluation criterion of effectiveness, each level representing an increasingly more precise measure of the effectiveness, and requiring more time-consuming data collection and more rigorous analysis. Apart from these four levels, it is also useful to consider other evaluation criteria, such as relevance, efficiency and sustainability.

Table 4.6 provides an example of focus, key questions and indicators for a training course. You can use the information here to develop a more specific set of questions relevant to the focus of the course. Using the feedback from your stakeholders and the data available to you, you will be able to determine which questions are important for your evaluation.

With reference to Table 4.6 you may want to focus on one criterion (e.g., impact) because of its importance to the continuation of the training course, or on the criteria of usability and accessibility because of their importance to the users. If accountability is the main purpose of the evaluation, you may want to limit the scope of the evaluation to the relevance, effectiveness and efficiency of the training course.

Drawing up a matrix like Table 4.6 shows how important it is to have access to good data to support your evaluation and, by extension, how important it is to maintain a good monitoring system of data relating to your training course.

Collecting the data

When you have determined your scope, focus and indicators, you will need to decide how to collect the data. It is important to develop a data collection strategy that ensures:

- that all relevant data will become available during the evaluation
- that no more data are collected than what is needed and can be analysed

Data collection methods for evaluating a training course could include the following:

- **Training needs survey:** This method would provide data on trainees and their training needs (see Box 4.2). The data would be useful for assessing the applicability of the course and defining areas of improvement, as well as for creating baseline data against which to measure the effectiveness and impact of the course.

- **Course registration:** This is an important instrument for collecting data from the trainees. These data could include name and address details, age, education and training, profession, organisation, position and course expectations.

- **Tests:** You can design an instrument to test the trainees' knowledge and skills at the end of the course. It can be either formal or informal. It can be used not only to measure their level of ability, but also to provide you with useful data, particularly if you also tested them at the start of the course.

- **Evaluation forms and group discussions:** Evaluation forms for the trainees to complete at the end of the course provide interesting data on how the course was implemented. However, they tend to measure trainee satisfaction with different aspects of the course, rather than giving precise information on learning and application. Group discussions at the end of the course can provide a better understanding of why trainees were satisfied/dissatisfied with certain issues.

**Table 4.6
Determining the focus, key questions and indicators for the evaluation of a training course, using some evaluation criteria as examples**

EVALUATION CRITERIA (SCOPE)	KEY QUESTIONS (FOCUS)	INDICATORS	STAKEHOLDER INTEREST	DATA ACCESSIBILITY
IMPACT	Has application of skills, knowledge and attitudes improved trainees' performance?	% of trainees showing improved performance	High	Low
RELEVANCE	Did the training address a major need among trainees?	% of trainees and their managers indicating that the course addressed a major need	High	Medium
ACCESSIBILITY	Were trainees able to get onto the course easily?	% trainees who experienced problems in applying, being accepted and getting time off to attend	High	High
	Were the venue and logistical arrangements satisfactory?	% of trainees satisfied with the venue and logistics	Medium	High
	Were course fees set at a reasonable level for these trainees?	% of trainees satisfied with the costs	High	High
	Was length of course adequate? (this links to ease of access; if course is too long, people might not get time off)	% of trainees satisfied with the duration of the course	Medium	High
	Was language of course one that all could readily understand and communicate in?	% of trainees happy with the language used and style of language	High	High
USABILITY	Were training materials easy to follow?	% of trainees who were able to follow materials when on the course, and after the course	High	High
EFFECTIVENESS Outputs	How many and what type of people participated?	No. of trainees trained, by category (age, education, etc.)	High	High
	How many courses were run?	No. of courses	High	High
Satisfaction	How satisfied were the trainees with the course content?	% of trainees satisfied with the course content	High	High
	Did the course meet trainees' expectations and learning needs?	% of trainees whose needs were met	High	High
	Were trainees satisfied with the training methodology?	% of trainees satisfied with the training approach	Medium	High
	How satisfied were trainees with the resource persons, including trainers?	% of trainees satisfied with skills and knowledge of resource persons	Medium	High
Learning	Did the course improve trainees' knowledge and skills?	% of trainees passing final exam or test	High	Medium
		% of trainees who could identify specific skills/knowledge item that they obtained	High	Medium
	Has the course changed trainees' attitudes in any way?	% of trainees demonstrating a change in attitude	High	Low
Transfer	Are trainees applying the knowledge/skills they obtained?	% of trainees saying they had applied the knowledge and skills learned	High	High
	Have trainees shared their knowledge?	% of trainees indicating knowledge sharing	High	High
EFFICIENCY	Was the training worth the time and costs (e.g., in terms of absence from work)?	% of trainees who felt the training worth the time and cost involved	High	Low
SUSTAINABILITY	Are the training institution and its financiers committed to continuing to run the course?	Willingness of managers of training institution and financing agency to continue support for course; indications in their strategic plans; budget allocations	High	High

Box 4.2
Example of conducting a training needs survey

A training institution ran a wide range of training courses. They found it useful to carry out needs surveys to determine whether their courses filled a gap and met demand. They surveyed the trainees at various stages:

- before the course took place, to see what the trainees expected from the course

- on completion of the course, to see if the trainees' expectations had been met

- after 3–6 months, to see the extent to which the trainees had been able to apply their new knowledge in practice; after several months, trainees are usually able to give a more realistic picture about the usefulness and effectiveness of the course (you need to bear in mind that to conduct a survey at this stage does require more resources)

Follow up: This can take the form of questionnaires, interviews and observations. Questionnaires can generate data on the extent to which the trainees were able to apply the knowledge and skills learned during the course in their daily work practice. Interviews (individual or group) are more time-intensive than questionnaires, and make it possible to get more detailed answers, providing insight into the application of new knowledge and skills and what is needed to improve the level of application. Observation can sometimes be done during the course, providing a very direct way of assessing the effectiveness of the course and the opportunity to correct mistakes on the spot.

Impact study: To determine the impact of training, it is not only necessary to know that trainees applied the lessons learnt, but also to assess whether there has been a positive change in their work performance. This requires defining performance indicators related to the training course (e.g., if the training includes communication skills aimed at improving the way extension officers offer advice to farmers, it would be necessary to assess whether or not farmers are more satisfied with the advice given).

Analysing the data

It is advisable to think about data analysis tools and methods before starting the data collection. This will help to ensure that the right types of data are being collected.

Table 4.8 will help you to start thinking in this way. For example, if you want to know what trainees think about the course, you should already be thinking about ways to interview them, individually or in groups.

In designing the data analysis for a training course evaluation, you should ask the following questions:

- Which analytical tools should be used? (e.g., a table featuring the type of questions versus the type of trainees, a graph showing development of trainees over time, or specific analytical tools such as a problem tree or a SWOT analysis)
- Which collection methods will provide the necessary data for each of the tools?
- What type of observations do you expect to make for each tool?
- What type of conclusions do you expect to reach using these tools?

Table 4.7
Example of data collection methods for evaluating a training course

DATA COLLECTION METHOD	INFORMATION SOURCE	KEY ISSUES / QUESTIONS	ANSWERS EXPECTED AND CONCERNS
Desk study	Registration forms/course reports	No. and background of trainees No. of training sessions Trainee satisfaction with the course, materials, methodology, resource persons, timing, venue and logistics Did the training course meet trainees' expectations and learning needs? Were there any topics that should have been included but were not? Were the course fees set at a reasonable level? Did the course improve trainees' knowledge? Did the course improve their skills? Has the course changed their behaviour and/or opinions ?	No., age, education, experience Very satisfied – very dissatisfied Fully, partly, not at all Topics and how often mentioned Very reasonable – unreasonable Very much – not at all Very much – not at all Very much – not at all
	Accounts department	What is the cost per trainee?	Average per participant
	Similar case studies (internet)	What alternative approaches to the training course are there?	Compare with on-the-job training
	Project documents	What were the original objectives and indicators?	Potential deviations and different insights
Questionnaire	Follow up questionnaire to all participants	Are trainees using the skills obtained? Has the course changed trainees' opinions? Do they see improvement of their performance? Have they applied their new skills to change their project or organisation? Have they trained other people in the new skills?	Ways trainees use the skills Hindrances encountered Suggestions
Interviews	Randomly selected trainees	Are the trainees using the skills obtained? Has the course changed their behaviour and/or opinions? Do they see an improvement in their performance? Have they applied their new skills to change their project or organisation? Have they trained other people in the new skills?	Ways trainees use the skills Hindrances to applying skills Suggestions
Observations	Randomly selected trainees	Are the trainees using the skills obtained?	Type of skills used/not used and reasons
Workshop	Selected trainees	Strengths, weaknesses, opportunities and threats of extension work Contribution of present training course New training opportunities and needs	Avoid wish list Verify that needs are real needs

Once you have designed the data analysis, it is important to see if your data collection includes all elements. The results from some data collection methods (e.g., interviews) could be specifically meant for checking and/or interpreting other data. Explain why you were unable to gather certain data.

Table 4.8
Example of a data analysis design for a training course evaluation

ANALYTICAL TOOLS AND TABLES	RESULTS FROM COLLECTION METHOD USED	TYPE OF OBSERVATIONS TO MAKE	TYPE OF CONCLUSIONS TO REACH
Table 1. Information on the participants and the course (quantitative results)	Desk study	Categories of participants that are over/under-represented	Categories to give more attention to
Table 2. Participant satisfaction	Desk study Questionnaires Interviews	Elements of high and low satisfaction	Priorities for improvement
Table 3. Participant learning and application: areas of application	Questionnaires Interviews Observations	Areas of good/ weak application	Areas for improvement
Table 4. Usability of the course	Questionnaires Interviews Observations	Range of subjects covered adequately/inadequately	Areas for improvement; areas that are irrelevant
Figure 1 Participants' application: influencing factors (e.g., problem tree)	Questionnaires Interviews Observations Workshop	Hindrances to application of techniques learned	Areas for improvement
Table 5. Cost-effectiveness	Data from accounts	Costs per element of the training programme	Potential for reducing costs
Table 6. Impact stories	Interviews Observations Data extension agency	Impact examples Indication of increase/decrease in consultation	Improvement and continuation of the programme
Table 7. New training opportunities	Workshop	Strengths and weaknesses of the present training New training needs	Improvement of the programme New potential training programmes to develop and offer

Preparing a communication plan

Designing the communication plan is an important activity in the evaluation process to ensure that conclusions and recommendations from the evaluation are well understood and supported. In designing this strategy, you need to consider these issues:

- Which communication methods will suit which stakeholders, especially the primary stakeholders?

- What are the main issues to be discussed and reported, taking into consideration the communication method and target group?

An effective communication plan for critical reflection during an evaluation and reporting findings during and after the evaluation helps to create common understanding among stakeholders, providing a good basis for implementing recommendations. If your stakeholders don't accept the conclusions and recommendations resulting from the evaluation, it will be almost impossible to motivate them to make the required changes. However, if they have been included throughout the process, they are more likely to accept the conclusions.

During the process of critical reflection and reporting, you should ask:

- Do the stakeholders share the same views on the problems with the course?
- Do they have the same views on the solution(s)?
- Are they prepared to support the same solution(s)?
- What are the obstacles that will prevent them from implementing the solution(s) proposed?
- What can be done to address the obstacles they face?

There are various ways in which you can convey the results of the evaluation (e.g., providing a summary of your findings, organising a meeting, a memorandum).

If the stakeholders are properly involved in the evaluation process in terms of participation and input, then getting their agreement on the relevance, reliability and quality of the data collected, the adequacy of the analysis provided and the conclusions drawn should not be difficult. Be aware, however, that although there might be general acceptance of a proposed solution, you might not be able to implement the solution because of a lack of resources, time and/or capacity.

An important component of the communication process is to find out what difficulties the stakeholders expect and/or experience in implementing the recommendations. Where changes can be implemented without difficulty, it is advisable to implement them as quickly as possible.

Table 4.9
Example of a communication plan for reporting the findings from a training course evaluation

COMMUNICATION METHOD	STAKEHOLDERS TO REPORT TO	MAIN ISSUES TO DISCUSS / REPORT ON
Critical reflection meeting on draft report	Resource persons, extension agency, management	Adequacy of training course
Full report, including executive summary	Funding agency Training agency Extension agency	Quantitative outputs, trainee satisfaction, learning and application, Impact indication, cost-effectiveness, new or potential courses
Personal meeting	Management training agency	Report recommendations Feedback on individual trainers
Article	Professionals active in similar field of training and extension	Evaluation approach and results
Extension brochure	Farmers	Examples of new extension approach
Workshops / field days	Farmers	Feedback and discussion of findings
Training brochure	Extension officers	Training contents Effects of the training Examples of participants

Box 4.3
Evaluating a training course: guidelines checklist

These guidelines on evaluating a training course are covered above:

- Course concept and objectives
- Data needs and stakeholder participation
- Evaluation focus, questions and indicators
- Data collection
- Data analysis
- The communication plan

For more on:
- data analysis, see Part 2, page 60 and Part 3, 157-162
- data collection, see Part 2, pages 58-59 and Part 3, pages 106-115
- evaluation communication and follow-up, see Part 3, pages 163-173
- evaluation criteria (scope), see Part 2, pages 33-34
- indicators, see Part 3, pages 91-98
- logframe, see Part 3, pages 68-83
- logic model, see Part 3, pages 103-105
- stakeholder participation, see Part 1, pages 3-5
- terms of reference, see Part 2, pages 32-35

NEWSLETTER

> These guidelines relate to evaluating a newsletter, using the terms of reference (see Part 3, pages 99-103) as the basis of the evaluation and drawing on examples where appropriate.
>
> It is important to make the evaluation process as participatory as possible, involving colleagues and key stakeholders from the outset, including your primary stakeholders (see Part 1, pages 3-5). By doing this, you will find the experience more rewarding and more likely to result in a general acceptance of the evaluation findings, making it much easier to implement change.
>
> The notion of 'critical reflection' is discussed towards the end of the guidelines, but we advise you and your evaluation team to 'reflect' on the main findings and problems at each stage of the evaluation process, for learning purposes and to improve the way you conduct the evaluation. (See Part 1, pages 5-6).
>
> The background to the evaluation process in general – concepts, context, terms, trends and core ingredients – is described in Part 2. Do read that section if you're not familiar with certain concepts or terms that occur in these guidelines. And in Part 3 you will find more on the evaluation tools described here.

Before evaluating a newsletter, you need to be clear about:

- what the main elements of the newsletter are
- its concept(s) and objectives
- who the primary and secondary stakeholders are
- how to go about identifying the needs of primary and secondary stakeholders
- what the focus of the evaluation is, the questions to ask and the indicators to use
- how to collect the data and analyse them
- how to communicate with your key stakeholders, to critically reflect upon the evaluation results and to report the results in such a way that they will be accepted and acted upon

What is a newsletter?

A newsletter is a periodical publication with at least two issues per year. It usually contains news and announcements and is focused on a particular subject. Generally, it will have a limited circulation. Newsletters are often used to disseminate information and knowledge. They may be distributed by e-mail or by post. Material for newsletters can be drawn from various sources.

A newsletter usually has a defined target group. For example, the readers of a newsletter may be a professional audience of policy-makers, managers, intermediaries or a mixture of these. Other newsletters are targeted at institutions or at a more grassroots audience, such as farmers.

Determining the newsletter concept and objectives

You can't evaluate your newsletter unless you are clear what it is about. The concept (idea) behind the newsletter and the objectives it seeks to achieve need to be clearly stated, otherwise you can't compare its actual performance with its intended performance. Also, without a clear concept it is difficult to make the right choices during the evaluation process.

In determining a newsletter concept, you should ask these questions:

- Why was the newsletter launched?
- What were the main objectives (expected results) and problems at the time?
- What is the goal of the newsletter?
- What is the purpose of the newsletter?
- What are its core values?
- Who are the targeted readers?
- How have the newsletter format, language, style and content been determined, bearing in mind the target group?

In evaluating the newsletter, you need to ask yourself key questions related to the concept, such as:

- Do the expected results achieved reflect its core values and approach?
- Do they reflect the project purpose and contribute to the goal?
- Does the newsletter address the main objectives and problems it was supposed to?
- Are the correct messages being conveyed?

Box 4.4
Example of a concept behind a newsletter for farmers

Main problem: Extension officers from the Ministry of Agriculture have been using the farmers' newsletter to promote improved agricultural production techniques. The chief extension officer is interested in finding out if the newsletter is meeting the needs of the farmers, as well as determining what more needs to be done to increase its distribution.

Target group: Farmers in the region targeted.

Goal: To contribute to agricultural production and development.

Project purpose: Farmers provided with a newsletter containing appropriate, relevant and timely information.

Expected results: Improved newsletter content and format, and increased distribution and impact among farmers.

Main approach: Meet with farmers' groups and on a one-to-one basis during field visits to get feedback and promote the newsletter.

Core values: Relevance, effectiveness, impact, sustainability

The logical framework can help you clarify the newsletter objectives (see pages 68-83). Commonly known as the 'logframe', it helps to summarise a project in a logical sequence. If a project plan lacks a logframe, it is useful to construct one so that you have a good idea of your objectives and the consequent hierarchy of activities. An example of a logframe for a newsletter is given in Table 4.10.

If the newsletter is not seen as a project, but as an ongoing activity, the logic model (see pages 103-108) might be the more appropriate tool to use. It provides an overview of activities associated with the newsletter, the resources used, the outputs/results, the outcomes/effects and the impact. An example of a logic model applied to a newsletter is given in Table 4.11.

In using this framework, the key questions to see if the newsletter is meeting the stated objectives over time become evident. For example:

Table 4.10
Logical framework for a farmers' newsletter

	INTERVENTION LOGIC	OBJECTIVELY VERIFIABLE INDICATORS	MEANS OF VERIFICATION	ASSUMPTIONS
GOAL	To contribute to improved agricultural production			
NEWSLETTER PURPOSE	Newsletter on agricultural techniques for farmers developed, promoted and disseminated	After 2 years the number of readers doubles	Routine and existing records	Newsletter contributes directly to agriculture production
EXPECTED RESULTS	1. Newsletter structure and design developed 2. Improved newsletter content 3. Improved promotion and distribution of newsletter	- Feedback from readers (farmers) - Demand for newsletter increases by 100 % - Distribution of newsletter increased	- Survey - Letters to the editor - Subscription rates - Routine records showing distribution rates	The newsletter meets an important need
ACTIVITIES	1.1 Meet staff and selected stakeholders to discuss newsletter objectives, design and content; brainstorm to formulate questionnaire for feedback and strategy to obtain feedback from target group 1.2 Identify priority topics through questionnaires and meetings with key stakeholders and test newsletter design and content with target group(s) 1.3 Develop plan with stakeholders for the various issues for the year 2.1 Research to produce the articles for the newsletter in line with identified topics 2.2 Identify and liaise with contributors to the newsletter 2.3 Publish newsletter 3.1 Meet with staff and key stakeholders (publishers and extension staff) to develop promotion and distribution strategy for the newsletter 3.2 Implement strategy	(sometimes a summary of resources/means is provided in this box)	(sometimes a summary of costs/budget is provided in this box)	(if the activities are completed, what assumptions must hold true to deliver the expected results)
INPUTS	Project funding from donor agency and core funding from the Ministry of Agriculture	List resources available		

- Are readers satisfied with the newsletter?
- Does the newsletter content reflect its objectives?
- Has its readership increased?

Smart Toolkit for Evaluating Information Projects, Products and Services

Table 4.11
Logic model for a farmers' newsletter

FOCUS	RESOURCES	ACTIVITIES	OUTPUTS (indicators of results)	OUTCOMES (indicators of effects)	IMPACT INDICATORS
Planning and development					
Laying the groundwork for the newsletter	Staff, room facilities	Meeting to discuss the objectives/ ideas for the newsletter and identify key stakeholders	List of objectives/ ideas, list of initial key stakeholders	Draft newsletter concept and select which stakeholders to involve in the process	
Involving stakeholders	Time needed for representatives from the Ministry of Agriculture, key stakeholder institutions and farmers' organisations to meet. Stationery, transport, postage, fax, telephone, computer, printer	Brainstorm meetings to design newsletter and questionnaires for feedback and identify other stakeholders	Newsletter structure and design developed. Questionnaires distributed to stakeholders	Changes made to structure and design, and topics identified	
Process development	Time and willingness of staff and stakeholders to meet	Develop plan for the year for the various issues	List issues and topics to be addressed by the newsletter over the year	Operational plan for the year for the newsletter	
Funds	Funds from donor agency, Ministry of Agriculture and research institutes	Budget prepared for the preparation, publication, promotion and distribution of the newsletter	Budget. Financial report	Agreement on funds available for newsletter	
Implementation/operations					
Compiling the newsletter	Capable staff to research and produce materials for the newsletter. Key contributors from partner institutions or independent actors	Research to produce materials for the newsletter in line with feedback from questionnaires	Articles submitted for possible inclusion in the newsletter	No. of articles addressing the needs of farmers	
Publishing the newsletter	Staff to prepare newsletter for publication. Publishing skills and software	Edit, layout, typeset and publish newsletter	No. of newsletters published	Knowledge gained	% farmers changing their practices consequent on the newsletter
Promotional activities	Time of staff and key stakeholders	Meetings to develop promotion and distribution strategy	Strategy developed	% change in farmers receiving the newsletter	Increased requests for newsletters
Monitoring and evaluation					
Monitoring and evaluation	Time for staff to implement clear procedures to record routine data. Time for staff to input routine data	Determine indicators. Identify data collection methods. Design reporting formats to collect and analyse data	Development of a database to support M&E	Improved newsletter (in terms of effectiveness and efficiency) meeting farmers' needs	

Clarifying data needs and stakeholder participation

When preparing for an evaluation, you will need to know who your primary and secondary stakeholders are, so that you can determine your data needs and involve stakeholder representatives in the evaluation. The stakeholders should be taken into account at every stage of the evaluation, from its planning and design, to being part of the team as well as sources of information, and providing feedback on the evaluation results. It will be difficult to implement the evaluation recommendations if they are not acceptable to your stakeholders.

The range of stakeholders in a newsletter could include:

- demand side/primary stakeholders: individuals/institutions (paying and non-paying subscribers)
- supply-side/contributors: writers and graphic designers
- production-side: editors, printers, publishers, distributors
- resources: funding agencies and advertisers (financial), and staff (human)

The stakeholders will have a vested interest in the evaluation itself, and should be consulted and involved in some way. The input of the different groups will vary, depending on the particular situation. You should therefore take into account:

- their interests when designing the evaluation
- how they can actively contribute to the evaluation process
- how to include them as part of the evaluation team
- their role as a source of data (e.g., via questionnaires, interviews and workshops)
- their feedback on evaluation results

The users of the newsletter – the primary stakeholders – will be the people who subscribe to, read and use the newsletter, and (if applicable) the institutions they belong to. The newsletter producers need to have a clear idea who they are and who the secondary stakeholders are. One way of identifying these stakeholders is to conduct a stakeholder analysis. It helps you to identify the key stakeholders, how they benefit from and contribute to the newsletter and how to include them in the evaluation. Table 4.12 provides an example of a stakeholder analysis.

When considering the stakeholders' interests in the newsletter, be aware of the kind of questions that they would like to have answered. Table 4.13 gives an overview of the kind of key questions that might be asked. If you know your stakeholders really well, you can start the process by working with your colleagues to formulate the questions based on your knowledge of them. However, the stakeholders must become involved at some stage to ensure that you have their views. You can do this using interviews, workshops, and questionnaires with individuals or groups of stakeholders.

Defining the evaluation focus, questions and indicators

Most evaluation exercises need to be limited in focus to reflect time and budget limitations. It is not possible to cover all elements of a newsletter extensively every time you carry out an evaluation, so you need to choose the focus of your evaluation, based on stakeholders' key questions and the time and cost of accessing data.

The focus of the evaluation might stem from your desire to improve it, from low or declining circulation figures, from feedback from others or from a need to cut costs. There might be

Table 4.12
Stakeholder analysis for a newsletter for farmers

STAKEHOLDER CATEGORY	BENEFITS FROM THE PROJECT	CONTRIBUTIONS / SACRIFICES	INFLUENCE ON THE PROJECT	POTENTIAL INVOLVEMENT IN THE EVALUATION
Readers	Improved knowledge on agricultural production	Time to read newsletter Cost of newsletter	Determine newsletter content through feedback to the editor	Represented on the team Involved in analysis and decisions on actions for change An information source Informed about main findings
Contributors/ partners	Improved newsletter content Better targeted and improved distribution	Time and technical input	Newsletter content improved, stronger network of contributors/ partnership	Representation on the team Informed about main findings
Editors/staff/ management/ publishers	Improved newsletter Improved outreach Promotional effect	Time to develop newsletter and convince funding agency	Determine objectives, planning, management, implementation, and distribution of newsletter	Representation on the team, to be involved in planning the evaluation To be informed about the results
Funding agencies	Results to show to their stakeholders	Finance and time	Have input into objectives and plan, and through monitoring and evaluation	Informed about the evaluation and the results

Table 4.13
Key questions stakeholders could be interested in

STAKEHOLDER CATEGORY	QUESTIONS THEY ARE INTERESTED IN	POTENTIAL USE OF THE ANSWERS
Readers	Does the newsletter meet the needs of the readers? Is the target group aware of the newsletter? Is the newsletter timely? Is it satisfactory?	Decide whether to continue the newsletter Decide how to improve it
Contributors	Do contributors provide relevant and accurate information? Is there an incentive for the partners to promote the newsletter?	Look at ways of strengthening collaboration
Editors/staff/management/ publishers	How effective and efficient is the newsletter? (e.g., Is it meeting the needs of the readers? Are the articles well written? Is it cost-effective? Can it be produced on a sustainable basis?)	Decide whether to continue the newsletter Decide how to improve it Look at ways of reducing costs
Funding agency	Does the newsletter make a difference to the quality of lives of the readers? How sustainable is it, given the available resources? Do staff have the capacity to produce a good-quality newsletter?	Determine whether funding will be made available to produce the newsletter

concerns about the performance of the newsletter in comparison with a competitor. You might want to assess current achievements so as to determine strategies for future publications.

Other examples of areas of focus could include:

- a specific objective (e.g., providing information to extension officers)
- specific assessment criteria such as the newsletter's effectiveness and impact
- a specific problem area (e.g., distribution)
- the primary stakeholders, or stakeholders voicing problems about the newsletter
- a combination of all of these

In evaluating a newsletter, it useful to draw on the model developed by Donald Kirkpatrick (1994). You can use it to measure the effectiveness and impact of the newsletter (see Table 4.14).

Table 4.14
Applying Kirkpatrick's model to the evaluation of a newsletter

LEVEL	MEASURES	WHEN / HOW TO MEASURE
4. Impact	Has the newsletter helped to improve farming practices, etc.	A year after dissemination of the newsletter, ask whether adoptions have led to any benefits (through impact stories and focus group discussions)
3. Transfer/adoption	What practices have farmers adopted; how has the newsletter changed their behaviour	A few months later, go into the field to determine the level of adoption – use questionnaires and personal observations
2. Learning	To what extent the farmers understand the content of the newsletter and the practices it promotes	Before and after the dissemination of the newsletter, assess the situation in the field, through questionnaires, interviews, focus groups
1. Satisfaction	How satisfied the farmers are with the newsletter	After dissemination of the newsletter, interview farmers receiving the newsletter

See also Table 4.5

The levels of 'satisfaction', 'learning' and 'transfer/adoption' can also be considered as being part of the evaluation criterion of effectiveness, each level representing an increasingly more precise measure of the effectiveness, and requiring more time-consuming data collection and more rigorous analysis. Apart from these four levels, it is also useful to consider other evaluation criteria, such as relevance, efficiency and sustainability.

From Table 4.14 (under Measures), you can see how asking specific questions can help you to improve key areas of your newsletter. With each key question, you need to think about the indicators to help you answer that question. Indicators also determine the type of data you will need to collect. It is also important to consider the interests of the stakeholders and the ease of access you have to the data you require in terms of time and cost.

Table 4.15 provides an example of focus, key questions and indicators for a newsletter. You can use the information here to develop a more specific set of questions, relevant to the focus of the newsletter. Using the feedback from your stakeholders and the data available to you, you will be able to determine which questions are important for your evaluation.

Table 4.15
Determining the focus, key questions and indicators for the evaluation of a newsletter, using some evaluation criteria as examples

EVALUATION CRITERIA (SCOPE)	FOCUS	KEY QUESTIONS	INDICATORS	STAKEHOLDER INTEREST	DATA ACCESSIBILITY
IMPACT	Changed practices, policies, products at individual level	Have your attitudes or practices changed in any way?	% of readers who say that their own personal practices / policies / products have been changed by the knowledge gained from the newsletter	High	Medium
RELEVANCE	Design	Do the readers find the newsletter useful?	% of readers who find the newsletter useful % of readers who wish more topics to be included	High	Medium
USABILITY	Readability	Is the language used by the newsletter at the right level?	% of readers who feel that the use of language and style are appropriate	High	Medium
EFFECTIVENESS	User characteristics/ defining a profile of the user	Who and where are the readers of the newsletter?	% of readers in different professional groups % of readers in different age groups % of readers located in different geographical areas % of readers in terms of gender	Medium	Low
	Reach	What is the range of readership over time?	No. of persons reading each copy of the newsletter (be aware of multiple readers per copy) No. of newsletters distributed to target group No. of target group who say that they have read the newsletter	Medium	Medium
	Circulation/ distribution	How many newsletters are being distributed? Is the newsletter easily accessible in electronic and/or print form?	No. of copies circulated No. of copies printed No. of subscribers	Medium	High
	Appearance of the newsletter	Are readers satisfied with the quality of the paper/printing of the newsletter? Are readers able to share the newsletters with others?	% of readers satisfied with the paper and printing quality No. of readers who have been able to share their copy because the paper has been strong enough to hand around without disintegrating	High	Medium
	Reader satisfaction	Are the readers satisfied with the information provided in the newsletter?	% of readers satisfied with the newsletter overall % of readers who think that the newsletter is too long / too short / just right % of subscriptions cancelled	High	Medium

Table 4.15 (continued)

EVALUATION CRITERIA (SCOPE)	FOCUS	KEY QUESTIONS	INDICATORS	STAKEHOLDER INTEREST	DATA ACCESSIBILITY
EFFECTIVENESS	Learning	Did the newsletter help improve the reader's knowledge and skills?	% of readers who think that the newsletter helped improve knowledge and skills	Low	Low
	Adoption	Has the reader adopted the techniques promoted? Have they shared their knowledge	% of readers who say that they have applied knowledge and skills; % readers who say they've shared their knowledge	Low	Low
EFFICIENCY	Timeliness	Is the newsletter produced on a timely basis?	% of readers who say they receive the newsletter on a timely basis	High	Medium
	How much does it cost to produce the newsletter?	How many copiers are needed and what are the costs and the time involved to produce them?	What is the unit cost per newsletter? What is the average cost/time involved in producing the newsletter?	Medium	High
SUSTAINABILITY	To what extent can you access diverse resources to ensure sustainability of the newsletter?	Availability of funds/ human resources to produce the newsletter. Should the newsletter be continued?	Can the newsletter continue to be produced after funding from various sources is reduced or ends? Is there sufficient capacity in-house to produce the newsletter? What is the level of institutional commitment to support the newsletter? Are there competing newsletters on the market?	Medium	High

With reference to Table 4.15 you may want to focus on one criterion (e.g., impact) because of its importance to the continuation of the newsletter, or on the criterion of usability because of its importance of the readers. If accountability is the main purpose of the evaluation you may want to limit the scope of the evaluation to the relevance, effectiveness and efficiency of the newsletter.

Drawing up a matrix like Table 4.15 shows how important it is to have access to good data to support your evaluation and, by extension, how important it is to maintain a good monitoring system of data relating to your newsletter.

Collecting the data

When you have determined your scope, focus and indicators, you will need to decide how to collect the data. It is important to develop a data collection strategy that ensures that:

- all relevant data will become available during the evaluation
- no more data are collected than what is needed and can be analysed

Table 4.16 gives some guidance on which data collection tools are most appropriate to use for the indicators identified. Note that some of the tools needed for some indicators might be too expensive to use and you might have to find more creative ways to get the information you need or perhaps decide against using that particular indicator.

Many newsletter evaluations use questionnaires as their primary data collection tool. However, other tools can also be used. Below are some tips specific to a newsletter that you should take into consideration when conducting interviews, compiling routine records and analysing recent issues of the newsletter:

- **Desk study:** Analyse recent issues of the newsletter, reading each article that has been published to see if it adheres to the stated focus of the newsletter. The frequency of publication should also be reviewed, as should the timely delivery of recent issues. Recent letters to the editor could also be studied, including those letters that were not published. Many of them will give feedback that could be useful to the evaluation. But it is important to remember that letter writers do not necessarily form a typical selection of readers' opinions, so any findings from the letters to the publication should be verified, or at least treated with caution.

- **Interviews and questionnaires:** Background data such as the main objectives, core values, approach and working methods can be collected by interviewing publishers and editors. The most critical data will be provided by the target group, who will usually be interviewed or asked to complete a questionnaire.

Table 4.16
Example of data collection methods for evaluating a newsletter

DATA COLLECTION METHOD	INFORMATION SOURCE	KEY ISSUES / QUESTIONS	ANSWERS EXPECTED AND CONCERNS
Desk study	Letters to the editor; evaluation forms; subscription forms; recent issues of the newsletter	How satisfied are you with the newsletter? Is the newsletter making a difference to the users (primary stakeholders)? Is the newsletter addressing the areas it set out to do?	Level of satisfaction; Level of subscriptions and cancellations; Newsletter not making a difference in the field; Articles produced are not within the objectives of the newsletter
	Accounts department	What is the cost of producing the newsletter?	Unit cost of the newsletter is too high
Interviews	Questionnaires, focus groups (to follow up and get a better picture of target group experiences)	Can you get the newsletter easily? Is it timely? Is the newsletter useful? Is it easy to read? Are there other topics you want to see in the newsletter? Have you changed your attitude as a result of the newsletter?	Accessibility, timeliness and usefulness of the newsletter; Suggestions
Meetings	Partners/ stakeholders	How can collaboration be increased/strengthened?	Research institutes not willing to collaborate by supporting / contributing technical content

▌ **Routine and existing records:** Regardless of the scope of the evaluation, you need to be systematically collecting routine information that can be used for the general assessment of the newsletter. Routine records are an important source of data as they provide information on the how, where and when people use the newsletter. If you haven't been compiling the data on a regular basis, you should start right away.

Examples of the type of data you should be collecting include how many copies of newsletters are being produced and distributed monthly/quarterly/half-yearly/annually, and the number of subscriptions cancelled. Important sources of this type of data include: subscription forms (which give information on the readers) and evaluation forms (which give information on the reader's view on the relevance of the newsletter, etc.).

People cancelling their subscriptions comprise an interesting group to include in an evaluation. They will be able to share with you why they cancelled the subscription, which will provide you with interesting data. You can obtain these data by sending them a short questionnaire immediately on cancellation. Keep the questionnaire short. In general, these people have lost interest and loyalty, and will not want to invest a lot of time in providing you with information.

Analysing the data

It is advisable to think about data analysis tools and methods before starting the data collection. This will help to ensure that the right types of data are being collected.

You will often find that the data you've collected from your routine records, feedback and interviews is quite rich and the challenge will be to interpret the information accurately. Table 4.17 shows you some of the ways you could analyse and interpret your data.

In designing the data analysis for a newsletter evaluation, you should ask the following questions:

▌ Which analytical tools should be used? (e.g., a table featuring the type of questions versus the type of readers, a graph showing development of readers over time, or specific analytical tools such as a problem tree or a SWOT analysis)
▌ Which collection methods will provide the necessary data for each of the tools?
▌ What type of observations do you expect to make for each tool?
▌ What type of conclusions do you expect to reach using these tools?

Once you have designed the data analysis, it is important to see if your data collection includes all elements. The results from some data collection methods (e.g., interviews) could be specifically meant for checking and/or interpreting other data. Explain why you were unable to gather certain data (e.g., in some communities the interviewers were not allowed to interview the women).

Preparing a communication plan

Designing the communication plan is an important activity in the evaluation process to ensure that conclusions and recommendations from the evaluation are well understood and supported. In designing this strategy, you need to consider these issues:

▌ Which communication methods will suit which stakeholders, especially the primary stakeholders?
▌ What are the main issues to be discussed and reported, taking into consideration the communication method and target group?

Table 4.17
Example of a data analysis design for a newsletter evaluation

ANALYTICAL TOOLS AND TABLES	RESULTS FROM COLLECTION METHOD USED	TYPE OF OBSERVATIONS TO MAKE	TYPE OF CONCLUSIONS TO REACH
Table 1: Who are the readers?	Desk study, routine records	Categories of readers over/ under-represented	Categories of readers to give more attention to when collecting data
Table 2: (target group) Relevance	Desk study Questionnaires Interviews	How useful is the newsletter given the needs of the target group	Whether the newsletter is relevant or not
Table 3: Usability Readability	Desk study Questionnaires Interviews	How appropriate is the language used?	Whether the language used should change
Table 4: (target group) Effectiveness: - Reader satisfaction - Awareness - Reach - Appearance - Learning	Desk study Questionnaires Interviews Letters to the editor	- High and low satisfaction with the newsletter as a whole, content - Level of awareness of newsletter - Change in readership over time - Format appropriate - Does it promote learning?	Priorities for improvement Obstacles to improvement
Table 5: Efficiency	Data from accounts	Cost to produce the newsletter Time involved in its production	Potential areas for reducing costs/time
Graph: Process flow chart	Farmers' time / Procedures manual / Interviews	Bottlenecks in the process	Steps to improve the process
Table 6: Impact stories	In-depth interviews, case studies, feedback from correspondence	Personal stories of how lives have been affected by the newsletter Statistics showing change agricultural production, etc.	Determine whether there has been any change in the quality of life in farming communities

An effective communication plan for critical reflection during an evaluation and reporting findings during and after the evaluation helps to create common understanding among stakeholders, providing a good basis for implementing recommendations. If your stakeholders don't accept the conclusions and recommendations resulting from the evaluation, it will be almost impossible to motivate them to make the required changes. However, if they have been included throughout the process, they are more likely to accept the conclusions.

During the process of critical reflection and reporting, you should ask:

- Do the stakeholders have the same views on the problems with the newsletter?
- Do they have the same views on the solutions?
- Are they prepared to support the same solutions?
- What obstacles prevent them from implementing the solutions proposed?
- What can be done to address the obstacles they face?

There are various ways in which you can convey the results of the evaluation (e.g., providing a summary of your findings, organising a meeting, a memorandum). You might also want to consider the type of information you make available to the various target groups. The communication plan you use will depend on your circumstance and the facilities available to you. Consider sharing the results of your evaluation with your readers in the actual newsletter itself, so that if there are changes in terms of how the newsletter is managed or presented, they will not come as a surprise to the reader.

Whatever you decide, your findings and recommendations should be presented in a way that is easily understood and accepted by all so that the desired changes can be implemented (see Table 4.18).

Table 4.18
Example of a communication plan for reporting the findings from a newsletter evaluation

COMMUNICATION METHOD	STAKEHOLDERS TO REPORT TO	MAIN ISSUES TO DISCUSS / REPORT ON
SWOT analysis	Representatives of newsletter and key farmers	Critically reflecting on the results from the data collection
Brainstorming	Staff and management of the newsletter and selected stakeholders	Creative solutions to problems identified
Full report, including executive summary	Funding agency Partners Staff and management	Readers' development Readers' satisfaction Topics Costs and income Conclusions and recommendations
Personal meeting	Management	Conclusions and recommendations Feedback on individual staff members
Article in newsletter	Readers	Major findings

If the stakeholders are properly involved in the evaluation process in terms of participation and input, then getting their agreement on the relevance, reliability and quality of the data collected, the adequacy of the analysis provided and the conclusions drawn should not be difficult. Be aware, however, that although there might be general acceptance of a proposed solution, you might not be able to implement the solution fully because of a lack of resources, time and/or capacity.

An important component of the communication process is to find out what difficulties the stakeholders expect and/or experience in implementing the recommendations. Where changes can be implemented without difficulty, it is advisable to implement them as quickly as possible.

Box 4.5
Evaluating a newsletter: guidelines checklist

These guidelines on evaluating a newsletter are covered above:

- Newsletter concept and objectives
- Data needs and stakeholder participation
- Evaluation focus, questions and indicators
- Data collection
- Data analysis
- The communication plan

For more on:
- data analysis, see Part 2, page 60 and Part 3, 157-162
- data collection, see Part 2, pages 58-59 and Part 3, pages 106-115
- evaluation communication and follow-up, see Part 3, pages 163-173
- evaluation criteria (scope), see Part 2, pages 33-34
- indicators, see Part 3, pages 91-98
- logframe, see Part 3, pages 68-83
- logic model, see Part 3, pages 103-105
- stakeholder participation, see Part 1, pages 3-5
- terms of reference, see Part 2, pages 32-35

WEBSITE

> These guidelines relate to evaluating a website, using the terms of reference (see Part 3, pages 99-103) as the basis of the evaluation and drawing on examples where appropriate.
>
> It is important to make the evaluation process as participatory as possible, involving colleagues and key stakeholders from the outset, including your primary stakeholders (see Part 1, pages 3-5). By doing this, you will find the experience more rewarding and more likely to result in a general acceptance of the evaluation findings, making it much easier to implement change.
>
> The notion of 'critical reflection' is discussed towards the end of the guidelines, but we advise you and your evaluation team to 'reflect' on the main findings and problems at each stage of the evaluation process, for learning purposes and to improve the way you conduct the evaluation. (See Part 1, pages 5-6).
>
> The background to the evaluation process in general – concepts, context, terms, trends and core ingredients – is described in Part 2. Do read that section if you are not familiar with certain concepts or terms that occur in these guidelines. And in Part 3 you will find more on the evaluation tools described here.

Before evaluating a website, you need to be clear about:

- what the main elements of the website are
- its concept(s) and objectives
- who the primary and secondary stakeholders are
- how to go about identifying the needs of the primary and secondary stakeholders
- what the focus of the evaluation is, the questions to ask and the indicators to use
- how to collect the data and analyse them
- how to communicate with your key stakeholders, to critically reflect upon the evaluation results and to report the results in such a way that they will be accepted and acted upon

What is a website?

A website is a collection of online files (pages) on a particular subject that includes an opening file, the 'home page'. All websites have an address, known as a 'universal resource locator' (URL), which is their home page address.

A website can be viewed throughout the world by people with computers with very different specifications, so long as they have a working browser (e.g., Internet Explorer, Firefox or Safari). It can have multiple goals and target groups (e.g., an information site providing details of a service, organisation or company to the general public, or a retail site selling goods to particular groups, or a site that encourages the exchange of knowledge and experiences among a particular group of professionals). The goal(s) and audience(s) will determine the website content and design.

Determining the website concept and objectives

You can't evaluate your website unless you are clear what it is about. The concept (idea) behind the website and the objectives it seeks to achieve need to be clearly stated, otherwise you can't compare its actual performance with its intended performance. Also, without a clear concept it is difficult to make the right choices during the evaluation process.

In determining a website concept, you should ask these questions:

- Why was the website developed?
- What were the main objectives (expected results) and problems to be addressed at the time?
- What is the goal of the website?
- What is the purpose of the website?
- What are its core values?
- What target group(s) are you aiming for?
- How do you want to develop the website in terms of content, organisation, presentation, accessibility and technical competence, bearing in mind its target group(s)?

In evaluating the website, you need to ask yourself key questions related to the concept, such as:

- Do the expected results achieved reflect its core values and approach?
- Do they reflect the project purpose and contribute to the goal?
- Does the website address the main objectives and problems it was supposed to?
- Are the correct messages being conveyed?

Box 4.6
Example of a concept behind a soils data website

Main problem: A research institute specialising in the collection of primary world soils data wants its clients to have easy access to its database and its publications.

Target group: Researchers, scientists, planners and students.

Goal: To contribute to improved agricultural and environmental planning through the provision of relevant and appropriate information on soils of the world.

Purpose: A good source of scientific information and knowledge on world soils, allowing visitors to access and share information developed.

Expected results: Increased awareness and understanding of key issues in soils.

Main approach: To provide an interactive website where users can access information and ask soils-related questions in an easy and user-friendly way.

Core values: Relevance, accessibility, usability and effectiveness

The logical framework can help you clarify the website objectives (see page 68-83). Commonly known as the 'logframe', it helps to summarise a project in a logical sequence. If a project plan does not have a logframe, it is useful to construct one so that you have a good idea of your objectives and the consequent hierarchy of activities. An example of a logframe for a website is given in Table 4.19.

Table 4.19
Logical framework for a soils data website

	INTERVENTION LOGIC	OBJECTIVELY VERIFIABLE INDICATORS	MEANS OF VERIFICATION	ASSUMPTIONS
GOAL	To contribute to improved agricultural and environmental planning through the provision of information on soils of the world			
WEBSITE PURPOSE	A good source of scientific information and knowledge on world soils, which allows visitors to access and share information developed	After 2 years the number of visitors increases fourfold	Routine and existing records, including web statistics	Contributes to improved agriculture and environmental planning
EXPECTED RESULTS	Increased awareness and understanding of key issues in soils and use of data	Feedback from visitors on key soil issues	Interviews Letters/emails to the organisation Web statistics Contributions to the website	Is relevant Increased awareness leads to increased visits to the website
ACTIVITIES	1.1 Meet staff and selected stakeholders to discuss website objectives, design and content, brainstorm to formulate strategy to obtain feedback from target group(s) 1.2 Identify priority areas for target group(s) 1.3 Put information on the website 1.4 Develop and carry out strategy for promoting and sharing soil information with stakeholders	(sometimes a summary of resources/means is provided in this box)	(sometimes a summary of costs/budget is provided in this box)	(if the activities are completed, what assumptions must hold true to deliver the expected results)
INPUTS	Project funding from donor agencies	List resources available		

If the website is not seen as a project, but as an ongoing activity, the logic model might be the more appropriate tool to use. It provides an overview of activities associated with the course, the resources used, the outputs/results, the outcomes/effects and the impact.

An example of a logic model applied to a website is given in Table 4.20.

In using this framework, the key questions to ask to see if the website is meeting the stated objectives become evident. For example:

- Are users satisfied with the website?
- Does the website content reflect its objectives?
- Is the website easy to navigate?
- Have visits to the website increased?

Table 4.20
Logic model for a soils data website

FOCUS	RESOURCES	ACTIVITIES	OUTPUTS (indicators of results)	OUTCOMES (indicators of effects)	IMPACT INDICATORS
Planning and development					
In-house	Staff Facilities	Meeting to discuss idea behind the website and how to go about its development	List of ideas, list of key stakeholders	Concept for website developed, who to involve	
Involving key stakeholders	Time needed for staff from key stakeholder institutions and national soils institutes to meet/discuss Stationery, transportation, postage, fax, telephone, computer, printer	Brainstorm meetings to design site and questionnaires to obtain feedback and identify other stakeholders	Structure and design of website developed Questionnaires sent to stakeholders	Feedback on website	
Process development	Time and willingness of staff and stakeholders to meet	Develop plan to place information on the website and update it regularly	Plan to identify information for the website	Operational plan for the website	
Funds	Funds from donor governments	Budget prepared for the development of the website	Budget; financial report	Agreement on funds available for the website	
Implementation/operations					
Designing website	Staff to modify design of website Capable staff to research and contribute content for the website Key contributors from partner institutions or independent actors	Modification of website based on feedback Materials identified for the website in line with feedback from questionnaires	Website modified No. of items submitted for possible inclusion on the website	New 'look' for website Key items selected for the website	Information addressing the needs of the target group
Launching the website	Staff to put information on the website	Set up the website and input data	Website online	Knowledge and information made accessible	% target users changing their practices consequent on the website
Promotional activities	Time of staff and key stakeholders	Meetings to develop promotion and distribution strategy	Strategy developed	Percentage change in the number of website visitors	Increased visits to the website
Monitoring and evaluation					
Monitoring and evaluation	Time staff need to implement clear procedures to record routine data Time staff need to input routine data	Determine indicators Identify appropriate data-collection methods Design reporting formats to collect and analyse data	Development of a database to support monitoring and evaluation	Improved website (in terms of its effectiveness and efficiency) to meet the needs of the users	

Clarifying data needs and stakeholder participation

When preparing for an evaluation, you will need to know who your primary and secondary stakeholders are, so that you can determine your data needs and involve stakeholder representatives in the evaluation. The stakeholders should be taken into account at every stage of the evaluation, from its planning and design, to being part of the team as well as sources of information, and providing feedback on the evaluation results. It will be difficult to implement the evaluation recommendations if they are not acceptable to your stakeholders.

The range of stakeholders in a website could include:

- target users (be aware that the visitors to your website are not necessarily those visitors you have defined as the website target group)
- webmaster
- test group
- content manager
- partners

The users of the website – the primary stakeholders – will be individuals looking for information on your organisation and/or information produced by your organisation. Who they are should be identified by whoever is responsible for developing the website content and design. One way of identifying these stakeholders is to conduct a stakeholder analysis. Table 4.21 provides an example of a stakeholder analysis.

When considering the stakeholders' interests in the website, be aware of the kind of questions that they would like to have answered. Table 4.22 gives an overview of the kind of key questions that

Table 4.21
Stakeholder analysis for a soils data website

STAKEHOLDER CATEGORY	BENEFITS FROM THE PROJECT	CONTRIBUTIONS / SACRIFICES	INFLUENCE ON THE PROJECT	POTENTIAL INVOLVEMENT IN THE EVALUATION
Website users/ test group	Improved knowledge on soil issues and access to soil data	Time to navigate the website Cost to access the service Time to contribute	Format (navigation) of website Content of website	Represented on the team Involved in analysis and decisions on actions for change An information source Told about main findings
Webmaster, content manager	Better information for and feedback from target groups, networking	Time and technical input	Concept, structure, design and contents of website	Represented on the team, involved in the planning, evaluation and findings
Management of soils research institute	Better information for and from target group Improved image	Time and costs	Website concept	Represented on the team, involved in the planning, evaluation and findings
Partners	Improved information, networking	Time and effort to support the process	Quality of information made available	Represented on the team, involved in the planning, evaluation and findings
Funding agencies	Results to show to their clientele	Finance and time	Project concept and plan Monitoring and evaluation	Informed about the evaluation and its findings

Table 4.22
Key questions stakeholders could be interested in

STAKEHOLDER CATEGORY	QUESTIONS THEY ARE INTERESTED IN	POTENTIAL USE OF THE ANSWERS
Website users/ test group	Is the information provided relevant, timely and applicable? Does it meet their needs? Is the website easy to navigate?	Should the website be modified? Should it be recommended to others?
Webmaster, content manager	Does it serve its target group well? Does it have enough statistical information to allow for visitor analysis? What other information might be useful on the website? How relevant and effective is the website? What are its strengths, weaknesses, opportunities and threats? Is it informative, popular and well presented?	How should we continue with the website?
Management of soils research institute	Is the target group better informed? Is there improved feedback from the target group? Does the website contribute to our image? What resources are needed?	Should we continue with the website? And if so, how?
Partners	What information should be on the website? How relevant and effective is the website? Is it informative, popular and well presented? Is there an incentive for partners to promote it?	Should we continue to support the website?
Funding agencies	Does the website have an impact on agricultural planning? How sustainable is it if we stop funding it?	Should we continue, reduce or increase our funding? In what areas can/should we assist?

might be asked. If you know your stakeholders really well, you can start the process by working with your colleagues to formulate questions based on your knowledge of them. But the stakeholders must become involved at some stage to ensure that you have their views. You can do this using interviews, workshops, and questionnaires with individual or groups of stakeholders.

Defining the evaluation focus, questions and indicators

Most evaluation exercises need to be limited in focus to reflect time and budget limitations. It is not possible to cover all elements of a website extensively every time you carry out an evaluation, so you need to choose the focus of your evaluation, based on stakeholders' key questions and the time and cost of accessing data.

Among the main reasons for wanting to conduct an evaluation might be to improve your website and serve your users better. Evaluating a website is not an easy task. In general, your users are unknown and could be scattered around the world. On the other hand, you can easily obtain a lot of data at very little cost, and you only need to analyse these data to be able to transform them into valuable information. Asking specific questions will also help you to improve key areas of your

Table 4.23
Determining the focus, key questions and indicators for the evaluation of a website, using some evaluation criteria as examples

EVALUATION CRITERIA (SCOPE)	FOCUS	KEY QUESTIONS	INDICATORS	STAKEHOLDER INTEREST	DATA ACCESSIBILITY
IMPACT		How has the information helped to change soil management practices?	Improvements achieved in agriculture	High	Low
RELEVANCE	Information needs of visitors	Do visitors find the website useful?	% of visitors who find the website useful % of visitors who want more information on the website Most visited parts of the website Least visited parts of the website	High	Medium
ACCESSIBILITY	Technology	How well constructed is the website? How long does it take to download the website?	Browser compatibility Average loading time in partner countries Technology used to develop the website – Flash, Java, Javascript, etc; also look at HTML (HyperText Markup Language)/XTML compatibilities, CSS, RSS feeds, printer friendly formats, etc.	Low	Medium
USABILITY	Learnability	How easy is it for visitors to accomplish basic tasks the first time they encounter the design? Basic tasks include for example, finding the latest issue of the Soils newsletter, or a soil map of Africa, etc	% of visitors who find it easy to do the basic tasks the first time they go to the website	High	Medium
	Efficiency	Once visitors to the website have learned the design, how quickly can they perform the tasks?	Perceived time taken to perform the tasks, does it take too long, is it adequate?	Medium	Medium
	Memorability	When visitors return to the website after a period of not using it, how easily can they re-establish proficiency?	Was it easy or difficult to use the website again?	Medium	Medium
	Satisfaction	How pleasant is it to use the design?	% of visitors indicating their satisfaction with the design of the website	High	Medium
	Readability	Can visitors understand the language on the website (i.e., is it pitched at the right level, or too difficult, or too easy)?	% of visitors who say that they understand the language used on the website % of visitors who report that they are satisfied with the language used	High	Medium

Table 4.23 (continued)

EVALUATION CRITERIA (SCOPE)	FOCUS	KEY QUESTIONS	INDICATORS	STAKEHOLDER INTEREST	DATA ACCESSIBILITY
USABILITY	Overall user satisfaction	Are visitors satisfied with the website? Which areas of the website are they satisfied with? Which areas of the website are they not satisfied with? How would you improve the website?	% of users satisfied with the website overall % of users satisfied with specific sections (bits) of the website Itemise them Areas suggested for improvement	High	Medium
	Navigability	How easy is it for visitors to find what they want to know? Why is navigation structured the way it is?	% of visitors who say it was easy to find the information Average loading time in partner countries Browser compatibility Drop-down menus used Search engines used Number of links within the website that are not working ('link rot')	High	Low
EFFECTIVENESS	Usage	How many visitors go to the website? How many resources accessed?	No. of visits to the website No. of resources accessed	High	Medium
	Content and accuracy	Is the website regularly updated? Is the information provided accurate?	Frequency of updating of content, depending on the type of information provided (e.g., news sites will need to be updated more often, but an old report of a meeting can't be updated) Feedback from the users	High	Medium
	Reach	Does the website reach a wide range of people?	No. of visitors and return visitors Average time spent on the website Percentage of users who say that they have passed the website URL on to others	Medium	Low
	Networking	Why do people go to the website? How easy is it to find the website?	Ranking of the website pages in search engines (e.g., Yahoo, AltaVista and Google) No. of referrals to your website Users of interactive parts of your website (see Online community)	Medium	Low

website (e.g., you might want to know how relevant your website is versus its accessibility and usability).

The type of technology used is also important to consider in your evaluation. For example:

- Does it use Flash, Shockwave, Java, Javascript or ASP?
- Is there a good content management system?
- Does it use HTML/XTML compatibilities, and/or offer interesting newsfeeds and printer-friendly formats?

Table 4.23 provides an example of focus, key questions and indicators for a website evaluation. You can use the information here to develop a more specific set of questions, relevant to the focus of the website. Using the feedback from your stakeholders and the data available to you, you will be able to determine which questions are important for your evaluation. Whatever your focus is, you should link it to primary stakeholder (user) considerations, your ease of access to data and your resources in terms of time and costs.

Table 4.23 shows that the evaluation of the website could focus on factors such as relevance, usability and impact primarily because of their importance to the stakeholders and those responsible for the website. The scope of the evaluation can always be broadened to areas such as the sustainability of the website if, for example, a strategic decision on its continuity has to be made.

It is evident that access to good, relevant data to support your evaluation is important. By extension it is also important to maintain a good monitoring system on information relating to your website. Some general data about your website that you might want to collect routinely includes: number of users and their user profiles (i.e., data about the users, such as country, organisation, gender, area of employment, language, age (category), specialisation, equipment used, reasons for visiting the site, and expectations). These data allow you to draw meaningful conclusions from the evaluation results in relation to your user groups and are useful when looking at various evaluation criteria.

Not all data can be routinely collected, however. It might be necessary to conduct extensive surveys among your users. Some key questions you might want to ask are:

- Do you know about the website?
- Do you find it relevant?
- Are you satisfied with it?
- Has it helped you in any way?

Collecting the data

When you have determined your scope, focus and indicators, you will need to decide how to collect the data. It is important to develop a data collection strategy that ensures:

- that all relevant data will become available during the evaluation
- that no more data are collected than what is needed and can be analysed

Table 4.24 gives some guidance on which data collection tools are most appropriate to use for the indicators identified. Note that some of the tools needed for some indicators might be too expensive to use and you might have to find more creative ways to get the information you need or decide against using that particular indicator.

Table 4.24
Example of data collection methods for evaluating a website

DATA COLLECTION METHOD	INFORMATION SOURCE	KEY ISSUES / QUESTIONS	ANSWERS EXPECTED AND CONCERNS
Desk study	Feedback from emails and web statistics Automated tests	Are visitors satisfied with the website? Is the website addressing the areas it set out to address? Who are the visitors? Which sections of the website are they most interested in? Are the website links up-to-date?	Level of satisfaction Website not being visited by your target groups
	Accounts department	How much time and resources are needed for developing and maintaining the website?	Time and money to develop and maintain a website can vary widely
Interviews / online questionnaire	Visitors to the website and test group	How did you find the website? How easy was it to find the information you wanted? Do you find the website useful? Have you learned anything on your visits to the website?	Online questionnaires are immediate and less expensive, but the drawback is that you're getting feedback from visitors who already know your website (and even these may not be a representative sample of visitors)
Direct observation	Identify 5 users to actually test the website by assigning set tasks to do	How easy is it to find the information asked? Were there problems in downloading documents? Is the website pleasant to look at? Suggestions	Difficulty in getting the 'right' testers for your website
Meetings	Production personnel, NGOs, government agencies	What do you think about the message, format, and presentation of the website?	Difficulty in getting partners to work with your organisation. How to improve collaboration?

Do remember to:

- use individual page views, as a measurement rather than website hits,
- check which pages are visited the most
- use a reliable web statistics programme
- look at the number of other websites linking to yours
- seek the opinions of other people on what changes are needed, especially if you were involved in developing the website

You might also want to consider:

- whether your web pages are recognised by search engines such as Yahoo, AltaVista and Google
- whether your website uses graphics that allow for quick loading
- taking advantage of new technology where appropriate (even if that means leaving some users behind)

Some other data collection tools specific to websites can also be used. These include:

- **Log-file data and web statistics:** Websites have a great advantage over most other information products in that they can provide you with the statistics on your website's performance. If you have not worked with web statistics before, you will need some help in their interpretation. Most internet service providers (ISPs) can provide you with log-files and web statistics, which will feed your evaluation.

Before analysing your log-files, you need a 'good' sample to work with. Log-files register all requests made by the web server, so you need to clean them up by removing some 'statistical noise'. This is done by excluding robots and crawlers from the analysis because they don't involve any human interaction and by identifying and excluding staff from the analysis. Google Analytics offers a service that filters data in this way, so you might want to try using it.

- **Automated tests:** For some mechanical aspects of website performance, web-based analysis tools can be used. Automated website tests are useful to evaluate purely mechanical features (e.g. whether or not a link works) that would be tedious or impossible to measure by eye.

- **Testing and browsing the website:** Many evaluation questions can be answered simply by browsing the website. Testing with actual users, who are undertaking real-world tasks, is one of the best methods for evaluating websites. For example, to find out how long a person takes to find specific information, you could ask a user to find the document on the website that you know has that information; you can see how the user starts searches for the document, if he or she finds it, and how long it takes them.

- **Surveys online and face-to-face:** You would use a survey to ask the users questions because this is more feasible when the target group is scattered all over the world and it is useful for finding out people's general opinions.

An online questionnaire is a cost-effective way to obtain information from people who might be difficult to reach via other means. The disadvantage is that you reach only those people who already know your website. It is a good idea for a user survey to be a permanent feature of your website, but keep it posted for at least 3 months before attempting to analyse the results. Surveys receive the largest response if they are prominent and/or offer an incentive. Examples of incentives include allowing the user access to a protected area of the website, subscription to a newsletter, an RSS feed, etc. You can also increase the response by creating a pop-up hyperlink to the survey on your website, and/or notify by e-mail all registered members of your website. It is worth using *SurveyMonkey* to publish your questionnaire online; for more on this, go to www.surveymonkey.com.

Table 4.25
Example of web statistics obtained for a website

LOCATION	PAGE VIEWS	VISITORS	TOTAL TIME SPENT BY VISITORS (dd:hh:mm:ss)	AVERAGE TIME SPENT PER VISITOR (hh:mm:ss)	PAGE VIEWS
Jamaica	2,500	150	01.50.00	00:00:43	16.67
Ghana	10,580	600	05:40:00	00:00:34	17.63
The Netherlands	70,567	7,000	1d 2:50:00	00:00:14	10.08

The last column is most telling. It gives an indication of the amount of interest the website generates for the different geographic groups of users. It is important to monitor this, because if the number of page views increases over time, it could mean that these countries are an important target group for the website.

If you have access to information centres, you can use face-to-face interviews with users. This will take more time, but you will get more questionnaires completed. It would also be a good opportunity to observe some users carrying out specific tasks on the website.

Analysing the data

It is advisable to think about data analysis tools and methods before starting the data collection. This will help to ensure that the right types of data are being collected.

Table 4.26 will help you to start thinking in this way. For example, if you want to know what staff think about the website, you should already be thinking that you might have to interview staff individually or in focus groups.

In designing the data analysis for a website evaluation, you should ask the following questions:

- Which analytical tools should be used? (e.g., a table featuring the type of questions versus the type of users, a graph showing visitor use over time, or specific analytical tools such as a problem tree or a SWOT analysis)
- Which collection methods will provide the necessary data for each of the tools?

Table 4.26
Example of a data analysis design for a website evaluation

ANALYTICAL TOOLS AND TABLES	RESULTS FROM COLLECTION METHOD USED	TYPE OF OBSERVATIONS TO MAKE	TYPE OF CONCLUSIONS TO REACH
Table 1: No. and type of visitors	Desk study Web statistics	Categories of visitors over/under-represented	Categories of visitors to give more attention to
Table 2: Relevance	Desk study Questionnaires Interviews	How useful the website is given the needs of the target group	Whether the website needs to be overhauled
Table 3: User access	Interviews	Level of access of the target group to the internet Access barriers	Can determine whether the website should be changed
Table 4: Usability Satisfaction of the users	Questionnaires Interviews Direct observation of how users use the website	Is the website attractive? Can visitors easily navigate the website and find the information they want? Can they understand the language used? High and low satisfaction with the website Whether the users are happy with website Quality (accuracy) of information provided	Whether the website needs to be modified, areas for improvement
Table 5: Efficiency	Data from accounts	Cost to produce and maintain the website	Potential areas for reducing costs/time
Graph: Process flow chart	Website procedures manual, interviews	Bottlenecks in the process	Process steps to improve
Table 6: Impact stories	In-depth interviews, case studies, feedback from emails, online questionnaires	Information being provided by the website is making a difference to people's lives	Determine whether there has been some change in the way communities manage their resource

- What type of observations do you expect to make for each tool?
- What type of conclusions do you expect to get from the tools?

Once you have designed the data analysis, it is important to see if your data collection includes all elements. The results from some data collection methods (e.g., interviews) could be specifically meant for checking and/or interpreting other data. Explain why you were unable to gather certain data (e.g., in some communities internet access was very erratic).

Preparing a communication plan

Designing the communication plan is an important activity in the evaluation process to ensure that conclusions and recommendations from the evaluation are well understood and supported. In designing this strategy, you need to consider these issues:

- Which communication methods will suit which stakeholders, especially the primary stakeholders?
- What are the main issues to be discussed and reported, taking into consideration the communication method and target group?

An effective communication plan for critical reflection during an evaluation and reporting findings during and after the evaluation helps to create common understanding among stakeholders, providing a good basis for implementing recommendations. If your stakeholders don't accept the conclusions and recommendations resulting from the evaluation, it will be almost impossible to motivate them to make the required changes. However, if they have been included throughout the process, they are more likely to accept the conclusions.

During the process of critical reflection and reporting, you should ask:

- Do the stakeholders share the same views on the problems with the website?
- Do they have the same views on the solution(s)?
- Are they prepared to support the same solution(s)?
- What are the obstacles that will prevent them from implementing the solution(s) proposed?
- What can be done to address the obstacles they face?

An important component of a communication plan is to find out what difficulties stakeholders have in implementing changes. In the case of websites, the stakeholders to focus on here would be the designers, donors and content providers, rather than the primary stakeholders - the users.

There are various ways in which you can convey the results of the evaluation (e.g., providing a summary of your findings, organising a meeting, internal communication via e-mail, a memorandum). You might also consider sharing the results on the website, so that if there are changes in terms of how the website is presented, they will not come as a surprise to the user. Table 4.27 provides an example of a communication strategy for a website evaluation.

If the stakeholders are properly involved in the evaluation process in terms of participation and input, then getting their agreement on the relevance, reliability and quality of the data collected, the adequacy of the analysis provided and the conclusions drawn should not be difficult. Be aware, however, that although there might be general acceptance of a proposed solution, you might not be able to implement the solution because of a lack of resources, time and/or capacity.

An important component of the communication process is to find out what difficulties the stakeholders expect and/or experience in implementing the recommendations. Where changes can be implemented without difficulty, it is advisable to implement them as quickly as possible.

Table 4.27
Example of a communication plan for reporting the findings from a website evaluation

COMMUNICATION METHOD	STAKEHOLDERS TO REPORT TO	MAIN ISSUES TO DISCUSS / REPORT ON
Critical reflection	Staff, key partners	Critically reflecting on the results from the data collection and any other issues which may arise
Summary report	Partners	Results from data collection
Full report, including executive summary	Funding agency Staff and management	Main messages of the evaluation: relevance, satisfaction, awareness, access, reach
Personal meeting	Staff and management	Conclusions and recommendations Feedback on individual staff members
Short report of the evaluation on the website	Users	Main findings in broad terms and how they will affect staff and management

Box 4.7
Evaluating a website: guidelines checklist

These guidelines on evaluating a website are covered above:

- Website concept and objectives
- Data needs and stakeholder participation
- Evaluation focus, questions and indicators
- Data collection
- Data analysis
- The communication plan

For more on:
- data analysis, see Part 2, page 60 and Part 3, 157-162
- data collection, see Part 2, pages 58-59 and Part 3, pages 106-115
- evaluation communication and follow-up, see Part 3, pages 163-173
- evaluation criteria (scope), see Part 2, pages 33-34
- indicators, see Part 3, pages 91-98
- logframe, see Part 3, pages 68-83
- logic model, see Part 3, pages 103-105
- stakeholder participation, see Part 1, pages 3-5
- terms of reference, see Part 2, pages 32-35

QUESTION-AND-ANSWER SERVICE

> These guidelines relate to evaluating a question-and-answer service (QAS), using the terms of reference (see Part 3, pages 99-103) as the basis of the evaluation and drawing on examples where appropriate.
>
> It is important to make the evaluation process as participatory as possible, involving colleagues and key stakeholders from the outset, including your primary stakeholders (see Part 1, pages 3-5). By doing this, you will find the experience more rewarding and more likely to result in a general acceptance of the evaluation findings, making it much easier to implement change.
>
> The notion of 'critical reflection' is discussed towards the end of the guidelines, but we advise you and your evaluation team to 'reflect' on the main findings and problems at each stage of the evaluation process, for learning purposes and to improve the way you conduct the evaluation. (See Part 1, pages 5-6).
>
> The background to the evaluation process in general – concepts, context, terms, trends and core ingredients – is described in Part 2. Do read that section if you are not familiar with certain concepts or terms that occur in these guidelines. And in Part 3 you will find more on the evaluation tools described here.

Before evaluating a question-and-answer service (QAS), you need to be clear about:

- what the QAS consists of
- its concept(s) and objectives
- who the primary and secondary stakeholders are
- how to go about identifying the needs of the primary and secondary stakeholders
- what the focus of the evaluation is, the questions to ask and the indicators to use
- how to collect the data and analyse them
- how to communicate with your key stakeholders, to critically reflect upon the evaluation results and to report the results in such a way that they will be accepted and acted upon

What is a QAS?

When an information centre or library systematically responds to questions from users, they are offering a question-and-answer service (QAS). A QAS provides tailor-made answers, often complemented with photocopies of documents or information on useful contacts. It can be a stand-alone service or part of a package of information services offered by an organisation (e.g., a newsletter, a library and a radio programme).

A QAS could be offered for a particular reason or combination of reasons, such as:

- it could be a part of an institution's knowledge transfer strategy
- it could be a service complementing another service
- it could be part of a promotional strategy
- it could be an income-generating activity

A QAS can focus on any subject field. An agriculture-oriented QAS might have been set up to:

- offer practical answers to everyday problems in order to support the improvement of agricultural practices and ultimately help to eradicate hunger and poverty

- help people to become self-sufficient in agricultural production
- promote the use of existing information and research findings
- complement and strengthen extension, training and research efforts
- gain insight into the information needs of users, in order to select the focus of extension, training and research initiatives
- document farmer experiences
- strengthen the link between farmers, institutions and government.

Determining the QAS concept and objectives

You can't evaluate your QAS unless you are clear what it is about. The concept (idea) behind the service and the objectives it seeks to achieve need to be clearly stated, otherwise you can't compare its actual performance with its intended performance. Also, without a clear concept it is difficult to make the right choices during the evaluation process.

In determining a QAS concept, you should ask these questions:

- What is the background to the QAS?
- What were the main objectives (expected results) and problems to be addressed at the time?
- What is the goal of the QAS?
- What is the purpose of the QAS?
- What are its core values?
- What is the main approach used to obtain questions and deliver answers?

In conducting the evaluation, you will need to assess whether the QAS concept is valid by asking, for example:

- Do the expected results achieved reflect the QAS core values and approach?
- Do they reflect the project purpose and contribute to the goal of the QAS?
- Does the QAS address the main objectives and problems it was supposed to?

Box 4.8
Example of a concept behind a Ministry of Agriculture QAS

Main problem: The QAS in the Ministry of Agriculture was set up to address the lack of available agricultural information for people involved in farming, agro-processing and produce marketing. It appeared that existing information was not adequately used.

Goal: To enhance the agricultural development process and increase agricultural production, processing and marketing.

Purpose: Relevant and appropriate information on a timely basis provided to assist farmers, extension workers, researchers, students and development agencies.

Expected results: Awareness among the primary stakeholders created, and an adequate resource base and network with partner organisations developed.

Main approach: To invite primary stakeholders to use the service and submit their questions, and provide answers through appropriate channels of communication, directly from main QAS or, where appropriate, using partner organisations to answer questions.

Core values: Relevance, effectiveness and efficiency.

The logical framework is a useful tool that can help you clarify the project objectives (see pages 68-93). Commonly known as the 'logframe', it helps to summarise a project in a logical sequence. If a project plan does not have a logframe, it is useful to construct one so that you have a good idea of your objectives and the consequent hierarchy of activities.

An example of a logframe for a QAS is given in Table 4.28.

Where the QAS is not seen as a project, but as an ongoing activity, the logic model might be the more appropriate tool to use. It provides an overview of activities associated with the QAS, the resources used, the outputs/results, the outcomes/effects and the impact. An example of a logic model applied to a QAS is given in Table 4.29.

In using this framework, the key questions to ask to see if the QAS is meeting the stated objectives become evident. For example:

- Is adequate agricultural information more accessible?
- Is the QAS directly or indirectly reaching the farmers, researchers, etc.?
- Does it contribute to increased agricultural production?
- Has awareness of the QAS increased?
- Is there more information flow from farmers, extensionists, researchers, etc.?
- Are the answers the QAS provides timely, relevant and cost-effective?

Clarifying data needs and stakeholder participation

When preparing for an evaluation, you will need to know who your primary and secondary stakeholders are, so that you can determine your data needs and involve stakeholder representatives in the evaluation. The stakeholders should be taken into account at every stage of the evaluation, from its planning and design, to being part of the team as well as sources of information, and providing feedback on the evaluation results. It will be difficult to implement the evaluation recommendations if they are not acceptable to your stakeholders.

The range of stakeholders in a QAS could include:

- users (primary stakeholders, e.g., farmers, extension officers, researchers, students, policy-makers)
- QAS staff and management
- partners in delivering the answers (e.g., research institutes, government agencies, experts, extension officers)
- information suppliers (e.g., magazines, agricultural databases)
- funding agencies/donors

Your stakeholders will play different roles depending on the focus of the evaluation. You should therefore take into account:

- their interests (stake) when designing the evaluation
- how they can actively contribute to the design of the evaluation
- how to include them in the evaluation team
- their role as a source of information (e.g., via questionnaires, interviews, workshops)
- their feedback on evaluation results

Smart Toolkit for Evaluating Information Projects, Products and Services

One way of identifying your primary and secondary stakeholders is to conduct a stakeholder analysis. It helps you to identify the key stakeholders, how they benefit from and contribute to the QAS and how to include them in the evaluation. Table 4.30 provides an example of a stakeholder analysis.

Table 4.28
Logical framework for a QAS

	INTERVENTION LOGIC	OBJECTIVELY VERIFIABLE INDICATORS	MEANS OF VERIFICATION	ASSUMPTIONS
GOAL	To contribute to improved national agricultural production			
QAS PURPOSE	Availability of agricultural information increased	After 3 years, no. of users increased to 200 per month	Management information system (MIS) (routine records)	QAS contributes to increased production
EXPECTED RESULTS	Improved awareness among stakeholders Improved availability of appropriate information materials Improved feedback on farmers' needs to researchers	After 3 years: 50% of primary stakeholders aware of QAS. 60% of questions can be addressed with available information materials 75% agri-researchers aware of priority information needs of farmers	Survey MIS (routine records) Survey	Increased awareness leads to increased use Researchers take farmers' needs seriously
ACTIVITIES	1.1 Organise meetings with stakeholders to discuss QAS and its promotion 1.2 Develop promotional campaign with stakeholders 1.3 Implement campaign 2.1 Conduct user needs survey of stakeholders to identify priority areas that the QAS should be addressing and the type of materials needed 2.2 Develop implementation plan to increase resources to information access based on needs identified 2.3 Access resources to build QAS 3.1 Identify information gaps that researchers need to be addressing for farmers 3.2 Feed results of farmer needs to researchers through meetings	(sometimes a summary of resources/means is provided in this box)	(sometimes a summary of costs/budget is provided in this box)	(if the activities are completed, what assumptions must hold true to deliver the expected results)
INPUTS	Project funding from donor agencies	List resources available		

Table 4.29
Logic model for a QAS

FOCUS	RESOURCES	ACTIVITIES	OUTPUTS (indicators of results)	OUTCOMES (indicators of effects)	IMPACT INDICATORS
Planning and development					
User needs identification	Open-minded staff transport, postage, copies Willingness of users to participate	Design and administer questionnaires and interviews Conduct meetings Analyse data and draw conclusions	No. of questionnaires administered No. of interviews conducted No. of meetings conducted	Information needs of target users No. of changes made based on user needs analysis	
Involving stakeholders	External-oriented staff Transport Willingness of stakeholders to be involved	Calls, visits, meetings with external partners Develop agreements	No. of calls and visits made and meetings organised No. of new external experts involved	Agreements made and network developed to support QAS	
Process development	Dedicated staff, view from client perspective Willingness to address bottlenecks	Process analysis Address bottlenecks Develop procedures and forms	No. of bottlenecks reduced Procedures manual compiled Request form designed Evaluation form designed Follow-up form designed	Time and costs per question reduced User satisfaction increased	
Developing information sources	Own resources (books, reports, databases), Partners Internet databases	Identify and select information resources Develop access to resources	No. of new relevant books, full text articles and brochures made accessible	% of questions that can be fully answered	
Budgeting and financing	Capable staff Support of management and donor agencies Organisational guidelines	Make a financial plan Specify activities Calculate the budget	Clear financial proposal Clear financial report	Funds available Expenditure within budget limits Staff and management agree on financial priorities	
Implementation/operations					
Promotional activities	Motivated, skilled staff Promotional materials (website, cards, brochures) Relationship with media	Posters/cards/brochures distributed Meetings organised Websites maintained Media informed	No. of designed cards, brochures distributed No. of meetings and participants No. of QAS users No. of press releases	% of potential target groups aware of the service Number of partners (experts involved) increases	Increase in no. of questions asked; Decrease in % of questions asked outside scope
Delivery of services	Motivated, skilled staff Office space, equipment database, information sources Contracts with experts Relations with other information centres Adequate procedures	Questions received and registered Search for answers Relate with experts Refer to other QAS's Questions answered Answers followed up	No. of questions answered No. of unique users increased No. of answers followed up	% of users being satisfied with the answers % of users with new requests.	% of users able to implement the answer. % of farmers able to improve agricultural production as a result of the QAS
Monitoring and evaluation					
Monitoring and evaluation	Capable staff Clear procedures Adequate registration Indicators of quality, effectiveness, efficiency	Design report formats Organise data collection Generate statistics and reports	Clear management information system (MIS) reports produced every month, 3 months and 12 months	Improved effectiveness and efficiency of the service	

Table 4.30
Stakeholder analysis for a QAS

STAKEHOLDER CATEGORY	BENEFITS FROM THE PROJECT	CONTRIBUTIONS / SACRIFICES	INFLUENCE ON THE PROJECT	POTENTIAL INVOLVEMENT IN THE EVALUATION
Users	Improved knowledge about agricultural production and marketing	Time Cost to access the service	Through needs assessment	Represented on the team Involved in analysis and decisions on actions for change An information source Informed about main findings
Partners (research, extension, other libraries)	Improved services Improved outreach Feedback	Expertise, time and costs involved Change of approach	Through contracts/ agreements Through evaluation	Representation in team To be informed about the main findings
QAS management and staff	Improved services Improved outreach Promotional effect	Time to develop concept/convince funding agency Extra efforts	Through project plan, project management and implementation	To be involved in planning To be in the team To be informed about results
Funding agencies	Results to show to their clientele	Finance and time	Project concept and plan Through monitoring and evaluation	To be informed about evaluation planning To be informed about results

Table 4.31
Key questions stakeholders could be interested in

STAKEHOLDER CATEGORY	QUESTIONS THEY ARE INTERESTED IN	POTENTIAL USE OF THE ANSWERS
Users	Is the information provided relevant, timely and applicable? Is it provided in an appropriate format? Is the overall service satisfactory?	Continue/discontinue using the QAS Recommend the QAS to others
Partners (extension, research, other libraries)	How effective and efficient is the QAS? Does it enhance their own service? Does it generate adequate feedback on information needs?	Continue collaboration with the QAS
QAS management and staff	How effective and efficient is the QAS? Which target groups and themes provide possibilities to expand the service or to improve its quality? What are the strengths, weaknesses, opportunities and threats? How can the QAS be financed in future?	Continue or discontinue the QAS Identify areas of expansion or improvement of the QAS Identify ways to increase income and reduce costs
Funding agency	Does the QAS have an impact on agricultural production and marketing? How sustainable is the QAS after we stop funding?	Decide whether to continue, reduce or increase funding for the QAS Identify areas of assistance

When considering the stakeholders' interests in the QAS, it is important to be aware of the kind of questions that they would like to have answered. To ensure that you have their views on what questions they are interested in you need to work with them to make an inventory of these questions.

You can do this using interviews, workshops, and questionnaires with individual or groups of stakeholders. If you know your stakeholders really well, you can start the process by working with your colleagues to formulate the questions based on your knowledge of them.

Table 4.31 gives an overview of the kind of key questions this initial work might produce.

Defining the evaluation focus, questions and indicators

Most evaluation exercises need to be limited in focus to reflect time and budget limitations. It is not possible to cover all elements of a QAS extensively every time you carry out an evaluation, so you need to choose the focus of your evaluation, based on stakeholders' key questions and the time and cost of accessing data.

The focus of the evaluation may be on:

- one or more of the key evaluation criteria (i.e., accessibility, impact, relevance, sustainability, usability, utility, effectiveness, efficiency)
- one or more of the primary stakeholder groups (e.g., livestock farmers, extension officers, policy-makers)
- one or more themes (e.g., poultry keeping, soil erosion)
- one or more steps in the delivery of the QAS (e.g., timeliness, follow-up)

Besides the general questions you need to ask during your QAS evaluation (e.g., who are the actual users, what type of information is in most demand), asking specific questions will help you to improve key areas of the QAS (e.g., Are you providing appropriate information to livestock farmers, one of your key stakeholder groups?).

With each key question, you need to think about the indicators that will help answer that question and determine the type of data you need to collect. Remember to consider the interests of the stakeholders and the ease of access you have to the data you need in terms of time and cost.

Table 4.32 provides an example of the focus, key questions and indicators for a QAS evaluation. You can use the information here to develop a more specific set of questions, relevant to the focus of the QAS. Using the feedback from your stakeholders and the data available to you, you will be able to determine which questions are important for your evaluation.

With reference to Table 4.32 you may want to focus on one criterion (e.g., impact) because of its importance to the continuation of the QAS, or on the criteria of usability and accessibility because of their importance to the users. If accountability is the main purpose of the evaluation you may want to limit the scope of the evaluation to the relevance, effectiveness and efficiency of the QAS.

It is clear that access to good, relevant data depends, to a large extent, on how well your QAS registration and monitoring system functions. However, certain aspects, such as impact, relevance and awareness, require an extensive survey amongst users and/or potential users. If the QAS carries out regular user needs surveys and follow-up activities, it is possible that some of these data already exist and can be used to determine impact, relevance, awareness, and so on.

Table 4.32
Determining the focus, key questions and indicators for the evaluation of a QAS, using some evaluation criteria as examples

EVALUATION CRITERIA (SCOPE)	FOCUS	KEY QUESTIONS	INDICATORS	STAKEHOLDER INTEREST	DATA ACCESSIBILITY
IMPACT	General	Have QAS users been able to use the service for improving productivity?	% of users who have been able to use answers for improving productivity	High	Low
RELEVANCE	Information needs of users	To what extent does the QAS address main information needs of its users?	% of users indicating that the QAS addresses one of their main information needs	High	Low
EFFECTIVENESS	Volume	What is the volume of the QAS?	No. and type of questions received / No. and type of questions answered	High	High
	Awareness	Are target groups aware of the service?	% of target group indicating awareness of the service	High	Low
ACCESSIBILITY	Ease of access	Is the service accessible to target groups?	% of target group that does not have easy access to one of the QAS communication channels.	High	Medium
-USABILITY		Were the answers provided easily understood?	% of users saying that the answers were prepared in in a way that was easily understood	High	Medium
		Were answers provided to users in an appropriate format?	% of users being satisfied with the format of the answer	High	Medium
	User satisfaction	Were they satisfied with the content of the answer?	% of users who were satisfied with the content of answer	High	Medium
		Are users satisfied with the QAS?	% of users being satisfied with the QAS	High	Medium
EFFICIENCY	Time and costs	Is the service delivered in a timely and cost-efficient way?	Average cost and time spent per question by the QAS staff	Medium	Medium
	Methodology used	Is the methodology adequate?	Weaknesses and complaints indicated by stakeholders on methods used to promote and to deliver	Medium	Medium
	Information sources	Are the information sources used adequate?	% of relevant questions that can't be adequately answered	Medium	High
SUSTAINABILITY	Potential for continuation	What is the potential for continuation of the QAS?	No. of years of guaranteed funding / % and growth rate of self-financing	Medium	Medium

Collecting the data

When you have determined your scope, focus and indicators, you will need to decide how to collect the data. It is important to develop a data collection strategy that ensures:

- that all relevant data will become available during the evaluation
- that no more data are collected than what is needed and can be analysed

Table 4.33 gives some guidance on which data collection tools are most appropriate to use for the indicators identified. Note that some of the tools needed for some indicators might be too expensive to use, you might have to find more creative ways to get the information you need or decide against using that particular indicator.

You need to check that all the questions relevant to your focus are included in your data collection design.

Table 4.33
Example of data collection methods for evaluating a QAS

DATA COLLECTION METHOD	INFORMATION SOURCE	KEY ISSUES / QUESTIONS	ANSWERS EXPECTED AND CONCERNS
Desk study	QAS records	What is the volume of the service? No. and type of users No. and type of questions Are users satisfied with: - the service as a whole - the relevance of the answer - the information format - the timeliness? % of answers being late % users implementing answers	Check reliability of registration
	Accounts department	What is the cost per question? What is the time spent per step in the QAS process?	Total cost of the QAS divided by no. of questions answered gives you the cost per question Time spent from the time of the registration system
	Bureau of Statistics	No. of farmers and extension workers Access to communication channels (post, radio, telephone, internet etc.)	Check reliability of data
Focus group discussion	Selected users	What helps or hinders using the QAS? What helps or hinders the implementation of QAS answers?	Time consuming to include large enough random sample
Interviews	Staff and partners	Strengths, weaknesses, opportunities and threats of the QAS, in particular, in information sources, delivery process, promotion and partnerships	Interviews can also be used to help forge linkages
Workshop	Partners	Strengths, weaknesses, opportunities and threats of the QAS Possibilities to improve collaboration	Aim to finalise workshop with clear statement on what to improve and who will do what

For acceptance and learning purposes, you should include the stakeholders, as far as possible, in your data collection activities. This increases their involvement in the evaluation process, and they will learn directly from the feedback they get, and will be less likely to challenge the results.

Workshops are useful not only for data collection purposes, but also for data analysis and reporting purposes.

Analysing the data

It is advisable to think about data analysis tools and methods before starting the data collection. This will help to ensure that the right types of data are being collected.

Table 4.34 will help you to start thinking in this way. For example, if you want to know what users think about the QAS, you should already be thinking about ways to select interviewees and to interview them.

In designing the data analysis for a QAS evaluation, you need to ask the following questions:

- Which analytical tools should I use? (e.g., a table featuring type of questions versus the type of users, a graph showing increase in users over time, or specific analytical tools such as a problem tree, process flow chart or SWOT analysis)

Table 4.34
Example of a data analysis design for a QAS evaluation

ANALYTICAL TOOLS AND TABLES	RESULTS FROM COLLECTION METHOD USED	TYPE OF OBSERVATIONS TO MAKE	TYPE OF CONCLUSIONS TO REACH
Table 1: Effectiveness: Type of questions and type of users	Desk study	High or low total output Categories of participants who are over/under-represented	Overall conclusion on results Categories to give more attention to
Table 2: Effectiveness: Awareness	Desk study Questionnaires Interviews	Awareness of the service	Whether the service needs to be more aggressively promoted
Table 3: Usability: User satisfaction	Desk study Interviews	High and low satisfaction in relation to: the service as a whole The language used in the answer Format Completeness of the answer	Priorities for improvement
Table 3: Efficiency	Data from accounts	Costs per question Time per process step	Potential areas for reducing costs/time
Figure 1: Process flow chart	QAS procedures manual Interviews	Bottlenecks in the process	Process steps to improve
Figure 2: Problem tree	Questionnaires Interviews Workshop	Hindrances in implementing the QAS effectively	Areas for improvement
Figure 3: SWOT analysis	Workshop with staff and stakeholder representatives	Strengths, weaknesses, opportunities and threats of the QAS	New QAS strategy

- Which collection methods will provide the necessary information for each of the tools?
- What type of observations do you expect to make from each tool?
- What type of recommendations do you expect to get from it?

Once you have designed the data analysis, it is important to see if your data collection includes all elements. The results from some data collection methods (e.g., interviews) could be specifically meant for checking and/or interpreting other data.

Preparing a communication plan

Designing the communication plan is an important activity in the evaluation process to ensure that conclusions and recommendations from the evaluation are well understood and supported. In designing this strategy, you need to consider these issues:

- Which communication methods will suit which stakeholders, especially the primary stakeholders?
- What are the main issues to be discussed and reported, taking into consideration the communication method and target group?

An effective communication plan for critical reflection during an evaluation and reporting findings during and after the evaluation helps to create common understanding among stakeholders, providing a good basis for implementing recommendations. If your stakeholders don't accept the conclusions and recommendations resulting from the evaluation, it will be almost impossible to motivate them to make the required changes. However, if they have been included throughout the process, they are more likely to accept the conclusions.

During the process of critical reflection and reporting, you should ask:

- Do the stakeholders share the same views on the problems with the QAS?
- Do they have the same views on the solution(s)?
- Are they prepared to support the same solution(s)?
- What are the obstacles that will prevent them from implementing the solution(s) proposed?
- What can be done to address the obstacles they face?

There are various ways in which you can convey the results of the evaluation (e.g., providing a summary of your findings, organising a meeting, a memorandum, a web page). Table 4.35 gives an example of a communication strategy for a QAS evaluation.

If the stakeholders are properly involved in the evaluation process in terms of participation and input, then getting their agreement on the relevance, reliability and quality of the data collected, the adequacy of the analysis provided and the conclusions drawn should not be difficult. Be aware, however, that although there might be general acceptance of a proposed solution, you might not be able to implement the solution because of a lack of resources, time and/or capacity.

An important component of the communication process is to find out what difficulties the stakeholders expect and/or experience in implementing the recommendations. Where changes can be implemented without difficulty, it is advisable to implement them as quickly as possible.

Table 4.35
Example of a communication plan for reporting the findings from a QAS evaluation

COMMUNICATION METHOD	STAKEHOLDERS TO REPORT TO	MAIN ISSUES TO DISCUSS / REPORT ON
SWOT analysis	Representatives of the QAS and partners	Critically reflecting on the results from the data collection
Brainstorming	QAS staff and management and selected partners	Creative solutions to problems identified
Full report, including executive summary	Funding agency QAS management	Quantitative and qualitative outputs, user satisfaction Impact indication, cost-effectiveness
Personal meeting	QAS management	Conclusions and recommendations Feedback on individual staff members
Follow-up workshop	Representatives of QAS and partners	Decisions by management Addressing obstacles to implementation
Article on experiences of the QAS	Professionals active in similar fields	Evaluation approach and results
QAS brochure	Farmers	Examples of QAS impact stories

Box 4.9
Evaluating a QAS: guidelines checklist

These guidelines on evaluating a QAS are covered above

- QAS concept and objectives
- Data needs and stakeholder participation
- Evaluation focus, questions and indicators
- Data collection
- Data analysis
- The communication plan

For more on:

- data analysis, see Part 2, page 60 and Part 3, 157-162
- data collection, see Part 2, pages 58-59 and Part 3, pages 106-115
- evaluation communication and follow-up, see Part 3, pages 163-173
- evaluation criteria (scope), see Part 2, pages 33-34
- indicators, see Part 3, pages 91-98
- logframe, see Part 3, pages 68-83
- logic model, see Part 3, pages 103-105
- stakeholder participation, see Part 1, pages 3-5
- terms of reference, see Part 2, pages 32-35

SMALL LIBRARY / RESOURCE CENTRE

> These guidelines relate to evaluating a small library or resource centre, using the terms of reference (see Part 3, pages 99-103) as the basis of the evaluation and drawing on examples where appropriate.
>
> It is important to make the evaluation process as participatory as possible, involving colleagues and key stakeholders from the outset, including your primary stakeholders (see Part 1, pages 3-5). By doing this, you will find the experience more rewarding and more likely to result in a general acceptance of the evaluation findings, making it much easier to implement change.
>
> The notion of 'critical reflection' is discussed towards the end of the guidelines, but we advise you and your evaluation team to 'reflect' on the main findings and problems at each stage of the evaluation process, for learning purposes and to improve the way you conduct the evaluation. (See Part 1, pages 5-6).
>
> The background to the evaluation process in general – concepts, context, terms, trends and core ingredients – is described in Part 2. Do read that section if you are not familiar with certain concepts or terms that occur in these guidelines. And in Part 3 you will find more on the evaluation tools described here.

Before evaluating a small library or resource centre, you need to be clear about:

- what the main elements of the library or resource centre are
- its concept(s) and objectives
- who the primary and secondary stakeholders are
- how to go about identifying the needs of primary and secondary stakeholders
- what the focus of the evaluation is, the questions to ask and the indicators to use
- how to collect the data and analyse them
- how to communicate with your key stakeholders, to critically reflect upon the evaluation results and to report the results in such a way that they will be accepted and acted upon

What is a small library or resource centre?

A library is more than a large organised collection of books for reading or reference – it is an entity that provides access to knowledge and learning. It is also an information service that responds to the needs of a particular group of people and is central to knowledge management. It can be an organisation in itself, or part of an organisation.

With the increased availability of new technologies such as the internet, library services have evolved to take advantage of new opportunities. Collections are no longer restricted to books and journals; there is now online access to databases and a wide range of publications from all over the world. Thus, the difference between a small library and a resource centre has narrowed, and can now be regarded as more or less the same. Here, we regard them as the same, and use the term 'library' to cover both small libraries and resources centres.

Determining the library concept and objectives

You can't evaluate your library unless you are clear what it is about. The concept (idea) behind the library and the objectives it seeks to achieve need to be clearly stated, otherwise you can't compare its actual performance with its intended performance. Also, without a clear concept it is difficult to make the right choices during the evaluation process.

In determining a library concept, you should ask these questions:

- Why was the library established?
- What were the main objectives (expected results) and main problems to be addressed at the time?
- What is the goal of the library?
- What are its core values?
- Who are the target users?

In evaluating the library, you need to ask yourself key questions related to the concept, such as:

- Do the expected results achieved reflect its core values and approach?
- Do they reflect the project purpose and contribute to the overall objective?
- Does the library address the main objectives and problem it was supposed to?
- Are the correct messages being conveyed?

Box 4.10
Example of a concept behind a library focusing on economic planning

Main problem: The DocCentre was established to support the National Planning Agency in carrying out macro-economic planning. A new chief librarian was hired to oversee operations in the DocCentre, and was faced with the challenge of building its resources and developing links with other key information providers to support the government in its efforts to meet the demands of an increasingly globalised world.

Goal: To support macro-economic planning through the provision of information to government officers.

Purpose: Economists, policy-makers and planners provided with appropriate information to support their planning, research and modelling activities to help the government formulate appropriate policies and to help decision-making processes.

Expected results: Services improved to meet the information needs of the policy-makers, planners and economists within the government service.

Main approach: Questionnaires have been sent out and meetings planned for the stakeholders to identify their data needs and ways in which they can help strengthen the information flow process. Also, librarians are being trained to use appropriate information technologies to access global information resources.

Core values: Relevance, effectiveness, impact

The logical framework can help you clarify the project objectives (see pages 68-83). Commonly known as the 'logframe', it helps to summarise a project in a logical sequence. If a project plan does not have a logframe, it is useful to construct one so that you have a good idea of your objectives and the consequent hierarchy of activities. An example of a logframe for a library is given in Table 4.36.

Table 4.36
Logical framework for a library focusing on economic planning

	INTERVENTION LOGIC	OBJECTIVELY VERIFIABLE INDICATORS	MEANS OF VERIFICATION	ASSUMPTIONS
GOAL	To promote macro-economic planning of the economy through the provision of information	Reports produced to support the decision-making process	Quarterly and yearly reports on the performance of the economy	
LIBRARY PURPOSE	Access to a wide range of information to support planning and policy-making provided	After 2 years key resources acquired to support economic planning and policy analysis Feedback from the users	Routine and existing records Interviews, questionnaires	Library contributes to better economic planning and policy analysis
EXPECTED RESULTS	1. Improved resources 2. Improved awareness among stakeholders	Level of satisfaction of users Feedback from library users Increase level of visits	Interviews/ questionnaire routine and existing records	Library is important to stakeholder needs Increased awareness leads to increased visits
ACTIVITIES	1.1 Develop and administer questionnaire to identify priority areas important to the stakeholders 1.2 Meet with librarians, staff, partners and primary stakeholders to discuss objectives, and needs in line with feedback so as to develop the library resources 1.3 Identify and acquire resources 2.1 Develop and implement plan with stakeholders on how to promote the library	(sometimes a summary of resources/means is provided in this box)	(sometimes a summary of costs/budget is provided in this box)	(if the activities are completed, what assumptions must hold true to deliver the expected results)
INPUTS	Project funding from donor agency and core funding from the Ministry of Finance and Planning	List resources available		

Where the library is not seen as a project, but as an ongoing activity, the logic model might be the more appropriate tool to use. It provides an overview of activities associated with the library, the resources used, the outputs/results, the outcomes/effects and the impact. An example of a logic model applied to a library is given in Table 4.37.

In using this framework you can see the key questions to ask to see whether the library is meeting its objectives over time. For example:

- Are the expected results that have been achieved in line with its core values and approach?
- Are the expected results in line with the project purpose and do they contribute to the goal?
- Does the library address the main problem it was supposed to?
- Have visits to the library increased?
- Are users satisfied with the library?

Regular evaluation will help you to ensure your library's continued relevance to its primary stakeholders, and suggest ways in which you might improve it. Be aware, however, that librarians have differing views on the approach an evaluation should take. Approaches to consider include:

Table 4.37
Logic model for a library

FOCUS	RESOURCES	ACTIVITIES	OUTPUTS (indicators of results)	OUTCOMES (indicators of effects)	IMPACT INDICATORS
Planning and development					
Identify stakeholders' needs	Staff Facilities to hold meetings, transportation	Meeting to discuss development of the library, identify key stakeholders and their needs	List of ideas, list of initial key stakeholders	Draft library concept and who to involve - stakeholders	
Involve key stakeholders	Time needed by staff from key stakeholder institutions to meet/discuss via telephone, email Stationery, transportation, postage, fax, telephone, computer, printer	Brainstorming meetings to develop questionnaires for feedback and to identify other stakeholders	Library objectives Number of questionnaires sent to stakeholders	Agreed objectives Feedback on library	
Process development	Time and willingness of stakeholders to meet	Develop plan to improve library's facilities	Plan to expand resources and range of library's services	Operational plan for library	
Funds	Funds from organisations to support the library	Budget prepared for the development of the library	Budget financial report	Agreement on funds available for the library	
Implementation/operations					
Implementation of the library services	Time and assistance of additional expertise to help librarians provide a range of services Library resources and facilities	Accessing resources and placing additional services in the library to help users access information in an easier way	Additional resources made available to users	Knowledge gained	% of primary stakeholders changing their practices as a result of using the library facilities
Promotional activities	Time of staff and key stakeholders	Meetings to develop promotion of the library	Strategy developed	% change in visits to the library	Increased visits and enquiries
Monitoring and evaluation					
Monitoring and evaluation	Time for staff to implement clear procedures to record routine data Time for staff to input routine data	Determine indicators Identify appropriate data collection methods Design reporting formats to collect and analyse data	Development of a database to support monitoring and evaluation	Improved library services (in terms of effectiveness and efficiency) to meet stakeholder needs	

- an objective-oriented approach which looks at the library's goals and objectives so as to determine the extent to which they have been achieved
- a management-oriented approach, which tries to identify and meet the information needs of management
- an expertise-oriented approach, which relies on professional expertise to determine the quality of the library service
- a participant-oriented approach, which emphasises the role of stakeholders in the whole evaluation process

Here, we describe a combination of the objective- and participant-oriented approaches.

Clarifying data needs and stakeholder participation

When preparing for an evaluation, you will need to know who your primary and secondary stakeholders are, so that you can determine your data needs and involve stakeholder representatives in the evaluation. The stakeholders should be taken into account at every stage of the evaluation, from its planning and design, to being part of the team as well as sources of information, and providing feedback on the evaluation results. It will be difficult to implement the evaluation recommendations if they are not acceptable to your stakeholders.

The range of stakeholders in a library could include:

- individuals using the library (e.g., researchers, journalists, students, teachers, farmers) – the primary stakeholder group
- organisation that houses the library (e.g., university, research institute)
- librarian(s)
- local authorities
- funding agencies

One way of identifying your primary and secondary stakeholders is to conduct a stakeholder analysis. It helps you identify key stakeholders, how they benefit from and contribute to the library and how to include them in the evaluation. Table 4.38 ges an example of a stakeholder analysis.

When considering the stakeholders' interests in the library, be aware of the kind of questions that they would like to have answered. Table 4.39 gives an overview of the kind of key questions that might be asked. If you know your stakeholders really well, you can start the process by working with your colleagues to formulate the questions based on your knowledge of them. But the stakeholders must become involved at some stage to ensure that you have their views. You can do this using interviews, workshops, and questionnaires with individual or groups of stakeholders.

Defining the evaluation focus, questions and indicators

Most evaluation exercises need to be limited in focus to reflect time and budget limitations. It is not possible to cover all elements of a library extensively every time you carry out an evaluation, so you need to choose the focus of your evaluation, based on stakeholders' key questions and the time and cost of accessing data.

Evaluations of libraries can vary greatly in scale and style. They might cover the whole range of library activities, or focus on an individual activity, such as the enquiry service. Thus, the evaluation might take more than a week or it might take only a day.

Table 4.38
Stakeholder analysis for a library focusing on economic planning

STAKEHOLDER CATEGORY	BENEFITS FROM THE PROJECT	CONTRIBUTIONS / SACRIFICES	INFLUENCE ON THE LIBRARY	POTENTIAL INVOLVEMENT IN THE EVALUATION
Users	Improved knowledge and access to economic data	Time to access the service Cost to access the service	How the service is delivered Range of services offered	Represented on the team Involved in analysis and decisions on actions for change An information source Informed about main findings
Librarians, management, staff	Better information for their target groups Networking	Time and technical input	Library service improved	Representation on the evaluation team Need to be informed about the evaluation results
Partners	Improved information Networking	Time and effort to provide information and promote the library	Quality of information made available	Could be included on the evaluation team Need to be consulted during the evaluation and informed of key results
Funding agencies	Results to show to their clientele	Finance and time	On project concept and plan and monitoring and evaluation	Should be informed about the evaluation results

Table 4.39
Key questions stakeholders could be interested in

STAKEHOLDER CATEGORY	QUESTIONS THEY ARE INTERESTED IN	POTENTIAL USE OF THE ANSWERS
Users	Is the information provided relevant, timely, and applicable?	Will they use the library? Are they likely to recommend it to others?
Staff (librarians) and management of the library	How relevant and effective is the library? Is it informative, popular, well presented?	How should we maintain/develop the library?
Partners	How relevant and effective is the library?	Should we continue to support the library?
Funding agencies	Does the library have an impact on policy-making and planning? How sustainable is the library if we stop funding?	Should we continue, reduce or increase our funding? In what areas can/should we assist?

Examples of key questions include: How can the library have more impact? Who is using the library? Which of the target groups are not accessing it, and why? Obtaining such information could help you to introduce innovations to attract more users. By documenting the books used, you can find out what to do to increase usage by buying more relevant resources.

With each key question, you need to think about the indicators you will need to help you answer that question. Indicators also determine the type of data you will need to collect. Table 4.40

Table 4.40
Determining the focus, key questions and indicators for the evaluation of a library, using some evaluation criteria as examples

EVALUATION CRITERIA (SCOPE)	FOCUS	KEY QUESTIONS	INDICATORS	STAKEHOLDER INTEREST	DATA ACCESSIBILITY
RELEVANCE	Usefulness	Do the users find the library useful? Which of the target groups use it most?	% of users who find the library useful % of users who want more resource material in the library The most used resources in the library	High	High
ACCESSIBILITY		How easy is it to access the library resources? Are the opening hours appropriate?	% of users who have no difficulty accessing the library's resources % of users who say that the opening hours are appropriate	High	High
USABILITY	Overall satisfaction of library service	Are you satisfied with the library's services?	% of users satisfied with the overall library % of users satisfied with specific services of the library	High	Medium
	Facilities	Are the library's collections appropriate for the target groups' needs? (right level, up-to-date, etc.) Are the library's resources organised in a way that you can easily find them? Is the library's building sufficient for the proposed services? (space, storage, security, etc.)	Satisfaction level of feedback from library staff and users % who say they are satisfied with library's facilities	High	High
	Services	Are the staff competent enough to give satisfactory service to all library users?	% of users who say that they are satisfied with the library staff's level of service	High	Medium
EFFECTIVENESS	Awareness	Do you know about the library? How did you find out about it?	% of visitors who say that they know about the library Ways in which users find out about the library (e.g., via colleagues, friends, newsletters, publications, website, etc.)	High	Medium
IMPACT	Improved knowledge	Have the attitudes or practices of the users changed in any way?	% of users who say that they gained knowledge from the materials consulted and changed their attitude as a result % who say they have passed on their knowledge to others	High	Low

provides an example of focus, key questions and indicators for a library evaluation. You can use the information here to develop a more specific set of questions, relevant to the focus of the library. Using the feedback from your stakeholders and the data available to you, you will be able to determine which questions are important for your evaluation.

With reference to Table 4.40 you may want to focus on one criterion (e.g., impact) because of its importance to the continuation of the library or on the criteria of usability and accessibility because of their importance to the users. If accountability is the main purpose of the evaluation you may want to limit the scope of the evaluation to the relevance, effectiveness and efficiency of the library.

Drawing up a matrix like Table 4.40 shows how important it is to have access to good data to support your evaluation and, by extension, how important it is to maintain a good monitoring system of data relating to your library.

Collecting the data

When you have determined your scope, focus and indicators, you will need to decide how to collect the data. It is important to develop a data collection strategy that ensures:

- that all relevant data will become available during the evaluation
- that no more data are collected than what is needed and can be analysed

Table 4.41 gives some guidance on which data collection tools are most appropriate to use for the indicators identified. Note that some of the tools needed for some indicators might be expensive to use and you might have to find more creative ways to get the information you need or perhaps decide against using that particular indicator.

It is helpful if you have been collecting data on the library on a regular basis. Routine monitoring records can provide a lot of data at no cost, and most of the data can be easily transformed into valuable information.

Table 4.41
Example of data collection methods for evaluating a library focusing on economic planning

DATA COLLECTION METHOD	INFORMATION SOURCE	KEY ISSUES / QUESTIONS	ANSWERS EXPECTED AND CONCERNS
Desk study	Library records Internal memoranda on meetings with colleagues, letters/emails	No. and type of users What are their main subjects of interest Is the service making a difference to research, planning and policy-making? Is the service doing what it set out to do? Are the users satisfied?	Some economists, planners do not have access to the service Very satisfied to very dissatisfied
	Accounts department	How much time and money are involved in accessing and updating resources?	Time and money to develop a library might vary widely
Interviews and questionnaires	Economists, planners, etc.	Are the users using the information? Has the quality of papers/ policy briefs/ analyses of the economy improved?	Time consuming and expensive Self-administered questionnaires are less expensive, but the respondents might not complete them correctly
Workshop	Partners, international agencies (e.g., World Bank, commodity agencies)	Strengths, weaknesses, opportunities and threats relating to the library Possibilities for improving collaboration	How to improve collaboration

Table 4.42
Example of routine data to collect for a library, to support evaluations

FOCUS	ROUTINE INFORMATION TO COLLECT
Physical facilities and services for the public	No. of (new) books, periodicals, reports, slide sets, posters, audio-cassettes, videos, CD-ROMs, etc. No. of desks and seats No. of rooms No. of photocopy machines No. of computers, with or without CD-ROM Access to Internet Access to information sources (also a virtual library)
Assistance	No. of enquiries per month (as against expected number of enquiries) Materials used to answer enquiries
Information sources	No. of materials for which new editions have been obtained No. of materials thrown away over time No. of new acquisitions as a result of efforts made by staff No. of materials donated or exchanged for publications No. of materials obtained that are published regularly in the country No. of materials added to each subject area of the collection on a regular basis
Availability	No. of hours intended to be open per month (or quarter or year) No. of hours actually open per month (or quarter or year)
Visitors	No. of visitors each month No. of male/female visitors Average no. of visits made by each user each month Average no. of visits made each day that the library is open No. of visits made each month by different categories of users
Materials used	Subject areas most often requested or used in the past month Types of materials most often requested or used in the past month Types of services used No. of times the various services offered to visitors are used per month (e.g., lending, photocopying, use of the database, document supply, or literature searches)
Services used	No. of resources consulted/lent on a regular basis (e.g., monthly, quarterly) No. of enquires made on a regular basis No. of photocopies made on a regular basis
Feedback	Information on how visitors became aware of the service Opinions on the service provided Areas for improvement

Your routine records could contain, for example, name, age, gender, profession, time entering and leaving library, average time spent in library, materials consulted, subjects, and remarks (see Table 4.42). You could also position cards strategically in the library, asking users for feedback. The data from all these records can be tabulated, and mapped over time. Other methods can be used to explore further the patterns or trends emerging from these data.

Analysing the data

It is advisable to think about data analysis tools and methods before starting the data collection. This will help to ensure that the right types of data are being collected.

Table 4.43 will help you to start thinking in this way. For example, if you want to know what staff think about the library, you should already be thinking that you might have to interview staff individually or in focus groups.

In designing the data analysis for a library evaluation, you should ask the following questions:

- Which analysis tools should I use? (e.g., a table featuring type of questions versus the type of users, a graph showing increase in users over time, or specific analytical tools such as a problem tree, process chart or SWOT analysis)
- Which collection methods will provide the necessary data for each tool?
- What type of observations do you expect to obtain from each tool?
- What type of conclusions do you expect to reach using each tool?

Once you have designed the data analysis, it is important to see if your data collection includes all elements. The results from some data collection methods (e.g., interviews) could be specifically meant for checking and/or interpreting other data.

Table 4.43
Example of a data analysis design for a library evaluation

ANALYTICAL TOOLS AND TABLES	RESULTS FROM COLLECTION METHOD USED	TYPE OF OBSERVATIONS TO MAKE	TYPE OF CONCLUSIONS TO REACH
Table 1: Who are the users of the library?	Desk study Routine records	Range of the users of the library	Category of users to give more attention to Type of resources that would be of interest to the users
Table 2: Relevance	Desk study Questionnaires Interviews	How useful is the library given the needs of the group?	Whether the library provides information that is relevant or not
Table 3: Usabilty of the service	Desk study Questionnaires Interviews	Are the users satisfied with the quality of the service in terms of materials offered, building and services of staff	Whether the resources, building, and staff assistance provided are adequate Priorities for improvement, obstacles Can determine direction the library should take
Table 4: Effectiveness Awareness of the library	Desk study Questionnaires Interviews	Level of awareness of library High and low satisfaction with library	Promotion strategy
Table 5: Efficiency	Data from accounts	Cost to equip and maintain the library	Potential areas for reducing costs/time
Figure 1: Process flow chart	Library procedures manual, interviews	Bottlenecks in the process	Process steps to improve
Table 6: Impact stories	In-depth, interviews, case studies, feedback cards, letters to the organisation in which the library is housed	Provision of resource materials is making a difference in the quality of analysis in terms of the economy's performance and the way decision-making, policy-making and planning is carried out	Determine whether there has been some change in the quality of work done by the users

Preparing a communication plan

Designing the communication plan is an important activity in the evaluation process to ensure that conclusions and recommendations from the evaluation are well understood and supported. In designing this strategy, you need to consider these issues:

- Which communication methods will suit which stakeholders, especially the primary stakeholders?
- What are the main issues to be discussed and reported, taking into consideration the communication method and target group?

An effective communication plan for critical reflection during an evaluation and reporting findings during and after the evaluation helps to create common understanding among stakeholders, providing a good basis for implementing recommendations. If your stakeholders don't accept the conclusions and recommendations resulting from the evaluation, it will be almost impossible to motivate them to make the required changes. However, if they have been included throughout the process, they are more likely to accept the conclusions.

During the process of critical reflection and reporting, you should ask:

- Do the stakeholders share the same views on the problems with the library?
- Do they have the same views on the solution(s)?
- Are they prepared to support the same solution(s)?
- What are the obstacles that will prevent them from implementing the solution(s) proposed?
- What can be done to address the obstacles they face?

There are various ways in which you can convey the results of the evaluation (e.g., providing a summary of your findings, organising a meeting, a brochure, a memorandum, a web page). You might also consider sharing the results with members of your staff and with library users, so that if there are changes or new additions to the library, they will not come as a surprise to them.

Table 4.44
Example of a communication plan for reporting the findings from a library evaluation

COMMUNICATION METHOD	STAKEHOLDERS TO REPORT TO	MAIN ISSUES TO DISCUSS / REPORT ON
SWOT analysis	Library staff	Critically reflecting on the results from the data collection
Brainstorming	Library staff and key stakeholders	Solutions to problems identified
Summary report	Partners, users	Results from the data collection
Full report, including executive summary	Management, funding agency	Main messages of the evaluation: relevance, satisfaction, awareness, sustainability
Short report on the evaluation of the library	Users	Main findings in broad terms and how they will affect the library
A few paragraphs about the evaluation in the organisation's annual report	Anyone interested in the organisation	Give main findings of the evaluation

If the stakeholders are properly involved in the evaluation process in terms of participation and input, then getting their agreement on the relevance, reliability and quality of the data collected, the adequacy of the analysis provided and the conclusions drawn should not be difficult. Be aware, however, that although there might be general acceptance of a proposed solution, you might not be able to implement the solution because of a lack of resources, time and/or capacity.

An important component of the communication process is to find out what difficulties the stakeholders expect and/or experience in implementing the recommendations. Where changes can be implemented without difficulty, it is advisable to implement them as quickly as possible.

Box 4.11
Evaluating a library: guidelines checklist

These guidelines on evaluating a library are covered above:

- Library concept and objectives
- Data needs and stakeholder participation
- Evaluation focus, questions and indicators
- Data collection
- Data analysis
- The communication plan

For more on:

- data analysis, see Part 2, page 60 and Part 3, 157-162
- data collection, see Part 2, pages 58-59 and Part 3, pages 106-115
- evaluation communication and follow-up, see Part 3, pages 163-173
- evaluation criteria (scope), see Part 2, pages 33-34
- indicators, see Part 3, pages 91-98
- logframe, see Part 3, pages 68-83
- logic model, see Part 3, pages 103-105
- stakeholder participation, see Part 1, pages 3-5
- terms of reference, see Part 2, pages 32-35

ONLINE COMMUNITY

> These guidelines relate to evaluating an online community, using the terms of reference (see Part 3, pages 99-103) as the basis of the evaluation and drawing on examples where appropriate.
>
> It is important to make the evaluation process as participatory as possible, involving colleagues and key stakeholders from the outset, including your primary stakeholders (see Part 1, pages 3-5). By doing this, you will find the experience more rewarding and more likely to result in a general acceptance of the evaluation findings, making it much easier to implement change.
>
> The notion of 'critical reflection' is discussed towards the end of the guidelines, but we advise you and your evaluation team to 'reflect' on the main findings and problems at each stage of the evaluation process, for learning purposes and to improve the way you conduct the evaluation. (See Part 1, pages 5-6).
>
> The background to the evaluation process in general – concepts, context, terms, trends and core ingredients – is described in Part 2. Do read that section if you are not familiar with certain concepts or terms that occur in these guidelines. And in Part 3 you will find more on the evaluation tools described here.

Before evaluating an online community, you need to be clear about:

- what the main elements of the online community are
- its concept(s) and objectives
- who the primary and secondary stakeholders are
- how to go about identifying the needs of the primary and secondary stakeholders
- what the focus of the evaluation is, the questions to ask and the indicators to use
- how to collect the data and analyse them
- how to communicate with your key stakeholders, to critically reflect upon the evaluation results and to report the results in such a way that they will be accepted and acted upon

What is an online community?

In recent years, as a result of the increased adoption of information and communication technologies (ICTs), particularly e-mail and group-ware, existing and new networks have taken to online interaction. In the development field, these online communities are flourishing. They include 'communities of ideas', 'communities of practice' and 'communities of purpose', and are being used to:

- upgrade the quality of the activities, outputs and impact of development organisations
- facilitate a collective learning process
- share information on development activities with national and international audiences

These communities generally have two main elements: a discussion list, and a platform that carries posted messages and provides access to useful resources such as documents and websites.

Online communities can:

- serve as a place where people with similar goals, interests, problems and approaches can learn from each other

- provide a forum where people can respond rapidly to individual enquiries from fellow community members with specific answers
- develop and transfer best practices on specific topics, through the sharing of knowledge
- influence development outcomes by promoting greater and better-informed dialogue
- link diverse groups of people from different disciplines
- promote innovative approaches to address specific development challenges

Determining the online community concept and objectives

You can't evaluate your online community unless you are clear what it is about. The concept (idea) behind the online community and the objectives it seeks to achieve need to be clearly stated, otherwise you can't compare its actual performance with its intended performance. Also, without a clear concept it is difficult to make the right choices during the evaluation process.

In determining an online community concept, you should ask these questions:

- Why was the online community developed?
- What were the main objectives (expected results) and problems to be addressed at the time?
- What is the goal of the online community?
- What are its core values?
- Who are the target users?

In evaluating the online community, you need to ask yourself key questions related to the concept, such as:

- Do the expected results achieved reflect its core values and approach?
- Do they reflect the project purpose and contribute to the goal?
- Does the online community address the main objectives and problems as it was supposed to?
- Are the correct messages being conveyed?

The logical framework can help you clarify the online community objectives (see pages 68-83). Commonly known as the 'logframe', it helps to summarise a project in a logical sequence. If a project plan does not have a logframe, it is useful to construct one so that you have a good idea of your objectives and the consequent hierarchy of activities. An example of a logframe for an online community is given in Table 4.45

Where the online community is not seen as a project, but as an ongoing activity, the logic model might be the more appropriate tool to use. It provides an overview of activities associated with the online community, the resources used, the outputs/results, the outcomes/effects and the impact. An example of a logic model applied to an online community is given in Table 4.46.

In using this framework you can see the key questions to ask to see if the online community is meeting the stated objectives over time. For example:

- Do the expected results achieved reflect its core values and approach?
- Do they reflect the project purpose and contribute to the goal?
- Does the online community address the main problem it was supposed to?
- Are the members satisfied with the online community?
- Has the community developed in line with its objectives?
- Has community membership increased?

> **Box 4.12**
> **Example of a concept behind an online community of practice**
>
> **Main problem:** EVAL is an online community of practice of information practitioners and evaluation experts. The members of the community have been working together to promote monitoring and evaluation practice for information products and services. EVAL is a joint initiative of five key development agencies. Since 2005, the members have worked on various initiatives, exchanging experiences and approaches. Initially, there was intense collaboration among members, but recently EVAL has not been very active.
>
> **Goal:** To have an online community on evaluation practice which supports development practitioners in the field of information products and services.
>
> **Project purpose:** Information specialists, evaluators and practitioners provided with a platform to communicate, exchange experiences and collaborate on the evaluation of information products and services.
>
> **Expected results:** EVAL, an online community practice established to support exchange of information and knowledge sharing among practitioners on evaluation of information products and services.
>
> **Main approach:** A Dgroup (this is a place on the internet where individuals and development organisations can come together and interact with one another) has been developed, where practitioners can exchange information and communicate with other members of the group. Face-to-face meetings have also been planned to help strengthen links and work on collaborative activities.
>
> **Core values:** Relevance, effectiveness, sustainability

Clarifying data needs and stakeholder participation

When preparing for an evaluation, you will need to know who your primary and secondary stakeholders are, so that you can determine your data needs and involve stakeholder representatives in the evaluation. The stakeholders should be taken into account at every stage of the evaluation, from its planning and design, to being part of the team as well as sources of information, and providing feedback on the evaluation results. It will be difficult to implement the evaluation recommendations if they are not acceptable to your stakeholders.

The range of stakeholders in an online community could include:

- Platform providers
- Funding agencies (e.g., banks, student award schemes, research institutions)
- Community moderators and facilitators
- Community members and their organisations (e.g., practitioners, researchers, policy-makers, managers) – the primary stakeholders (and other groups, such as people known as 'lurkers' who don't contribute to the postings but benefit from reading them)

One way of identifying your primary and secondary stakeholders is to conduct a stakeholder analysis. It helps you to identify the key stakeholders, how they benefit from and contribute to the online community and how to include them in the evaluation. Table 4.47 provides an example of a stakeholder analysis.

Table 4.45
Logical framework for an online community

	INTERVENTION LOGIC	OBJECTIVELY VERIFIABLE INDICATORS	MEANS OF VERIFICATION	ASSUMPTIONS
GOAL	To contribute to improved evaluation practices in development efforts			
ONLINE COMMUNITY PURPOSE	Exchange of knowledge and experiences on evaluation to better manage information projects promoted	After 3 years, a considerable amount of resource material and sharing of experiences documented	Routine and existing records Contributions to the online community	Online community contributes to better information project management
EXPECTED RESULTS	1. Online community to support information practitioners in the field of evaluation strengthened	Threefold increase in online community membership Facilitators and providers aware of the needs of the online community 100% increase in the level of interaction Feedback of members	Web statistics and routine records show level of interaction within the community, and resources available Survey	Online community is relevant Increased awareness leads to increased visits to the online community
ACTIVITIES	1.1 Meet moderator /facilitator and selected stakeholders (providers, development agencies) to discuss Dgroup objectives, structure 1.2 Brainstorm to formulate questionnaire for feedback and develop strategy to obtain feedback from target group 1.3 Identify priority areas for target group(s) 1.4 Develop plan with stakeholders on how to develop the Dgroup 1.5 Place resources on the Dgroup platform and invite members to add their own resources	(sometimes a summary of resources/means is provided in this box)	(sometimes a summary of costs/budget is provided in this box)	(if the activities are completed, what assumptions must hold true to deliver the expected results)
INPUTS	Project funding from donor agency and core funding from the Ministry of Agriculture	List resources available		

When considering the stakeholders' interests in the online community, be aware of the kind of questions that they would like to have answered. Table 4.48 gives an overview of the kind of key questions that might be asked.

If you know your stakeholders really well, you can start the process by working with your colleagues to formulate the questions based on your knowledge of them. But the stakeholders must become involved at some stage to ensure that you have their views. You can do this using interviews, workshops, and questionnaires with individual or groups of stakeholders.

Table 4.46
Logic model for an online community

FOCUS	RESOURCES	ACTIVITIES	OUTPUTS (indicators of results)	OUTCOMES (indicators of effects)	IMPACT INDICATORS
Planning and development					
Identify users' needs	Staff Facilities	Meeting to discuss the online community and how to go about it and determine who should be involved	List of ideas, list of initial key stakeholders	Draft concept of online community, who to involve	
Involve key stakeholders	Time staff need from key stakeholder institutions to meet/discuss via telephone, email Stationery, transportation, postage, fax, telephone, computer, printer	Brainstorm meetings to develop online community and questionnaires for feedback and identifying other stakeholders	Objectives and structure of the online community developed No.of questionnaires sent to stakeholders	Agreed to objectives and structure; key materials also identified Access rights to the online community, membership profile developed	
Process development	Time and willingness of stakeholders to meet	Develop plan to facilitate community, place information and update it regularly	Plan to identify information sources and obtain information from the members	Operational plan for the community	
Funds	Funds from organisations to support the online community	Budget prepared for the development of the online community	Budget; financial report	Agreement on funds available for the online community	
Implementation/operations					
Implementation of the online community	Facilitator to put information online	Accessing site to input data and to facilitate	Community online	Knowledge gained	% of users changing their practices as a result of the online community
Promotional activities	Time required from staff and key stakeholders	Meetings to develop promotion of the community	Strategy developed and implemented	% change in the no. of members	Increased membership and enquiries
Monitoring and evaluation					
Monitoring and evaluation	Time required by staff to implement clear procedures to record routine data Time required by staff to input routine data	Determine indicators Identify appropriate data collection methods Design reporting formats to collect and analyse data	Development of a database to support monitoring and evaluation	Improved online community (in terms of its effectiveness and efficiency) to meet the needs of the members	

Defining the evaluation focus, questions and indicators

Many development organisations are investing in online communities, but the benefits from these investments are by no means clear. As these communities are relatively new, there are no generally accepted standards with regard to evaluation, except that existing principles apply. Anecdotal evidence and lessons indicate that the success of online communities is related to the human

Table 4.47
Stakeholder analysis for an online community

STAKEHOLDER CATEGORY	BENEFITS FROM THE PROJECT	CONTRIBUTIONS / SACRIFICES	INFLUENCE ON THE PROJECT	POTENTIAL INVOLVEMENT IN THE EVALUATION
Members/ organisations (users)	Improved knowledge on evaluation issues as they relate to information services and products	Time, knowledge and expertise involved in participating in the community	Format of the community Topics for discussion	Represented on the team Involved in analysis and decisions on actions for change An information source Informed about main findings
Platform provider (Dgroup)	Better information for their target groups, networking	Time and technical input	Dgroup platform improved	Represented on the team Informed about main findings
Moderators/ facilitators	Improved information, networking	Time and effort to support the process	Quality of information made available	Represented on the team Involved in the evaluation planning, implementation and findings
Funding agencies	Results to show to their clientele	Finance and time	On project concept and plan and monitoring and evaluation	Informed about the evaluation results

Table 4.48
Key questions stakeholders could be interested in

STAKEHOLDER CATEGORY	QUESTIONS THEY ARE INTERESTED IN	POTENTIAL USE OF THE ANSWERS
Members/ organisations (users)	Is the information provided relevant? Is the target group aware of the online community? Does the community meet target group needs? Is it easy for users to ask questions and/or contribute? Is the target group satisfied with the community?	Will they continue to be part of the online community? Are they likely to recommend it to others?
Platform provider (Dgroup)	How relevant and effective is the platform? Is it user-friendly, informative, popular, well presented? Is it doing what it was set up for? Do providers of information contribute relevant and accurate information? Is there an incentive for members to promote the online community?	How should we continue with the platform?
Moderators/ facilitators	Is the platform adequate? How relevant and effective is the community? Is the platform pleasing to look at? What information should it carry? Is the information accurate, relevant and up-to-date? Is it easy to reach the target group?	Should we continue with this platform? Should we continue to facilitate the community?
Funding agencies	Does the community have an impact on evaluation practice? How sustainable is it if we stop funding? Does it contribute in some way to the promotion of the evaluation of information products and services? Should we continue to fund it?	Should we continue, reduce or increase our funding? In what areas can/should we assist?

relationships within these communities. This means that, when conducting an evaluation, you will need to find indicators relating to people's experience of interaction.

Most evaluation exercises need to be limited in focus to reflect time and budget limitations. It is not possible to cover all elements of an online community extensively every time you carry out an evaluation, so you need to choose the focus of your evaluation, based on stakeholders' key questions and the time and cost of accessing data.

When evaluating, you must be clear about why you are doing it. How will the information affect your future actions? What difference will the evaluation make? Some issues are more straightforward to interpret and translate into action than others. For example, it is easier to count the number of community members than it is to measure 'trust and reciprocity'; these are complex matters and are likely to mean different things to different people. The kinds of questions you could ask include:

- Is the content relevant?
- Who are the main members of the online community in terms of profession and organisation?
- How many 'lurkers' vis-à-vis active members are there?
- Are best practices being shared and disseminated?
- Which are the lead organisations and who are the key individuals?
- How easy is it for you to contribute ideas and follow through on them?

Table 4.49 provides an example of focus, key questions and indicators for an online community evaluation. You can use the information here to develop a more specific set of questions, relevant to the focus of the online community. Using the feedback from your stakeholders and the data available to you, you will be able to determine which questions are important for your evaluation. Whatever your focus is, you should link it to primary stakeholder (user) considerations, your ease of access to data and your resources in terms of time and costs.

With reference to Table 4.49 you may want to focus on one criterion (e.g., impact) because of its importance to the continuation of the online community or on the criteria of usability and accessibility because of their importance to the users. If accountability is the main purpose of the evaluation you may want to limit the scope of the evaluation to the relevance, effectiveness and efficiency of the online community.

Drawing up a matrix like Table 4.49 shows how important it is to have access to good data to support your evaluation and, by extension, how important it is to maintain a good monitoring system of data relating to your online community.

Collecting the data

When you have determined your scope, focus and indicators, you will need to decide how to collect the data. It is important to develop a data collection strategy that ensures:

- that all relevant data will become available during the evaluation
- that no more data are collected than what is needed and can be analysed

Table 4.50 gives some guidance on which data collection tools are most appropriate to use for the indicators identified. Note that some of the tools needed for some indicators might be too

Table 4.49
Determining the focus, key questions and indicators for the evaluation of an online community, using some evaluation criteria as examples

EVALUATION CRITERIA (SCOPE)	FOCUS	KEY QUESTIONS	INDICATORS	STAKEHOLDER INTEREST	DATA ACCESSIBILITY
IMPACT	Change in the knowledge and practice in the field of the evaluation of information projects	Have you improved in terms of knowledge and professional practice?	% of members who conduct evaluations of their projects % who publish on evaluation of information projects, or who have joint publications, shared models, shared language, new collaborative approaches Change in dialogue and issues discussed	High	Low
RELEVANCE	Content and contact	Are the contacts made useful? Are the resources provided useful?	% of members who see the contacts as relevant % of members who see the content as relevant	High	Low
ACCESSIBILITY	Access to content and contacts	How much contact is there between the members? How willing are members to share their resources	Frequency of contact between members Level of access to peers and experts Level of access to insider tacit and explicit knowledge e.g. non-public/confidential reports and documents	High	Low
EFFECTIVENESS	Facilitation	How well is the facilitation done?	No. of messages sent by facilitator Response time by the facilitator % of members satisfied with the facilitator	High	High
	Participation	Are members leaving? If so, why? How active are the members? Where is leadership located? How easy is it to contribute? What are the obstacles to participation?	% of members who cancelled their membership Balance of contributions (e.g., in terms of gender, location, profession) No. of messages posted by no. of people No. of resources posted by no. of people	High	High
	Trust	Is there a high level of trust, reciprocity and willingness among the members of the community?	% of members who perceive trust within the community	Low	Medium
	Reach	Where do members come from, which organisations are represented?	No. of members (both individual and institutional) No. of organisations No. of national cultures Ratio experts : practitioners	Medium	High

Table 4.49 (continued)

EVALUATION CRITERIA (SCOPE)	FOCUS	KEY QUESTIONS	INDICATORS	STAKEHOLDER INTEREST	DATA ACCESSIBILITY
USABILITY	Technology/design. Extent to which you can access resources to ensure sustainability of the community	Are the users satisfied with the design of the Dgroup? Is the technology used appropriate for the community? Is it easy to upload and download documents? Was it easy for the members to learn to use the platform?	% of members satisfied with the design. % of members satisfied with the navigability	High	Medium
SUSTAINABILITY		What resources are required to maintain the community?	Amount and type of resources required to maintain the community	Low	Low

expensive to use and you might have to find more creative ways to get the information you need or perhaps decide against using that particular indicator.

Online communities have a great advantage over many other information products in that almost all web hosts can provide you with the statistics from your platform. These are routinely produced reports. If you have never worked with web statistics before, you will need some help in their interpretation.

Table 4.50
Example of data collection methods for evaluating an online community

DATA COLLECTION METHOD	INFORMATION SOURCE	KEY ISSUES / QUESTIONS	ANSWERS EXPECTED AND CONCERNS
Desk study (technology and design)	Software information. Online comments. Web statistics/routine data	Is the community easy to access? Is it easy to navigate? Who are the members?	Some target groups don't have access to the internet
	Accounts department	How much time and resources are involved in facilitating and maintaining the community?	Time and money to facilitate and maintain an online community can vary widely
Interviews /online questionnaire	Members of the community. Partners	Is the community useful? Are you satisfied with it? Have you learned anything since joining it? Who are your members? Are you reaching those you want to?	Level of satisfaction
Face-to-face meetings		What do you think about the way the community is designed and run? How can collaboration be improved?	Organisations not willing to support the community

Analysing the data

It is advisable to think about data analysis tools and methods before starting the data collection. This will help to ensure that the right types of data are being collected. Table 4.51 will help you to start thinking in this way. For example, if you want to know what members think about the online community, you should already be thinking about ways to interview them.

In designing the data analysis for the online community, you should ask the following questions:

- Which analysis tools should be used? (e.g., a table featuring type of questions versus the type of members, a graph showing increase in members over time, or specific analytical tools such as a problem tree, process chart or SWOT analysis)
- Which collection methods will provide the necessary data for each tool?
- What type of observations do you expect to obtain from each tool?
- What type of conclusions do you expect to reach using each tool?

Preparing a communication plan

Designing the communication plan is an important activity in the evaluation process to ensure that conclusions and recommendations from the evaluation are well understood and supported. In designing this strategy, you need to consider these issues:

Table 4.51
Example of a data analysis design for an online community evaluation

ANALYTICAL TOOLS AND TABLES	RESULTS FROM COLLECTION METHOD USED	TYPE OF OBSERVATIONS TO MAKE	TYPE OF CONCLUSIONS TO REACH
Table 1: Who are the members joining the community	Desk study Routine records	Range of the members	Category of members to give more attention to Type of resources that would be of interest to the members
Table 2: Relevance	Desk study Questionnaires Interviews	How useful is the community given the needs of the group	Whether the online community is relevant or not
Table 3: Effectiveness Awareness of community Facilitation Participation	Desk study Questionnaires Interviews	Level of awareness of community Quality (accuracy) of information provided Is there a lot of interaction within the community?	Promotion strategy Priorities for improvement, obstacles Can determine how community should be changed
Table 4: Efficiency	Data from accounts	Cost to facilitate and maintain the community	Potential areas for reducing costs/time
Figure 1: Process flow chart	Community procedures manual, interviews	Bottlenecks in the process	Process steps to improve
Table 5: Impact stories	In-depth interviews, case studies, feedback from emails, online questionnaires	Interaction in the community is making a difference to the way people practice their profession	Determine whether there has been some change in the way people manage their information projects

- Which communication methods will suit which stakeholders, especially the primary stakeholders?
- What are the main issues to be discussed and reported, taking into consideration the communication method and target group?

An effective communication plan for critical reflection during an evaluation and reporting findings during and after the evaluation helps to create common understanding among stakeholders, providing a good basis for implementing recommendations. If your stakeholders don't accept the conclusions and recommendations resulting from the evaluation, it will be almost impossible to motivate them to make the required changes. However, if they have been included throughout the process, they are more likely to accept the conclusions.

During the process of critical reflection and reporting, you should ask:

- Do the stakeholders share the same views on the problems with the online community?
- Do they have the same views on the solution(s)?
- Are they prepared to support the same solution(s)?
- What are the obstacles that will prevent them from implementing the solution(s) proposed?
- What can be done to address the obstacles they face?

There are various ways in which you can convey the results of the evaluation (e.g., providing a summary of your findings, organising a meeting, a memorandum). You might also consider sharing the results on the community platform, so that if there are changes in terms of how it is presented, they will not come as a surprise to the members. Table 4.52 gives an example of a communication strategy for an online community evaluation.

If the stakeholders are properly involved in the evaluation process in terms of participation and input, then getting their agreement on the relevance, reliability and quality of the data collected, the adequacy of the analysis provided and the conclusions drawn should not be difficult. Be aware, however, that although there might be general acceptance of a proposed solution, you might not be able to implement the solution because of a lack of resources, time and/or capacity.

Table 4.52
Example of a communication plan for reporting the findings from an online community evaluation

COMMUNICATION METHOD	STAKEHOLDERS TO REPORT TO	MAIN ISSUES TO DISCUSS / REPORT ON
Critical reflection	Staff, selected partners	Critically reflect on results from the data collection
Summary report/ internet page	Partners, members	Results from the data collection
Full report, including executive summary	Funding agency	Main messages of the evaluation: relevance, satisfaction, awareness, access, reach, sustainability
Short report of the evaluation of the online community	Members of the online community	Main findings in broad terms and how it will affect the community
Articles	Potential partners and members	Main messages of the evaluation, lessons learned
Face-to-face meetings	Members of the online community	Main findings and the implication for the community

An important component of the communication process is to find out what difficulties the stakeholders expect and/or experience in implementing the recommendations. Where changes can be implemented without difficulty, it is advisable to implement them as quickly as possible.

Box 4.13
Evaluating an online community: guidelines checklist

These guidelines on evaluating an online community are covered above:

- Online community concept and objectives
- Data needs and stakeholder participation
- Evaluation focus, questions and indicators
- Data collection
- Data analysis
- The communication plan

For more on:
- data analysis, see Part 2, page 60 and Part 3, 157-162
- data collection, see Part 2, pages 58-59 and Part 3, pages 106-115
- evaluation communication and follow-up, see Part 3, pages 163-173
- evaluation criteria (scope), see Part 2, pages 33-34
- indicators, see Part 3, pages 91-98
- logframe, see Part 3, pages 68-83
- logic model, see Part 3, pages 103-105
- stakeholder participation, see Part 1, pages 3-5
- terms of reference, see Part 2, pages 32-35

RURAL RADIO

> These guidelines relate to evaluating a programme for rural radio, using the terms of reference (see Part 3, pages 99-103) as the basis of the evaluation and drawing on examples where appropriate.
>
> It is important to make the evaluation process as participatory as possible, involving colleagues and key stakeholders from the outset, including your primary stakeholders (see Part 1, pages 3-5). By doing this, you will find the experience more rewarding and more likely to result in a general acceptance of the evaluation findings, making it much easier to implement change.
>
> The notion of 'critical reflection' is discussed towards the end of the guidelines, but we advise you and your evaluation team to 'reflect' on the main findings and problems at each stage of the evaluation process, for learning purposes and to improve the way you conduct the evaluation. (See Part 1, pages 5-6).
>
> The background to the evaluation process in general – concepts, context, terms, trends and core ingredients – is described in Part 2. Do read that section if you are not familiar with certain concepts or terms that occur in these guidelines. And in Part 3 you will find more on the evaluation tools described here.

Before evaluating your rural radio programme, you need to be clear about:

- what the main elements of the radio programme are
- its concept(s) and objectives
- who the primary and secondary stakeholders are
- how to go about identifying the needs of the primary and secondary stakeholders
- what the focus of the evaluation is, the questions to ask and the indicators to use
- how to collect the data and analyse them
- how to communicate with your key stakeholders, to critically reflect upon the evaluation results and to report the results in such a way that they will be accepted and acted upon

What is a rural radio?

Rural radio is a broadcasting system in which programmes are tailored for rural areas. It aims to facilitate development by helping to identify, debate and discuss issues of concern and provide information on ways of addressing the issues, relying on local knowledge systems and information communication tools. In Africa, rural radio has taken on many forms, the most recent being the 'community' type local rural radio.

Whether it is called local or community radio, or free or participative radio, it is the process used to produce the programmes, together with their content, which determines if it can be called 'rural radio'. Rural radio should have the following features:

- the programmes are constructed around the needs of the communities they serve
- in a highly participatory process, various people and organisations contribute to their production
- exchanges are interactive
- local culture and knowledge are valued and developed

Rural radio is therefore a community's means of expression. It has most influence where it is inclusive, accessible and trusted by the community. It is also important if the community has a sense of ownership of the service that it has an element of sustainability.

How do you know if rural radio is meeting the needs of the community? How do you know if the programmes have been developed properly or not? Evaluating rural radio programmes will help you find answers to these questions. It will also help you to find out who is listening and when, and what difference the programmes make to the community. It can also provide feedback on the production process, improve your relationship with the listeners, demonstrate value for money and provide ideas for future programmes.

Determining a rural radio programme concept and objectives

You can't evaluate your radio programme unless you are clear what it is about. The concept (idea) behind the radio programme and the objectives it seeks to achieve need to be clearly stated, otherwise you can't compare its actual performance with its intended performance. Also, without a clear concept it is difficult to make the right choices during the evaluation process.

In determining the concept of a rural radio programme, you should ask these questions:

- Why was the rural radio programme developed?
- What were the main objectives (expected results) and problems to be addressed at the time?
- What is the goal of the rural radio programme?
- What is the project purpose of the radio programme?
- What are the core values of the radio programme?
- Who is the target group?

In evaluating your rural radio programme, you need to ask yourself key questions related to the concept, such as:

- Do the expected results achieved reflect its core values and approach?
- Do they reflect the project purpose and contribute to the goals?
- Does the rural radio programme address the main objectives and problems it was supposed to?
- Are the correct messages being conveyed?

The logical framework can help you clarify the radio programme objectives (see pages 68-83). Commonly known as the 'logframe', it helps to summarise a project in a logical sequence. If a project plan does not have a logframe, it is useful to construct one so that you have a good idea of your objectives and the consequent hierarchy of activities.

An example of a logframe for a radio prgramme is given in Table 4.53.

Where the rural radio programme is not seen as a project, but as an ongoing activity, the logic model might be the more appropriate tool to use. It provides an overview of activities associated with the programme, the resources used, the outputs/results, the outcomes/effects and the impact.

An example of a logic model applied to a rural radio programme is given in Table 4.54.

> **Box 4.14**
> **Example of a concept behind a rural radio programme on health issues**

> **Main problem:** The public relations department in the Ministry of Health developed the HealthTime radio programme to address the limited access that some population groups have to basic health information.
>
> **Goal:** To improve the quality of life of the population in rural communities.
>
> **Project purpose:** Rural communities (particularly women, children, and health and social workers) provided with relevant and appropriate health information on a timely basis.
>
> **Expected results:** Awareness created among target groups; information provided in such a way that the target groups will be able to understand and act upon it.
>
> **Main approach:** To transmit the radio programme in an attractive way in the main local language, providing simple health messages and aired at a time slot favoured by women and children.
>
> **Core values:** Relevance, effectiveness, efficiency and impact

Clarifying data needs and stakeholder participation

When preparing for an evaluation, you will need to know who your primary and secondary stakeholders are, so that you can determine your data needs and involve stakeholder representatives in the evaluation. The stakeholders should be taken into account at every stage of the evaluation, from its planning and design, to being part of the team as well as sources of information, and providing feedback on the evaluation results. It will be difficult to implement the evaluation recommendations if they are not acceptable to your stakeholders.

The range of stakeholders in a rural radio programme could include:

- listeners (including specific targets such as women, children, and health and social workers) – the primary stakeholder group
- volunteers, contributors
- advisors
- NGOs
- production personnel
- broadcasters
- government agencies
- funding sources (e.g., donor agency)

One way of identifying your primary and secondary stakeholders is to conduct a stakeholder analysis. It helps you to identify the key stakeholders, how they benefit from and contribute to the programme and how to include them in the evaluation. Table 4.55 provides an example of a stakeholder analysis.

When considering the stakeholders' interests in the rural radio programme, be aware of the kind of questions that they would like to have answered. Table 4.56 gives an overview of the kind of key questions that might be asked. If you know your stakeholders really well, you can start the process

Table 4.53
Logical framework for a rural radio programme on health issues

	INTERVENTION LOGIC	OBJECTIVELY VERIFIABLE INDICATORS	MEANS OF VERIFICATION	ASSUMPTIONS
GOAL	To contribute to improved living conditions in rural communities	After 5 years: migration rate in communities reduced by 20%; incidence of water-borne diseases and other basic illnesses reduced by 40%	National statistics on population, health and living standards	
RADIO PROGRAMME PURPOSE	Availability of health information to women and children in rural communities increased	After 3 years, no. of listeners increased threefold % of households following recommended practices: - 80% boil drinking water - 90% immunise children against polio - 70% use pit latrine to dispose of human waste No. of listeners and range of listenership	Routine records at the radio station National statistics Field visits Interviews, case studies, diaries	Rural radio programme contributes to improvement in living conditions
EXPECTED RESULTS	1. Improved availability of health information 2. Improved awareness among the listeners	Level of listenership aware of programme content	Routine records Questionnaires Interviews	Increase in awareness leads to increased listenership
ACTIVITIES	1.1 Meet staff and selected stakeholders to discuss programme objectives and presentation and increase programme exposure 1.2 Draft questionnaire for feedback and develop strategy to obtain feedback from target group 1.3 Identify priority health issues, key information on how to improve the programme through questionnaires and meetings with key stakeholders 1.4 Develop plan with stakeholders for a series on health issues for the year 1.5 Produce series of programmes with stakeholders reflecting identified health issues 2.1 Meet staff and key stakeholders to develop promotion and distribution strategy for programme 2.2 Implement strategy to promote it, such as preparing brochure, advertising on billboards and on website, organising competitions	(sometimes a summary of resources/means is provided in this box)	(sometimes a summary of costs/budget is provided in this box)	(if the activities are completed, what assumptions must hold true to deliver the expected results)
INPUTS	Funding from donor agency; core funding from Ministry|	List resources available		

Table 4.54
Logic model for a rural radio programme on health issues

FOCUS	RESOURCES	ACTIVITIES	OUTPUTS (indicators of results)	OUTCOMES (indicators of effects)	IMPACT INDICATORS
Planning and development					
1. Laying the groundwork for the rural radio programme	Capable staff	Conduct meetings to discuss rural radio programme and decide who to involve	List of ideas and key stakeholders	Draft rural radio programme concept and who to involve	
2. Involving stakeholders	Representatives from the Ministry of Health, key stakeholders (inc. women) from representative communities targeted External-oriented staff Transport, photocopies Willingness of partners	Brainstorm with partners to determine rural radio format Develop questionnaire for feedback and ideas	Rural radio format developed Questionnaire developed and administered	Changes made to rural radio programme format in response to the feedback obtained	
3. Process development	Committed staff and partners Time and willingness to address bottlenecks	Process analysis Identify priority health messages Address bottlenecks Develop procedures and forms	No. of bottlenecks reduced Procedures manual compiled		
4. Producing the radio programme	Resources (books, reports, databases) from Ministry of Health and partners Internet databases Storyboard writer to develop sketches	Identify information resources Develop access to resources Write the story to support the message	No. of short stories written around special themes suited for radio drama along with information packet Information resources identified and consulted		
5. Budgeting and financing	Capable staff Support of management, donors and NGOs	Budget for all activities to support the production and airing of the programme	Budget Financial report	Funds available Costs in budget limits Staff and management agree on financial priorities	
Implementation/operations					
6. Promotional activities	Motivated, skilled staff Promotional materials (website, brochures) Relationship with media	Posters/cards/brochures developed Meetings organised Media informed	No. of brochures sent No. of meetings and participants No. of press releases	% of potential target groups aware of service No. of partners (experts involved) increases	Increase in no. of questions asked Decrease in % of questions asked outside scope
7. Delivery of radio programme	Motivated, skilled staff Office space, equipment Database, information sources Writer, actor contracts Relations with other radio stations	Broadcasting rural radio programme via various radio stations Liaise with experts Feedback followed up	No. of radio programmes aired No. of responses to feedback followed up	% of listeners listening to the programme % of listeners satisfied with the programme	% of listeners implementing what they've learned
Monitoring and evaluation					
8. Monitoring and evaluation	Capable staff Clear procedures Adequate registration Indicators of quality, effectiveness, efficiency	Define indicators Design report formats Organise data collection Generate statistics and report	Clear routine for recording reports (updated regularly, daily, weekly, monthly quarterly, yearly)	Improved effectiveness and efficiency of the radio programme	

by working with your colleagues to formulate the questions based on your knowledge of them. But the stakeholders must become involved at some stage to ensure that you have their views. You can do this using interviews, workshops, and questionnaires with individual or groups of stakeholders.

Table 4.55
Stakeholder analysis for a rural radio programme on health issues

STAKEHOLDER CATEGORY	BENEFITS FROM THE PROJECT	CONTRIBUTIONS / SACRIFICES	INFLUENCE ON THE LIBRARY	POTENTIAL INVOLVEMENT IN THE EVALUATION
Listeners	Improved knowledge on relevant health issues	Time listening to the radio Cost to access the service (radio)	Format and content of the programme	Represented on the team Involved in analysis and decisions on actions for change An information source Informed about main findings
Volunteers, NGOs, contributors, advisors, health and community groups	Better information for their target groups	Time and technical input	Rural radio programme improved, sharper	Should be represented on the evaluation team Informed about main findings
Broadcasters, government agencies, production personnel	Improved programme Improved outreach Promotional effect	Time to develop programme concept and convince funding agency Extra efforts	Through project, plan project management and implementation, distribution of programme	Should be involved in the programme planning and evaluation Should be informed about evaluation findings
Funding agencies	Results to show to their clientele	Finance and time	On project concept and plan and monitoring and evaluation	Should be informed about the evaluation findings

Table 4.56
Key questions stakeholders could be interested in

STAKEHOLDER CATEGORY	QUESTIONS THEY ARE INTERESTED IN	POTENTIAL USE OF THE ANSWERS
Listeners	Is the rural radio programme relevant and timely? Is the information provided in an appropriate format? Is the programme satisfactory?	Will they continue to listen to the programme Are they likely to recommend it to others?
Volunteers, NGOs, contributors, advisors, health and community groups	How effective and efficient is the programme?	Should we continue to collaborate with its producers
Broadcasters, government agencies, production personnel	How effective and efficient is the programme? What are its strengths, weaknesses, opportunities and threats? Is it informative, popular and well presented? How can it be financed in the future?	Should we continue with the programme? What should we do to improve it? What should we do to reduce costs and increase income?
Funding agencies	Does the programme have an impact on the health of the target population? How sustainable is the programme after funding is stopped?	Should we continue, reduce or increase the funding? In what areas can/should we assist?

Defining the evaluation focus, questions and indicators

Most evaluation exercises need to be limited in focus to reflect time and budget limitations. It is not possible to cover all elements of a rural radio programme extensively every time you carry out an evaluation, so you need to choose the focus of your evaluation, based on stakeholders' key questions and the time and cost of accessing data.

The focus of the evaluation might stem from your desire to improve it, from low or declining listenership, from feedback from others, or from a need to cut costs. There might be concerns about the programme in comparison with a competitor. You might want to assess current achievements so as to determine strategies for future publications. Other examples of areas of focus include:

- a specific objective (i.e., providing information to certain vulnerable groups)
- specific assessment criteria (e.g., effectiveness and impact of the programme, or a focus on those criteria that are most problematic)
- the primary stakeholders or those experiencing the most problems
- a combination of all of these

Asking specific questions will help you to improve key areas of the radio programme. With each key question, you need to think about the indicators you will need to help you answer that question. Indicators also determine the type of data to collect. Remember to consider the interests of the stakeholders and the ease of access you have to the data you need in terms of time and cost.

All this information can give you insight on how to schedule the programme better, or target it to specific groups. It may seem simply common sense, but often mistakes are made in scheduling or targeting. By checking that your assumptions are right, and that you are reaching the people you intend to reach, you can ensure that the programme has the maximum impact.

Table 4.57 provides an example of the focus, key questions and indicators for a rural radio programme. You can use the information here to develop a more specific set of questions, relevant to the focus of the programme. Using the feedback from your stakeholders and the data available to you, you will be able to determine which questions are important for your evaluation.

With reference to Table 4.57 you may want to focus on one criterion (e.g., impact) because of its importance to the continuation of the radio programme or on the criteria of usability and accessibility because of their importance to the listeners. If accountability is the main purpose of the evaluation you may want to limit the scope of the evaluation to the relevance, effectiveness and efficiency of the radio programme.

Drawing up a matrix like Table 4.57 shows how important it is to have access to good data to support your evaluation and, by extension, how important it is to maintain a good monitoring system of data relating to your radio programme.

Collecting the data

When you have determined your scope, focus and indicators, you will need to decide how to collect the data. It is important to develop a data collection strategy that ensures:

- that all relevant data will become available during the evaluation
- that no more data are collected than what is needed and can be analysed

Table 4.57
Determining the focus, key questions and indicators for the evaluation of a rural radio programme, using some evaluation criteria as examples

EVALUATION CRITERIA (SCOPE)	FOCUS	KEY QUESTIONS	STAKEHOLDER INTEREST	DATA ACCESSIBILITY
IMPACT	Has the health of the target population improved?	Percentage of target group who have changed their attitudes/behaviour (e.g., hygiene, eating habits) as a result of the programme Changes in the programming: the extent to which the programme gives opportunities to the target group to contribute to programming	High	Low
RELEVANCE	Needs of the target group	Percentage of target group indicating that the programme addresses their information needs Percentage who want more issues to be addressed	High	Medium
ACCESSIBILITY	Access	Percentage of target group who have access to a working radio?	High	Medium
USABILITY	Listener satisfaction	Percentage of target group satisfied with the programme Percentage of the target group satisfied with specific sections of the programme Feedback from listeners on: - what they thought the main message of the programme was - if the programme is the right length - if it's in the right language	High	Medium
EFFECTIVENESS	Awareness	Percentage of target group aware of the programme Percentage of target group who say they learned from the programme	High	Medium
	Message Format Duration Presentation	Feedback from staff on what they thought the main message of the programme was and what it should have been, whether the programme is appropriate for the target audience, right length, right language and well presented	High	Low
	Reach	Percentage and range of the target group who listen to the programme over time	High	Medium
EFFICIENCY	Expenditure	Average cost to produce and air the programme	High	Low

Data collection therefore requires careful preparation. Defining the scope of the evaluation to use as the basis for designing the evaluation questions and indicators allows you to see clearly what data are required and the most appropriate data collection methods to use.

The data collection methods for a radio programme include:

- **Internal interviews:** Interview both volunteers and staff, asking them their opinion about the programme. This inclusion will assist buy-in and ownership, and provide valuable information. You need to reassure them that their input is confidential. This method can be applied informally, or it could be structured around a simple questionnaire.

- **Audience market research:** Many stations will not be able to do this because it is a large-scale and costly activity. But you could conduct the research via a partner (e.g., if you're working with a large NGO, it might have access to market research analysts; or in your local university there might be students on marketing or related courses who could conduct a study as part of their course work).

- **Listener feedback analysis:** Document the number and time of all the phone calls taken during phone-in programmes, or in response to competitions. Get some details about the caller, such as where they live and their age (preferably their age category). Record all the feedback the station receives.

- **Vox pops:** Conduct on-the-street interviews systematically, asking the same questions of a range of people. Vox pops are a quick and easy way to gauge public opinion on an issue or programme.

- **In-depth interviews/case studies:** Conducting in-depth interviews with a small, carefully selected group of people might provide information that is just as useful as a large statistical survey. Use a checklist of topics to guide the interview, but follow up any unexpected or negative responses. For an in-depth case study, you could identify a group of listeners representative of your target audience, and then visit them regularly (weekly, monthly) to obtain their feedback on the programmes after they are broadcast.

- **Listener club feedback:** Many successful radio projects use listener clubs to listen in regularly and report back on programmes that are broadcast. This works particularly well in rural areas and with women's groups. The members of a club gather regularly to listen to a programme, discuss it and provide feedback.

- **Listener diaries:** These can be useful for collecting information on women and people living in remote areas. Encourage representative members of the target group to write listener diaries, recording their reactions to programmes, what information they thought most or least useful, and whether they put into practice any of the advice they heard. This can be time-consuming, so it is often appropriate to offer modest incentives, such as running a competition.

Do remember to include the 'silent audience' – those people who never contact a radio station but listen to its programmes, as well as those people in your target audience who don't listen to any of the programmes, to find out why.

Table 4.58 gives some guidance on which data collection tools are most appropriate to use for the indicators identified. Note that some of the tools needed for some indicators might be too expensive to use and you might have to find more creative ways to get the information you need or perhaps decide against using that particular indicator.

Analysing the data

It is advisable to think about data analysis tools and methods before starting the data collection. This will help to ensure that the right types of data are being collected.

Table 4.59 will help you to start thinking in this way. For example, if you want to know what listeners think about the programme, you should already be thinking about ways to interview them.

In designing the data analysis for a radio programme evaluation, you should ask the following questions:

- Which analytical tools should be used? (e.g., a table featuring the type of questions versus the type of listeners, a graph showing increase in listeners over time, or specific analytical tools such as a problem tree, process chart or SWOT analysis)
- Which collection methods will provide the necessary data for each of the tools?

Table 4.58
Example of data collection methods for evaluating a rural radio programme

DATA COLLECTION METHOD	INFORMATION SOURCE	KEY ISSUES / QUESTIONS	ANSWERS EXPECTED AND CONCERNS
Desk study	Programme records Internal memoranda on meetings with colleagues, letters, emails, recordings of the programme	Are colleagues satisfied with the radio programme? Are the targeted listeners satisfied with it? Is it making a difference in communities? Is it addressing the areas it set out to do?	Some communities don't have access to a working radio Listeners who give feedback might not be in the target group Need to test the findings by looking at the listener profiles
	Accounts department	How much time is involved in producing each programme? What is the cost of production?	Time and money to produce a programme can vary widely
Interviews/case studies/vox pops/ questionnaires	Selected listeners	Are you aware of the programme? Is the programme useful? Is it broadcast at an appropriate time? Have you changed your attitude as a result of the programme?	Time consuming, expensive Self-administered questionnaires are less expensive, but the respondent may fill in the questionnaire incorrectly or not at all Use the radio station to encourage listeners to contact you for an interview by broadcasting your address and telephone number, and organising competitions. A short intercept interview by the receptionist who, for example, takes music requests can also help (e.g., name, sex, address, opinion of programme)
Informal interviews	Advisors, staff and volunteers	What is their opinion on how the programme was produced and content?	Need to ensure that feedback is confidential to encourage trust and openness
Listener club feedback	Target listeners	Ask a group of listeners to regularly give feedback on the programme	Listeners are close to the material and therefore not objective in their feedback
Listener diaries	Target listeners	Ask listeners to record their reactions to the programme in terms of what was useful and what was not useful	Time consuming
Meetings	Production personnel, NGOs, government agencies	What do you think about the message, format, duration, and presentation of the programme? How to improve collaboration?	Difficulty in getting partners to work with your organisation

- What type of observations do you expect to make for each tool?
- What type of conclusions do you expect to reach from using the tools?

Once you have designed the data analysis, it is important to see if your data collection includes all elements. The results from some data collection methods (e.g., interviews) could be specifically meant for checking and/or interpreting other data. Explain why you were unable to gather certain data.

Table 4.59
Example of a data analysis design for a rural radio programme evaluation

ANALYTICAL TOOLS AND TABLES	RESULTS FROM COLLECTION METHOD USED	TYPE OF OBSERVATIONS TO MAKE	TYPE OF CONCLUSIONS TO REACH
Table 1: (target group) Listenership by age, location, programme penetration by group	Desk study	Categories of listeners who are over-/ under-represented	Categories of listeners to give more attention to
Table 2: (target group) Relevance	Desk study Questionnaires Interviews	How useful the programme is given the needs of the target group	Whether the programme has outlived its purpose
Table 3: Usability: - Listener satisfaction	Desk study Questionnaires Interviews Listener club feedback Listener diaries	High and low satisfaction with the programme as a whole	Areas for attention
Table 4: (target group) Effectiveness: - Awareness - Access - Reach	Desk study Questionnaires Interviews	Level of awareness of the programme Level of access of the target group to a working radio Change in number of target listeners who listen to the programme over time	Priorities for improvement Obstacles to improvement
Table 5: (staff, partners) Effectiveness: - Message - Format - Duration - Presentation	Interviews	Whether staff and partners are happy with the programme	Can determine whether the radio has to change its way of programming
Table 6: Efficiency	Data from accounts	Cost to produce the programme Time involved in the production process	Potential areas for reducing costs/time
Figure 1: Process flow chart	Programme procedures manual, interviews	Bottlenecks in the process	Process steps to improve
Table 7: Impact stories	In-depth interviews, case studies, feedback from letters, emails, call-ins, health statistics	Personal stories of how lives have been affected by the programme Statistics showing, e.g., fewer children getting water-borne diseases	Determine whether there has been some change in the quality of life in communities

Preparing a communication plan

Designing the communication plan is an important activity in the evaluation process to ensure that conclusions and recommendations from the evaluation are well understood and supported. In designing this strategy, you need to consider these issues:

- Which communication methods will suit which stakeholders, especially the primary stakeholders?
- What are the main issues to be discussed and reported, taking into consideration the communication method and target group?

An effective communication plan for critical reflection during an evaluation and reporting findings during and after the evaluation helps to create common understanding among stakeholders, providing a good basis for implementing recommendations. If your stakeholders don't accept the conclusions and recommendations resulting from the evaluation, it will be almost impossible to motivate them to make the required changes. However, if they have been included throughout the process, they are more likely to accept the conclusions.

During the process of critical reflection and reporting, you should ask:

- Do the stakeholders share the same views on the problems with the rural radio programme?
- Do they have the same views on the solution(s)?
- Are they prepared to support the same solution(s)?
- What are the obstacles that will prevent them from implementing the solution(s) proposed?
- What can be done to address the obstacles they face?

There are various ways in which you can convey the results of the evaluation (e.g., providing a summary of your findings, organising a meeting, a memorandum).

Table 4.60
Example of a communication plan for reporting the findings from a rural radio programme evaluation

COMMUNICATION METHOD	STAKEHOLDERS TO REPORT TO	MAIN ISSUES TO DISCUSS / REPORT ON
Critical reflection	Staff, selected partners	Critically reflect on results from the data collection
Summary report	Representatives from health and rural communities and partners	Results from data collection
Full report, including executive summary	Funding agency; Programme management	Message, content, duration, presentation listenership, relevance, satisfaction, awareness, access, reach, impact, cost-effectiveness
Personal meeting	Programme management	Conclusions and recommendations; Feedback on individual staff members
Short report of the evaluation aired on the programme	Listeners	Main findings in broad terms and how they will affect the programme
Article on experiences of the programme	Professionals active in similar fields	Evaluation approach and results
Programme promotional brochure	Target listeners	Examples of programme impact stories

If the stakeholders are properly involved in the evaluation process in terms of participation and input, then getting their agreement on the relevance, reliability and quality of the data collected, the adequacy of the analysis provided and the conclusions drawn should not be difficult. Be aware, however, that although there might be general acceptance of a proposed solution, you might not be able to implement the solution because of a lack of resources, time and/or capacity.

An important component of the communication process is to find out what difficulties the stakeholders expect and/or experience in implementing the recommendations. Where changes can be implemented without difficulty, it is advisable to implement them as quickly as possible.

Box 4.15
Evaluating a rural radio programme: guidelines checklist

These guidelines on evaluating a rural radio programme are covered above:

- Rural radio programme concept and objectives
- Data needs and stakeholder participation
- Evaluation focus, questions and indicators
- Data collection
- Data analysis
- The communication plan

For more on:

- data analysis, see Part 2, page 60 and Part 3, 157-162
- data collection, see Part 2, pages 58-59 and Part 3, pages 106-115
- evaluation communication and follow-up, see Part 3, pages 163-173
- evaluation criteria (scope), see Part 2, pages 33-34
- indicators, see Part 3, pages 91-98
- logframe, see Part 3, pages 68-83
- logic model, see Part 3, pages 103-105
- stakeholder participation, see Part 1, pages 3-5
- terms of reference, see Part 2, pages 32-35

DATABASE

> These guidelines relate to evaluating a database, using the terms of reference (see Part 3, pages 99-103) as the basis of the evaluation and drawing on examples where appropriate.
>
> It is important to make the evaluation process as participatory as possible, involving colleagues and key stakeholders from the outset, including your primary stakeholders (see Part 1, pages 3-5). By doing this, you will find the experience more rewarding and more likely to result in a general acceptance of the evaluation findings, making it much easier to implement change.
>
> The notion of 'critical reflection' is discussed towards the end of the guidelines, but we advise you and your evaluation team to 'reflect' on the main findings and problems at each stage of the evaluation process, for learning purposes and to improve the way you conduct the evaluation. (See Part 1, pages 5-6).
>
> The background to the evaluation process in general – concepts, context, terms, trends and core ingredients – is described in Part 2. Do read that section if you are not familiar with certain concepts or terms that occur in these guidelines. And in Part 3 you will find more on the evaluation tools described here.

Before evaluating a database, you need to be clear about:

- what the main elements of the database are
- its concept(s) and objectives
- who the primary and secondary stakeholders are
- how to go about identifying the needs of the primary and secondary stakeholders
- what the focus of the evaluation is, the questions to ask and the indicators to use
- how to collect the data and analyse them
- how to communicate with your key stakeholders, to critically reflect upon the evaluation results and to report the results in such a way that they will be accepted and acted upon

What is a database?

A database is a large, regularly updated file of digitised information (e.g., bibliographic records, abstracts, full-text documents, directory entries, images, statistics) related to a specific subject or field. It consists of records of uniform format organised for ease and speed of search and retrieval and is managed with the aid of database management system software.

Every database has been created with a specific goal. They are usually stored in one location and made available to several users at the same time for various applications involving rapid search and retrieval. There are also databases that can only be accessed online. Databases can also be stored in a machine-readable form (on magnetic tape, disk or optical disk), or printed on paper (as in a book). Common databases include:

- project databases (these include details of projects for one or more institutions)
- bibliographic databases (these include bibliographic records, with or without abstracts)
- contact databases (these include details of individuals and institutions relevant to an organisation's work; sometimes, these data are shared among a group of organisations)

If it takes too long to find the required information in a database, or people need expertise to conduct an adequate search, then the intended users will not be able to access it. To encourage greater use of databases, search and retrieval processes need to be efficient.

Determining the database concept and objectives

You can't evaluate a database unless you are clear what it is about. The concept (idea) behind the database and the objectives it seeks to achieve need to be clearly stated, otherwise you can't compare its actual performance with its intended performance. Also, without a clear concept it is difficult to make the right choices during the evaluation process.

In determining the database concept, you should ask these questions:

- Why was the database developed?
- What were the main objectives (expected results) and main problems to be addressed at the time?
- What is the goal of the database?
- What are its core values?
- Who are the targeted readers?
- Is it a database that your institution has developed, or one that your institution is subscribing to?

In evaluating the database, you need to ask yourself key questions related to the concept, such as:

- Do the expected results achieved reflect its core values and approach?
- Do they reflect the project purpose and contribute to the goal?
- Does the database address the main objectives and problems it was supposed to?
- Are the correct messages being conveyed?

> **Box 4.16**
> **Example of a concept behind a database to support scientific research**
>
> **Main problem:** A Scientific Research Institute has been documenting its work since its inception in 1990 and trying to build up its resources to support scientific research in the country. A few years ago, the institute received funds to boost its library resources on the condition that it made its database accessible to the wider scientific community. Since then, it has acquired scientific literature and access to key scientific bibliographic databases. The director is uncertain, however, if the current database is meeting the needs of his institute and other stakeholders. If it is not, he wants to know what needs to be done so that the database can better meet the needs of staff and other stakeholders.
>
> **Goal:** To contribute to raising the level of scientific research through the establishment of a reliable database with extensive resources for scientists, researchers and other stakeholders to support national development and production.
>
> **Project purpose:** Access to current and reliable information to support the research and scientific investigations of scientists, researchers and students provided.
>
> **Expected results:** Comprehensive database which is available and accessible to the scientific community developed.
>
> **Main approach:** To meet staff and key stakeholders to identify their needs and document their experiences in using the current database.
>
> **Core values:** Relevance, effectiveness, efficiency and impact

The logical framework can help you clarify the database objectives (see pages 68-83). Commonly known as the 'logframe', it helps to summarise a project in a logical sequence. If a project plan does not have a logframe, it is useful to construct one so that you have a good idea of your objectives and the consequent hierarchy of activities. An example of a logframe for a database is given in Table 4.61.

Where the database is not seen as a project, but as an ongoing activity, the logic model might be the more appropriate tool to use. It provides an overview of activities associated with the database, the resources used, the outputs/results, the outcomes/effects and the impact. An example of a logic model applied to a database is given in Table 4.62.

Table 4.61
Logical framework for a scientific database

	INTERVENTION LOGIC	OBJECTIVELY VERIFIABLE INDICATORS	MEANS OF VERIFICATION	ASSUMPTIONS
GOAL	To raise the level of scientific research for improved national production			
DATABASE PURPOSE	Access of scientists, researchers and students to a wide range of resources increased	After 3 years, number of users increased by 50%	Routine records	Access to the database contributes to increased national production
EXPECTED RESULTS	1. Improved awareness among stakeholders about the database 2. Improved availability of adequate scientific information	After 3 years, 90% of target group aware of the database; 75% can access the database; and there is a 50% increase in number of publications written	Survey Routine records	Increased awareness leads to increased use of the database
ACTIVITIES	1.1 Organise meeting with partners to discuss the database and its promotion 1.2 Develop promotional campaign with partners 1.3 Promote the database using researchers/scientists who use it 1.4 Implement campaign 2.1 Conduct user needs survey of selected researchers, scientists and students 2.2 Identify gaps in the database 2.3 Acquire appropriate resources	(sometimes a summary of resources/means is provided in this box)	(sometimes a summary of costs/budget is provided in this box)	(if the activities are completed, what assumptions must hold true to deliver the expected results)
INPUTS	Funding from donor agency; core funding from Ministry	List resources available		

Table 4.62
Logic model for a scientific database

FOCUS	RESOURCES	ACTIVITIES	OUTPUTS (indicators of results)	OUTCOMES (indicators of effects)	IMPACT INDICATORS
Planning and development					
1. User needs identification	Open-minded staff Transport, postage, photocopies Users willing to participate	Design and administer questionnaires/interviews Conduct meetings Analyse data and draw conclusions	No. of questionnaires sent No. of interviews conducted No. of meetings conducted	No. of changes made based on user needs analysis	
2. Involving stakeholders	External-oriented staff Transport, photocopies Willingness of partners	Calls, visits, meetings with external partners Develop agreements	No. of calls/visits made and meetings organised No. of external agencies involved	Stronger network; awareness and number of information sources increased	
3. Development of the database	Dedicated staff, database expert, view from client perspective, Willingness to address bottlenecks	Process analysis Address bottlenecks Develop database structure and content Develop updating and user registration procedures	No. of bottlenecks reduced Procedures manual compiled Database developed Evaluation form made Follow-up form made	Time and costs providing the information User satisfaction increased	
4. Developing information sources	Own resources (books, reports, databases) Partners Internet databases	Identify information sources (e.g., bibliographic databases) Select information resources Develop access to resources	Broader range of literature offered	% increase in the volume of information available	
5. Budgeting and financing	Capable staff Support of management and donor agencies Organisational guidelines Donors' financial guidelines	Make a financial plan Specify activities Calculate the budget	Clear financial proposal Clear financial report	Funds available Expenditure within budget limits Staff and management agree on financial priorities	
Implementation/operations					
6. Promotional activities	Motivated, skilled staff Promotional materials (website, posters, brochures)	Posters/ brochures developed Meetings organised Media informed	No. of brochures sent No. of meetings and participants No. of press releases	% of potential target groups aware of service No. of partners (experts involved) increases	% change in no. of user profiles developed to meet the needs of users % users who share information received from the database
7. Delivery of services	Motivated, skilled staff Office space, equipment Database, information sources Registration and updating procedures	Registration of users Regularly sending out information when new material available Updating and maintaining the database	No. of persons using the database More, better targeted literature/ bibliographic references offered	% of users being satisfied with the information available	% change in the volume of published and unpublished papers
Monitoring and evaluation					
8. Monitoring and evaluation	Capable staff Clear procedures Adequate registration Indicators of quality, effectiveness, efficiency	Designing report formats Organising data collection Generating statistics & reports	Routine records regularly updated monthly, quarterly, yearly	Improved effectiveness and efficiency of the database	

In using this framework, some key questions to see if the database is meeting the stated objectives over time become evident. For example:

- Is the research and scientific community aware of the database?
- Do researchers and scientists have access to the database?
- Is the database useful?
- Does the database contribute to an increased number of local scientific publications/research materials ?
- Is the information provided in a timely and cost-effective way?

Clarifying data needs and stakeholder participation

When preparing for an evaluation, you will need to know who your primary and secondary stakeholders are, so that you can determine your data needs and involve stakeholder representatives in the evaluation. The stakeholders should be taken into account at every stage of the evaluation, from its planning and design, to being part of the team as well as sources of information, and providing feedback on the evaluation results. It will be difficult to implement the evaluation recommendations if they are not acceptable to your stakeholders.

The range of stakeholders in a database could include:

- researchers/scientists
- extension workers
- farmers
- community workers
- policy-makers
- database manager
- content manager
- funding agencies
- implementing agency
- partners

The stakeholders will have a vested interest in the evaluation itself, and should be consulted and involved in some way. The input of the different groups will vary, depending on the particular situation. You should therefore take into account:

- their interests when designing the evaluation
- how they can actively contribute to the evaluation process
- how to include them as part of the evaluation team
- their role as a source of data (e.g., via questionnaires, interviews and workshops)
- their feedback on evaluation results

One way of identifying these stakeholders is to conduct a stakeholder analysis. It helps you to identify the key stakeholders, how they benefit from and contribute to the database and how to include them in the evaluation. Table 4.63 provides an example of a stakeholder analysis.

When considering the stakeholders' interests in the database, be aware of the kind of questions that they would like to have answered. Table 4.64 gives an overview of the kind of key questions that might be asked. If you know your stakeholders really well, you can start the process by working with your colleagues to formulate the questions based on your knowledge of them. But

Table 4.63
Stakeholder analysis for a scientific database

STAKEHOLDER CATEGORY	BENEFITS FROM THE PROJECT	CONTRIBUTIONS / SACRIFICES	INFLUENCE ON THE PROJECT	POTENTIAL INVOLVEMENT IN THE EVALUATION
Implementing agency	Improved database Improved outreach Promotional effect	Time and expertise to develop the database concept/ convince funding agency Extra efforts	Through project, plan project management and implementation of the database	Involve staff in the evaluation and inform staff of the findings
Users	Improved knowledge on issues they are researching	Time to search the database Cost to access the database	Contents and accessibility of the database	Represented on the team Involved in analysis and decisions on actions for change An information source Informed about main findings
Database manager/ content manager	Feedback of users	Time and expertise to develop the database and make it accessible	Concept, structure and contents of the database	Part of the evaluation team Should be involved in all stages of the evaluation Informed about main findings
Partners, NGOs	Better information for their target groups	Time and technical input	Improved database	Involve key partners in the evaluation and inform them of the main findings
Funding agencies	Results to show to their clientele	Finance and time	On project concept and plan, as well as monitoring and evaluation	Inform them of the main findings of the evaluation

Table 4.64
Key questions stakeholders could be interested in

STAKEHOLDER CATEGORY	QUESTIONS THEY ARE INTERESTED IN	POTENTIAL USE OF THE ANSWERS
Users	Is the database relevant and timely? Is the information provided in an appropriate format? Is the overall database satisfactory?	Should the database be used/recommended?
Partners, NGOs	How effective and efficient is the database?	Decide on whether to continue collaboration with staff of the database
Implementing agency (agency management and database management)	How effective and efficient is the database? What are its strengths, weaknesses, opportunities and threats? Is it popular and well presented? How can it be financed in the future?	Should the database be continued? What should be done to improve it? What should be done to reduce costs and increase income?
Funding agencies	Does the database have an impact on the quality of the scientific research produced? How sustainable is the database after we stop funding?	Should funding be continued, reduced or increased? In what areas is assistance needed?

the stakeholders must become involved at some stage to ensure that you have their views. You can do this using interviews, workshops, and questionnaires with individual or groups of stakeholders.

Defining the evaluation focus, questions and indicators

Most evaluation exercises need to be limited in focus to reflect time and budget limitations. It is not possible to cover all elements of a database extensively every time you carry out an evaluation, so you need to choose the focus of your evaluation, based on stakeholders' key questions and the time and cost of accessing data.

The focus of the evaluation might stem from your desire to improve the database, from low or declining use, from feedback from others, or from a need to cut costs. There might be concerns about the database in comparison with a competitor. Other examples of areas of focus include:

- a specific objective (i.e. providing information on particular subjects)
- specific assessment criteria (e.g., relevance and impact of the database)
- the primary stakeholders or those experiencing the most problems
- a combination of all of these

Asking specific questions will help you to improve key aspects of the database. With each key question, you need to think about the indicators you will need to help you answer that question. Indicators also determine the type of data to collect. Remember to consider the interests of the stakeholders and the ease of access you have to the data you need in terms of time and cost.

Table 4.65 provides an example of the focus, key questions and indicators for a database. You can use the information here to develop a more specific set of questions, relevant to the focus of the database. Using the feedback from your stakeholders and the data available to you, you will be able to determine which questions are important for your evaluation.

With reference to Table 4.65 you may want to focus on one criterion (e.g., impact) because of its importance to the continuation of the database or on the criteria of usability and accessibility because of their importance to the users. If accountability is the main purpose of the evaluation you may want to limit the scope of the evaluation to the relevance, effectiveness and efficiency of the database.

Drawing up a matrix like Table 4.65 shows how important it is to have access to good data to support your evaluation and, by extension, how important it is to maintain a good monitoring system of data relating to your database.

Collecting the data

When you have determined your scope, focus and indicators, you will need to decide how to collect the data. It is important to develop a data collection strategy that ensures:

- that all relevant data will become available during the evaluation
- that no more data are collected than what is needed and can be analysed

Data collection therefore requires careful preparation. It happens too often that too much data are collected, or that insufficient 'good' data are collected to draw the relevant conclusions. Properly

Table 4.65
Determining the focus, key questions and indicators for the evaluation of a database, using some evaluation criteria as examples

EVALUATION CRITERIA (SCOPE)	FOCUS	KEY QUESTIONS	INDICATORS	STAKEHOLDER INTEREST	DATA ACCESSIBILITY
IMPACT	Change in the quality of research	Have researchers/scientists been able to improve the quality of their research? Have they been able to produce the type of information needed to increase production?	% of researchers/scientists who say that the quality of their research has improved. % of researchers producing information relevant for increasing production	High	Low
RELEVANCE	Usefulness	Do users find the database useful?	% of users who find the database useful. % of users who find the information of little use	High	Medium
ACCESS	Accessibility/ reliability	Are there any restrictions to accessing the database (e.g., language, browser required)? Is there a charge to access the database? How do charges compare with other services? Is the service reliable and reasonably fast to access? Is there online help? What is the source of the information? (If it is a bibliographic database, ask if it is from a reputable publisher)	Rules governing usage of the database. % of users who say that the database is easy to access and reliable	High	Medium
	Technology/ media	How often is the hardware updated/maintained? What software is used?	Type of media used: CD-ROM, web-based, etc. Whether the following are available: - thesaurus searching - support for non-traditional (non-Boolean) searching - possibility for Boolean operators to be used - nested Boolean searches accepted to support complex searches	Low	Medium/ High
USABILITY	Learnability	How easy is it for you to use the database the first time you use it?	% of users who find it easy to use database	High	High
	Efficiency	Once you use the database how easy is it to find the information you need?	Perceived time taken to find the information, does it take too long, is it adequate?	Medium	Medium
	Memorability	When you return to the database after a period of not using it, how easily can you re-establish proficiency?	Was it easy or difficult to use the database again?	Medium	Medium
	Satisfaction	Is the database design pleasant to use?	% of users who are satisfied with the database	Medium	Medium

Table 4.65 (continued)

EVALUATION CRITERIA (SCOPE)	FOCUS	KEY QUESTIONS	INDICATORS	STAKEHOLDER INTEREST	DATA ACCESSIBILITY
USABILITY	Content	Is there a full-text resource? Indexes and abstracts? Index only? Quality of information/ accuracy; contents up to date?	Type of database in place % of users who say that the database is accurate and up-to-date	High	Medium
	Retrieval	What are the search features? Can indexes be browsed and terms selected for searching? Can a combination of fields be searched simultaneously? Can search limits be applied (by year, language, publication type)?	Itemise	High	Low
	User satisfaction	Are the users satisfied with the information provided? Are the users satisfied with the personal service offered?	% of users satisfied with the information provided % of users satisfied with the personal service from those operating the database	High	High
EFFECTIVENESS	Awareness	Do you know about the database?	% of scientists / researchers who know about the database	High	Medium

defining the scope of the evaluation to use as the basis for designing the evaluation questions and indicators allows you to see clearly what data are required and the most appropriate data collection methods to use.

It should be possible to generate automatically much of the data required to evaluate your database. In addition, routine records on dates of updating and numbers of records should also be easily accessible.

Table 4.66 gives some guidance on which data collection tools are most appropriate to use for the indicators identified. Note that some of the tools needed for some indicators might be too expensive to use and you might have to find more creative ways to get the information you need or perhaps decide against using that particular indicator.

Analysing the data

It is advisable to think about data analysis tools and methods before starting the data collection. This will help to ensure that the right types of data are being collected.

Table 4.67 will help you to start thinking in this way. For example, if you want to know what the users think about the database, you should already be thinking about ways to interview them.

Table 4.66
Example of data collection methods for evaluating a database

DATA COLLECTION METHOD	INFORMATION SOURCE	KEY ISSUES / QUESTIONS	ANSWERS EXPECTED AND CONCERNS
Desk study	Feedback from users (e.g., letters, emails)	Are users satisfied with the database? Is the database making a difference to the type and quality of research being done? Is the database addressing the objectives it set out to do?	Some users may not have access to a database. Users who give feedback may not be the target group. Need to test the findings by looking at the user profile (i.e., in this case researchers, scientists and students)
	Accounts department	How much time is involved in developing and updating the database? What is the cost of production?	
Interviews/questionnaires/ self-administered questionnaire Informal interviews	Selected users Staff, partners	Are you aware of the database? Is the database useful? How have you changed/improved your research as a result of the database? What is your opinion on how the database was produced and content included?	Time consuming, expensive Self-administered questionnaire less expensive; but the respondent may not fill in the questionnaire correctly or at all Need to ensure that feedback is confidential to encourage trust and openness
Direct observation	Identify 5 users to test the database by assigning set tasks to do	How easy is it to find the information asked? Were there problems in accessing the information requested?	
Meetings	Staff, NGOs, government agencies	What do you think about the structure, content, interactive use of the database? How to improve collaboration?	Difficulty in getting partners to work with your organisation

In designing the data analysis for a database evaluation, you should ask the following questions:

- Which analytical tools should be used? (e.g., a table featuring the type of questions versus the type of users, a graph showing development of users over time, or specific analytical tools such as a problem tree, process chart or SWOT analysis)
- Which collection methods will provide the necessary data for each of the tools?
- What type of observations do you expect to make for each tool?
- What type of conclusions do you expect to reach from using the tools?

Once you have designed the data analysis, it is important to see if your data collection includes all elements. The results from some data collection methods (e.g., interviews) could be specifically meant for checking and/or interpreting other data. Explain instances where you were unable to gather certain data.

Preparing a communication plan

Designing the communication plan is an important activity in the evaluation process in order to ensure that the conclusions and recommendations from the evaluation are well understood

Table 4.67
Example of a data analysis design for a database evaluation

ANALYTICAL TOOLS AND TABLES	RESULTS FROM COLLECTION METHOD USED	TYPE OF OBSERVATIONS TO MAKE	TYPE OF CONCLUSIONS TO REACH
Table 1: Type of users	Desk study	Categories of users that are over/under-represented	Categories of users to give more attention to
Table 2: (target group) Relevance to the target group	Desk study Questionnaires Interviews	How useful is the database given the needs of the target group	Whether the database has outlived its purpose
Table 3: (target group) Access	Desk study Questionnaires Interviews	High and low satisfaction with the database as a whole Level of awareness of the database Level of access of the target group to the database	Priorities for improvement, obstacles
Table 4: Usabilty Learnability Efficiency Memorability Satisfaction of target group Content Retrieval	Interviews	Whether staff and partners are happy with the database	Can determine whether the database has to be modified
Table 5: Efficiency	Data from accounts	Cost to produce the database Time involved in the production process	Potential areas for reducing costs/time
Figure 1: Process flow chart	Database management procedures manual Interviews	Bottlenecks in the process	Process steps to improve
Table 6: Impact stories	In-depth interviews, case studies, feedback from correspondence	Personal stories of how research has improved because of increased access to the database Statistics showing, for example, change type and quality of research undertaken	Determine whether there has been some change in the quality and number of research papers produced

and supported. In designing this communication strategy, you need to consider the following issues:

- Which communication methods will suit which stakeholders, especially the primary stakeholders?
- What are the main issues to be discussed and reported taking into consideration the communication method and target group?

An effective communication plan for critical reflection during an evaluation and reporting findings during and after the evaluation helps to create common understanding among stakeholders, providing a good basis for implementing recommendations.

If your stakeholders don't accept the conclusions and recommendations resulting from the evaluation, it will probably be almost impossible to motivate them to make the required

Table 4.68
Example of a communication plan for reporting the findings from a database evaluation

COMMUNICATION METHOD	STAKEHOLDERS TO REPORT TO	MAIN ISSUES TO DISCUSS / REPORT ON
Critical reflection	Staff, selected partners	Critically reflect on results from the data collection
Summary report	Representatives from the users and partners	Results from data collection
Full report, including executive summary	Funding agency Database management	Impact, effectiveness and efficiency and conclusions and recommendations
Personal meetings	Database management	Conclusions and recommendations
Database promotional brochure	Target users	Main findings in broad terms and how the database has changed in response to the needs of users Examples of database impact stories

changes. However, if they have been included throughout the process, they are more likely to accept the conclusions.

During the process of critical reflection and reporting, you should ask:

- Do stakeholders have the same views on the problems with the database?
- Do they have the same views on the solutions?
- Are they prepared to support the same solutions?
- What obstacles prevent them from implementing the solutions proposed?
- What can be done to address the obstacles they face?

There are various ways in which you can convey the results of the evaluation (e.g., providing a summary of your findings, organising a meeting, a memorandum, an internet page). You might also want to consider the type of information you make available to the various target groups. The communication plan you use will depend on your circumstance and the facilities available to you. You might also want to consider sharing the results of your evaluation with your users, so that if there are changes to the database they will not come as a surprise to the users.

If the stakeholders are properly involved in the evaluation process in terms of participation and input, then getting their agreement on the relevance, reliability and quality of the data collected, the adequacy of the analysis provided and the conclusions drawn should not be difficult. Be aware, however, that although there might be general acceptance of a proposed solution, you might not be able to implement the solution because of a lack of resources, time and/or capacity.

An important component of the communication process is to find out what difficulties the stakeholders expect and/or experience in implementing the recommendations. Where changes can be implemented without difficulty, it is advisable to implement them as quickly as possible.

Box 4.17
Evaluating a database: guidelines checklist

These guidelines on evaluating a database are covered above:

- Database concept and objectives
- Data needs and stakeholder participation
- Evaluation focus, questions and indicators
- Data collection
- Data analysis
- The communication plan

For more on:

- data analysis, see Part 2, page 60 and Part 3, 157-162
- data collection, see Part 2, pages 58-59 and Part 3, pages 106-115
- evaluation communication and follow-up, see Part 3, pages 163-173
- evaluation criteria (scope), see Part 2, pages 33-34
- indicators, see Part 3, pages 91-98
- logframe, see Part 3, pages 68-83
- logic model, see Part 3, pages 103-105
- stakeholder participation, see Part 1, pages 3-5
- terms of reference, see Part 2, pages 32-35

SELECTIVE DISSEMINATION OF INFORMATION (SDI) SERVICE

> These guidelines relate to evaluating an SDI service, using the terms of reference (see Part 3, pages 99-103) as the basis of the evaluation and drawing on examples where appropriate.
>
> It is important to make the evaluation process as participatory as possible, involving colleagues and key stakeholders from the outset, including your primary stakeholders (see Part 1, pages 3-5). By doing this, you will find the experience more rewarding and more likely to result in a general acceptance of the evaluation findings, making it much easier to implement change.
>
> The notion of 'critical reflection' is discussed towards the end of the guidelines, but we advise you and your evaluation team to 'reflect' on the main findings and problems at each stage of the evaluation process, for learning purposes and to improve the way you conduct the evaluation. (See Part 1, pages 5-6).
>
> The background to the evaluation process in general – concepts, context, terms, trends and core ingredients – is described in Part 2. Do read that section if you're not familiar with certain concepts or terms that occur in these guidelines. And in Part 3 you will find more on the evaluation tools described here.

Before evaluating an SDI service, you need to be clear about:

- what the main elements of the SDI service are
- its concept(s) and objectives
- who the primary and secondary stakeholders are
- how to go about identifying the needs of the primary and secondary stakeholders
- what the focus of the evaluation is, the questions to ask and the indicators to use
- how to collect the data and analyse them
- how to communicate with your key stakeholders, to critically reflect upon the evaluation results and to report the results in such a way that they will be accepted and acted upon

What is an SDI service?

An SDI service is a current awareness service that provides users with up-to-date and relevant information on a regular basis: monthly, bi-monthly or quarterly. Libraries and information services often provide such a service. It is based on profiles that describe the users' information needs.

A profile is compiled by the user in conjunction with the information professionals who provide the service. The profile is a symbolic description of a documentary/information requirement represented by a search equation. It can be a standard profile designed for a group of users sharing a common information need, or a personalised profile designed for an individual user. The profile is used as the starting point to select relevant information for the user. The profiles are run on multiple databases to ensure optimum recall based on subject, geographical and linguistic coverage. The service usually sends users newly recorded bibliographic records, including abstracts corresponding to their respective profiles.

An SDI service is often coupled with a document delivery service that allows users to order documents of particular interest. The service is usually provided by information centres, and is frequently run by larger organisations.

The establishment of an SDI service represents a significant investment in both human and financial resources. It is therefore essential to ensure that this service is meeting the objectives for which it was established.

Determining the SDI service concept and objectives

You can't evaluate your SDI service unless you are clear what it is about. The concept (idea) behind the service and the objectives it seeks to achieve need to be clearly stated, otherwise you can't compare its actual performance with its intended performance. Also, without a clear concept it is difficult to make the right choices during the evaluation process.

In determining an SDI service concept, you should ask these questions:

- Why was the SDI service developed?
- What were the main objectives (expected results) and main problems to be addressed at the time?
- What is the goal of the service?
- What are its core values?
- What is the project purpose of the service?

In evaluating the SDI service, you need to ask yourself key questions related to the concept, such as:

- Do the expected results achieved reflect its core values and approach?
- Do they reflect the project purpose and contribute to the overall objective?
- Does the SDI service address the main objectives and problems it was supposed to?
- Are the correct messages being conveyed?

Box 4.18
Example of a concept behind an SDI service supporting economic development

Main problem: Researchers and scientists in developing countries have limited access to the requisite academic literature to support their research activities and to develop appropriate technologies needed to support the development of their country's economies.

Goal: To improve the quality of research and development of appropriate technologies to improve the quality of life of the population.

Purpose: Access of information to researchers and scientists improved.

Expected results: An appropriate SDI service for the target group provided.

Main approach: To provide the service to key institutions concerned with research and scientific development within the country.

Core values: Relevance, usability, effectiveness

The logical framework can help you clarify the SDI service objectives (see pages 68-83). Commonly known as the 'logframe', it helps to summarise a project in a logical sequence. If a project plan lacks a logframe, it is useful to construct one so that you have a good idea of your objectives and the consequent hierarchy of activities. An example of a logframe for an SDI service is given in Table 4.69.

Where the SDI service is not seen as a project, but as an ongoing activity, the logic model might be the more appropriate tool to use. It provides an overview of activities associated with the service, the resources used, the outputs/results, the outcomes/effects and the impact. An example of a logic model applied to an SDI service is given in Table 4.70.

Clarifying data needs and stakeholder participation

When preparing for an evaluation, you will need to know who your primary and secondary stakeholders are, so that you can determine your data needs and involve stakeholder representatives in the evaluation. The stakeholders should be taken into account at every stage of the evaluation, from its planning and design, to being part of the team as well as sources of information, and providing feedback on the evaluation results. It will be difficult to implement the evaluation recommendations if they are not acceptable to your stakeholders.

The range of stakeholders in an SDI service could include:

- users (primary stakeholders, e.g., researchers, lecturers, policy-makers, extension workers, farmers, groups/organisations including women's groups and farmer associations, input suppliers, students, training institutions)
- partners (organisations with resources needed for the success of the SDI service)
- policy-makers (those who have approved the implementation of the service)
- implementing agency
- funding agencies (e.g., development organisations, NGOs, government ministries)

The stakeholders will have a vested interest in the evaluation itself, and should be consulted and involved in some way. The input of the different groups will vary, depending on the particular situation. You should therefore take into account:

- their interests when designing the evaluation
- how they can actively contribute to the evaluation process
- how to include them as part of the evaluation team
- their role as a source of data (e.g., via questionnaires, interviews and workshops)
- their feedback on evaluation results

One way of identifying these stakeholders is to conduct a stakeholder analysis. It helps you to identify the key stakeholders, how they benefit from and contribute to the SDI service and how to include them in the evaluation. Table 4.71 provides an example of a stakeholder analysis.

When considering the stakeholders' interests in the SDI service, be aware of the kind of questions that they would like to have answered. Table 4.72 gives an overview of the kind of key questions that might be asked. If you know your stakeholders really well, you can start the process by working with your colleagues to formulate the questions based on your knowledge of them. But the stakeholders must become involved at some stage to ensure that you have their views. You can do this using interviews, workshops, and questionnaires with individual or groups of stakeholders.

Table 4.69
Logical framework for an SDI service

	INTERVENTION LOGIC	OBJECTIVELY VERIFIABLE INDICATORS	MEANS OF VERIFICATION	ASSUMPTIONS
GOAL	To contribute to improved quality of life of the population through research and development of appropriate technologies			
SDI SERVICE PURPOSE	Availability of information to researchers and scientists improved	After 3 years number of users tripled	Routine records	Access to SDI contributes to increased production
EXPECTED RESULTS	Improved awareness among users and partners. Improved availability of adequate information materials	After 3 years: - 90% of users and partners aware of the SDI - 75% of requests can be addressed with existing information resources - 50% increase in number of publications written	Survey Routine records	Increased awareness leads to increased use
ACTIVITIES	1.1 Organise meeting with partners to discuss SDI and its promotion 1.2 Develop promotional campaign with partners 1.3 Implement campaign 2.1 User needs survey and discussions with key stakeholders 2.2 Formulate project proposal 2.3. Generate donor interest and funding to strengthen SDI 2.4 Develop implementation plan 2.5 Acquire additional resources	(sometimes a summary of resources/means is provided in this box)	(sometimes a summary of costs/budget is provided in this box)	(if the activities are completed, what assumptions must hold true to deliver the expected results)
INPUTS	Funding from donor agency; core funding from Ministry	List resources available		

Defining the evaluation focus, questions and indicators

Most evaluation exercises need to be limited in focus to reflect time and budget limitations. It is not possible to cover all elements of an SDI service extensively every time you carry out an evaluation, so you need to choose the focus of your evaluation, based on stakeholders' key questions and the time and cost of accessing data.

The focus of the evaluation might stem from your desire to improve the SDI service, from low or declining use, from feedback from others, or from a need to cut costs. There might be

Part 4: EVALUATION GUIDELINES: Selective dissemination of information (SDI) service

Table 4.70
Logic model for an SDI service

FOCUS	RESOURCES	ACTIVITIES	OUTPUTS (indicators of results)	OUTCOMES (indicators of effects)	IMPACT INDICATORS
Planning and development					
1. User needs identification	Open-minded staff Transport, postage, photocopies Willingness of users to participate	Design and administer questionnaires/interviews Conduct meetings Analyse data and draw conclusions	List of user needs, list of ideas identified, list of stakeholders who should be involved	Changes based on user needs analysis	
2. Involving stakeholders and partners	External-oriented staff Transport, copies Willingness of partners	Calls, visits, meetings with external partners	No. of calls and visits made and meetings organised No. of new external agencies involved	Increased level of awareness of role of SDI No. of information sources increased	
3. Process development	Dedicated staff, view from client perspective, Willingness to address bottlenecks	Developing agreements Process analysis Address bottlenecks Develop/update procedures and user profiles	Bottlenecks reduced Procedures manual compiled User profile database developed Evaluation form made Follow up form made	Time and costs of providing the information User satisfaction increased	
4. Developing information sources	Own resources (books, reports, databases) Partners Internet databases	Identify and select information resources Develop access to resources	Broader range of literature offered	% increase in the volume of information available	
5. Budgeting and financing	Capable staff Support of management and donor agencies. Organisational guidelines Donor financial guidelines	Make a financial plan Specify activities Calculate the budget Implementation/operations	Clear financial proposal Clear financial report	Funds available Expenditure within budget limits Staff and management agree on financial priorities	
Implementattion/operations					
6. Promotional activities	Motivated, skilled staff Promotional materials (website, posters, brochures)	Posters/brochures developed Meetings organised Websites maintained Media informed	No. of brochures sent No. of meetings and no. of participants in meetings No. of website visitors No. of press releases	% of potential target groups being aware of the service No. of partners (experts involved) increases	% change in number of user profiles developed to meet the needs of users % of users who share information received from SDI
7. Delivery of services	Experts Database of information sources, user profiles Alerting/message tools to regularly send out information Full-text documents	Liaise with experts Regularly sending out information based on the user profiles Update user profiles	No. of requests for full text papers increases More, better targeted literature/bibliographic references offered	% of users being satisfied with the information received	% change in the volume of published and unpublished papers
Monitoring and evaluation					
8. Monitoring and evaluation	Capable staff Clear procedures Adequate registration Indicators of quality, effectiveness, efficiency	Define indicators Design report formats Organise data collection Generate statistics & reports	Routine records regularly updated (monthly, quarterly, yearly)	Improved effectiveness and efficiency of the service	

Table 4.71
Stakeholder analysis for an SDI service

STAKEHOLDER CATEGORY	BENEFITS FROM THE PROJECT	CONTRIBUTIONS / SACRIFICES	INFLUENCE ON THE PROJECT	POTENTIAL INVOLVEMENT IN THE EVALUATION
Users (e.g., researchers, scientists, students, farmers)	Improved knowledge on issues they are investigating	Time to look through the information Cost to access the service	Content, form of delivery, format of the information provided	Represented on the team Involved in analysis and decisions on actions for change An information source Informed about main findings
Policy-makers and partners (e.g., libraries and research institutes)	Better information for the scientific and research community	Time and support for the service, costs are also involved	Through contracts and agreements	Source of information Represented on the team Informed about main findings
Implementing agency	Improved service Improved outreach Promotional effect	Time to develop SDI concept and convince funding agency	Through project plan, project management and implementation, provision of service	Represented on the team Involved in the planning Should be informed of the findings
Funding agencies (e.g., NGOs, ministries, development agencies)	Results to show to their clientele	Finance and time	On project concept, planning and monitoring and evaluation	Should be informed of the findings

Table 4.72
Key questions stakeholders could be interested in

STAKEHOLDER CATEGORY	QUESTIONS THEY ARE INTERESTED IN	POTENTIAL USE OF THE ANSWERS
Users (e.g., researchers, scientists, students, farmers)	Is the information provided relevant, timely and applicable? Is the information provided in an appropriate format? Is the overall service satisfactory?	Will they continue to use the service? Are they likely to recommend it to others?
Policy-makers and partners (e.g., libraries, research institutes)	How effective and efficient is the service?	Should we continue to collaborate with the organisation implementing the service?
Implementing agency	How effective and efficient is the service? How can the service be financed in the future?	Should we continue with the service? What should we do to improve it? What should we do to reduce costs and increase income?
Funding agencies (e.g., NGOs, ministries, development agencies)	Does the service have an impact on the quality of research and development in the country? How sustainable is the service after we stop funding?	Should we continue, reduce or increase our funding? In what areas can/should we assist?

concerns about the SDI service in comparison with a competitor. Other examples of areas of focus include:

- a specific objective (i.e., providing information on particular subjects)
- specific assessment criteria (e.g., relevance and impact of the service)
- the primary stakeholders or those experiencing the most problems
- a combination of all of these

Asking specific questions will help you to improve key aspects of the SDI service. With each key question, you need to think about the indicators you will need to help you answer that question. Indicators also determine the type of data to collect. Remember to consider the interests of the stakeholders and the ease of access you have to the data you need in terms of time and cost.

Table 4.73 provides an example of the focus, key questions and indicators for an SDI service. You can use the information here to develop a more specific set of questions, relevant to the focus of the SDI service. Using the feedback from your stakeholders and the data available to you, you will be able to determine which questions are important for your evaluation.

With reference to Table 4.73 you may want to focus on one criterion (e.g., impact) because of its importance to the continuation of the SDI service or on the criteria of usability and accessibility because of their importance to the users. If accountability is the main purpose of the evaluation you may want to limit the scope of the evaluation to the relevance, effectiveness and efficiency of the service.

Drawing up a matrix like Table 4.73 shows how important it is to have access to good data to support your evaluation and, by extension, how important it is to maintain a good monitoring system of data relating to your SDI service.

For an SDI service, it is particularly important to keep routine records, providing details of each user profile, when it was received, when updates were sent, the information provided (level, subject) and means of delivery. This will provide the basis for the evaluation. However, certain aspects such as impact, relevance and awareness require an extensive survey among users and potential users. So, depending on what you want to know, you will need to have evaluation questions that focus on the users' view of the service.

Collecting the data

When you have determined your scope, focus and indicators, you will need to decide how to collect the data. It is important to develop a data collection strategy that ensures:

- that all relevant data will become available during the evaluation
- that no more data are collected than what is needed and can be analysed

Data collection therefore requires careful preparation. It happens too often that too much data are collected, or that insufficient 'good' data are collected to draw the relevant conclusions. Properly defining the scope of the evaluation to use as the basis for designing the evaluation questions and indicators allows you to see clearly what data are required and the most appropriate data collection methods to use.

Good SDI evaluations should collect information from both the service provider and users to ensure that decisions made are based on comprehensive, accurate and relevant data. While absolute

Table 4.73
Determining the focus, key questions and indicators for the evaluation of an SDI service, using some evaluation criteria as examples

EVALUATION CRITERIA (SCOPE)	FOCUS	KEY QUESTIONS	INDICATORS	STAKEHOLDER INTEREST	DATA ACCESSIBILITY
IMPACT	Change in quality and type of research produced	Is there more local applied research aimed at improving production?	% of producers who are able to improve their production after having access to locally produced research and technology	High	Low
RELEVANCE	Information needs of users	Do the users find the service useful?	% of users who find the SDI useful % of users who find the information irrelevant	High	Medium
ACCESSIBILITY	Access	Are stakeholders able to subscribe to the service? Can users easily get the information needed from the service?	% of stakeholders who want to subscribe to the service, but can't % of researchers/scientists who face difficulties accessing information from the service	High	Medium
	Delivery	How was the service delivered?	No. of users who receive their information by paper, e-mail	Medium	High
	User satisfaction	Are the users satisfied with the information provided by the service? Are the users satisfied with the personal service offered?	% of users satisfied with the service % of users who are satisfied with the personal service they received from those operating the service	High	Medium
	User profile	Are the profiles up-to-date and cover user information needs?	No. of users who feel their profile reflected their regular information requirements	High	High
EFFECTIVENESS	Awareness	Do you know about the service?	% of scientists/researchers who know about the service	High	Medium
	Timeliness	Is the information needed produced on a timely basis?	% of users who receive the information on a timely basis No. of complaints received related to delays in receiving the right information	High	Medium
EFFICIENCY	Expenditure: How much does it cost to have access to the information?	How many profiles need to be developed/updated and what are the costs and the time involved to meet the information needs based on the profiles?	What is the unit cost per profile? What is the average cost/time involved in producing the information for the profiles?	Medium	High

Part 4: EVALUATION GUIDELINES: Selective dissemination of information (SDI) service

Table 4.74
Example of data collection methods for evaluating an SDI service

DATA COLLECTION METHOD	INFORMATION SOURCE	KEY ISSUES / QUESTIONS	ANSWERS EXPECTED AND CONCERNS
Desk study	SDI records Internal memoranda on meetings with colleagues, letters, emails	Number and type of users, subject interest Is the service making a difference to research and scientific development? Is the service doing what it set out to do? Are the users satisfied?	Some researchers and scientists don't have access to the service Very satisfied to very dissatisfied
	Accounts department	How much time and money are involved in developing the database, producing the information and delivering the services including the full-text documents?	Costs can vary depending on the number of requests for document deliveries
Interviews/questionnaires	Researchers, scientists	Are the users using the information? Have they written more papers or done more research as a result of increased access to the SDI?	Time consuming, expensive Self-administered questionnaires are less expensive; but the respondent may not fill in the questionnaire correctly or at all
Workshop	Partners, publishing houses	Strengths, weaknesses, opportunities and threats of the SDI Possibilities to improve collaboration	

numbers are important (to determine the size of the need, for comparison between groups and over time), you should also calculate percentages.

Table 4.74 gives some guidance on which data collection tools are most appropriate to use for the indicators identified. Note that some of the tools needed for some indicators might be too expensive to use and you might have to find more creative ways to get the information you need or decide against using that particular indicator.

Analysing the data

It is advisable to think about data analysis tools and methods before starting the data collection. This will help to ensure that the right types of data are being collected.

Table 4.75 will help you to start thinking in this way. For example, if you want to know what users think about the SDI service, you should already be thinking about ways to interview them.

In designing the data analysis for an SDI service evaluation, you should ask the following questions:

- Which analytical tools should be used? (e.g., a table featuring the type of questions versus the type of users, a graph showing increase in users over time, or specific analytical tools such as a problem tree, process chart or SWOT analysis)
- Which collection methods will provide the necessary data for each of the tools?
- What type of observations do you expect to make for each tool?
- What type of conclusions do you expect to reach from using the tools?

Table 4.75
Example of a data analysis design for an SDI service

ANALYTICAL TOOLS AND TABLES	RESULTS FROM COLLECTION METHOD USED	TYPE OF OBSERVATIONS TO MAKE	TYPE OF CONCLUSIONS TO REACH
Table 1: Type of questions and type of users	Desk study	Categories of users that are over/under-represented	Categories of users to give more attention to
Table 2: (target group) Relevance	Desk study Questionnaires Interviews	How useful is the service given the needs of the target group	Whether or not the SDI is providing the 'right' information
Table 3: Accessibility	Desk study Questionnaires Interviews	Whether the target group is able to access the service	Need to devise ways of increasing access to target group
Table 4: Usabilty User satisfaction	Desk study Questionnaires Interviews	High and low satisfaction with the service as a whole	Areas for improvement
Table 5 (target group) Effectiveness: - Awareness - Coverage	Desk study Questionnaires Interviews	Level of awareness of the service Level of access of the target group to the service Range of topics covered by the SDI	Priorities for improvement Obstacles to improvement
Table 6: Efficiency	Data from accounts	Cost to produce the information	Potential areas for reducing costs/time
Figure 1: Problem tree	Questionnaires, interviews, workshop	Constraints in the process	Process steps to improve
Table 7: Impact stories	In-depth interviews, case studies, feedback from users	Anecdotal evidence that locally produced scientific material is promoting development in certain areas of the economy	Continue/redirect the SDI
Figure 2: SWOT analysis	Workshop with staff, stakeholders	Strengths, weaknesses, opportunities and threats of the SDI	New strategy for the SDI

Once you have designed the data analysis, it is important to see if your data collection includes all elements. The results from some data collection methods (e.g., interviews) could be specifically meant for checking and/or interpreting other data. Explain instances where you were unable to gather certain data.

Preparing a communication plan

Designing the communication plan is an important activity in the evaluation process to ensure that conclusions and recommendations from the evaluation are well understood and supported. In designing this strategy, you need to consider these issues:

- Which communication methods will suit which stakeholders, especially the primary stakeholders?
- What are the main issues to be discussed and reported, taking into consideration the communication method and target group?

An effective communication plan for critical reflection during an evaluation and reporting findings during and after the evaluation helps to create common understanding among stakeholders, providing a good basis for implementing recommendations. If your stakeholders don't accept the conclusions and recommendations resulting from the evaluation, it will be almost impossible to motivate them to make the required changes. However, if they have been included throughout the process, they are more likely to accept the conclusions.

During the process of critical reflection and reporting, you should ask:

- Do stakeholders have the same views on the problems with the service?
- Do they have the same views on the solutions?
- Are they prepared to support the same solutions?
- What obstacles prevent them from implementing the solutions proposed?
- What can be done to address the obstacles they face?

There are various ways in which you can convey the results of the evaluation (e.g., providing a summary of your findings, organising a meeting, a memorandum, an internet page). You might also want to consider the type of information you make available to the various target groups. The communication plan you use will depend on your circumstance and the facilities available to you.

Whatever you decide, your findings and recommendations should be presented in a way that is easily understood and accepted by all so that the desired changes can be implemented (see Table 4.76).

If the stakeholders are properly involved in the evaluation process in terms of participation and input, then getting their agreement on the relevance, reliability and quality of the data collected, the adequacy of the analysis provided and the conclusions drawn should not be difficult. Be aware, however, that although there might be general acceptance of a proposed solution, you might not be able to implement the solution because of a lack of resources, time and/or capacity.

Table 4.76
Example of a communication plan for reporting the findings from an SDI service

COMMUNICATION METHOD	STAKEHOLDERS TO REPORT TO	MAIN ISSUES TO DISCUSS / REPORT ON
Critical reflection	Staff, selected partners	Critically reflect on results from the data collection
SWOT analysis	Representatives of SDI, partners, other key stakeholders	Critically reflecting on the results from the data collection
Brainstorming	Evaluation team	Problematic issues as they arise
Summary report	Users of the service	Results from data collection in terms of whether the service is useful or not; positives; constraints
Full report, including executive summary	Funding agency, SDI management	Relevance, satisfaction, awareness, access, reach Impact indication, cost-effectiveness
Personal meeting	SDI management	Conclusions and recommendations Feedback on individual staff members
SDI promotional brochure	Target users	Examples of SDI impact stories

An important component of the communication process is to find out what difficulties the stakeholders expect and/or experience in implementing the recommendations. Where changes can be implemented without difficulty, it is advisable to implement them as quickly as possible.

> **Box 4.17**
> **Evaluating an SDI service: guidelines checklist**
>
> These guidelines on evaluating an SDI service are covered above:
>
> - SDI service concept and objectives
> - Data needs and stakeholder participation
> - Evaluation focus, questions and indicators
> - Data collection
> - Data analysis
> - The communication plan
>
> For more on:
>
> - data analysis, see Part 2, page 60 and Part 3, 157-162
> - data collection, see Part 2, pages 58-59 and Part 3, pages 106-115
> - evaluation communication and follow-up, see Part 3, pages 163-173
> - evaluation criteria (scope), see Part 2, pages 33-34
> - indicators, see Part 3, pages 91-98
> - logframe, see Part 3, pages 68-83
> - logic model, see Part 3, pages 103-105
> - stakeholder participation, see Part 1, pages 3-5
> - terms of reference, see Part 2, pages 32-35

ANNEXES

ANNEX 1   Toolkit background

ANNEX 2   Toolkit contributors

ANNEX 3   Workshop participants

ANNEX 4   Information sources

ANNEX 5   Glossary

ANNEX 1

Toolkit background

Since 2001, a group of information practitioners from development agencies have been working together on the evaluation of information projects, products and services. The lead agencies in this undertaking have been the ACP-EU Technical Centre for Agricultural and Rural Cooperation (CTA), the International Institute for Communication and Development (IICD) and the Royal Tropical Institute (KIT), working with a range of partner institutions. The group was referred to as the LEAP IMPACT partnership, after the name of the online community of practice.

The partnership examined the challenges facing the information professional who wants to evaluate his or her own information service, but does not have adequate experience and knowledge. This is mainly because:

- the literature that could act as a guide is highly dispersed, and the publications that are available tend not to be aimed at a self-help or practitioner audience

- there is often no evaluation culture or related evaluation expertise on which to build, with the result that carrying out an evaluation is often seen as intimidating

Although these challenges apply particularly to information professionals in a resource-poor or isolated situation, they are also valid for most information professionals working in the field of information for development. The ability to undertake an evaluation – and to look at one's own products and services in an analytical and systematic manner – strengthens the professional capacity of the information practitioner. Logically, this would lead to his or her professional empowerment and the improved management of information services in the organisation.

It was at the first meeting of the group in Bonn, Germany in 2001 that the idea for the first 'how to' manual on self-evaluation for information practitioners was conceived. The word 'smart' was chosen to emphasise the 'clever' or 'appropriate' aspects of the tools. It also referred to the SMART indicators (specific, measurable, achievable, realistic, time-bound) common in the evaluation literature.

Potential contributors were identified and a series of workshops were held to refine the content of the manual. The first edition was launched in 2005 in Tanzania. The feedback indicated that a second, revised edition was called for. Writing the second edition involved information practitioners from South and North, putting their experiences down on paper and also tapping into the knowledge of experts in the field of evaluation and information. In order to obtain comments on the draft version from other experts and practitioners, a workshop was held in Bonn in 2007, followed by an evaluation training workshop in St Lucia in 2008. The draft was also made available for peer review on a wiki page, enabling the contributors to easily exchange views and provide new inputs for the second edition.

The feedback from the workshops and reviews was incorporated into the draft, and it then underwent a final editing process prior to publication.

ANNEX 2

Toolkit contributors

The co-ordinators from the lead agencies involved in compiling this toolkit – CTA, IICD and KIT – have played a pivotal role in making the toolkit a reality, and the LEAP IMPACT community of practice were crucial in facilitating dialogue among all those involved.

The writers and collaborators who voluntarily contributed their time and energy to the development of the evaluation tools were drawn from both the South and North, representing governments, the private sector, non-governmental organisations and universities. Many are information specialists with a wide range of experience in the evaluation of information products.

The tools were tested in African, Caribbean and Pacific (ACP) countries, as well as in Asia, Europe and the USA, with many of the tool writers acting as supervisors and providing valuable guidance along the way. Many of the testers were drawn from networks developed as a result of the increased level of collaboration within the information community. These testers and supervisors contributed greatly to the further refinement of the toolkit.

Many of the tools were reviewed by a distinguished group of evaluators from the European Evaluation Society and the International Development Evaluation Association, who participated in electronic discussions and attended a workbench meeting to refine the manual.

The contributors to the second edition are listed here. This is followed by a list of contributors to the first edition, including test supervisors and reviewers.

SECOND EDITION

Co-ordinators
Heemskerk, Harry (KIT)
Khadar, Ibrahim (Dr) (CTA)
Nigten, Riet (IICD)

Writers and contributors
Akande, Modupe (Professor)
Alkemade, Bert
Batjes-Sinclair, Karen
op de Coul, Maartje
Cummings, Sarah
Davies, Jackie
Diallo, Alassane
Dumur, Dhaneswar
van Dyk, Herman
Gast, Lisette
Heemskerk, Harry
Hewlitt, Allison
Khadar, Ibrahim (Dr)
Kooijman, Margo
Kusters, Cecile
Lauckner, Bruce
Lenglet, Frans
McQuinn, Mark
Mook, Byron (Dr)
Nath, Shampa
Nigten, Riet
Okail, Nancy
Osei, Simon
Springer-Heinze, Andreas (Dr)
Vincent, Rob (Dr)
Visser-Mabogunje, Lola
Wigboldus, Seerp

Steering Committee
(Bonn workshop, October 2007)

Coordination and arbitration
Ayayi, Flora
Heemskerk, Harry
Keller, Mara
Khadar, Ibrahim (Dr)
Knipschild, Henning
Neun, Hansjörg (Dr)
Nigten, Riet

Content and development
Alkemade, Bert
Baguma, Sylvester
Batjes-Sinclair, Karen
Kebede, Gashaw (Dr)
Kusters, Cecile
Lauckner, Bruce

Lombard, Huibre
Pamba, Petro
Sam, Joel
Thieba, Daniel (Dr)

Editorial and production
Blackman, Rachel
Herrema, Auke
Matturi, Jenessi
Parr, Martin (Dr)

Outreach and collaboration
Assigbley, Yawo
Bernard, Marc
Byer, Mark
Kagoiya, Rachel
Mondé, Prosper
Nath, Shampa
Portegies Zwart, Robert

FIRST EDITION

Co-ordinators
Cummings, Sarah (KIT)
Gast, Lisette (IICD)
Visser-Mabogunje, Lola (CTA)

Writers and contributors
Akande, Modupe (Professor)
Batjes-Sinclair, Karen
op de Coul, Maartje
Cummings, Sarah
Davies, Jackie
Diallo, Alassane
Dumur, Dhaneswar
van Dyk, Herman
Gast, Lisette
Hewlitt, Allison
Khadar, Ibrahim (Dr)
Kooijman, Margo
Lauckner, Bruce
Lenglet, Frans
McQuinn, Mark
Mook, Byron (Dr)
Okail, Nancy
Osei, Simon
Springer-Heinze, Andreas (Dr)
Vincent, Rob (Dr)
Visser-Mabogunje, Lola

Collaborators
Chakanyuka, Jaison
Diaw, Boubacar
Dumur, Dhaneswar
van Dyk, Herman
Hendriks, Stefan
Kalume, Christine
Lauckner, Bruce
McQuinn, Mark
Phipps, Andy
Richardson, Victoria
Sam, Joel
Singh, Alec
Visser-Mabogunje, Lola

Testers
Ayinla, Alayande
de Chassy, Stephanie
Chibomba, Kelvin
De Frietas, Claudette
Diabate, Dembélé
Ebong, Geoffrey
Hattotuwa, Sanjana
Kasuga, Richard
Muinde, Francis
Nachibinga, Golden

Namponya, Clemens
Ogunsumi, Lucy
Okello, Dorothy
Prasad, Daniel
Sow, Fatoumata
van den Wollenberg, Lidwien

Test supervisors
Akande, Modupe (Professor)
op de Coul, Maartje
Cummings, Sarah
Diaw, Boubacar
van Dyk, Herman
Asaba, Jane Frances
Kooijman, Margo
Lauckner, Bruce
Lufadeju, E.A. (Professor)
Mbabu, Adiel (Dr)
Okello, Dorothy
Tiémogo, Ibrahim (Dr)

Visser-Mabogunje, Lola
Umar, Mohammed (Dr)

Editorial and production
Batjes-Sinclair, Karen
Allen, Ann
Budhram, Dowlat (Dr)
Pinder, Richard

Peer reviewers
Budhram, Dowlat (Dr)
Chakanyuka, Jaison
Khadar, Ibrahim (Dr)
Lauckner, Bruce
Lenglet, Frans
Mbeng, Martin
McQuinn, Mark
Niang, Thiendou (Dr)
Okail, Nancy
Pinder, Richard
Schiefer, Ulrich (Professor Dr)

ANNEX 3

Workshop participants

Bonn Workshop
9–12 October 2001

Guest participants
De Haas, Hans-Joachim (Dr)
Engel, Paul (Dr)
Franzen, Hubertus (Dr)
Greenidge, Carl B.
Kuby, Thomas
Suden, Wilhem (Dr)

Participants
Adupa, Joyce
Akande, Modupe (Professor)
Alexaki, Nancy
Asiamah, Helen
Badji, Moussa (Dr)
Batjes-Sinclair, Karen
Cummings, Sarah
Ducastel, Nathan
van Dyk, Herman
Esterhuysen, Anriette
Flanagan, Jim
Gast, Lisette
Graham-Knight, Natasha
Hagenaars, M.J.L.J. (Dr)
Hewlitt, Alison
Kalume, Christine
Kanfi, Shady
Kanyunyuzi-Asaba, Jane Frances
Khadar, Ibrahim (Dr)
Kooiman, Margo
Lauckner, Bruce
Lafadeju, Emmanuel A. (Professor)
Mbabu, Adiel Nkonge (Dr)
Mbaye, Ndiaga (Dr)
Mchombu, Kingo (Professor)
Medhine, Yohannes Gebre (Dr)
Menou, Michel (Professor)
Mook, Byron (Dr)
Mukhebi, Adrian Wekulo (Dr)
Nadeau, Charles Andrew
Redecker, Monika
Sanou, Fernand (Professor)
Springer-Heinze, Andreas (Dr)
Vogel, Isabel (Dr)

Amsterdam Workshop
19–22 November 2002

Addison, Chris
Akande, Modupe (Professor)
Batjes-Sinclair, Karen
Belt, John
op de Coul, Maartje
Cummings, Sarah
Diaw, Boubacar
van Dyk, Herman
Gast, Lisette
Hardon, Anne
Hewlitt, Alison
Kalume, Christine
Khadar, Ibrahim (Dr)
Kooijman, Margo
Kulis, Ivan
Lauckner, Bruce
Mbabu, Adiel Nkonge (Dr)
Mchombu, Kingo (Professor)
Mook, Byron (Dr)
Osei, Simon K.
Sam, Joel
Springer-Heinze, Andreas (Dr)
Thieba, Daniel (Dr)
Visser-Mabogunje, Lola

Annex 3

Wageningen Workshop
8–12 September 2003

Akande, Modupe (Professor)
Budhram, Dowlat (Dr)
Coul, Maartje
Cummings, Sarah
Davies, Rick (Dr)
Diaw, Boubacar
Dyk van, Herman
Engel, Paul (Dr)
Gast, Lisette
Khadar, Ibrahim (Dr)
Kooijman, Margo
Lauckner, Bruce
Lufadeju, E.A. (Professor)
Mbabu, Adiel Nkonge (Dr)
Mook, Byron (Dr)
Niang, Thiendou (Dr)
Osei, Simon
Richardson, Victoria
Shadrach, B.
Singh, Alec
Thieba, Daniel (Dr)
Thioune, Alioune
Umar, Mohammed (Dr)
Vincent, Rob (Dr)
Visser-Mabogunje, Lola
Webster, Christine

Workbench Meeting, Wageningen
14–15 February 2005

Akande, Modupe (Professor)
Allen, Ann
Batjes-Sinclair, Karen
Blok, Lucie (Dr)
Budhram, Dowlat (Dr)
op de Coul, Maartje
Cummings, Sarah
Khadar, Ibrahim (Dr)
Kooijman, Margo
Lauckner, Bruce
Lenglet, Frans
Gast, Lisette
Mbeng, Martin
McQuinn, Mark
Nthuku Muinde, Francis
Niang, Thiendou (Dr)
Okail, Nancy
Pinder, Richard
Schiefer, Ulrich (Professor, Dr)
Tiémogo, Ibrahim (Dr)
Visser-Mabogunje, Lola

ANNEX 4

Information sources

General references

Batjes-Sinclair, K. and Cummings, S. (2003) *Smart Tools for Evaluating the Performance of Information Products and Services.* Proceedings of a KIT/CTA/IICD/LEAP IMPACT technical consultation. Amsterdam, the Netherlands, 19–22 November 2002. CTA Working document 8029. CTA, Wageningen, The Netherlands

Batjes-Sinclair, K and Khadar, I. (2002) *Assessing the Performance and Impact of Agricultural Information Products and Services: Summary Report and Recommendations of a Technical Consultation.* Bonn, Germany, 9–12 October 2001. CTA, Wageningen, The Netherlands

Boissière, N. (2000) Assessing methodologies in studies of the impact of information: a synthesis. In: *Defining and Assessing the Impact of Information on Development: Building Research and Action Agendas.* Horton, F.W. Jr (ed.) FID Occasional Paper 16. pp 49–64. IFID, The Hague, The Netherlands

Botswana National Library Service (2002) *Revitalisation of Public Libraries.* Monitoring and evaluation workshop, 14–17 May 2002. Botswana National Library Service, Gaborone. Botswana

Caldwell, R. (2002) *Project Design Handbook.* CARE International, Atlanta, USA

Change Management Learning Centre. http://www.change-management.com/tutorial-adkar-overview.htm (accessed 1 October 2009)

CTA (1998) *Assessing the Impact of Information and Communication Management on Institutional Performance.* Proceedings of a CTA workshop, Wageningen, the Netherlands, 27–29 January 1998. CTA, Wageningen, The Netherlands

CTA (2002) *Technical Consultation on Assessing the Performance and Impact of Agricultural Information Products and Services.* Proceedings of a CTA/IICD/LEAP IMPACT Technical Consultation, Bonn, Germany, 9–12 October 2001. CTA Working Document 8027. CTA, Wageningen, The Netherlands

CTA (2004) *CTA Annual Report 2003.* CTA, Wageningen, The Netherlands

Conole, G., Oliver, M. and Harvey, J. (2000) *Toolkits as an Approach to Evaluating and Using Learning Materials.* www.ascilite.org.au/conferences/coffs00/papers/grainne_conole.pdf (accessed 1 October 2009)

Cummings, S. (2002a) Conceptual frameworks and methodologies used for evaluating agricultural information products and services. In: *Technical Consultation on Assessing the Performance and Impact of Agricultural Information Products and Services.* Proceedings of a CTA/IICD/LEAP IMPACT Technical Consultation, Bonn, Germany, 9–12 October 2001. CTA Working document 8027. CTA, Wageningen, The Netherlands

Cummings, S. (2002b) Inventory: conceptual frameworks and methodologies used for evaluating agricultural information products and services. In: *Technical Consultation on Assessing the Performance and Impact of Agricultural Information Products and Services*. Proceedings of a CTA/IICD/LEAP IMPACT Technical Consultation, Bonn, Germany, 9–12 October 2001. CTA Working document 8027. CTA, Wageningen, The Netherlands

Cummings, S. and Mchombu, K. (2003) Developing evaluation practice in the information sector: Introduction to the special issue. *Information Development* 19 (2)

DAC (2002) *Glossary of Key Terms in Evaluation and Results-based Management*. OECD/DA, Paris, France

DANIDA (1999) *Evaluation Guidelines*. Ministry of Foreign Affairs, Denmark

Danish Management et al. (2001) *Handbook for Monitors*. EVA/1999/11, ALA/MED/ACP and Balkans Monitoring Project, for European Commission. EuropeAid Unit H6

Davies, R. and Dart, J. 2005. *The Most Significant Change (MSC) Technique: A Guide to its Use*. Davies and Dart, UK

EC (2004) *Aid Delivery Methods. Volume 1: Project Cycle Management Guidelines*. EC, Brussels, Belgium

EC (2005) *Evaluation of EU Activities: An Introduction*. EC, Brussels, Belgium.

Engel, P.G.H. and Salomon, M.L. (1997) *The Social Organization of Innovation: A Focus on Stakeholder Interaction. A RAAKS Resource Box*. KIT/CTA/STOAS, Amsterdam, The Netherlands

EuropeAid (2001) *Manual of Project Cycle Management*. European Commission, Brussels, Belgium.

FAO (2001) *Project Cycle Management Technical Guide: Socio-Economic and Gender Analysis Programme (SEAGA)*. FAO, Rome, Italy

Gittinger, J.P. (1982) *Economic Analysis of Agricultural Projects* (2nd edn) Johns Hopkins University Press Baltimore, MD, USA

Hiatt, J.M. (2006) *ADKAR: A model for change in Business, government and our community: How to implement successful change in our personal lives and professional careers*. Prosci Research, CO, USA

Herman, J., Morris, L. and Fitz-Gibon, C. (1987) *Evaluator's Handbook*. Sage Publications Newbury Park, CA, USA

Horton, D., Ballantyne, P., Peterson, W., Uribe, B., Gapasin, D. and Sheridan, K. (1993) *Monitoring and Evaluating Agricultural Research: A Source Book*. CAB International/ISNAR, Wallingford, UK

Horton, D. et al. (2003) *Evaluating Capacity Development: Experiences from Research and Development Organisations around the World*. ISNAR/CTA/IDRC, Wageningen, The Netherlands

IADB (1997) *Evaluation in the Bank*. Office of Evaluation and Oversight, IADB, Washington, DC, USA

IFAD (2004) *A Guide for Project M&E: Managing for Impact in Rural Development*. IFAD, Rome, Italy

Johnson, R. and Redmond D. (1998) *The Art of Empowerment*. Financial Times/Prentice Hall, London, UK

Katzenback, J.R. and Smith, D.H. (1993) *The Wisdom of Teams, Creating the High Performance Organisation.* Harper Business, New York, USA

Kellogg Foundation. Using Logic Models to Bring Together Planning, Evaluation, and Action: Logic Model Development Guide. Available at http://www.wkkf.org/Pubs/Tools/Evaluation/Pub3669.pdf. (accessed 1 October 2009)

Khadar, I. (2002) Evaluation concepts and terminology: a discussion note. In: *Technical Consultation on Assessing the Performance and Impact of Agricultural Information Products and Services.* Proceedings of a CTA/IICD/LEAP IMPACT Technical Consultation, Bonn, Germany, 9–12 October 2001. CTA Working document 8027. CTA, Wageningen, The Netherlands

Khadar, I. (2004). An evaluation framework for evaluating the performance and impact of information projects, products and services. In: *Smart Tools for Evaluating the Performance of Information Products and Services.* Proceedings of a KIT/CTA/IICD/LEAP IMPACT technical consultation. Amsterdam, the Netherlands, 19–22 November 2002. CTA Working Document 8029. CTA, Wageningen, The Netherlands

Kirkpatrick, D.L. 1994. *Evaluating Training Programs.* Berrett-Koehler, San Francisco, USA

Kolb, D.A. (1984) *Experiential Learning: Experience as the Source of Learning and Development.* Prentice Hall, Englewood Cliffs, NJ, USA

Kusek, J. and Rist, R. (2004) *Ten Steps to a Results-Based Monitoring and Evaluation System.* IBRD, Washington, DC, USA: World Bank

Laurence., A. and Hawthorne, W. (2006) *Plant Identification: Creating User-Friendly Field Guides for BioDiversity Management.* Earthscan, London, UK

Levi, D. 2001. *Group Dynamics for Teams.* Sage Publications, London UK

Lewin, K. 1943, Defining the 'field at a given time'. *Psychological Review* 50: 292-310

MacKay, K. (2005) *Influential Evaluations: Detailed Case Studies.* Washington, DC, USA: Operations Evaluation Department, World Bank

Mbabu, A. (2002) Principles of evaluation. *Technical Consultation on Assessing the Performance and Impact of Agricultural Information Products and Services.* Proceedings of a CTA/IICD/LEAP IMPACT Technical Consultation, Bonn, Germany, 9–12 October 2001. CTA Working document 8027. CTA, Wageningen, The Netherlands

Mchombu, K. (2002) Key issues on the characteristics of agricultural information. In: *Technical Consultation on Assessing the Performance and Impact of Agricultural Information Products and Services.* Proceedings of a CTA/IICD/LEAP IMPACT Technical Consultation, Bonn, Germany, 9–12 October 2001. CTA Working document 8027. CTA, Wageningen, The Netherlands

Mook, B.T. (2003) *Evaluating Information: A Letter to a Project Manager.* CTA/ISNAR, Wageningen, The Netherlands. Available at: http://www.ifpri.org/isnararchive/Publicat/PDF/rmg8.pdf

Moss Kanter R. (1994) *The Change Masters.* Free Press, New York, USA

Osborn, A. 1953. *Applied Imagination: Principles and Procedures of Creative Problem Solving.* Scribner, New York, USA.

OECD (1992) *Development Assistance Manual: DAC Principles for Effective Aid.* OECD, Paris, France

OECD (2001) *Evaluation Feedback for Effective Learning and Accountability*. Report of DAC Tokyo workshop on 'Evaluation feedback for effective learning and accountability', 26–28 September 2000. OECD/DAC Paris, France

OECD (2002) *Glossary of Key Terms in Evaluation and Results Based Management*. OECD, Paris, France

Oomkes, F. and Thomas, R. H. (1992) *Cross cultural communication: A trainers manual*. Gower, Aldershot, UK.

Open University (2000) *Technique Library*. Prepared by J. Martin and R. Bell. Open University, Milton Keynes, UK

Powell, M. (2003) *Information Management for Development Organisations*. Oxfam, Oxford, UK

Pretty, J. (1994) Alternative systems for inquiry for a sustainable agriculture. *Institute of Development Studies Bulletin* 25 (9)

Project Management Institute. (2000) *A Guide to the Project Management Body of Knowledge (PMBOK Guide)*. Project Management Institute, Pennsylvania, USA

Roche, C. (1999) *Impact Assessment for Development Agencies: Learning to Value Change*. Oxfam, Oxford, UK

Royal Institute of the Tropics/World Bank. (2000) *Village Participation in Rural Development. The African Network on Participatory Approaches Manual*. KIT/World Bank, The Hague, The Netherlands

Sayce, K. and Norrish, P. (2006) *Perception and Practice: An Anthology of Impact Assessment Experiences*. CTA, Wageningen, The Netherlands

Schiefer, U. and Döbel, R. (2001) *MAPA-PROJECT: A Practical Guide to Integrated Project Planning and Evaluation*. Institute for Educational Policy/Open Society Institute, USA

Senge, P. (1994) *The Fifth Discipline*. Random House, New York, USA

SIDA (2004) *The Logical Framework Approach – A Summary of the Theory behind the LFA Method*. SIDA, Stockholm, Sweden

Springer-Heinze, A. (2003) Indicators: between hard measures and soft judgements. In: *Smart Tools for Evaluating the Performance of Information Products and Services*. Proceedings of a KIT/ CTA/ IICD/ LEAP IMPACT technical consultation. Amsterdam, the Netherlands, 19–22 November 2002. CTA Working document 8029. CTA, Wageningen, The Netherlands

Thomas, A., Chataway, J. and Wuyts, M. (eds) (1998) *Finding out Fast: Investigative Skills for Policy and Development*. Sage/Open University, London, UK

UNESCO (1989) Measuring the Performance of Public Libraries. UNESCO, Paris, France

UNEP (2005) *Project Manual: Formulation, Approval, Monitoring and Evaluation*. UNEP, New York, USA

Westat, J.L. et al. (2002) *The 2002 User Friendly Handbook for Project Evaluation*. National Science Foundation, Virginia, USA

References on information evaluation

Association of College and Research Libraries. (1998) *Task Force on Academic Library Outcomes Assessment Report*. ACRL, USA. Available at: http://www.ala.org/acrl/outcome.html

Baark, E. and Heeks, R. (1998) *Evaluation of Donor-funded Information Technology Transfer Projects in China: A Life-cycle Approach*. Institute for Development Policy and Management, University of Manchester, UK

Bellamy, M. (2000) *Approaches to Impact Evaluation (assessment) in Agricultural Information Management: Selective Review of the Issues, the Relevant Literature and Some Illustrative Case Studies.* CTA, Wageningen, The Netherlands.

Burroughs, C.M. and Wood, F.B. (2000) *Measuring the difference: guide to planning and evaluating health information outreach.* National Network of Libraries of Medicine, University of Washington, Seattle, Washington, USA

CIDA (2000) *CIDA Evaluation Guide.* CIDA, Toronto, Canada

Correa, A.F., Ndiaye, D., Mchombu, K.J., Rodriguez, G.M., Rosenberg, D. and Yapa, N.U. (1997) *Rural Information Provision in Developing Countries: Measuring Performance and Impact.* UNESCO, Paris, France

CTA (1998) *Assessing the Impact of Information and Communication Management on Institutional Performance.* Proceedings of a CTA workshop. Wageningen, The Netherlands, 27–29 January, 1998. CTA, Wageningen, The Netherlands

DAC–OECD. (2001) Evaluation feedback for effective learning and accountability. *OECD Evaluation and Aid Effectiveness* No. 5, 117pp

Ernberg, J. (1998) *Integrated Rural Development and Universal Access: Towards a Framework for Evaluation of Multipurpose Community Telecentres.* ITU, Geneva, Switzerland

Gangapersad, G. (2000) *Assessing the Impact of Information and Communication to NAMDEVCO's Clientele through its Newsletter and a Hot Pepper Seminar.* Trinidad and Tobago

Gómez, R., Hunt, and P. Lamoureux, E. (1999) *Enchanted by Telecentres: A Critical Look at Universal Access to Information Technologies for International Development.* IDRC, Toronto, Canada

Hafkin, N. and Menou, M.J. (1996) *Impact of Electronic Communication on Development in Africa.* CABECA/IDRC, Toronto, Canada

Haravu, L.J. and Rajan, T.N. (1995) *Impact of the Semi-Arid Tropical Crops Information Service* SATCRIS/ICRISAT, India

Harris, R.W. *Evaluating Telecentres within National Policies for ICTs in Developing Countries.* Faculty of Information Technology, University of Sarawak, Malaysia

HealthLink World-wide. Monitoring and evaluation. In: *Resource Centre Manual. How to Set Up and Manage a Resource Centre.* HealthLink. UK

Hudson, H.E. *Designing Research for Telecentre Evaluation.* Acacia Program, IDRC, Toronto, Canada

Kidane, S. *Report of Evaluation of HealthNet Service.* Nuffield Institute Health Resource Centre, University of Leeds, Sheffield, UK.

Mchombu, K. (1995) *Impact of Information on Rural Development: Background, Methodology and Progress.* IDRC, Toronto, Canada

Menou, M. (1993) *Indicators and Assessment Methods.* IDRC, Toronto, Canada

Menou, M. (1993) *Preliminary Framework for Impact Assessment.* IDRC, Toronto, Canada

Menou, M. (1999) Impact of the Internet: Some conceptual and methodological issues, or how to hit a moving target behind the smoke screen. In: Nicholas, D. and Rowlands, I., (eds) *The Internet: Its Impact and Evaluation.* Aslib, London, UK.

Møller Rasmussen, A.. (2001) Information and development: the information effect. *Information Development* vol 17(1)

Mook, B. (2001) *Evaluating Information: A Letter to a Project Manager.* CTA, Wageningen, The Netherlands.

Parker, S. (2000) Knowledge is like light – information is like water. *Information Development* 16(4). Pages: 233–236

Saunders, M. (2000) Beginning an evaluation with RUFDATA: theorising a practical approach to evaluation planning. *Evaluation: the International Journal of Theory, Research and Practice* 2000 6 (1)

Tague-Sutcliffe, J., Vaughan, L. and Sylvain, C. (1995) *Using LISREL to Measure the Impact of Information on Development: London site pilot study.* IDRC, Toronto, Canada

Vincent, R. (2001) *Beyond Circles in Square Boxes: Lessons Learned from Health Communication Impact Evaluations.* Exchange, HealthLink Worldwide, London, UK

Vogel, I. (2001) An online impact assessment tool for research information: some preliminary concepts. *Information Development* 17 (2) 111-113.

Whyte, A. (1999a) *Indicators in Telecentre Studies.* IDRC, Toronto, Canada

Whyte, A. (1999b) *Understanding the Role of Community Telecentres in Development.* Mestor Associates, Canada

Wilson III, E.J. and Daly, J. (1998) *Internet Counts: Measuring the Impact of the Internet.* National Academy Press, Washington DC, USA

Selected references for tools, products and services

These references relate to the tools described in Part 3 and the products and services described in Part 4

Evaluation tools

LOGICAL FRAMEWORK

AusGUIDElines The Logical Framework Approach. Available at: http://portals.wi.wur.nl/files/docs/ppme/ausguidelines-logical%20framework%20approach.pdf (accessed 1 October 2009)

Caldwell, R. (2002) *Project Design Handbook.* CARE International, Atlanta, USA

Checkland, P.B. and Scholes, J. (1990) *Soft Systems Methodology in Action.* John Wiley, Chichester, UK

EuropeAid (2001) *Manual of Project Cycle Management.* European Commission, Brussels, Belgium

EC. (2004) *Aid Delivery Methods. Volume 1: Project Cycle Management Guidelines.* EC, Brussels, Belgium

FAO (2001) *Project Cycle Management Technical Guide: Socio-Economic and Gender Analysis Programme (SEAGA).* FAO, Rome, Italy

GTZ. (2000) *Guidelines for Impact Monitoring in Economic and Employment Promotion Projects with Special Reference to Poverty Reduction Impacts.* GTZ, Eschborn, Germany

Hambly Odame, H. (2001) *Engendering the Logical Framework.* ISNAR, The Hague, The Netherlands

IADB (1997) *Evaluation: A Management Tool for Improving Project Performance (A Logical Framework).* IFAD, Washington, DC.

IFAD (2004) *A Guide for Project M&E: Managing for Impact in Rural Development.* IFAD, Rome, Italy

IUCN (1997) *Designing Projects and Project Evaluations using the Logical Framework Approach.* IUCN, Gland, Switzerland

Schiefer, U. and Döbel, R. (2001) *MAPA-PROJECT: A Practical Guide to Integrated Project Planning and Evaluation.* Institute for Educational Policy/Open Society Institute, USA

SIDA (2004) *The Logical Framework Approach – A Summary of the Theory behind the LFA Method.* SIDA, Stockholm, Sweden

UNEP. (2005) *Project Manual: Formulation, Approval, Monitoring and Evaluation.* UNEP, New York, USA

RESULTS-BASED MANAGEMENT

ELI Monitoring & Evaluation. (2000) *Results Based Management for ELI: A Primer.* ELI, World Bank, Washington DC, USA

Kusek, K.Z. and Rist, R.C. (2004) *Ten Steps to a Results-Based Monitoring and Evaluation System.* World Bank, Washington, DC, USA

Schiavo-Campo, S. (1999) Performance in the public sector. *Asian Journal of Political Science* 7 (2): 75–87

BENCHMARKING

Camp, R.C. (1989) *Benchmarking: The Search for Industry Best Practices that lead to Superior Performance.* ASQ Quality Press, Milwaukee, WI, USA

Camp, R.C. (1995) *Business Process Benchmarking: Finding and Implementing Practices.* ASQ Quality Press, Milwaukee, WI, USA

Kaplan, R.S. and Norton, D.P. (1992) The balanced scorecard – measures that drive performance. *Harvard Business Review* Jan/Feb: 71–79

Paton, R. (2001) The performance of social enterprises. In: *Materials from TU870 Course Capacities for Managing Development.* Open University, Milton Keynes, UK: Open University

Russell, P.J. (1998) *Quality Management Benchmark Assessment.* ASQ Quality Press, Milwaukee, WI, USA

Spendolini, M. (1992) *The Benchmarking Book.* AMACOM, New York, NY, USA

INDICATORS

CIDA. (1999) *Results-based Management in CIDA: An Introductory Guide to the Concepts and Principles.* CIDA, Ottawa, Canada

Jaeger, R. (1978) About educational indicators. *Review of Research in Education* 6, 276–315

Moldan, B. and Billharz, S. (eds) (1997) *Sustainability Indicators: Report of the Project on Indicators.* Ministry of the Environment, Prague, Czech Republic

Mook, B.T. (2003) *Evaluating Information: A Letter to a Project Manager.* CTA/ISNAR, Wageningen, The Netherlands

TERMS OF REFERENCE

DANIDA (1999) *Evaluation Guidelines.* Ministry of Foreign Affairs, Denmark

EC (2001) *Evaluation in the European Commission: A Guide to the Evaluation Procedures and Structures Currently Operational in the Commission's External Cooperative Programme.* EC, Brussels, Belgium

EC (2004) *Aid Delivery Methods. Volume 1: Project Cycle Management Guidelines.* EC, Brussels, Belgium

FAO (2001) *Project Cycle Management Technical Guide: Socio-Economic and Gender Analysis Programme (SEAGA).* FAO, Rome, Italy

Mook, B.T. (2003) *Evaluating Information: A Letter to a Project Manager.* CTA/ISNAR, Wageningen, The Netherlands

LOGIC MODEL

Caldwell, R. (2002) *Project Design Handbook.* CARE International, Atlanta, USA

Kellogg Foundation. Using Logic Models to Bring Together Planning, Evaluation, and Action: Logic Model Development Guide

University of Wisconsin. Program Development and Evaluation: Logic Model. Program Development and Evaluation

SWOT ANALYSIS

Balamuralikrishna, R. and Dugger, J.C. (1995) SWOT analysis: a management tool for initiating new programs in vocational schools. *Journal of Vocational and Technical Education* 12(1) (e-journal)

Berkowitz, E.N., Kerin, R.A., Hartley, S.W. and Rudelius, W. (2000) *Marketing.* (6th edn) Irwin/McGraw Hill, Boston, MA, USA

FOCUS GROUP DISCUSSIONS

Dawson S. and Manderson, L. (1993) *A Manual for the Use of Focus Groups.* INFDC, Boston, MA, USA

Gibbs, A. (1997) Focus groups. *Social Research Update 19.* (e-journal) Available at: http://www.soc.surrey.ac.uk/sru/SRU19.html (accessed 1 October 2009)

Kitzinger, J. (1995) Introducing focus groups. *British Medical Journal* 311: 299-302

Krueger, R.A. and Casey, M.A. (2000) *Focus Groups: A Practical Guide for Applied Research* (3rd edn). Sage, Thousand Oaks, CA, USA

CASE STUDIES

Tellis, W. (1997) Introduction to case study. *The Qualitative Report* 3 (2). Available at: http://www.nova.edu/ssss/QR/QR3-2/tellis1.html (accessed 1 October 2009)

Whittemore, C.T. (1995) Teaching interpersonal and transferable skills to students of agriculture: a case study. *European Journal of Agricultural Education and Extension* 1: 87–106

World Bank/OECD. (2005) *Influential Evaluations: Detailed Case Studies.* World Bank/OECD, Washington DC, USA

Yin, R.K (2003) *Case Study Research, Design and Methods.* (3rd edn) Sage, London, UK

INDIVIDUAL INTERVIEWS

Consumer Health Care Information Workgroup 'Techniques for Testing and Evaluation'. Available at: http://www.talkingquality.gov/docs/section5/5_3.htm#Qualitative%20Methods (accessed 1 October 2009)

McDowell, D. (1997) *Process Guide #6: Interview Techniques.* Available at: http://projects.edtech.sandi.net/staffdev/tpss99/processguides/interviewing.html (accessed 1 October 2009)

Robinson, M. and Thin, N. (1993) *Project Evaluation: A Guide for NGOs.* ODA, East Kilbride, UK

PARTICIPATORY AND CREATIVE TOOLS

IIED (2003) *Learning and Teaching Participation. Tips for Trainers.* PLA Notes 48: IIED, London, UK

IIED/ODA (1994) Participatory reflection and action methods. In: *Whose Eden? An Overview of Community Approaches to Wildlife Management.* IIED/ODA, London, UK

World Bank. 2004. Participatory video: Rural people document their knowledge and innovations. *IK Notes.* No. 71, August 2004. Available at: http://www.worldbank.org/afr/ik/iknt71.pdf (accessed 1 October 2009)

AFTER ACTION REVIEW

Collison, C. and Parcell, G. (2001). *Learning to Fly.* Capstone Publishing, Milford, CT, USA

Darling, M.J. and Parry, C.S. (2001) *From Post-mortem to Living Practice: An In-depth Study of the Evolution of the After Action Review.* Signet Consulting Group, Boston, MA, USA: Signet Consulting Group

DATA ANALYSIS

den Boer, D.-J., Bouwman, H., Frissen, V. and Houben, M. (1994) *Methodologie en Statistiek voor Communicatie-onderzoek.* Bohn Stafleu Van Loghum. Zavetem Houten, The Netherlands

Coghlan, D. and Brannick, T. (2005) *Doing Action Research in Your Own Organisation.* Sage, London, UK

Miles, M.B. and Huberman, A.M. (1994) *Qualitative Data Analysis: An Expanded Sourcebook.* Sage, London, UK

Patton, M.Q. (2002) *Qualitative Research and Evaluation Methods.* Sage, Thousand Oaks, CA, USA

Voelkl, K. and Gerber, S. (1999) *Using SPSS for Windows. Data Analysis and Graphics.* Springer Verlag, New York, NY, USA

WRITING AND DISSEMINATING AN EVALUATION REPORT

ISNAR/IDRC/CTA. (2003) *Evaluating Capacity Development: Experiences from Research and Development Organisations around the World.* Arlington Press, UK

Schiefer, U. and Döbel, R. (2001) *MAPA-PROJECT: A Practical Guide to Integrated Project Planning and Evaluation.* Institute for Educational Policy/Open Society Institute, USA

UNICEF. *A UNICEF Guide for Monitoring and Evaluation: Making a Difference?* UNICEF, New York USA. Available at: http://www.unicef.org/reseval/mande4r.html (accessed 1 October 2009)

PROMOTING THE USE OF EVALUATION FINDINGS

ISNAR/IDRC/CTA. (2003) *Evaluating Capacity Development: Experiences from Research and Development Organisations around the World.* Arlington Press, UK

OECD (2001) *Evaluation Feedback for Effective Learning and Accountability.* Report of DAC Tokyo workshop on 'Evaluation feedback for effective learning and accountability', 26–28 September 2000. OECD/DAC Paris, France

TRANSLATING EVALUATION FINDINGS

Open University (2000) *Technique Library.* Prepared by J. Martin and R. Bell. Open University, Milton Keynes, UK

Tubbs, S.L. (2004) *Decision-making Processes.* McGraw-Hill, New York, USA

Information products and services

TRAINING COURSE

Casly, D.J. and Lang, D.A. (1982) *Monitoring and Evaluation of Agricultural and Rural Development Projects.* World Bank, Washington, DC, USA

Mook, B.T. (2003) *Evaluating Information: A Letter to a Project Manager.* CTA/ISNAR, Wageningen, The Netherlands

UN (1984) *Guiding Principles for the Design and Use of Monitoring and Evaluation in Rural Development Projects and Programmes.* FAO, Rome, Italy

Winfrey, E.C. (1999) Kirkpatrick's four levels of evaluation. In B. Hoffman (ed.) *Encyclopedia of Educational Technology.*

NEWSLETTER

Mook, B.T. (2003) *Evaluating Information: A Letter to a Project Manager.* CTA/ISNAR, Wageningen, The Netherlands.

Winfrey, E.C. (1999) Kirkpatrick's four levels of evaluation. In B. Hoffman (ed.) *Encyclopedia of Educational Technology.*

WEBSITE

Additional evaluation and repair software for web accessibility is available from
http://www.w3.org/WAI/ER/existingtools.html (accessed 1 October 2009)

CGIAR. *Evaluating the Impact of Your Website: A guide for CGIAR Centers to Evaluate the Usage, Usability and Usefulness of Their Websites.* ICT-KM Guide, version 1.0, November 2007. Available at:
http://ictkm.cgiar.org/archives (accessed 1 October 2009)

Evaluation framework. Available at:
http://www.urbandevelopmentforum.org/WebsiteEvaluation/docs/WebsiteEvaluationFramework.html (accessed 1 October 2009)

QUESTION-AND-ANSWER SERVICE

Bellamy, M. (2000) *Approaches to Impact Evaluation (assessment) in Agricultural Information Management: Selective Review of the Issues, the Relevant Literature and Some Illustrative Case Studies.* CTA, Wageningen, The Netherlands

CTA (2001). *Manual for the Management of Question and Answer Services.* CTA, Wageningen, The Netherlands

Mook, B.T. (2003) *Evaluating Information: A Letter to a Project Manager.* CTA/ISNAR, Wageningen, The Netherlands

SMALL LIBRARY / RESOURCE CENTRE

ACRL. (1998) *Task Force on Academic Library Outcomes Assessment Report.* ACRL, USA

CTA (1998) *Assessing the Impact of Information and Communication Management on Institutional Performance.* Proceedings of a CTA workshop, Wageningen, the Netherlands, 27–29 January 1998. CTA, Wageningen, The Netherlands

Mook, B.T. (2003) *Evaluating Information: A Letter to a Project Manager.* CTA/ISNAR, Wageningen, The Netherlands

ONLINE COMMMUNITY

Church, M., Bitel, M., Armstrong, K. Fernando, P. Gould, H. Joss, S., Marwaha-Diedrich, M. Torre de la, A.L. and Vouhé, C. (2000) *Participation, Relationships and Dynamic Change: New Thinking on Evaluating the Work of International Networks.* A Development Planning Unit Project. University College London, UK

Cummings, S., Heeks, R. and Huysman, M. (2003) *Knowledge and Learning in Online Communities in Development: A Social Capital Perspective.* Development Informatics Working Paper Series No. 16, Institute for Development Policy and Management, Manchester, UK

RURAL RADIO

Adam, G. and Harford, N. (1998) *Health on Air – A Guide to Creative Radio for Development.* Health Unlimited, London, UK

Adam, G. and Harford, N. (1999) *Radio and HIV/AIDS: Making a Difference.* Joint United Nations Programme on HIV/AIDS (UNAIDS) and Media Action International. UNAIDS, Geneva, Switzerland

AMARC. *The African Community Radio Manager's Handbook: A Guide to Sustainable Radio.* AMARC Africa. Available at: http://www.apc.org/apps/img_upload/29f7440303691f46ae6e48c35512ccf2/AMARC_manual_for_managers.doc (accessed 1 October 2009)

OneWorld Radio, resources section on evaluation. Available at: www.oneworld.net/radiohttp://radio.oneworld.net/index.php?fuseaction=cms.trainingResourcePage

SELECTIVE DISSEMINATION OF INFORMATION SERVICE

CTA (1998) *Assessing the Impact of Information and Communication Management on Institutional Performance.* Proceedings of a CTA workshop, Wageningen, the Netherlands, 27–29 January 1998. CTA, Wageningen, The Netherlands

McKimmie, T. (1994) *Evaluation of a Current Awareness Service in an Academic Library.* New Mexico State University, Mexico

Mook, B.T. (2003) *Evaluating Information: A Letter to a Project Manager.* CTA/ISNAR, Wageningen, The Netherlands

Niang, T. (2001) Information services to agricultural research management at the Technical Centre for Agricultural and Rural Cooperation. In Vernon, R. (ed) *Knowing Where You're Going: Information Systems for Agricultural Research Management.* ISNAR, The Hague, the Netherlands

Poncelet, J. (1980) *Guide for the Establishment and Evaluation of Services for Selective Dissemination of Information.* UNESCO UNISIST, Paris, France

ANNEX 5

Glossary

These terms are defined within the context of information projects, products and services.

Accessibility: The extent to which the target groups have access to a product or service.

Accountability test: Traditionally, the main focus of an evaluation. This exercise generally assesses the extent to which available resources have been spent according to set procedures and for the intended activities. It now also includes accountability to clients.

Accuracy: A measure of the quality of the information.

Appraisal: Analysis of a proposed project to determine its merits and acceptability in accordance with established criteria. It assesses whether the project is feasible practically, the objectives are appropriate and the costs are reasonable. Common synonyms: feasibility study, *ex ante* evaluation.

Assumptions: External factors that could affect the progress of the project, but over which the project manager has no direct control.

Attribution problem: Whether changes observed after project implementation can be directly attributed to the project.

Beneficiaries: People and/or institutions that benefit, in one way or another, from the implementation of a project. They include:
- Implementing organisations (those receiving financial means to carry out a project)
- Intermediate beneficiaries (those supported in the project to better deliver services to the target group)
- Target groups (the primary stakeholders, whose lives will be directly affected by the project and with whom project staff will work closely)
- Final beneficiaries (those in the wider society who will benefit from the project in the long term)

Cost–benefit: Relates inputs into the information system to impact.

Cost-effectiveness: Relates inputs to the information system to usage of the outputs.

Data-collection tools: The methods used to identify information sources of data and to collect those data.

Effectiveness: Relates outputs of the information system to usage.

Efficiency: Measures the outputs (qualitative and quantitative) in relation to the inputs. It is a term that signifies that the project uses the least costly resources in order to achieve the desired results.

Evaluation: An assessment, as systematic and objective as possible, of ongoing and completed projects, in terms of their design, implementation and results. It is generally carried out before a project begins (sometimes called *ex ante*); in mid-cycle (mid-term); or at the end when impact can be measured (sometimes called *ex post*). It is usually undertaken as an independent examination of the background, objectives, results, activities and means deployed, with a view of drawing lessons to guide future decision-making.

Feasibility study: This assesses whether a proposed project is well-founded and is likely to meet the identified needs of its intended target groups.

Formative evaluation: This is designed to increase understanding in order to improve performance.

Gender approach: The socio-cultural construct that refers to roles, responsibilities, characteristics, attitudes and beliefs about men and women. They are defined, supported and reinforced by societal structures and institutions, and are learned and change over time, varying within and between cultures. Factors such as education, technology, economics and crises such as war and famine often bring about changes in gender roles.

Gender analysis: An organised assessment aimed at understanding how men and women relate to each other in terms of roles and responsibilities, access and control. The purpose is to ensure that project activities fully incorporate the roles, needs and participation of women and men. It requires separate data and information by gender and age.

Goals: Clear statements of success that a project is working to achieve.

Impact: Long-term effects (economic, social and environmental), anticipated or unanticipated, positive or negative, at the individual or organisational level, brought about by a development intervention. Relates use of information outputs to transformation of the users or their environment.

Indicators: Measurable elements that indicate whether project efforts are successful. They help to define what information must be collected to answer evaluation questions.

Logical framework (logframe): A methodology for planning, managing and evaluating projects, involving stakeholder analysis, problem analysis, analysis of objectives, analysis of strategies, and preparation of the logframe matrix and the activity and resource schedules.

Monitoring: A continuous process of collecting and analysing data for performance indicators, to compare a project's progress against intended results.

Objectives: Interim, measurable goals that can be achieved within a defined period.

Outcomes: The differences a project makes to the target group. They should flow directly from the project's goal or purpose.

Outputs: Reflect measurable products of a project. They can include anything that can be counted, such as people, activities, materials and time. Outputs measure quantity, not quality.

Performance: Quality of the way a project functions.

Productivity: The output in relation to the input.

Purpose: The direct outcome to be achieved as a result of the outputs produced by the project.

Relevance: The extent to which project objectives are consistent with the target group's needs.

Results: The products of the activities undertaken.

Self-evaluation: An evaluation by those responsible for the design and implementation of a project.

Stakeholders: Agencies, organisations, individuals or groups who have a direct or indirect interest in a project and its evaluation.

Summative evaluation: Measures overall performance against external standards or intended achievements.

Sustainability: The likelihood of a continuation in the products/services delivered by the project, after the project itelf has ended.

SWOT analysis: Analysis of an organisation's strengths and weaknesses, and the opportunities and threats that it faces.

Target group: The people whose lives a project seeks to positively affect.

Terms of reference: Defines the tasks and parameters that the agency implementing a project should adhere to, indicating the objectives, planned activities, expected outputs, budget, timetable and job descriptions.

Transformation path: Stages an idea must go through before visible impact among the primary stakeholders is attained.

Utility: The extent to which the project can be successfully replicated in another location or among different stakeholders.

ACRONYMS AND ABBREVIATIONS

AAR	after-action review
ACP	African, Caribbean and Pacific Group of States
AIDS	acquired immune deficiency syndrome
APC	Association for Progressive Communications
ARIS	Agricultural Research Information Service
ASARECA	Association for Strengthening Agricultural Research in Eastern and Central Africa
CABI	Centre for Agriculture and Biosciences International
CAQDAS	Computer-Assisted Qualitative Data Analysis
CARDI	Caribbean Agricultural Research and Development Institute
CIDA	Canadian International Development Agency
CORAF	Conférence des responsables de recherche agronomique africains
CSO	civil society organisation
CTA	Technical Centre for Agricultural and Rural Cooperation
CTRL	control
DAC	Development Assistance Committee (OECD)
DANIDA	Danish International Development Assistance
DFID	Department for International Development
EC	European Commission
ECART	European Consortium for Agricultural Research in the Tropics
ECDPM	European Centre for Development Policy Management
EU	European Union
FAKT	Fördergesellschaft für Angepasste Techniken
FAQs	frequently asked questions
FID	International Federation for Information and Documentation
GDC	Gabriima Development Centre (SWOT tool)
GTZ	Gesellschaft für Technische Zusammenarbeit
HIV	human immunodeficiency virus
HTML	hypertext mark-up language
ICT	information and communication technology
IDRC	International Development Research Centre
IDS	Institute of Development Studies, University of Sussex, UK
IEC	information, education and communication
IICD	International Institute for Communication and Development
IK	indigenous knowledge
INFDC	International Nutrition Foundation for Developing Countries
ISNAR	International Service for National Agricultural Research
IUCN	International Union for the Conservation of Nature
KISS	keep it short and simple
KIT	Royal Tropical Institute
LEAP	Learning and Evaluation Action Program
M&E	monitoring and evaluation
MDF	Management Development Foundation
MOV	means of verification (Logframe)
NGO	non-governmental organisation
NUD*IST	Non-numerical, Unstructured Data Indexing, Searching and Theory-building
OECD	Organisation for Economic Cooperation and Development
OVI	objectively verifiable indicator (Logframe)
PCM	project cycle management
PRA	participatory rural approach
R&D	research and development
RBM	Results-based management
QAS	Question-and-Answer Service

RUFDATA	reasons and purposes, uses, focuses, data and evidence, audience, timing, agency
SAR	specific actionable recommendations
SDI	Selective Dissemination of Information
SMART	specific, measurable, achievable, realistic, time-bound
SWOT	strengths, weaknesses, opportunities and threats
ToR	terms of reference
UK	United Kingdom
UNECA	United Nations Economic Commission for Africa
UNESCO	United Nations Educational, Scientific and Cultural Organisation
URL	uniform resource locator
USA	United States of America
USAID	United States Agency for International Development
WWW	World Wide Web

INDEX

accessibility *see* evaluation criteria
accountability v, vii, viii, 33
action plan 61-62
ADKAR model 63
After Action Review 40, 106, 109, 155-157
analysis *see* data analysis, gender analysis, objectives analysis, problem analysis, situation analysis, stakeholder analysis, strategy analysis, SWOT analysis
assumptions 11, 13 *see also* logical framework

baseline data 24, 76
benchmarking 67, 88-91
brainstorming 171-173
budget 3, 30, 43-46, 79

cascading projects 76-77
case studies 106, 109, 136-139
change, managing 63-64
communication strategy 26, 30, 41-42, 45, 46, 54-56, 188-189, 217-218, 229-230, 241-242, 252-254, 266-267, 277-279, 290-292
CREAM 50, 87
criteria, evaluation *see* evaluation criteria
critical reflection *see* reflection, critical

data analysis 25, 26, 30, 32, 45-46, 52-54, 60, 106, 157-162, 186-188, 201-203, 216-217, 228-229, 239-241, 252, 263-265, 276-278, 289-290
data collection 17, 20, 25, 26, 30-32, 37-41, 45, 46, 48-49, 52, 58-59, 106-115, 181-186, 195-201, 209-216, 221-228, 235-239, 245-251, 257-263, 272-276, 283-289
data, baseline *see* baseline data
data, qualititative *see* qualititative data
data, quantitative *see* quantitative data
database evaluation x, 176, 268-280
design, evaluation *see* evaluation design
drawing 145-147

effectiveness *see* evaluation criteria
efficiency *see* evaluation criteria
evaluation
    context 1-27
    criteria 16, 33-34, 51, 80-82
    definition 2 *see also* M&E
    design 19, 30-31, 46-54
    ex ante 19
    ex post 19
    external viii
    findings 66, 163-173, 163 *see also* communication strategy
    focus 46, 49-51, 182-186, 195-199, 210-213, 225-226, 235-238, 247-249, 261-262, 274-275, 284-288
    follow-up 20, 30-31, 61-64
    implementation x, 8, 20, 30-31, 58-62, 66, 106-162
    internal viii

objectives 10, 11, 24
participatory *see* stakeholder participation
planning 8, 9, 26, 30, 32, 43-45, 67
process 29-64
purpose 24, 32-33, 45
questions 49, 59 *see also* evaluation focus
recommendations 63
report 26, 30, 33, 42, 45, 55, 60-61, 163-167 *see also* communication strategy
scope 24, 32, 33-35, 45
team 35, 43
tools x, 65-173
ex ante evaluation *see* evaluation, ex ante
ex post evaluation *see* evaluation, ex post
expected results *see* logical framework
external evaluation *see* evaluation, external

feedback 27
findings, evaluation *see* evaluation findings
focus group discussions 40, 106, 109, 128-132
focus, evaluation *see* evaluation focus
follow-up, evaluation *see* evaluation follow-up
force-field analysis 170-173

Gantt chart 78
gender analysis 70
goal *see* logical framework
group dynamics 56-58

impact assessment v, 2, 3, 8-10, 21-27, 186 *see also* evaluation criteria
implementation, evaluation *see* evaluation implementation
indicators viii, 11, 13, 25, 47, 49-51, 67, 91-98 *see also* logical framework, SMART indicators, SPICED indicators
information needs *see* data collection
inputs 10, 11, 13 *see also* logical framework
internal evaluation *see* evaluation, internal
intervention logic *see* logical framework
interviews 106, 109, 141-144, 200, 262-263

key questions 49-51 *see also* evaluation focus
Kirkpatrick's model 183, 197
Kolb's learning cycle 5-6

learning v, vii, viii, 2, 5-8, 30
logic model 67, 99, 103-106, 180-181, 194, 208, 223, 234, 247, 259, 271, 285
logical framework 3, 11-14, 47, 67, 68-81, 179, 193, 207, 222, 233, 246, 258, 270, 284

M&E, definition of 2
means of verification 11, 13 *see also* logical framework
methodology 38-40, 45, 52-54, 60 *see also* data collection, data analysis
monitoring viii, 2, 3, 8, 16-18, 24-27, 87

newsletter evaluation x, 37, 48, 53-56, 176, 191-204

objectives analysis 71-72
objectives, evaluation *see* evaluation objectives

online community evaluation x, 176, 243-254
outcomes v, 10 *see also* logical framework
outputs v, 10, 11, 13, 45 *see also* logical framework

participatory and creative tools 106, 109, 144-154
participatory evaluation *see* stakeholder participation
participatory learning and action (PLA) 4, 40
participatory video 147-150
planning, evaluation *see* evaluation planning
problem analysis 71
process flowchart 106, 132-134
programme, definition of 8
project
    concept 24, 46-47
    cycle vii, 8-10
    definition of 8
    management x, 2, 36
    objectives 46-47
    plan viii, 2, 10-16, 66-98
purpose, evaluation *see* evaluation purpose

qualitative/quantitative data 106-107, 158-162
qualitative/quantitative methods *see* methodology
question-and-answer service evaluation x, 16, 176, 219-230
questionnaires 40, 106, 109, 120-127, 200

radio evaluation *see* rural radio evaluation
rapid appraisal 40
recommendations, evaluation *see* evaluation
reflection, critical 8, 9, 25, 42, 45, 55, 60-61
relevance *see* evaluation criteria
report, evaluation *see* evaluation report
resource centre evaluation *see* small library / resource centre evaluation
results, evaluation *see* evaluation findings
results-based management 67, 83-88
review, critical *see* reflection, critical
rich pictures 150-152
role-play 145-147
rural radio evaluation x, 176, 255-267

sampling 109-112
scope, evaluation *see* evaluation scope
selection dissemination of information (SDI) service evaluation x, 176, 281-292
self-evaluation vii, viii, 3, 30
situation analysis 8, 9
small library / resource centre evaluation x, 176, 231-242
SMART indicators viii, 50, 96
Smart Toolkit background vii-xi, 294
Smart Toolkit contributors 295-297
Smart Toolkit workshops 298-299
SPICED indicators 50, 96
stakeholder analysis 3-5, 68-70, 182, 196, 209 *see also* stakeholder participation
stakeholder participation x, 2, 3-5, 23, 30, 35-37, 38, 45, 181-182, 195, 209-210, 221-225, 235-236, 245-248, 257-260, 272-274, 283-286
stakeholders 3, 4, 18, 24, 27, 32, 34-37, 47 *see also* stakeholder participation

strategic positioning 8, 9
strategy analysis 73
surveys 22, 184, 215
sustainaibility *see* evaluation criteria
SWOT analysis 40, 106, 109, 115-119

team, evaluation *see* evaluation team
terms of reference 30, 32-46, 99-103
theory of action 11-12, 47
tools, evaluation *see* evaluation tools
training course evaluation x, 9, 34, 176, 177-190

usability *see* evaluation criteria
utility *see* evaluation criteria

Venn diagrams 152-154

web statistics 214-215
website evaluation x, 176, 205-218